DATE DUE

ARBA In-depth:
Children's and Young Adult Titles

ARBA In-depth Series:

Children's and Young Adult Titles

Economics and Business

Health and Medicine

Philosophy and Religion

ARBA In-depth:
Children's and Young Adult Titles

Dr. Martin Dillon, EDITOR IN CHIEF

Shannon Graff Hysell, ASSOCIATE EDITOR

LIBRARIES
UNLIMITED
A Member of the Greenwood Publishing Group

Westport, Connecticut • London

Library of Congress Cataloging-in-Publication Data

ARBA In-depth. Children's and young adult titles / edited by Martin Dillon and Shannon
  Graff Hysell.
   p. cm.
   "Consists of reviews chosen from the past six volumes of American reference books
   annual (ARBA)—years 1997-2003 ... reviews of reference books, CD-ROMS, and websites"—P.
   Includes index.
   ISBN 1-59158-162-1
   1. Children's reference books—Reviews. 2. Children's literature—Book reviews. 3. Young
   adult literature—Book reviews. 4. Children's electronic reference sources—Reviews. 5.
   Children's Web sites—Reviews. 6. Children's libraries—Book lists. 7. Young adults'
   libraries—Book lists. 8. School libraries—Book lists. I. Title: Children's and Young adult
   titles. II. Dillon, Martin, 1938- III. Graff Hysell, Shannon. IV. American reference books
   annual. V. Series.
   Z1037.1.A73 2004
   028.1'62—dc22   2003065943

British Library Cataloguing in Publication Data is available.

Library of Congress Catalog Card Number: 2003065943
ISBN: 1–59158–162–1

First published in 2004

Libraries Unlimited, 88 Post Road West, Westport, CT 06881
A Member of the Greenwood Publishing Group, Inc.
www.lu.com

Printed in the United States of America

The paper used in this book complies with the
Permanent Paper Standard issued by the National
Information Standards Organization (Z39.48–1984).

10   9   8   7   6   5   4   3   2   1

Contents

Introduction

The staff of *American Reference Books Annual* is pleased to announce the first edition of *ARBA In-depth: Children's and Young Adult Titles.* The fourth in this series of companion volumes to ARBA, this work is designed to assist academic, public, and school libraries in the systematic selection of suitable reference materials for their collections. As with all publications in this series, its purpose is to aid in the evaluation process by presenting critical and evaluative reviews in all areas of children's and young adult resources. The increase in the publication of reference resources in the United States and Canada, in combination with the decrease in library budgets, makes this guide an invaluable tool.

ARBA In-depth: Children's and Young Adult Titles consists of reviews chosen from the past six volumes of *American Reference Books Annual* (ARBA)—years 1997-2003. This work provides reviews of reference books, CD-ROMs, and Websites published in the United States and Canada, along with English-language titles from other countries. ARBA has reviewed more than 55,000 titles since its inception in 1970. Because it provides comprehensive coverage of reference resources in all subject areas, not just selected or recommended titles, many titles in ARBA are of interest only to large academic and public libraries. Thus, *ARBA In-depth: Children's and Young Adult Titles* has been developed as an abridged version of ARBA with selected reviews of resources that are candidates for school and public collections as well as university libraries with children's and young adult collections. Titles reviewed in *ARBA In-depth: Children's and Young Adult Titles* include dictionaries, encyclopedias, directories, bibliographies, guides, and other types of ready-reference tools appropriate for children in grades K-12.

This volume provides 560 unabridged reviews selected from ARBA 1997 through ARBA 2003. Some 100 subject specialists throughout the United States and Canada have contributed these reviews. Reviewers are asked to examine the resources and provide well-documented critical comments, both positive and negative. Coverage usually includes the usefulness of a given work; organization, execution, and pertinence of contents; prose style; format; availability of supplementary materials (e.g., indexes, appendixes); and similarity to other works and previous editions. All reviews provide complete ordering and bibliographic information, including title, publisher, price, and ISBN. References to all reviews published in periodicals during the year of coverage are appended to the reviews (see page xix for journals cited). All reviews are signed and the title and affiliation of all reviewers at the time the review was published can be found on page xi. Comprehensive author/title and subject indexes can be found at the end of the volume.

The present volume contains 27 chapters that follow the organization of ARBA. Chapter 1, "General Reference Works," is subdivided by form: bibliography, biography, dictionaries and encyclopedias, handbooks and yearbooks, and so on. The remaining chapters are arranged alphabetically by subject (e.g., Area Studies, Literature, Science and Technology in General) and then by reference type (e.g., dictionaries and encyclopedias, directories, handbooks and yearbooks, indexes).

The ARBA staff is continually striving to improve both the accessibility and timeliness of this resource, while at the same time retaining the quality reviews that librarians have come to expect. ARBA and its companion volume *Recommended Reference Books for Small and Medium-sized Libraries and Media Centers* have been favorably reviewed in such journals as *Library Journal*, *Booklist*, and *Journal of Academic Librarianship*. In 2002, Libraries Unlimited launched

ARBAonline (www.arbaonline.com), a searchable database that provides more than 11,000 reviews of both print and electronic resources from the past seven years. The editors continue to strive to make the companion volumes in this series valuable acquisition tools for academic, public, and special libraries as well.

On behalf of our readers and Libraries Unlimited, I would like to express my gratitude to the contributors whose reviews appear in this volume. ARBA and its companion volumes would not be possible without their dedication and continued involvement. I would also like to thank the staff members of Libraries Unlimited who have been instrumental in the preparation of this work, and particularly Associate Editor Shannon Hysell, for her contribution to this volume.

Martin Dillon, Editor in Chief

Contributors

Stephen H. Aby, Education Bibliographer, Bierce Library, Univ. of Akron, Ohio.

Anthony J. Adam, Reference Librarian, Prairie View A & M Univ., Coleman Library, Tex.

January Adams, Asst. Director/Head of Adult Services, Franklin Township Public Library, Somerset, N.J.

Donald Altschiller, Reference Librarian, Boston Univ.

Elizabeth L. Anderson, Part-Time Instructor, Lansing Community College, Mich.

Mary A. Axford, Reference Librarian, Georgia Institute of Technology, Atlanta.

Jan Bakker, Resource Center Director, North Central Regional Educational Laboratory, Oak Brook, Ill.

Robert M. Ballard, Professor, School of Library and Information Science, North Carolina Central Univ., Durham.

Helen M. Barber, Reference Librarian, New Mexico State Univ., Las Cruces.

Mark T. Bay, Electronic Resources, Serials, and Government Documents Librarian, Hagan Memorial Library, Cumberland College, Williamsburg, Ky.

Craig W. Beard, Reference Librarian, Mervyn H. Sterne Library, Univ. of Alabama, Birmingham.

Leslie M. Behm, Reference Librarian, Michigan State Univ. Libraries, East Lansing.

Laura J. Bender, Science Librarian, Univ. of Arizona, Tucson.

Kenneth W. Berger, Team Leader, Reference/ILL Home Team, Perkins Library, Duke Univ., Durham, N.C.

Bernice Bergup, Humanities Reference Librarian, Davis Library, Univ. of North Carolina, Chapel Hill.

Teresa U. Berry, Reference Coordinator, Univ. of Tennessee, Knoxville.

Barbara M. Bibel, Reference Librarian, Science/Business/Sociology Dept., Main Library, Oakland Public Library, Calif.

Adrienne Antink Bien, Medical Group Management Association, Lakewood, Colo.

Terry D. Bilhartz, Assoc. Professor of History, Sam Houston State Univ., Huntsville, Tex.

Richard Bleiler, Reference Librarian, Univ. of Connecticut, Storrs.

Marcia Blevins, Reference Supervisor, McMinnville Public Library, Oreg.

Edna M. Boardman, Bismark, N.D.

Mary Pat Boian, Assoc. Editor, *Foster's Botanical & Herb Review*, Beaver, Ark.

Mary L. Bowman, Reference Librarian, Noel Memorial Library, Louisiana State Univ., Shreveport.

William Bright, Research Associate in Linguistics, Univ. of Colorado, Boulder.

Georgia Briscoe, Assoc. Director and Head of Technical Services, Law Library, Univ. of Colorado, Boulder.

Natalie Brower-Kirton, (formerly) Staff, Libraries Unlimited.

Sue Brown, Reference Librarian, Louisiana State Univ., Shreveport.

Vik Brown, Assoc. Professor, Music Librarian, Southern Utah Univ. Library, Cedar City.

Patrick J. Brunet, Library Manager, Western Wisconsin Technical College, La Crosse.

Betty Jo Buckingham, (retired) Consultant, Iowa Dept. of Education, Des Moines.

John R. Burch Jr., Director of Library Services, Cambellsville Univ., Ky.

Frederic F. Burchsted, Reference Librarian, Widener Library, Harvard Univ., Cambridge, Mass.

E. Wayne Carp, Professor of History, Pacific Lutheran Univ., Tacoma, Wash.

Boyd Childress, Reference Librarian, Ralph B. Draughon Library, Auburn Univ., Ala.

Dene L. Clark, (retired) Reference Librarian, Auraria Library, Denver, Colo.

Juleigh Muirhead Clark, Public Services Librarian, John D. Rockefeller, Jr. Library, Colonial Williamsburg Foundation, Williamsburg, Va.

Stella T. Clark, Professor, Foreign Languages, California State Univ., San Marcos.

Joshua Cohen, Director for Outreach and Continuing Education, Mid-Hudson Library System, Poughkeepsie, N.Y.

Donald E. Collins, Assoc. Professor, History Dept., East Carolina Univ., Greenville, N.C.

Barbara Conroy, Career Connections, Santa Fe, N.Mex.

Kay O. Cornelius, (formerly) Teacher and Magnet School Lead Teacher, Huntsville City Schools, Ala.

Bob Craigmile, Information Technology Librarian, Jackson County Library System, Medford, Oreg.

Mark J. Crawford, Consulting Exploration Geologist/Writer/Editor, Madison, Wis.

Erin C. Daix, Reference Librarian, Univ. of Delaware Library, Newark.

Joseph W. Dauben, Professor of History and History of Science, City Univ. of New York.

Gail de Vos, Adjunct Assoc. Professor, School of Library and Information Studies, Univ. of Alberta, Edmonton.

Margaret Denman-West, Professor Emeritus, Western Maryland College, Westminster.

R. K. Dickson, MFA Candidate, Wichita State Univ., Kans.

Tara L. Dirst, Technology Coordinator, Abraham Lincoln Historical Digitization Project, Northern Illinois Univ., DeKalb.

Margaret F. Dominy, Information Services Librarian, Drexel Univ., Philadelphia.

Diane Donham, Reference Librarian, Library of Michigan, Lansing.

G. Kim Dority, (formerly) Staff, Libraries Unlimited.

John A. Drobnicki, Assoc. Professor and Head of Reference Services, City Univ. of New York—York College, Jamaica.

David J. Duncan, Reference Librarian, Humanities, Wichita State Univ., Ablah Library, Kans.

Bradford Lee Eden, Head of Cataloging, Univ. of Nevada at Las Vegas.

Jean Engler, Reference Librarian, Koelbel Public Library, Englewood, Colo.

Edward Erazo, Head of Reference, Florida Atlantic Univ., Boca Raton.

Patricia A. Eskoz, (retired) Catalog Librarian, Auraria Library, and Asst. Professor Emeritus, Univ. of Colorado, Denver.

Lorraine Evans, Instruction and Reference Librarian, Auraria Library, Denver, Colo.

G. Edward Evans, Univ. Librarian, Charles Von der Ahe Library, Loyola Marymount Univ., Los Angeles, Calif.

Elaine Ezell, Library Media Specialist, Bowling Green Jr. High School, Ohio.

Kathleen Farago, Reference Librarian, Cleveland Heights-University Heights Public Library, Ohio.

Evan Ira Farber, College Librarian Emeritus, Earlham College, Richmond, Ind.

Lesley S. J. Farmer, Library Media Teacher, Tamalpais UHSD, Corte Madera, Calif.

Michael Florman, Staff, Libraries Unlimited.

Michael A. Foley, Honors Director, Marywood College, Scranton, Pa.

Harold O. Forshey, Assoc. Dean, Miami Univ., Oxford, Ohio.

David K. Frasier, Asst. Librarian, Reference Dept., Indiana Univ., Bloomington.

Susan J. Freiband, Assoc. Professor, Graduate School of Librarianship, Univ. of Puerto Rico, San Juan.

David O. Friedrichs, Professor, Univ. of Scranton, Pa.

Paula Frosch, Assoc. Museum Librarian, Thomas J. Watson Library, Metropolitan Museum of Art, New York.

Jeanne D. Galvin, Chief of Reference, Kingsborough Community College, City Univ. of New York, Brooklyn, N.Y.

Vera Gao, Catalog Librarian, Auraria Library, Univ. of Colorado, Denver.

Joan Garner, (formerly) Staff, Libraries Unlimited.

Pamela J. Getchell, (formerly) Staff, Libraries Unlimited.

John T. Gillespie, College Professor and Writer, New York.

Lois Gilmer, Library Director, Univ. of West Florida, Fort Walton Beach.

Barbara B. Goldstein, Media Specialist, Magothy River Middle School, Arnold, Md.

Pamela M. Graham, Latin American and Iberian Studies Librarian, Columbia Univ., New York.

Laurel Grotzinger, Professor, Univ. Libraries, Western Michigan Univ., Kalamazoo.

Blaine H. Hall, English Language and Literature Librarian, Harold B. Lee Library, Brigham Young Univ., Provo, Utah.

Deborah Hammer, Head, History, Travel and Biography Div., Queens Borough Public Library, Jamaica, N.Y.

Chauncy D. Harris, Samuel N. Harper Distinguished Service Professor Emeritus of Geography, Univ. of Chicago.

Kimberley D. Harris, Public Librarian, Newman Riga Library, Churchville, N.Y.

Ann Hartness, Asst. Head Librarian, Benson Latin American Collection, Univ. of Texas, Austin.

Fred J. Hay, Belk Library, Appalachian State Univ., Boone, N.C.

Lucy Heckman, Reference Librarian (Business-Economics), St. John's Univ. Library, Jamaica, N.Y.

Carol D. Henry, Librarian, Lyons Township High School, LaGrange, Ill.

Diana Tixier Herald, Librarian, Freelance Writer, Grand Junction, Co.

Mark Y. Herring, Dean of Library Services, Winthrop Univ., Dacus Library, Rock Hill, S.C.

Susan Davis Herring, Reference Librarian, Univ. of Alabama Library, Huntsville.

Janet Hilbun, Student, Texas Woman's Univ., Denton.

Susan Tower Hollis, Assoc. Dean and Center Director, Central New York Center of the State Univ. of New York.

Leslie R. Homzie, Reference Librarian, Brandeis Univ., Waltham, Mass.

Shirley L. Hopkinson, Professor, Div. of Library and Information Science, San Jose State Univ., Calif.

Marilynn Green Hopman, Librarian, NASA Johnson Space Center, Scientific and Technical Information Center, Houston, Tex.

Mihoko Hosoi, Public Services Librarian, Cornell Univ., Ithaca, N.Y.

Jonathan F. Husband, Program Chair of the Library/Reader Services Librarian, Henry Whittemore Library, Framingham State College, Mass.

Shannon Graff Hysell, Staff, Libraries Unlimited.

Barbara Ittner, Staff, Libraries Unlimited.

Scott Johnston, Reference Librarian and Asst. Professor, CUNY Graduate Center, New York.

Florence W. Jones, Librarian, Auraria Campus Library, Denver, Colo.

Suzanne Julian, Public Services Librarian, Southern Utah Univ. Library, Cedar City.

Elaine F. Jurries, Coordinator of Serials Services, Auraria Library, Denver, Colo.

John Laurence Kelland, Reference Bibliographer for Life Sciences, Univ. of Rhode Island Library, Kingston.

Barbara E. Kemp, Asst. Dean for Public Services, M. D. Anderson Library, Univ. of Houston, Tex.

Sung Ok Kim, Senior Asst. Librarian/Social Sciences Cataloging Librarian, Cornell Univ., Ithaca, N.Y.

Norman L. Kincaide, Citation Editor, Shepard's/McGraw-Hill, Inc., Colorado Springs, Colo.

Lori D. Kranz, Freelance Editor, Chambersburg, Pa.

Marlene M. Kuhl, Library Manager, Baltimore County Public Library, Reisterstown Branch, Md.

Keith Kyker, Educational Media Specialist, Okaloosa County Schools, Valparaiso, Fla.

Robert V. Labaree, Reference/Public Services Librarian, Von KleinSmid Library, Univ. of Southern California, Los Angeles.

Binh P. Le, Reference Librarian, Abington College, Pennsylvania State Univ., University Park.

John A. Lent, Drexel Hill, Pa.

Jeffrey R. Luttrell, Leader, Humanities Cataloging Team, Princeton Univ. Library, N.J.

Barbara MacAlpine, Science Librarian, Coates Library, Trinity Univ., San Antonio, Tex.

Theresa Maggio, Head of Public Services, Southwest Georgia Regional Library, Bainbridge.

Kay Mariea, (formerly) Staff, Libraries Unlimited.

Judith A. Matthews, Physics-Astronomy/Science Reference Librarian, Main Library, Michigan State Univ., East Lansing.

Judy Gay Matthews, (formerly) Staff, Libraries Unlimited.

Christopher Michael McDonough, Lecturer, Dept. of Classics, Princeton Univ., N.J.

Dana McDougald, Lead Media Specialist, Learning Resources Center, Cedar Shoals High School, Athens, Ga.

Susan V. McKimm, Business Reference Specialist, Cuyahoga County Library System, Maple Heights, Ohio.

Lynn M. McMain, Instructor/Reference Librarian, Newton Gresham Library, Sam Houston State Univ., Huntsville, Tex.

Lillian R. Mesner, Mesner Information Connections, Nebraska City, Nebr.

G. Douglas Meyers, Chair, Dept. of English, Univ. of Texas, El Paso.

Elizabeth M. Mezick, CPA/Asst. Professor, Long Island Univ., Brookville, N.Y.

Robert Michaelson, Head Librarian, Seeley G. Mudd Library for Science and Engineering, Northwestern Univ., Evanston, Ill.

Elizabeth B. Miller, Instructor, College of Library and Information Science, Univ. of South Carolina, Columbia.

Richard A. Miller, Professor of Economics, Wesleyan Univ., Middletown, Conn.

Terri Tickle Miller, Slavic Bibliographer, Michigan State Univ. Libraries, East Lansing.

Paul A. Mogren, Head of Reference, Marriott Library, Univ. of Utah, Salt Lake City.

Janet Mongan, Research Officer, Cleveland State Univ. Library, Ohio.

Terry Ann Mood, Professor Emeritus, Univ. of Colorado, Denver.

Gerald D. Moran, Director, McCartney Library, Geneva College, Beaver Falls, Pa.

Betty J. Morris, Assoc. Professor, State Univ. of West Georgia.

Craig A. Munsart, Teacher, Jefferson County Public Schools, Golden, Colo.

Madeleine Nash, Reference Librarian, Spring Valley, N.Y.

Deborah L. Nicholl, Asst. Professor, Coates Library, Trinity Univ., San Antonio, Tex.

Christopher W. Nolan, Asst. University Librarian, Elizabeth Huth Coates Library, Trinity Univ., San Antonio, Tex.

Carol L. Noll, Volunteer Librarian, Schimelpfenig Middle School, Plano, Tex.

O. Gene Norman, Head, Reference Dept., Indiana State Univ. Libraries, Terre Haute.

David G. Nowak, Asst. Professor and Reference Librarian, Mississippi State Univ. Libraries, Mississippi State.

Marshall E. Nunn, Professor, Dept. of History, Glendale Community College, Calif.

Barbara J. O'Hara, Adult Services Librarian, Free Library of Philadelphia.

Lawrence Olszewski, Manager, OCLC Information Center, Dublin, Ohio.

Robert Palmieri, Professor Emeritus, School of Music, Kent State Univ., Ohio.

J. Carlyle Parker, Librarian and Univ. Archivist Emeritus, Library, California State Univ., Turlock.

Gari-Anne Patzwald, Freelance Editor and Indexer, Lexington, Ky.

Julia Perez, Biological Sciences Librarian, Michigan State Univ. Libraries, East Lansing.

Kevin W. Perizzolo, (formerly) Staff, Libraries Unlimited.

Glenn Petersen, Professor of Anthropology and International Affairs, Graduate Center and Baruch College, City Univ. of New York.

Phillip P. Powell, Asst. Reference Librarian, Robert Scott Small Library, College of Charleston, S.C.

Ann E. Prentice, Dean, College of Library and Information Services, Univ. of Maryland, College Park.

Randall Rafferty, Reference Librarian, Mississippi State Univ. Library, Mississippi State.

Varadaraja V. Raman, Professor of Physics and Humanities, Rochester Institute of Technology, N.Y.

Nancy P. Reed, Information Services Manager, Paducah Public Library, Ky.

Allen Reichert, Electronic Access Librarian, Courtright Memorial Library, Otterbein College, Westerville, Ohio.

Jo Anne H. Ricca, (formerly) Staff, Libraries Unlimited.

Constance Rinaldo, Ernst Magr Library, Museum of Comparative Zoology, Harvard Univ., Hanover, N.H.

Cari Ringelheim, (formerly) Staff, Libraries Unlimited.

William B. Robison, Asst. Professor, History, Southeastern Louisiana Univ., Hammond.

Deborah V. Rollins, Reference Librarian, Univ. of Maine, Orono.

Samuel Rothstein, Professor Emeritus, School of Librarianship, Univ. of British Columbia, Vancouver.

Michele Russo, Acting Director, Franklin D. Schurz Library, Indiana Univ., South Bend.

Edmund F. SantaVicca, Librarian, Phoenix College, Ariz.

Willa Schmidt, (retired) Reference Librarian, Univ. of Wisconsin, Madison.

John P. Schmitt, Regis Univ. Library, Denver, Colo.

Ralph Lee Scott, Assoc. Professor, East Carolina Univ. Library, Greenville, N.C.

Margretta Reed Seashore, Professor of Genetics and Pediatrics, Yale Univ. School of Medicine, New Haven, Conn.

Susan K. Setterlund, Science/Health Science Librarian, Florida Atlantic Univ., Boca Raton.

Ravindra Nath Sharma, Library Director, West Virginia State College, Institute.

Leena Siegelbaum, Bibliographer of Eastern European Law, Harvard Univ., Cambridge, Mass.

Stephanie C. Sigala, Head Librarian, Richardson Memorial Library, St. Louis Art Museum, Mo.

Esther R. Sinofsky, Library Media Teacher, Alexander Hamilton High School, Los Angeles, Calif.

Mary Ellen Snodgrass, Freelance Writer, Charlotte, N.C.

Karen Y. Stabler, Head of Information Services, New Mexico State Univ. Library, Las Cruces.

Kay M. Stebbins, Coordinator Librarian, Louisiana State Univ., Shreveport.

Norman D. Stevens, Director Emeritus, Univ. of Connecticut Libraries, Storrs.

Bronwyn Stewart, Reference Librarian, Sam Houston State Univ., Huntsville, Tex.

John W. Storey, Professor of History, Lamar Univ., Beaumont, Tex.

Mila C. Su, Senior Asst. Librarian, Pennsylvania State Univ., Altoona.

Timothy E. Sullivan, Asst. Professor of Economics, Towson State Univ., Md.

Nigel Tappin, (formerly) General Librarian, North York Public Library, Ont.

Sharon Thomerson, Patron Services Librarian, Villa Library, Jefferson County Public Library, Lakewood, Colo.

Angela Marie Thor, Simmons Institute of Funeral Service, Librarian, Syracuse, N.Y.

Linda D. Tietjen, Senior Instructor, Instruction and Reference Services, Auraria Library, Denver, Colo.

David A. Timko, Head Reference Librarian at the U.S. Bureau of Census Library.

Andrew G. Torok, Assoc. Professor, Northern Illinois Univ., De Kalb.

Mary L. Trenerry, Media Specialist, Millard Public Schools, Omaha, Neb.

Diane J. Turner, Science/Engineering Liaison, Auraria Library, Univ. of Colorado, Denver.

Michele Tyrrell, Media Specialist, Arundel Senior High School, Gambrills, Md.

Arthur R. Upgren, Professor of Astronomy and Director, Van Vleck Observatory, Wesleyan Univ., Middletown, Conn.

Judith A. Valdez, Instructor/Reference Librarian, Auraria Library, Univ. of Colorado, Denver.

Nancy L. Van Atta, Dayton, Ohio.

Debra S. Van Tassel, Reference Librarian, Univ. of Colorado, Boulder.

Vang Vang, Reference Librarian, Henry Madden Library, California State Univ. Fresno.

Vandelia L. VanMeter, Professor and Library Director, Spalding Univ., Louisville, Ky.

Jennie Ver Steeg, Education Liaison/Social Science Librarian, Northern Illinois Univ., De Kalb.

Anthony F. Verdesca Jr., Reference Librarian, Florida Atlantic Univ., Boca Raton.

Dario J. Villa, Reference Librarian/Bibliographer, Ronald Williams Library, Northeastern Illinois Univ., Chicago.

Ed Volz, Director, Estes Park Public Library, Estes Park, Colo.

Kathleen Weessies, Maps/GIS Librarian, Michigan State Univ., East Lansing.

Karen T. Wei, Head, Asian Library, Univ. of Illinois, Urbana.

Arlene McFarlin Weismantel, Reference Librarian, Michigan State Univ., East Lansing.

Lynda Welborn, Director of Libraries, Colorado Academy, Denver.

Andrew B. Wertheimer, Asst. Professor, Library and Information Science Program, Univ. of Hawai'i—Manoa, Honolulu.

Lee Weston, Assoc. Professor/Reference Librarian, James A. Michener Library, Univ. of Northern Colorado, Greeley.

Lucille Whalen, Dean of Graduate Programs, Immaculate Heart College Center, Los Angeles, Calif.

Jan Squire Whitfield, Fayetteville State Univ., N.C.

Robert L. Wick, Asst. Professor and Fine Arts Bibliographer, Auraria Library, Univ. of Colorado, Denver.

Nancy L. Widmann, Consultant/Preservation and Public History, Denver, Colo.

Wiley J. Williams, Professor Emeritus, School of Library Science, Kent State Univ., Ohio.

Mark A. Wilson, Professor of Geology, College of Wooster, Ohio.

Terrie L. Wilson, Art Librarian, Michigan State Univ., East Lansing.

Glenn R. Wittig, Director of Library Services, Criswell College, Dallas, Tex.

Julienne L. Wood, Head, Research Services, Noel Memorial Library, Louisiana State Univ. in Shreveport.

Neal Wyatt, Collection Management Librarian, Chesterfield County Public Library, Va.

Bohdan S. Wynar, (formerly) Staff, Libraries Unlimited.

Hope Yelich, Reference Librarian, Earl Gregg Swem Library, College of William and Mary, Williamsburg, Va.

Arthur P. Young, Director, Northern Illinois Libraries, Northern Illinois Univ., De Kalb.

Anita Zutis, Adjunct Librarian, Queensborough Community College, Bayside, N.Y.

Journals Cited

FORM OF CITATION	JOURNAL TITLE
ARBA	*American Reference Books Annual*
BL	*Booklist*
BR	*Book Report*
C&RL	*College and Research Libraries*
C&RL News	*College and Research Libraries News*
Choice	*Choice*
EL	*Emergency Librarian*
LJ	*Library Journal*
RUSQ	*Reference & User Services Quarterly*
RBB	*Reference Books Bulletin*
SLJ	*School Library Journal*
SLMQ	*School Library Media Quarterly*
TL	*Teacher Librarian*
VOYA	*Voice of Youth Advocates*

1 General Reference Works

ALMANACS

1. **Information Please Almanac, Atlas, & Yearbook, 1996.** 49th ed. Otto Johnson, ed. New York, Houghton Mifflin, 1995. 1024p. illus. maps. index. $24.95; $10.95pa. ISBN 0-395-75525-5; 0-395-75524-7pa. ISSN 0073-7860.

In the 1996 *Information Please Almanac*, a section entitled "Gender Issues" replaces the section on women's issues. The new section incorporates many of the significant topics that had been in the women's issues section. In this reviewer's opinion, when viewed with the section "Family Matters" that follows, "Gender Issues" gives a much better and more balanced coverage of issues of concern to women and all people. Articles on sexual harassment, the Equal Rights Amendment, and the Women's Hall of Fame with selected honorees remain. Articles about gender in the workplace, the fatherhood movement, and spousal abuse are superior to those that they replace.

As a compendium of miscellaneous facts and statistics, the *Information Please Almanac* serves its purpose well. Forty percent of the pages cover three sections alone: "Countries of the World," "U.S. States, Cities, and Statistics," and "Sports." Other sections with information exclusively on the United States include "Business and the Economy," "Consumer Resources," "U.S. History," "Presidential Elections," "Cabinet Members," "Executive Departments and Agencies," and "Presidents of the U.S. (Biographies)." Whether it be environmental issues, the topic of slavery, Native Americans, employment statistics, or birth and death rates, the almanac provides a compilation of useful and current information on the population of the United States.

The United States is the primary focus, but sections on geography, space exploration, awards including Nobel prize-winners, and current events help provide a more international orientation. The "Headline History" section provides brief summaries of human development from antiquity to the present day. The charts and tables with lists of superlatives and significant persons, places, or things are too numerous to review. References and sources can easily be verified using both print and online sources. The *Information Please Almanac* is well indexed and easy to use. Surprisingly the words or terms *CD-ROM*, *e-mail*, and *online* did not appear in the index. While they were defined in the section entitled "Computer Notes," they were otherwise absent from the text. The almanac would not be an ideal selection for current events of a topical nature, but it is an excellent source of current and factual information about geographic localities and significant past events and records, including athletics.—**Robert M. Ballard**

2. **The New View Almanac.** By Jenny Tesar. Bruce S. Glassman, ed. Woodbridge, Conn., Blackbirch Press, 1996. 608p. illus. maps. index. $24.95. ISBN 1-56711-123-8.

This statistical almanac of the United States is divided into 12 major subject areas, such as "Health and Nutrition," "Politics and Government," "Drugs and Crime," and "Agriculture and Natural Resources." The areas are further subdivided into shorter, more specific topics. Each of these topics is introduced by a brief narrative summary and a set of "Fingertip Facts" for understanding the upcoming group of graphs and charts. The almanac contains more than 2,000—mainly black-and-white but also some color—charts, graphs (mostly bar and pie graphs), and maps. Many outline maps of the United States are used to illustrate state data on a given topic. The book contains a detailed table of contents and a subject index.

This almanac is visually striking, including quite a few clever graphs, such as a watch shape depicting leisure time and U.S. apple production shown on an apple-shaped graph. The sources of the graphs vary from U.S. government publications to special associations to popular magazines. While sources are cited, there is not enough detail to verify the accuracy of any graph. The latest date for the data is 1993. More detail on some graphs would be welcome; when state data are given for a certain topic, they are usually for the top and bottom 5 or 10 states. The data are more useful when comparing regions of the country on any given topic. This almanac is not as comprehensive as *Statistical Abstract of the United States* (118th ed.; see ARBA 2000, entry 784), and therefore can be best used as a supplementary source in high school and public libraries. [R: BR, Sept/Oct 96, p. 58; LJ, Feb 96, p. 144; RQ, Summer 96, pp. 561-62; SLJ, Aug 96, p. 183]—**Kathleen Farago**

3. **Scholastic Book of World Records 2002.** New York, Scholastic, 2001. 320p. illus. $9.95. ISBN 0-439-31398-8.

Answers to questions researchers might have relating to record-holders in seven broad categories are accessed through a loosely defined table of contents page and an eight-page, end-of-the-book index. The categories—or sections of the book—named in the table of contents are "Nature Records," "Human-Made Records," "U.S. Records," "Science and Technology Records," "Money and Business Records," "Sports Records," and "Popular Culture Records." Entries in some of the sections are alphabetized while in others they are not. One page is devoted to each world record presented.

No rationale is given for inclusion in this book of world records. However, the following explanation is given for the graphs accompanying the text on each page: "In most cases, the graphs in this book represent the top five record holders in each category. However, in some graphs, we have chosen to list well-known or common people, places, animals, or things that will help you better understand how extraordinary the record holder is . . ." (verso of the title page).

World records can be found in other sources, but the graphs, text, and color pictures illustrating each of the 306 entries in this book make it unique. Unlike most reference books, it is fun to browse and its low price makes it very affordable for school, public, and home libraries.—**Lois Gilmer**

4. **The World Almanac for Kids 1999.** Elaine Israel, ed. Mahwah, N.J., World Almanac Books, 1998. 320p. illus. maps. index. $8.95pa. ISBN 0-88687-826-8.

The *World Almanac for Kids 1999* is an easy-to-follow, comprehensive guide to facts and information about many subject areas. Art, computers, and health and science are just a few of the chapters, which are arranged alphabetically with subdivisions of the major points of interest. There is even a brief description of the approaching millennium that informs the reader the new millennium does not actually begin until January 1, 2001. "Facto the Factosaurus" leads readers to many interesting and eye-catching facts. Photographs, illustrations, graphs, and charts supplement the multitude of information given by the almanac. Color maps also complement the "Countries" and "United States" chapters.

Besides factorial information, the almanac also provides important information on life. It supplies pertinent advice on health, AIDS, and even what to do when offered drugs. The "Money and Business" chapter has a section that discusses budgets. In addition, the almanac addresses environmental issues such as air pollution and recycling.

Overall, the book is a good resource for miscellaneous facts and information. It provides important information while also being fun and entertaining for children. It is not, however, the best source for in-depth research. Even though it is well organized, finding a particular fact can be troublesome. The index is not as complete as one would like. As a research tool, it would be best to supplement the almanac with other, more detailed sources. [R: BL, 15 Oct 98, p. 442-443]—**Cari Ringelheim**

BIOGRAPHY

5.   **Contemporary Heroes and Heroines, Book III.** Terrie M. Rooney and Karen E. Lemerand, eds. Farmington Hills, Mich., Gale, 1998. 699p. illus. index. $63.00. ISBN 0-7876-2215-X.

Contemporary Heroes and Heroines, Book III adds 100 profiles of men and women whose exemplary achievements will interest and inspire young adults to previously published *Book I* and *Book II* (see ARBA 93, entry 45, and ARBA 91, entry 12). Each entry includes a photograph; basic statistics about each hero and heroine; a discussion about motivations, ambitions, and accomplishments; and a mailing address for those still living. Each profile is concluded with a list of sources used.

The entries are alphabetic in the body of the volume. The table of contents is an alphabetic list of the included individuals with a brief description of their claim to fame. The contents pages are followed by the heroes and heroines listed by their field of endeavor. The index of this volume covers all three volumes of the series. This set is a handy source of biographical information in compact form, a useful tool for small or financially challenged libraries. This Gale publication is also available through Lexis-Nexis under "Gale Biographies." [R: BL, 15 Nov 98, p. 610]—**Sue Brown**

6.   **The Grolier Library of International Biographies.** Danbury, Conn., Grolier, 1996. 10v. illus. index. $319.00/set. ISBN 0-7172-7527-2.

This 10-volume set of biographies covers activists; athletes; entrepreneurs, inventors, and discoverers; explorers; performing artists; political and military leaders; scholars and educators; scientists; visual artists; and writers. It is a beautifully organized and well-written set for children and young adults; adults may find it useful as well. The inclusiveness of its contents speaks well for the research efforts of the editors; as they state in the introduction, the set is a "mosaic that spans time and geography while overcoming boundaries of gender, race, and class."

Entries are arranged alphabetically in each volume, sometimes including a photograph of or a quotation from the subject. The life achievements of each are placed in a historical context, and the necessary facts are summarized in a concise fashion. One of the attractive features of this set is the brevity and clarity of the writing, along with the ease of use. Appendixes include a glossary that refers to the words in bold typeface in each entry (for performers, for instance, there is a definition of *glitter rock* and *diva*; for explorers, there is *avalanche* and *malaria*). Another appendix provides a "Sources and Further Reading" list for each person profiled, and a general index includes locations, types of occupations, and people.

Whether the set is describing Italian mountaineers or Mongolian cosmonauts, French actors or African musicians, the editors succeed in supplying a well-rounded and readable addition to any library. It is highly recommended. [R: BR, Sept/Oct 96, p. 57; RBB, 1 April 96, p. 1388; SLJ, May 96, p. 145]—**Barbara J. O'Hara**

7.   Harris, Laurie Lanzen, and Cherie D. Abbey. **Biography Today: Profiles of People of Interest to Young Readers, 1999 Annual Cumulation.** Detroit, Omnigraphics, 2000. 446p. illus. index. $56.00. ISBN 0-7808-0370-1.

As with past editions of *Biography Today*, this 1999 volume features 30 people who have made news and peaked public interest in 1999. The books are designed specifically with young readers (ages nine and above) in mind and the choice of biographees reflects this audience's interests. The 1999 volume features such celebrities as Jennifer Aniston, Ben Affleck, and Sarah Michelle Gellar; sports heroes such as Mark McGwire and Venus Williams; musicians such as Shania Twain; and authors such as Sharon Draper. Obituaries of the famous are also noted here, including King Hussein, Shari Lewis, Frank Sinatra, and Gene Siskel.

Each biography is six to seven pages in length and contains at least one photograph. The entries feature the person's childhood, career, and home and personal life, along with some special anecdotes. This set from Omnigraphics will continue to be well used in school and public libraries catering to children and young adults.—**Shannon Graff Hysell**

8.   **Heroes and Pioneers.** Judy Culligan, ed. New York, Macmillan Library Reference/Simon & Schuster Macmillan, 1998. 414p. illus. index. (Macmillan Profiles, v.3). $75.00. ISBN 0-02-865059-X.

Volume 3 of the Macmillan Profiles series *Heroes and Pioneers* provides brief biographies for 137 multicultural figures from ancient times through the present and is written especially for the older elementary or middle school student. Those personages who are included in the volume were chosen based on their relevance to school curriculum, their importance in history, and their representation of a broad cultural range. The people featured in this volume include America's founding fathers; American and foreign national heroes; wartime heroes; reformers, humanitarians, and civil rights activists; crime fighters; peace activists; explorers and astronauts; and pioneers. Helpful page format design includes timelines, notable quotations, pull quotes highlighting essential facts, difficult words defined in sidebars, and additional sidebars amplifying topics. A table of contents, an index, a glossary, and a reading list for additional information about each person are provided. A list of contributors and sources is also given. Length of biographies runs from half a page to several pages depending on the contributions of the person. Although this volume is not useful for in-depth research by students, it provides concise biographies that give students the essential facts and contributions for each person included. The broad scope of the book makes it a worthwhile purchase for general school and public library use.—**Janet Hilbun**

9.   Madigan, Carol Orsag, and Ann Elwood. **When They Were Kids: Over 400 Sketches of Famous Childhoods.** New York, Random House, 1998. 326p. illus. index. $14.95pa. ISBN 0-375-70389-6.

Anecdotal sketches about the childhoods of celebrities, focusing on their home, school, and social life, compose this volume. It covers personalities throughout history and from many disciplines (e.g., art, science, entertainment, politics). Inclusion depends upon the quality of the stories and their suitability to existing subject categories. The aim throughout the work is to display factors important in their development and themes of childhood familiar to us all.

The 8 chapters, with topics such as "Thoughts and Aspirations," "Hard Knocks," and "Being Different," are divided into subsections, including past traumas and inspirations. Interspersed throughout are quotes from the personalities as well as black-and-white portraits. There is an extensive bibliography and an index, enabling access to all stories about a subject or person.

The arrangement of this book highlights common occurrences in childhood, rather than individual celebrities. Although such a slant provides a different perspective on famous figures, it also necessitates looking elsewhere if full biographical information is sought.—**Anita Zutis**

10. **100 Greatest.** Danbury, Conn., Grolier, 1997. 12v. illus. maps. index. $249.00/set. ISBN 0-7172-7691-0.

Although this attractive 12-volume set holds a great deal of appeal in terms of subject matter and presentation, it lacks substance. Each book focuses on 100 outstanding examples of a given topic or field (e.g., women, tyrants, disasters, inventions). Students will surely be attracted to such volumes as "100 Greatest Disasters" and "100 Amazing Animals," but the information offered is spare. Each entry is given a page of coverage, with approximately one or two paragraphs of description. These are supplemented by large color photographs and sidebars of interesting facts. In addition, each book has an index and several games or activities based on some of the information. Cataloging cards are provided with the set.

Some of the books are organized in topical sections. For example, in "100 Greatest Men," there are sections on humanitarians, scientists, musicians and composers, and so forth. Within these sections, entries are arranged chronologically. Other volumes are simply arranged chronologically. Criteria for selection are not stated, and therefore it is difficult to assess the choices. However, this type of reference is bound to raise questions about the inclusion (or exclusion) of specific people or events (e.g., Mikhail Gorbachev as one of the 100 greatest men of all time). Because the entries are brief, it is also unfortunate that they do not direct students to sources for further information.

The publicity information for this set states that it is aimed at readers in grades 5 or higher, but the typeface size, layout, and content (or lack thereof) seem geared to a younger audience. More important, most of the information contained in this collection can easily be found in a general encyclopedia, so librarians with limited budgets should give careful consideration to the purchase.—**Barbara Ittner**

11. **Prominent Women of the 20th Century.** Peggy Saari, ed. Detroit, U*X*L/Gale, 1996. 4v. illus. index. $115.00/set. ISBN 0-7876-0646-4.

Until recently, history books have focused almost exclusively on the achievements of men. Although recent publications have made an effort to include women and minorities, it is still sometimes difficult to find information about female heroes. This new reference work remedies that to a great extent. Aimed at students in grades 5-12, it gives young readers a glimpse at the many facets of greatness achieved by women around the world in the past century.

The 200 alphabetically arranged biographical sketches tell the stories of such great women as Aung San Suu Kyi, the political activist and human rights advocate from Myanmar (formerly Burma); African American poet Maya Angelou; and Ida Tarbell, the American writer who exposed corrupt practices in the oil industry in the early 1900s. Many of the names are familiar—Marie Curie, Anne Frank, Madonna, Gloria Steinem, Mother Teresa, Margaret Thatcher—but others are relatively unknown. For example, the book tells the story of Annie Dodge Wauneka, the tribal leader who eradicated tuberculosis among the Navajo, and Rosalind Franklin, who co-discovered the structure of DNA.

Emphasis is on U.S. women (encompassing African American, Asian American, Hispanic American, and Native American), but the work also covers women from other countries—China, France, Germany, Japan, India, Palestine, Poland, Russia, the former Yugoslavia, and so on. There are representatives from a variety of fields, such as sports, politics, social issues, the arts, and science. A nationality/ethnicity index and an index to fields of endeavor enable readers to access specific information. The profiles (approximately 5-8 pages in length) are written in journalistic style, and what they lack in finesse is made up for with factual information. Boldfaced headlines and handsome black-and-white photographs will spark the interest of casual browsers, and lists of resources will lead them to further study.

It seems inevitable in such a work as this one that there are some obvious names missing—Angela Davis, Judy Chicago, Billie Jean King—and one might wish for less of a U.S. bias or for a more thorough index. However, this ambitious endeavor is one that should be applauded. The stories will be sources of information and inspiration to students, and the work will supplement the information offered in history textbooks and other resources. While not affordable to all school and public libraries, the price is reasonable. Those seeking a less expensive alternative that covers U.S. women throughout history may consider *Amazing American Women* (Libraries Unlimited, 1995). [R: BR, Sept/Oct 96, p. 50; RBB, 1 May 96, pp. 1534-38; SLJ, May 96, p. 146]—**Barbara Ittner**

12. **U*X*L Biographies: Biographies and Portraits of 1,500 High-Interest People.** [CD-ROM]. Detroit, U*X*L/Gale, 1996. Minimum system requirements: IBM or compatible 286 (486SX or faster recommended). ISO 9660-compatible CD-ROM drive with cables, interface card, and MS-DOS CD-ROM Extensions 2.1 (double-speed drive or faster recommended). MS-DOS or PC-DOS 3.3. 640K RAM. 3MB hard disk space. VGA monitor and graphics card. Mouse (optional). Printer (optional). $325.00/stand-alone version; $450.00/2-8 users. ISBN 0-7876-0538-7. [Also available in Macintosh version.]

Designed for students in upper-elementary through middle school, *U*X*L Biographies* profiles 1,500 current and historical figures who represent an extremely broad range of endeavor. Although, as one would expect, there is strong representation of celebrities (especially athletes and entertainers), there are also entries for Black Elk, St. Francis of Assisi, Amelia Earhart, Vincent van Gogh, Václav Havel, Dean Koontz, Colin Powell, and Faye Wattleton. The entries range in length from 1,000 to 3,000 words and describe the individual's early years, key experiences, and adult careers. Sidebars highlight important events and provide factual summaries of each individual's career. Portraits are included with each entry, and many entries include not only other illustrations but also "fact boxes" that feature additional interesting information about the individual. Happily, the entries reflect the solid, consistent writing style found throughout the U*X*L series, and clearly are designed to engage the reader's interest. Each profile concludes with a list of sources to check for further information.

The software and search engine are simple to use and provide many options for "getting at" the kind of information students would be likely to look up. The main menu offers four search options: by name, by subject term, by personal data, and by custom search. Personal data include birth and death information; gender; nationality; ethnic group (African American, Arabic, Asian American, Hispanic American, and Native American); and occupation. Subject terms are derived from the subject term assigned to each individual based on his or her field(s) of endeavor. *U*X*L Biographies* supports use of Boolean operators and truncation, as well as offering full-text search options, printing and downloading (especially useful with the photographs and other illustrations), on-screen tutorials, and context-sensitive help buttons.

This is a well-executed, high-quality resource that belongs in every school and public library. Although an expensive purchase, it provides exceptionally strong value for its cost. It should prove to be a popular research tool for its target audience. [R: RBB, 1 Feb 96, p. 948; SLJ, Aug 96, p. 60]—**G. Kim Dority**

13. **U*X*L Encyclopedia of World Biography.** Laura B. Tyle, ed. Farmington Hills, Mich., U*X*L/Gale, 2003. 10v. illus. index. $399.00/set. ISBN 0-7876-6465-0.

This resource, designed with middle school and high school students in mind, provides biographical information for 750 influential people worldwide—both historical and contemporary. The 750 chosen are those believed to be the most studied figures at the middle and high school levels. The biographees come from a wide range of fields, from American and world history and government to the sciences, literature, and arts and entertainment.

Arranged alphabetically throughout 10 volumes beginning with Hank Aaron and ending with Paul Zindel, each individual is covered in two to three pages and each has a black-and-white photograph accompanying the text. Information includes their birth and death dates (if applicable), profession, information on their childhood and personal lives, career highlights, and a list for further reading. The biographies are well written and, although brief, provide information that will be interesting to young adults. An alphabetic list of individuals is listed in the table of contents, followed by a list of individuals by nationality.

School and children's public library collections have many sources to choose from for their biographical reference information. For those needing to expand their resources in this area or for those needing updated information, this will be a good selection.—**Shannon Graff Hysell**

CHRONOLOGY

14. Nowlan, Robert A. **Born This Day: A Book of Birthdays and Quotations of Prominent People Through the Centuries.** Jefferson, N.C., McFarland, 1996. 257p. index. $39.95. ISBN 0-7864-0166-4.

For those curious as to the famous or infamous who may have shared their birthday, Nowlan has selected seven prominent men or women—living or dead—from all places, times, and walks of life: authors, speakers, philosophers, statespeople, criminals, celebrities, anarchists, theologians, dancers, actors, athletes, and even murderers. Each entry consists of a brief capsule description of the person and a quotation, chosen to represent the person's outlook, ideas, or sense of humor. Inclusion decisions were made first on the quality of the quotation, then the prominence of the person, followed by an attempt to balance the periods of time represented. The quotations reflect universal truths, regrets, warnings, prophecies, memories, and fundamental questions, and include all subjects: love, death, freedom, sexuality, duty, right and wrong, hatreds, romance, optimism, pessimism, peace, religion, worries, fears. The statements reflect and encompass the contradictions, complexities, wisdom, humor, pleasure, and prejudices of human life. Also provided is a useful index of people, included in the calendar. Those libraries needing such a birthday book will find this a worthwhile acquisition, but much better and more extensive quotation books would be preferable if one needs a source of quotations. [R: RBB, 15 Nov 96, p. 608]—**Blaine H. Hall**

DICTIONARIES AND ENCYCLOPEDIAS

15. **The American Heritage High School Dictionary.** 4th ed. New York, Houghton Mifflin, 2002. 1636p. illus. $25.00. ISBN 0-618-17388-9.

Most high school students will find the *American Heritage High School Dictionary* daunting. In fact, the buyer should be aware that the *American Heritage High School Dictionary* differs from the *American Heritage College Dictionary* (4th ed.; see ARBA 2003, entry 30) in only a few trivial respects, such as the preface and the exclusion of a few vulgarities. Even the pagination is exactly the same. But those high school students who are not frightened off by the impressive list of editors, consultants, and contributors, or intimidated by the learned essay on usage by Geoffrey Nunberg will be rewarded.

It is difficult to know whether *The American Heritage High School Dictionary* should be treated as a dictionary designed for high school students, which it obviously is not, or instead as simply another general dictionary. But users already have *The American Heritage Dictionary of the English Language* (4th ed.; see ARBA 2001, entry 1011), which was generally well received when it appeared in 2000. So we are forced to treat the *High School Dictionary* as it is being billed, namely, for high school students. In many respects, it compares favorably with other similar dictionaries. The number of entries is impressive (more than 200,000, which is more than twice as many as most of its competition in the high school dictionary market). The number of photographs and etymologies are also generally greater than other dictionaries geared for the high school audience.

Like *The American Heritage Dictionary of the English Language*, the most distinctive aspects of this dictionary are the usage notes and detailed word histories that accompany hundreds of entries. A unique feature of American Heritage dictionaries is the reliance on a professional usage panel for determining correct usage, especially for controversial words such as "hopefully," "conflicted," and "impact" (the verb). The voting of the panel is noted, and disagreements acknowledged. This should provide attentive high school students with particularly valuable insight into the nature of language—even the authorities may disagree on correct usage and what is considered "right" and "wrong" is constantly changing. However, some (the present reviewer included) will sometimes still wish for clearer guidance in such matters.

Even unabridged dictionaries become dated within a generation; general interest dictionaries need revising much more frequently, and for that reason alone this updated and revised dictionary is worth acquiring. Even many colloquialisms that have become common only in recent years appear in the dictionary. The entry for "like," with its clearly stated alternative definitions (to mean "say" and a number of other things besides), is characteristic for its insight and utility.

This dictionary is, unfortunately, not for every high school student. But to the extent that it respects its user and does not compromise its standards, *The American Heritage High School Dictionary* deserves our attention and respect.—**David A. Timko**

16.   **The Chambers Encyclopedia.** Trevor Anderson and Una McGovern, eds. New York, Larousse Kingfisher Chambers, 2001. 957p. maps. index. $47.95. ISBN 0-550-13001-2.

Between the concise, mass market almanacs like the *World Almanac and Book of Facts* (2001 ed.; see ARBA 2002, entry 5) and the mammoth *Columbia Encyclopedia* (6th ed.; see ARBA 2001, entry 23), there is a group of single-volume, mid-sized encyclopedias that are roughly comparable in volume, price, and content. To this group should be added a new entry— *The Chambers Encyclopedia*. It is compiled by "an experienced team of researchers and editors" (preface) and, although English in origin, gives good coverage of American subjects.

This cornucopia of facts and statistics is organized into 14 main thematic sections, each subdivided by many smaller subjects. For example, the sciences are covered in sections titled "Space," "Earth," "Climate and Environment," "Natural History," "Human Body," and "Science and Technology." Each section is identified by running heads that appear at the sides of each page. The largest section (over 200 pages) alphabetically covers the world's nations from Afghanistan to Zimbabwe. The information given on each country is standard—about one page in length with a black-and-white map and basic information on topics like climate, government, economy, and history.

As in the rest of the book, coverage ends with 1999 or early 2000. The other sections are more amazing and daring in the range of material covered. For example, in "Thought and Belief," a relatively short section, there are lists of gods from various mythologies; an extensive glossary of names from myth and legend with four to five lines of identification each; a rundown on the world's great religions; a biographical dictionary of world religious leaders; population statistics by religion and country; lists of patron saints (by occupation), of movable feasts, and of Saint's days; and a section on religious symbols and the zodiac. This wide range of coverage is duplicated in the other sections. Fortunately, locating this material is made easy by a thorough, small-type index that is over 90 pages in length. *The Chambers Encyclopedia* contains some illustrations, but they are all black-and-white. It is therefore not as physically attractive as many of its competitors. This volume is recommended for homes and all types of libraries. [R: LJ, 1 Mar 02, p. 86; Choice, May 02, p. 1553]—**John T. Gillespie**

17.   **Children's Encyclopedia.** [CD-ROM]. New York, DK Multimedia, 1997. Minimum system requirements: IBM or compatible Pentium 75MHz. Quad-speed CD-ROM drive. Windows 95. 16MB RAM. 25MB hard disk space. 800 x 600 pixels, 16-bit color monitor. Mouse. 8-bit sound card. Loudspeakers or headphones. $39.95. ISBN 0-7894-2233-6. (Also available in Macintosh version: ISBN 0-7894-2236-0.)

The Dorling Kindersley (DK) Eyewitness book series has been a staple of school media centers and children's library collections for several years. Now, DK Multimedia offers the Eyewitness *Children's Encyclopedia* CD-ROM as a continuance of its high-concept publishing efforts.

Program installation is simple and quick. Although only newer machines will easily meet the system requirements, older school and library computers may fall short. When accessing the program, the user is given an option to access the DK Internet Website, DK Online. (An Internet connection is required to access this feature.) After a brief registration process, the user is given a list of linked Websites. Exiting the browser software takes the user back to the encyclopedia's start-up screen.

Each user must log on to the CD-ROM encyclopedia before accessing information. This process may prove tiresome to busy library personnel who typically load several different CD-ROM encyclopedias into the computer throughout the day. The user is then presented with the Navigator, a graphic interface to the information available through the encyclopedia. The easiest way to access the information is to use the "Search" function and type the desired topic. Users can access all media—articles, video, animations, and others—or restrict the search to a single presentation style.

The typical entry consists of about 100 words and at least one illustration of the topic. "Fact Files" and "Amazing Facts" sections are frequently offered. A helpful *see also* section is provided, which includes many topics. Almost any article can begin an exciting, eclectic knowledge quest. Such quests can also begin by investigating the 20 "virtual worlds." In these virtual reality presentations, users can click "world" elements to access certain sections of the encyclopedia. For example, by clicking the movie theater in the "City" world, the user can learn about motion pictures. Additionally, a slot machine-style button on the Navigator can send the user to a randomly selected article.

But what about the information? After spending a few hours on the program, one nine-year-old said, "It's fun, but I couldn't use it for a report." Although the Eyewitness *Children's Encyclopedia* is intuitive, fun, and beautifully made, its value as a research tool is limited. Several topics of interest to children (dogs, cats, horses) have minimal representation. Articles about countries contain only the information available in a print children's almanac, and states fare worse under the regional approach. Also missing are audio files. Although filled with sound effects, the sounds of animals, musical instruments, and vocal performers are missing.

Clearly designed for the casual elementary-age explorer, the Eyewitness *Children's Encyclopedia* is an inexpensive and professionally produced CD-ROM. However, a student requiring more than cursory information on most topics would quickly discover the program's inadequacies. —**Keith Kyker**

18.   **Children's Illustrated Encyclopedia.** 5th ed. New York, DK Publishing, 2000. 800p. illus. maps. index. $40.00. ISBN 0-7894-6498-5.
      This newly revised edition of the *Children's Illustrated Encyclopedia* has all the child-friendly attributes of DK Publishing's books—color illustrations, lively text, and easy-to-follow cross-referencing. This volume covers some 500 broad topics on everything from science and nature to art and history. The topics are further divided into 2,000 subentries, which ensures that a multitude of topics are discussed. For example, under the entry on John F. Kennedy there are subtopics for the Kennedy dynasty, the Cuban Missile Crisis, and the president's assassination, with cross-references to the Cold War, presidency, and World War II. The book is heavily illustrated with photographs, illustrations, and maps. Near the end of the volume is a 20-page fact finder that provides ready-reference information on world population, constellations, classification of living things, and U.S. statistics, to name a few.
      This children's reference will be valuable in both school and public libraries. The book is presented in an easy-to-browse and easy-to-read style that will be helpful to children and adults.—**Shannon Graff Hysell**

19.   **DK Concise Encyclopedia.** By John Farndon. New York, DK Publishing, 1999. 512p. illus. maps. index. $16.95pa. ISBN 0-7894-3948-4.
      This brief source, designed for children, contains selected basic facts, combined with DK's usual colorful illustrations and photographs, on nine general topics: space, planet earth, the living world, the human body, science and technology, transportation, the world (subdivided by region), people and society, and a history timeline. A reference section concludes the work. Although the occasional error creeps in—for instance a photograph of a Jersey cow is identified as a Guernsey—the brief treatments are commendably succinct and accurate. Although the source is most suitable for a small private collection where children are present, it may also serve as a popular reference or circulating item in a library's juvenile collection.—**Lee Weston**

20.   **DK Illustrated Oxford Dictionary.** New York, Oxford University Press and New York, DK Publishing, 1999. 1008p. illus. index. $50.00. ISBN 0-7894-3557-8.
      This work is a collaboration between DK Publishing and Oxford University Press. It is compiled from Oxford's U.S. Dictionaries Program and is easy to use. In keeping with the DK tradition, this dictionary is filled with photographs and illustrations.
      The front matter consists of a "How to Use the Dictionary" section, which is explicit, along with a "Key to Symbols," "Structure of Entries," a "Pronunciation Guide," and an "Abbreviations" list. The main body of the dictionary is user-friendly, and most pages have at least one photograph or illustration. Under some general terms there are sidebars of accompanying pertinent information. For example, under *flower* there is a sidebar with a close-up photograph of a flower with arrows pointing out various important aspects of the flower as well as photographs of other varieties of flowers.
      This work concludes with a reference section that includes political and physical maps of the world and the United States and Canada; countries of the world (which includes the flag and other pertinent information of each country); the constellations of the sky; measurements; lists of symbols, including chemistry and biological symbols; Braille; mathematical symbols; and even laundry codes. There is a map of the time zones, a list of birthday gems, wedding anniversary gifts, and

a section on grammar and style. This dictionary belongs in everyone's reference library. [R: LJ, Dec 98, p. 86]—**Pamela J. Getchell**

21.   **Encyclopaedia Britannica. http://www.eb.com/.** [Website]. Chicago, Encyclopaedia Britannica, 2002. Price negotiated by site. Date reviewed: Aug 2002.

     Encyclopaedia Britannica has a rich and well-respected 200-year history. It is well known as a scholarly encyclopedic source for both students and general researchers. This online version of the product lives up to its print counterpart's reputation. The simplest way to search for a topic is to enter a word or phrase and click on go. Users can also browse the encyclopedia alphabetically or by subject. The page with search results will display results located in *Encyclopedia Britannica*, *Britannica Student Encyclopedia* (for middle and high school students), and *Britannica Elementary Encyclopedia* (written for young students grades 1-5). It will also display related Websites—all of which have been reviewed by the editors—as well as videos and magazine articles. The user can then select the *Britannica* version they would like to read. The article will appear, along with links to the appropriate Websites and videos. Users can at any time look up the definition of a word in *Merriam-Webster's Collegiate Dictionary* and *Thesaurus* by double-clicking on the word. The encyclopedia also gives users access to many photographs, charts, and maps, all of which can be printed out or e-mailed to another computer.—**Shannon Graff Hysell**

22.   **The Encyclopedia Americana 2002.** international ed. Danbury, Conn., Grolier, 2002. 30v. illus. maps. index. $1,049.00/set. ISBN 0-7172-0135-X.

     Encyclopedia Americana has been a well-respected resource for academics for more than 173 years. This edition marks the sets 67th consecutive revision. After reading the set's preface as well as a review of the 2000 edition (see ARBA 2001, entry 24), it is easy to see that only moderate updates and no expansive revisions have been made to this latest edition.

     Hundreds of experts have contributed to this encyclopedia over the years, which boast 45,000 entries to date. The entries are both authoritative and objective and it is obvious there is collaboration between the editors and the experts as the reviews are written in an easy-to-understand language. Articles that have been updated by the editors of the publication have an asterisk by the author's name. After a brief preface, an extensive list of contributors, and a key to pronunciation and abbreviations, the entries are arranged in alphabetic order. The longer, more extensive entries provide a table of contents; for example, the entry on Africa is divided by geography, the economy, the people, the arts, and history. Many entries also provide cross-references to related articles (either within the article or at the end) and a bibliography listing resources for further research. A glossary of terms accompanies some of the more technical articles (e.g., electricity, stock exchange). There are thousands of black-and-white and color illustrations, photographs, and maps sprinkled throughout the volumes. Although the illustrations are not as extravagant as in other notable encyclopedias such as *World Book Encyclopedia* (see entry 28), they do add significantly to the text.

     This resource will continue to be a significant tool at the reference desk of academic and public libraries. Available in both print and electronic form (see entry 23) libraries will have their choice of how to retrieve its information.—**Shannon Graff Hysell**

23.   **Encyclopedia Americana. http://www.go.grolier.com.** [Website]. Bethel, Conn., Grolier Educational, 2002. Price negotiated by site. Date reviewed: Aug 2002.

     This new online edition of the well-respected *Encyclopedia Americana* is exceptionally easy to use and provides a wealth of information at the fingertips of the user. One of six online publications currently available from Grolier and Scholastic Library Publishing, this resource provides 45,000 articles written by more than 6,000 contributors. Many of these articles link directly into OCLC's WorldCat bibliographic database—up to 25 bibliographic citations per entry. This resource also gives users access to journal articles from the *Americana Journal*. About 250 articles are added weekly and many include photographs from the Associated Press.

Users can either browse the encyclopedia or they can search for specific topics either by article or journal. Users are first given the option to browse by specific subject (e.g., arts, society, geography, history), editors' pick (specific articles or Websites that the editors have found to be particularly useful or newsworthy), journal articles (which links to features stories or online news), and profiles (biographical portraits of 1,500 of *Encyclopedia Americana*'s most frequently searched people). For those needing to narrow their search, an advanced search option is also available.

Added features of this resource include cross-references and links to related articles, bibliographic citations to print and online resources, relevant periodical literature (access to the full text of more than 1,000 periodical articles from EBSCO), and a teacher's guide and student's guide for those articles found in *Americana Journal*. The teacher's guide and student's guide will be useful for those teaching at the high school level. The teacher can take one of the featured articles (or one of those in the archives) and have access to an introduction they can give their class, articles they can assign, activities they can assign, and lists of useful vocabulary. By using this as a teaching tool, one's students will not only learn more about current events but about the history behind them, how to research online and in printed volumes, and critical thinking skills.

Beginning with this online edition of *Encyclopedia Americana* Grolier is in the process of making this resource compliant with the rules of the Americans with Disabilities Act. They have provided a text-only version of this product, which includes all of the photographs, illustrations, maps, and flags, but excludes video and sound files. They are in the process of providing narration for video and animated content.

This encyclopedia will be well received in all high school, undergraduate, and some graduate libraries. It is easy to use and provides an incredible amount of information from credible sources. Those who can afford it should seriously consider its purchase.—**Shannon Graff Hysell**

24.   **Grolier Multimedia Encyclopedia 2002.** deluxe ed. [CD-ROM]. New York, Scholastic, 2002. Minimum system requirements: Pentium 100 or higher processor. Double-speed CD-ROM drive. Windows 95, Windows 98, Windows 2000, Me, XP, NT 4.0, or later. 16MB RAM, 25MB hard disk space. 16-bit color (640 x 480 resolution). 16-bit stereo SoundBlaster compatible card and speakers. Apple QuickTime 4.0 or higher. Direct X version 3.0 or higher. Mouse or compatible pointing device. $29.95. ISBN 0-439-35767-5.

The reasonable price of this two-disk CD-ROM set is only one of the attractive features of the 2002 edition of the *Grolier Multimedia Encyclopedia*. Unlike many other electronic databases, the set displays easy and intuitive navigation. Boasting material suitable for three reading levels, it is an effective reference resource for all age groups. The search system supports Boolean searching and is heavily cross-referenced. In the individual articles highlighted blue words lead the reader to further materials in related subjects. Many of the articles link to online resources selected particularly for research on the subject in question as well as articles in the *Encyclopedia Americana* (2002 ed.; see entry 22) and *The New Book of Knowledge* (see entry 26). "Ballet," for example, has five Internet sites linked to the article.

The multimedia is excellent, boasting still pictures, videos, and sound clips. All the media ran well, except for the Jesse Owens video, which performed an illegal operation. Particularly fascinating are the cutaways. For example, the cutaway of the White House shows the interior of the building a floor at a time. The accompanying teacher's guide crosses the curriculum in providing activities and projects developed for the three grade levels. Unfortunately, the manual is a looseleaf binder with poorly punched pages. It will not stand up to regular use without some reinforcing.

The encyclopedia is updated on the Internet regularly. A cursory check of the "Ballet" articles showed no major changes. There is an alphabetic listing entitled "New Articles," which is material that apparently did not make it onto the CD-ROM. All in all, this is an excellent multimedia encyclopedia and is recommended for purchase for public and school libraries.—**Nancy P. Reed**

25. **The Kingfisher First Encyclopedia.** New York, Larousse Kingfisher Chambers, 1996. 159p. illus. maps. index. $16.95. ISBN 0-7534-5010-0.

This first encyclopedia contains more than 80 entries that provide abundant information on a variety of subjects. Coverage includes entries on Africa, the arts, babies, computers, kings, the human body, and religion, to name a few. Each entry is enhanced by bold, bright, breathtaking illustrations. The information given is clear and concise. *See* references labeled "Find Out More" are offered for the more curious reader.

This is an excellent companion to the *Kingfisher Young World Encyclopedia*, published in 1995 (see ARBA 96, entry 50). It contains a table of contents, a glossary, and an index. This is an excellent source for seeking specific information and a great picture book for browsing. It is highly recommended for all libraries serving children. Preschools to primary schools will find this book delightfully useful. Children of all ages will appreciate it as a gift. [R: RBB, 1 Nov 96, p. 536]—**Mary L. Bowman**

26. **The New Book of Knowledge.** 2000 ed. Danbury, Conn., Grolier, 2000. 21v. illus. maps. index. $699.00/set. ISBN 0-7172-0531-2.

Compiled by an extensive staff of editors, contributors, and reviewers, *The New Book of Knowledge* continues to be an outstanding encyclopedic reference for children's and young adult library collections. Like past editions, the 21 volumes provide many illustrations, photographs, and maps to enhance the well-written text. Content for this encyclopedia is chosen by educators familiar with current curriculum standards, librarians familiar with the reading levels and research needs of children, and cultural specialists. The entries are written to be easily comprehended by young children, although those entries that are more technical in nature will most likely only be understood by the older children in the intended audience.

The volume is laid out alphabetically, with each entry containing one or more of the following to provided additional information: sidebars, diagrams, photographs, maps, chronological timelines, and *see also* references. The publisher has also made searching this encyclopedia easier with the use of word guides at the bottom of each page next to the page number and providing the index in each volume (set apart in blue paper). Many of the entries also contain "Wonder Questions," which will appeal to the natural curiosity of children. Besides the main volumes of the encyclopedia, readers also have access to a paperback supplement titled "Home and School Reading and Study Guides," which features an extensive bibliography as well as activities young users can do to become familiar with the encyclopedia.

What makes this encyclopedia so outstanding are the full-color illustrations, the well-written text, and the fact that the information provided works well with current curriculum standards. This set should be in all school library media centers and public libraries' children's reference collections. It should also be noted that Grolier provides *The New Book of Knowledge*, along with *Encyclopedia Americana* and the *Grolier Multimedia Encyclopedia*, in online versions.—**Shannon Graff Hysell**

27. **Pockets: Encyclopedia.** By John Farndon. New York, DK Publishing, 1997. 512p. illus. maps. index. (DK Pockets). $14.95 flexibinding. ISBN 0-7894-1498-8.

Want an encyclopedia that is both handy and unconventional? This well-illustrated, pocket-size encyclopedia is one of a series of fact-packed miniguides in a wide range of fields covering such diverse topics as aircraft, castles, clogs, gemstones, and many more. Unlike the others in the series, this is a general encyclopedia covering physical and biological sciences, technology, transportation, countries of the world, and history. Smaller topics are covered in two adjoining pages with outstanding color illustrations, captions, fact boxes, and timelines. For example, the section on galaxies has an informational beginning definition of the concept, four color illustrations including pictures of the different galaxy types, the Milky Way galaxy and the Andromeda galaxy, and two galaxy facts. A timeline of world history and a reference section with units of measurement, conversions, wars and battles, and good indexes end the book. This encyclopedia would be an excellent way to introduce students to concepts and a useful source for illustrations. Its unconventional size has drawbacks, but it will be attractive to students.—**Carol D. Henry**

28. **The World Book Encyclopedia.** Chicago, World Book, 2002. 22v. illus. maps. index. $1,065.00/set. ISBN 0-7166-0102-8.

29. **World Book: Special Census Edition.** Chicago, World Book, 2002. 160p. illus. maps. index. Free to schools and libraries with purchase of the *World Book Encyclopedia*. ISBN 0-7166-1294-1.

In publication since 1917, this well-known and well-respected encyclopedia now comprises 22 volumes, including a special research guide and index volume and a "Special Census Edition" with the results of the 2000 U.S. Census. The publishers claim that 30 percent of this 2002 edition has been updated—the most substantial update in the past 5 years—and that more than 125 articles have been completely revised. Many of the updates are to be expected because of the vast amount of new information that has emerged about them within the past year, such as the entries on the Internet and Mars. Others, such as the entry on Viet Nam, are expanded to represent their new importance as a world economic factor and place in the travel industry, instead of the typical U.S. focus on their role in the Vietnam War. Contributing to this update, more than 28,000 illustrations, photographs, and maps are presented here, including reproductions of fine art and well-drawn illustrations of the human anatomy.

World Book has a roster of 3,700 experts who work as contributors, authenticators, reviewers, and consultants. Content of the encyclopedia is determined by what the publisher refers to as the Classroom Research Project. This project allows for the publisher to poll students in 250 kindergarten through high school classrooms and find out what they are researching, how they are researching, and if the *World Book Encyclopedia* is useful in their research. This encyclopedia is based on the schools' curriculum needs and national and state standards. For this reason, this *Encyclopedia* is most useful in K-12 school media centers and children's reference departments of public libraries.

This edition of the *World Book Encyclopedia* features a special volume dedicated to the results of the 2000 U.S. Census. This information will be interesting to young people because it represents the American people as a whole and presents the information in a way that will allow for easy comparisons. The volume gives population statistics found on each state and the 10 largest cities and provides essays on the history of the Census, the population groups of the United States, the impact of minorities in the United States, and a history of the censuses taken around the world.

The *World Book Encyclopedia* is available on both CD-ROM and in an Internet version (by subscription) so libraries will have a choice of the most useful format for their library. Although the print version is bulky, it does provide stunning illustrations and will teach young users valuable research skills.—**Shannon Graff Hysell**

30. **World Book Student Discovery Encyclopedia.** Chicago, World Book, 2000. 13v. illus. maps. index. $299.00/set. ISBN 0-7166-7400-9.

Created for students who are reading at the middle school grade level or below, the *World Book Student Discovery Encyclopedia* is a simpler version of *The World Book Encyclopedia* (see entry 28). This general encyclopedia has thousands of color illustrations, phonetic spellings for harder words, clear cross-references, fact boxes and timelines, and hands-on activities. Articles are arranged alphabetically with prominent guide words for easy locating. An index and atlas with color maps are included in the last volume.

Every article has at least one color illustration or photograph—many have more. The article on sharks, for example, has four photographs, three color illustrations, and a chart comparing the size of different species of shark. The content of the articles is geared toward the interests of children—how many shark types there are, how they eat (ripping live fish apart), where they live, their body parts and teeth, how to be safe from shark attacks, and how people use sharks are covered. Articles could be read for pleasure or research.

The *World Book Student Discovery Encyclopedia* fills a void in the reference area. Children too young to read articles in a regular encyclopedia or off the Web will like this simply written, well-illustrated encyclopedia. Students in ESL classes and older students looking for pictures or illustrations will also find this encyclopedia useful. [R: SLJ, Aug 2000, p. 136]—**Carol D. Henry**

31.   **World Book's Childcraft: The How and Why Library.** Chicago, World Book, 2000. 15v. illus. maps. index. $229.00/set. ISBN 0-7166-0197-4.

World Book's Childcraft has been specially designed to meet the educational needs of young learners. It is intended as a teaching tool for parents to provide their children with the beginning skills they will need for learning. With this in mind, *Childcraft* is geared to be fascinating and enjoyable for children. The goals of this set are to stimulate the process of learning, to develop readiness to learn to read, to encourage natural curiosity, and to create a love of books.

Each volume in the set covers a separate topic that has been selected as a result of international research conducted to identify the subjects that children are most likely to study in school. The majority of the volumes focus on various areas of science such as earth and mechanical science, biology, zoology, astronomy, and geography. The first two volumes focus on reading skills through poems, rhymes, fairy tales, and folktales. There are also volumes on art and mathematics. Two volumes introduce children to cultures around the world, including beliefs and customs along with descriptions of various celebrations in the U.S. and other countries. Multiculturalism is a theme strongly represented throughout *Childcraft*. The publisher intends to annually add new volumes to the set. Along with the 15 volumes in the set there are also 2 handbooks to introduce users to *Childcraft* and to provide suggestions for using the set with children.

This work provides a good starting point for education, but it does seem to focus more heavily on science than on reading or any other subjects. This may be in part because science topics are a large part of children's curiosity and also because science is a subject with international scope. Further, history seems to be one subject that is strongly lacking from the set. This may be because World Book has produced this work for international audiences and U.S. or European history may not appeal to readers in other parts of the world. Perhaps future volumes may at least introduce children to world history topics. Despite this shortcoming, this set is a good teaching tool for parents, teachers, and librarians.—**Cari Ringelheim**

HANDBOOKS AND YEARBOOKS

32.   Ash, Russell. **Factastic Millennium Facts.** New York, DK Publishing, 1999. 128p. illus. index. $12.95pa. ISBN 0-7894-4710-X; 0-7894-4948-Xpa.

Factastic Millennium Facts is a chronological book of milestone events that have shaped history in the last millennium. Each 100 years, beginning with 1000 C.E., is given a broad title (e.g., 1000-1999 is "The Age of Religion") and for each year a specific event is given. The earlier years generally have only one historical milestone listed, but as the years progress and presumably better accounts were recorded, more facts are listed. From 1600 to 1999 several milestones are listed under each year. As with all DK Publishing books there are beautiful illustrations and photographs as well as plenty of sidebars with fascinating information. Often these sidebars compare the past with the present or give century statistics. Before each century's chapter are descriptions of events that make the century memorable, such as global war in the 1900s or exploration in the 1600s.

This work and the previous volumes by Ash titled *Factastic Book of 1001 Lists* (see entry 435) and *The Top Ten of Everything* (see entry 000) are worthwhile for children's reference collections but may be of more use if they can be browsed through by children and young adults.—**Shannon Graff Hysell**

33.   Ash, Russell. **Top 10 of Everything 2001.** New York, DK Publishing, 2000. 288p. illus. index. $24.95. ISBN 0-7894-5960-4.

This book is somewhat misleading in its title as it is less a volume of top 10s and more a volume of lists from every aspect of society. It contains over 1,000 lists in 10 categories: the universe and the earth, life on earth, the human world, town and country, culture and learning, music, stage and screen, the commercial world, on the move (transportation), and sports. More than one-half of the book is devoted to U.S. popular culture and includes many lists of questionable value, such as Bridget Fonda's top 10 movies or Wayne Gretsky's top 10 seasons.

Source information is unevenly provided—while some lists include their source and criteria for ranking, the author does not provide any information on how the list was compiled on others. The *Top 10 of Everything* has become an annual publication and compared to previous volumes there is a certain amount of overlap—some lists are included each year. However, these lists are updated with new information and a number of new lists appear in each volume. The book is a useful addition to any reference collections where such "list" questions are common and vexing, but a more international focus would improve future volumes.—**Terri Tickle Miller**

34.   Cohl, H. Aaron. **The Book of Mosts.** New York, St. Martin's Press, 1997. 340p. $22.95. ISBN 0-312-15482-8.

In the introduction, Cohl writes that his goal in this compilation was to present "the most brilliant, the most flamboyant, the most unbelievable facts" (p. ix). The facts are arranged in 22 subject areas including geography, money, crime, sports, air travel, and health. Information is generally presented as lists, with short introductions. The book includes such facts as the highest mountains, the biggest divorce settlement, hockey play with the most goals, the most romantic cruises, and the most watched television episodes. Brief citations are provided for the facts; the most recent information dates from 1995. As with any such compilation, some facts are already out of date. For example, the section on movies does not include *Titanic*, which would now top several of the lists.

This work is similar in coverage to other books of facts such as *The World Almanac and Book of Facts* (see ARBA 2002, entry 5) and *The Guinness Book of Records 1996* (Bantam, 1996) that include many of the same facts and are cited as the source of some of Cohl's facts. There is no clear organization of the material and, surprisingly, no index is provided. This work is really intended for casual browsing rather than ready-reference. *The Book of Mosts* may answer an occasional question, but for those libraries that own the titles mentioned above and the *Statistical*

Abstract of the United States (118th ed.; see ARBA 2000, entry 784), this is not a necessary purchase. [R: RBB, 1 Nov 97, pp. 506-508]—**Terry Ann Mood**

35.   **The FAQs of Life: Over 2,500 of the Most Frequently Asked Questions and Their Answers, on Every Topic Imaginable.** Camille N. Cline, ed. Kansas City, Mo., Andrews McMeel Publishing, 1997. 662p. index. $16.95pa. ISBN 0-8362-3574-6.

   The FAQs of Life is like a surf through the Internet, but it is all in one place and is quite reliable. It is like those "odd question" files that librarians have kept behind the desk on cards, slips of paper, or even online—but this book has it collected, authenticated, and indexed in one handy place.

   The book contains answers to 2,500 questions that the editor feels are the most commonly asked. Many questions about computers and alternative medicine give it a contemporary flavor, although other popular categories such as food, law, travel, and gardening are also well covered. The editor has divided the questions and answers into 18 chapters with numerous subheadings under each. There is a good index with useful terminology. Generally, the editor lists the sources and writes in a lively, engaging style. It is a great read—librarians will love it. Each entry is under half a page, making it just right for instant gratification. Even when the question does not have an answer (e.g., the Coca-Cola formula), the surrounding information is useful.

   Libraries should definitely select this title. At just $16.95 it is reasonably priced, and it should stand in reference collections along with such classics as *Famous First Facts* (see ARBA 2001, entry 21), the *New York Public Library Desk Reference* (3d ed.; see ARBA 2000, entry 47), and the *World Almanac and Book of Facts* (see ARBA 2002, entry 5). [R: LJ, 1 Feb 98, p. 76]—**Paul A. Mogren**

36.   Giblin, Nan J., and Barbara A. Bales. **Finding Help: A Reference Guide for Personal Concerns.** Springfield, Ill., Charles C. Thomas, 1995. 211p. $49.95; $29.95pa. ISBN 0-398-05995-0; 0-398-05996-9pa.

   As self-help books have become a major industry, and are presumably regularly used by many people to assist them with personal problems, the basic idea of a bibliographic guide to the best of the books in a number of major categories is a smart one. That kind of guide is exactly what Giblin and Bales have sought to produce. Their guide provides brief, and generally helpful, annotations for from roughly 6 to 10 titles in approximately 40 different areas grouped under such major headings as stress, aging, and sexual problems. Among the topics covered are burnout, career changes, divorce, menopause, sleep problems, cancer, and a variety of other ills that triumph over contemporary society.

   Because the idea for this volume is such a good one, it is unfortunate that the contents are, in the end, so disappointing. Apart from the fact that there is no index and that the annotations make for dull reading in comparison to the books being annotated, the titles covered are so out-of-date as to render this guide almost worthless. In today's publishing environment, there is no excuse for publishing a bibliographic guide in 1995 that covers very few books published after 1990. The result is that not only are outstanding books such as Sherwin Nuland's *How We Die* (Alfred A. Knopf, 1994) omitted, but in many cases, especially in areas such as AIDS/HIV (where no book after 1991 is listed), so much has changed in recent years that reliance on books published in the 1980s is a dangerous mistake.—**Norman D. Stevens**

37.   Langley, Andrew. **The Illustrated Book of Questions and Answers.** New York, Facts on File, 1996. 96p. illus. maps. index. $19.95. ISBN 0-8160-3561-X.

   Look out DK Publishing, Facts on File is moving into your territory. Langley's compendium of questions and answers about space, the world, nature, history, and science and technology adopts the characteristic DK Crayola-colors-on-white format. The reference work bursts with energy and data to cover 270 queries that a child may ask or ponder in private. Under the 5 main topics, the author pursues 45 subissues, such as great explorers, world wars, farming, sea mammals, exploring space, the Middle Ages, and habitats. Two-page spreads feature five to seven questions in bold typeface, followed by one-paragraph answers keyed to brightly colored drawings, cutaways, sidebars, maps, and multipart diagrams. A three-page index concludes the work.

Layout is the soul of Langley's work. The pacing is brisk and upbeat, and human features are lifelike. Violence is kept in perspective. Except in historical scenes, the faces tend to be Caucasian, and women play a token role in action shots. Vocabulary challenges readers to ponder such terms as *LCD, compound eye, stalagmite, plowshare, boreal forest, Inuit, Zimbabwe, moraine, lithography, smart card*, and *umbilical cord*. Most questions reflect a sensitivity to children's interests; for example, What is inside the earth? What is a fossil? Others sound more like editors making a hit-or-miss guess about what a youngster may want to know about a prechosen topic; for instance, What was Paris like in the fourteenth century? How did Greek culture spread? What are computer peripherals? These questions reflect what adults want children to know rather than the scope and wording of actual kid-originated questions. Overall, however, the book vibrates with charm and adventure.—**Mary Ellen Snodgrass**

38.　McWhirter, Norris. **Norris McWhirter's Book of Millennium Records: The Story of Human Achievement in the Last 2,000 Years.** London, Virgin; distr., New York, Sterling Publishing, 2000. 256p. illus. index. $24.95. ISBN 1-85227-805-6.

McWhirter has assembled a remarkable compendium of the achievements of world civilization—north and south, east and west—that reads more like a narrative of events, places, and people. Students of world history and trivia buffs will relish the wealth of interesting information that abounds here. McWhirter's experience as the founding editor of *The Guinness Book of Records* is evident on almost every page of this volume.

The work is arranged in 10 general categories that treat achievements in the arts, science, medicine and health, politics and government, building and engineering, transport, war, communication and media, sports, and everyday life. An introductory section provides a millennium timeline, accompanied by comparative essays focused on how the world was in 1000 B.C.E., 1 B.C.E., 1000 B.C.E., and 2000 B.C.E., and how it might be in 3000 B.C.E. This chronological framework is also used as the matrix for presenting information in each of the major sections, allowing the reader to better understand how much civilization has achieved, and at what pace.

Color photographs abound, as do charts that are historical, comparative, illustrative, or thematic. A separate index of people, accompanied by a general index, allow the user to locate every bit of information presented.

Given its low cost, readability, format, and scope of content, this volume should be included in every high school, public, and academic library. The range of areas covered are the same as many reference queries, and can quickly satisfy patron demands for succinct information. This work is highly recommended. [R: VOYA, April 2000, p. 68]—**Edmund F. SantaVicca**

QUOTATION BOOKS

39.　**Scholastic Treasury of Quotations for Children.** By Adrienne Betz. New York, Scholastic, 1998. 254p. $16.95. ISBN 0-590-27146-6.

Scholastic Treasury of Quotations for Children is an outstanding reference work for libraries and classroom use. A wonderful introduction to the concept of quotations, the book is targeted for a younger audience but is equally informative for adults. The book is divided into two main sections. The first section contains the quotations arranged by subjects. The second section has brief biographies of all the people quoted in the book and indicates the subject where they are quoted. The table of contents is arranged alphabetically by subject to help locate quotations about a specific topic. Some sections are highlighted in special boxes that contain more information about special quotations and the people who said them. There are cross-references at the end of some sections that point out similar topics containing related quotations.

Betz has provided an excellent introduction to the book. In it she explains the history of quotations and how books of quotations originated. Betz also discusses how one can use quotations in speaking and writing to introduce an idea; describe a person, place, or concept; add authority and support to opinions; borrow titles from old proverbs and literary works; twist a quotation to make a point; and use a favorite quotation to add style. The author selected quotations for this book because each says a lot in a few words. The goal was to create a balanced collection by including quotations that state clear and direct messages, present a variety of opinions, reflect knowledge and experiences of experts, and present famous statements from English and American literature and history.

Finally, Betz explains the difference between proverbs and quotations and provides several examples of books containing collections of proverbs. *Scholastic Treasury of Quotations for Children* is a compact, concise, and powerful resource book. It is a delightful browse and an equally serious study for those wanting quotations and information about quotations. It is a must-have for all schools and public libraries. [R: SLJ, Feb 99, p. 132]—**Mary L. Trenerry**

2 Area Studies

GENERAL WORKS

40. **Cultures of the World: Belarus, Guatemala, Liberia, New Zealand, Papua New Guinea, and Tanzania.** By Patricia Levy and others. Tarrytown, N.Y., Marshall Cavendish, 1998. 6v. illus. maps. index. (Cultures of the World). $136.52/set. ISBN 0-7614-0811-8 (Belarus); 0-7614-0812-6 (Guatemala); 0-7614-0810-X (Liberia); 0-7614-0808-8 (New Zealand); 0-7614-0813-4 (Papua New Guinea); 0-7614-0809-6 (Tanzania).

Cultures of the World is a multivolume set of books covering cultures of 96 countries. The newest set presents Belarus, Guatemala, Liberia, New Zealand, Papua New Guinea, and Tanzania. Each volume opens with a brief introduction to the country and continues with 12 topical chapters covering geography; history; government; the economy; the peoples of the country (for example, Belarusians, Liberians, Tanzanians); lifestyle; religion; language; the arts; leisure; festivals; and food. Immediately preceding the index are a map of the country, quick notes, a glossary, and a bibliography. The age levels for which the texts are targeted are identified as 4th grade and up; however, the simple vocabulary and excellent illustrations will appeal to younger readers as well. Olympic enthusiasts will enjoy reading about countries with whom they may be less familiar whose athletes are represented at the Games.

The entire set is highly recommended for purchase for all libraries serving children. The collection will add depth and quality of information on the 96 countries represented. It is also recommended for families who may want to select individual volumes for countries of special interest.
—**Margaret Denman-West**

41. **Culturgrams: The Nations Around Us.** Provo, Utah, Kennedy Center Publications, 1998. 2v. maps. $80.00pa./set. ISBN 0-89434-260-6.

Culturgrams is a reference book for finding brief information on various aspects of life in all countries of the world. It has been published in two volumes and includes a glossary of terms used in the book. Volume 1 includes all countries of the Americas and Europe and is arranged alphabetically, covering Albania to Yugoslavia. Volume 2 covers Africa, Asia, and Oceania. All entries are four pages long and have been arranged under broad headings and subheadings, such as background, history, people, customs and courtesies, lifestyle, society, and information about travelers. Special attention has been given to Canada, which has three entries—Canada-Atlantic; Canada-Ontario; and West, Canada-Quebec. The book has a few entries with wrong information and old information. For example, under India the map is old with many wrong names, such as Mumbai for Bombay, Pune for Poona, and Tamil Nudu for Madras. New names have not been shown in the map. The Muslims ruled over India from the eleventh century, not the eighth century. No dates have been given for British rule in India, and the name of France has not been mentioned under foreign powers in India. The information for all countries should be checked for accuracy before printing it. The book certainly gives a broad picture of the lifestyles of people in many countries and their history. [R: RBB, 1 May 98, p. 1532]—**Ravindra Nath Sharma**

42. **Eye Openers Series.** Woodbridge, Conn., Blackbirch Press, 2002. 12v. illus. maps. index. $24.95/vol.

This set from Blackbirch Press is a very simplistic approach to teaching children grades K-3 the concepts of geography and cultures. The front of each book in the series has the statement "Know Your World," indicating that these titles represent cultures from all over the world. The 12 titles in the series to date include the subjects of landmarks, food, clothing, animals, holidays, cities, land, homes, people, transportation, sports, and arts and crafts. For each title, information on the subject being discussed is given on 10 representative countries. For example, the chapter on landmarks has 10 two-page spreads on such countries as China (the Great Wall of China), India (the Taj Mahal), France (the Eiffel Tower), and the United States (the Statue of Liberty). By covering only 10 countries per book, the set does not come close to being comprehensive on any one subject. Some subjects and countries in fact are underrepresented. This set provides colorful photographs and maps that children would enjoy; however, at $24.95 per volume few school libraries will be able to afford this simplistic set.—**Shannon Graff Hysell**

43. **Fiesta!** Danbury, Conn., Grolier, 1997. 16v. illus. maps. index. $259.00/set. ISBN 0-7172-9099-9.

Fiesta is a Spanish word whose meaning—festival—is understood worldwide. As this book points out, there is more than merrymaking to festivals. These occasions for worship and revelry show what different groups of people around the world find important. In this 16-volume set, students can learn what different cultures around the world find important by studying their public celebrations.

Students will learn from this set how people live, eat, talk, think, and worship. It introduces students to a nation's geography, culture, and legends. Along with a description of each festival, each volume provides recipes for food associated with the festivity, songs for the occasion, and at least two traditional stories surrounding a celebration. The names of the holidays and words for songs are not written phonetically, which could hinder student's pronunciation of these foreign words and phrases.

Titles in the set include Brazil, China, Germany, India, Ireland, Israel, Italy, Jamaica, Japan, Korea, Mexico, Nigeria, Peru, Russia, Turkey, and Vietnam. Each volume is 32 pages, for a total of 512 pages in the set. *Fiesta!* also offers special learning features, including colorful global and local illustrations throughout the set; a master set index and glossary in each volume as well as activities designed to help students experience new languages, food, crafts, religions, traditions, and values; and lessons promoting understanding and tolerance in our multicultural world.

This set is aimed at all students from elementary school to high school. It is easy to use, and students will benefit from the material included in each volume. For more than 100 years, the Grolier name has been respected worldwide for signifying excellence in printed reference and research material. *Fiesta!* is another example of Grolier's commitment to producing superior books for students.—**Barbara B. Goldstein**

44. **Fiesta! 2.** Tessa Paul, ed. Danbury, Conn., Grolier, 1999. 16v. illus. index. $265.00/set. ISBN 0-7172-9324-6.

Each of the 16 slim books in this set, titled with a country name, is a resource for middle-grade students who study nations of the world and who like to learn about formal celebrations and cultural traditions. Each cover has a colored picture of an 8-or 10-year-old in traditional dress (for the United States it is western). Inside, an outline map identifies location, and a box contains "first impressions" (basic facts). In each volume there are traditional stories, recipes, songs with music (just the melody), about six words from the country's language, and pictures of items unique to the country (e.g., dishes, clothing, symbols, ritual items). Two crafts for each, which are doable by children under supervision, will make great classroom display items. Religious festivals, central in popular and national celebrations in much of the world, are included, and there is often a box briefly outlining a religion's basic tenets. This set will be a welcome addition to the multicultural studies shelf. Set 1, titled *Fiesta!* (see entry 43), has similar material for16 other countries.—**Edna M. Boardman**

45. **Junior Worldmark Encyclopedia of Cities.** Jill Copolla and Susan Bevan Gall, eds. Farmington Hills, Mich., U*X*L/Gale, 2000. 4v. illus. maps. index. $149.00/set. ISBN 0-7876-4870-1 (v.1); 0-7876-4871-X (v.2); 0-7876-4872-8 (v.3); 0-7876-4873-6 (v.4).

This reference publication, aimed primarily at middle school students, presents a wealth of information about 50 world cities, chosen to represent the continents and cultures of the world.

Even though this reference work provides information on 50 world cities, its primary emphasis is the United States. This collection presents information on 25 cities from North America (21 from the United States), 9 from Asia, 7 from Europe, 5 from Africa, and 4 from South America. Since only 50 cities are examined, there are definite limitations to the usefulness of this work, but the content on the cities is very informative.

The examination of the cities is broken up into 22 categories of investigation, including but not limited to general demographic information, history, government, economy, environment, shopping, and sports. One of its most valuable contributions is that each city includes a section called "For Further Study," which provides the reader with many resources for further research, including Websites, government offices, tourist offices, books, and other publications.

This four-volume reference collection includes many black-and-white maps, charts, and photographs. This set would better suit its audience if it included color photographs and provided more visual stimulation, but it provides useful, informative content on its subject. It is recommended for school and public libraries.—**Tara L. Dirst**

46. **Junior Worldmark Encyclopedia of the Nations.** Timothy L. Gall, Susan Bevan Gall, and others, eds. Detroit, U*X*L/Gale, 1996. 9v. illus. maps. index. $225.00/set. ISBN 0-7876-0741-X.

Young students will appreciate this well-organized set of information on countries of the world. The 35 numbered headings are consistent for all of the 193 entries, Afghanistan through Zimbabwe, making it possible for the user to quickly compare 2 or more countries. Headings cover geography and environment, history, population and culture, government, economy, health and education, recreation, famous people, and additional bibliographic sources for each.

Entries begin with illustrations of the national emblem and flag of the country in question; the name of the capital; and brief information about the anthem, currency, weights and measurement system, holidays, and international time difference. However, emblems and flags are displayed in black-and-white, and students must refer to a color symbol key at the beginning of the volume. This is one drawback in an otherwise excellent reference tool. The encyclopedia does not provide a heading for ethnic food, which would be helpful.

Each entry has a map of the country showing major cities and adjoining countries plus graphic presentation of some data, including a chart of social indicators comparing the country to averages for low-income and high-income countries and to the United States. More than 300 black-and-white photographs throughout the entire set reflect daily life and scenery one may expect to see in that country. All volumes end with a comprehensive glossary. Volume 9 contains an index to the full set.

This set is highly recommended for student use. The publisher also offers a companion set, four volumes of in-depth information about U.S. states and territories (*Junior Worldmark Encyclopedia of the States* [see entry 50]) for $110. [R: RBB, 1 May 96, p. 1530; SLJ, Aug 96, p. 182]—**Jean Engler**

47.   **Lands and Peoples.** Danbury, Conn., Grolier, 1999. 7v. illus. maps. index. $269.00/set. ISBN 0-7172-8021-7.

This set is organized by continent, and the individual volumes by countries. It could be argued that as a whole it deals with neither "lands" (in the sense of geographically, historically, or culturally distinct regions) nor "peoples" (in the sense of language or ethnic groups), but only with modern nation-states. Inasmuch as many current junior high school social studies texts have abandoned the artificially constricting criterion of United Nations membership as the most productive approach to understanding the world we live in, this set will not provide adequate support for students' work outside the classroom. On the other hand, because of its competent entries, written by a battery of capable scholars, its handy summaries of facts and figures, its flags and maps, and its generally representative photographs, it will be of great help to students eager to gather materials efficiently for school reports. All entries include materials on the landscape, language, religion, history, and government; countries deemed significant include topical discussions. If this set is intended for use in teaching beginning library skills, it will certainly serve. But programs that might consider it for use in reinforcing social studies lessons would do well to look elsewhere.—**Glenn Petersen**

48.   **The World Book Encyclopedia of People and Places.** Chicago, World Book, 2000. 6v. illus. maps. index. $229.00/set. ISBN 0-7166-3797-9.

This six-volume encyclopedia provides articles on the nations of the world. Each country's entry summarizes its history, geography, economy, culture, and politics. Many of the listings also give additional information on the nation's environment, major cities, arts, natural resources, industry, religion, indigenous peoples, and so on. Features include photographs, fact boxes with key socioeconomic data, maps, and timelines. Of particular interest is a pie chart showing each nation's average caloric intake compared to the recommended daily allowance. For example, this graphic shows that the population of Bhutan consumes 107 percent of the recommended daily intake of 2,345 calories.

The cumulative index is detailed and indicates topics by subject, such as the Masai Steppe, the Punic Wars, and Voltaire. Plus, there are subheadings under each country's name, such as agriculture in Chile. This is a useful general-interest reference. [R: BR, Sept/Oct 2000, p. 66; RUSQ, Winter 2000, pp. 193-194]—**Adrienne Antink Bien**

UNITED STATES

49.   **The Blackbirch Kid's Visual Reference of the United States.** Woodbridge, Conn., Blackbirch Press, 2002. 336p. illus. maps. index. $49.94. ISBN 1-56711-659-0.

This colorful, fact-filled work will be an ideal addition to elementary and middle school libraries as well as children's reference collections in public libraries. Everyone is bound to find something of interest here as well as learn something new about their own state. The work begins with a section titled "A Look at the 50 States," which shows with illustrative maps the most and least populated states, the states and cities with the highest and lowest temperatures, the largest and smallest states, the states with the longest rivers, the states with the highest and lowest per capita incomes, and even the cities with the worst traffic. From here the book alphabetically lists each state, providing each with a four-page entry. First readers will find information on the state's nickname, population, statehood, electoral votes, and capital. It then discusses the geography, its history, and how it is today. The information is supplemented with color photographs of the city and its people, charts and maps, and sidebars with facts. After the states are discussed the work also looks at the U.S. territories of American Samoa, Guam, the Northern Mariana Islands, Puerto Rico, and the U.S. Virgin Islands. A short list of resources for further information follows, which includes books and Websites, and an index.—**Shannon Graff Hysell**

50.   **Junior Worldmark Encyclopedia of the States.** 2d ed. Timothy L. Gall and Susan Bevan Gall, eds. Farmington Hills, Mich., U*X*L/Gale, 1999. 4v. illus. maps. index. $110.00/set. ISBN 0-7876-3796-3.
       This junior reference is a well-organized, clearly written presentation of basic information about the nation's 50 states, Washington, D.C., Puerto Rico, and U.S. Pacific and Caribbean dependencies. A final 44-page chapter, organized in similar fashion to the state chapters, is devoted to an overview of the United States. Based on the 4th edition of *Worldmark Encyclopedia of the States* (Eastword, 1997), the work is useful for fourth grade through junior high school readers. Each state's information is arranged under 40 numbered headings. Examples are "1 Location and Size," "5 Environmental Protection," "8 Languages," "19 Industry," "26 Energy and Power," "39 Famous People," and "40 Bibliography." A full-page state map appears early in each state chapter. All four volumes have an identical two-page glossary and a list of abbreviations and acronyms. Only the final volume carries the 11-page index.
       The 2d edition includes 2 features not found in the 1996 1st edition: a table of governors and the years they served is added to each state chapter, and Websites are added to each state's selected bibliography. The 2d edition's information is also updated and several new photographs are included. Photographs capture scenic views and highlight state attributes, such as the photographs of a farm in Dane County, Wisconsin, and a street in Park City, Utah, site of the 2002 Winter Olympics. Unfortunately, a few typographical errors slipped by the Gale editors. One was found in the governor's table titled "Colorado Governors: 1886-1999." Colorado became a state in 1876, a fact correctly reported on the first page on the Colorado chapter. The table was up-to-date, however, with the inclusion of the new Colorado governor elected in 1999. There are two strong reasons for recommending this reference tool for junior collections. One is the overall brevity, accuracy, and readability of the information. The other is that the set is organized so well that it would serve as an aid in teaching how to use multivolume reference works.—**Nancy L. Widmann**

51.   **Macmillan Color Atlas of the States.** By Mark T. Mattson. New York, Macmillan Library Reference/Simon & Schuster Macmillan, 1996. 377p. illus. maps. $100.00. ISBN 0-02-864659-2.
       Rich in facts and as inviting as a cornucopia, the Macmillan atlas spills out a pleasurable 4-color guided tour of the 50 states, Washington, D.C., Puerto Rico, the U.S. Virgin Islands, Guam, American Samoa, and the Northern Mariana Islands. The delightful layout and clear subheadings entice the student, teacher, parent, librarian, and general reader. Within this hefty volume are flap copy synopsizing the contents and a clever pictorial table of contents—a subdued U.S. map featuring red-lettered page numbers of entries alphabetized by state. The formal table of contents precedes acknowledgments. A surprisingly unattractive and unimaginative two-page introduction does a poor job of initiating young readers into the purpose and reference style of an atlas. Models and sidebars would help.
       Each state receives a seven-page entry. The first page of the entry features the seal and motto, which is translated into English. Legal holidays and a brief history of the state flag are followed by festivals and events and a small map situating the state in its region (e.g., Colorado set among Montana, Idaho, Wyoming, Utah, Nevada, Arizona, and New Mexico). Alongside the cluster

are figures comparing the other states in population and a list repeating state capitals. The right column covers revenues and expenditures and general financial data, such as per capita income and sales tax. A second map indicates the size, location, boundaries, and measurements of the state. A paragraph on facts includes the origin of the state name; the nickname; and the state song, bird, and tree. It is unusual for a quality reference work to pass up an opportunity to picture these last two details.

The second page offers a scale map featuring highways, cities, airports, lakes, state parks, welcome centers, county seats, and educational institutions. Cultural attractions are described more fully below. Additional pages cover weather, topography, land use, hydrology, history, events, population figures and projections, famous citizens, ethnicity, education, economy, and resources. A pie chart displays employment percentages. The body concludes with a handy columnar listing of facts by state. An unexplained one-page appendix discusses the environmental quality in six states.

Macmillan excels at layout and graphics. Page numbers in red are easy to spot, typefaces are clear, and maps are subtly shaded. The details are suited to young readers. Mattson has done a masterful job of using space to advantage. However, text is marred by unsubtle nuances (e.g., Arizona rejects the holiday honoring Martin Luther King Jr., frequent mention of polygamy in Mormon history); questionable priorities (e.g., biographer Katharine Anthony over Maya Angelou); and omissions (e.g., Black Hills revered as sacred ground, U.S. presidents born in North Carolina), all of which indicate the need for better editing. Historical content favors athletes, outlaws, politicians, and movie stars, and misses opportunities to pinpoint the Trail of Tears and the Long Walk and to honor great Native American speakers, philosophers, artisans, and leaders.

Overall, the writing is heavy-handed and male-centered. California's entry ignores Japanese internment at Camp Manzanar and the work of conservationist John Muir and the Sierra Club, but allots five lines to riots, two to assassination, six to earthquakes and fire, and seven to the O. J. Simpson trial. North Carolina's entry overemphasizes the absurdities of Jesse Helms but omits comment on evangelist Billy Graham. A library reference work costing $100 can do better. [R: RBB, 1 Nov 96, pp. 536-38]—**Mary Ellen Snodgrass**

52. **Scholastic Encyclopedia of the United States.** By Judy Bock and Rachel Kranz. New York, Scholastic, 1997. 139p. illus. maps. index. $17.95. ISBN 0-590-94747-8.

This encyclopedia is a slender, oversized, 1-volume work for middle-grade students needing a source for reports on individual U.S. states and territories. A two-page spread is allocated to each state or territory (e.g., Guam, Puerto Rico, American Samoa, and U.S. Virgin Islands). A blue-background sidebar on the left lists "basic" information—total population, area, and state bird. Another on the right gives "Fascinating Facts," which includes different information for each state or territory but usually lists famous people and some touch of humor. The large-print text endeavors to encapsulate the state's geography; history; industry; and cultural, racial, and ethnic makeup. It also often spots some controversial element, such as race, in each state's history or situation. In some entries, the authors note special tourist attractions. A small line map identifies the location of each state in relation to the whole.

Librarians and teachers should not depend on this work entirely to teach a unit on the states. The map work is extremely weak; there is not a single map showing physical features, or any place other than the state itself. Even the location of state capitals is not given. The map of the United States has Hawaii and a tiny Alaska as insets. The frequent reference to elements of controversy is unfortunate because the issues are never examined adequately. Black-and-white archival photographs do not always show places as they currently look. The appendixes include a limited bibliography for child readers and a state-by-state list of places to visit. There are no reference to or pictures of state flags.—**Edna M. Boardman**

AFRICA

53.   **Cultural Atlas of Africa.** rev. ed. Jocelyn Murray, ed. New York, Facts on File, 1998. 240p. illus. maps. index. $50.00. ISBN 0-8160-3813-9.

Africa's rapidly changing social climate requires reexaminations of cultural information, and former International African Institute's researcher Murray's volume should improve most libraries' resources. This update of the 1981 edition (see ARBA 82, entry 325), written by an international team of experts, prominently features 96 specially drawn maps and 284 color and 85 black-and-white illustrations, supplemented by textual commentary. A 12-page overview of Africa's physical background introduces the volume. Part 2, the cultural background, features excellent maps and photographs on languages, religion, history and archaeology, architecture, the arts, and literacy. The book's final half, part 3, covers individual nations, with 2 pages on each country given over to maps, short overview essays, and some statistical data. A gazetteer, index, and flag page conclude the volume.

As handsome as this work is upon first glance, closer examination reveals basic flaws. First, too many maps and photographs are split by the binding, making good photograph reproduction difficult. Second, statistical data are limited; any good almanac will provide more detail on the nations. Finally, some sections (e.g., "early man") do not reflect any research over the past 20 years, at least as is demonstrated by Murray's bibliography —a serious flaw for any volume on cultural studies. However, because this is the only up-to-date atlas focusing on African culture, *Cultural Atlas of Africa* is recommended for all public and academic libraries.—**Anthony J. Adam**

ASIA

54.   Blunden, Caroline, and Mark Elvin. **Cultural Atlas of China.** rev. ed. New York, Checkmark Books/Facts on File, 1998. 240p. illus. maps. index. $50.00. ISBN 0-8160-3814-7.

This is a well-crafted book that provides a visual and cultural overview of China, through a blend of readable text and vividly presented maps, illustrations, and photographs, most of which are in full color. The attractive maps, used for geographical, demographical, and historical purposes particularly stand out, as do interesting sidebars, such as that on the excavation of the underground army of the First Emperor of Quin, and the full, informative captions of illustrations and figures.

The book is divided into sections on space, time, and symbols and society. The "Space" section provides geographic and demographic contexts for the history that follows, using maps to trace the regional structure of China—typology, climate, agriculture, settlement patterns, and population density. The section titled "Time" surveys China from the Peking Man era to modern times, bringing in aspects of politics; society; and art of the archaic, imperial, and modern worlds. "Symbols and Society" is even more fascinating, as it uses a thematic approach to look at aspects of Chinese culture, including origins of the Chinese language and writing system; the traditions of poetry; philosophy and religion; architecture; principles of mathematics; the arts of theater, ceramics, and music; agriculture and cuisine; family life; and the interaction of China with the West. Also provided are a chronology, bibliography, gazetteer, and index.

This updated version of the 1983 volume *Cultural Atlas of China* has been amended to include new textual and visual information and three new features on Taiwan, the Chinese Diaspora, and China's "natural environment." The latter has an emphasis on water and the Three Georges Dam project. Because of the brevity of their treatment and the importance Taiwan and the Diaspora should be accorded, it would have been better to have not included these sections. This work is recommended for making this complex country accessible to the general public.—**John A. Lent**

55.   Clark, Donald N. **Culture and Customs of Korea.** Westport, Conn., Greenwood Press, 2000. 204p. illus. maps. index. (Culture and Customs of Asia). $45.00. ISBN 0-313-30456-4.

The United States had already fought three major wars, one of which was the Korean War, in Asia in the twentieth century. Today, Asia is not only one of America's leading trading partners, but also the ancestral homelands of one of America's fastest growing minorities. But for some reason, as the editor of the series has noted, Asia remains for most of us a relatively unfamiliar, if not stereotypical or even mysterious, "Oriental" land.

The work under review, *Culture and Customs of Korea*, should serve as an excellent introduction in helping Americans get a better understanding of one of Asia's major civilizations. It is organized into nine chapters, covering every aspect of Korea's culture and customs, such as thought and religion; arts and literature; performing arts; life in urban Korea; and gender, marriage, and the lives of Korean women. Although the information provided is rather brief, users should be able to learn virtually every essential characteristic of Korean culture and customs (rituals of courtship, traditional Korean marriage ceremony, traditional Korean costumes, funeral customs, and so on). The coverage of modern life in North Korea, however, is rather limited. Also included in the text are a chronology (2333 B.C.E.-2000 C.E.), a glossary, and a subject index.

High school and college students, business people, and tourists should find this work useful. School, public and academic libraries ought to purchase this publication in order that it may be used as a reference source or as an introductory textbook.—**Binh P. Le**

56.   Johnson, Gordon. **Cultural Atlas of India.** New York, Facts on File, 1996. 240p. illus. maps. index. $50.00. ISBN 0-8160-3013-8.

This excellent cultural atlas deals with the Indian subcontinent, which is the home of 20 percent of the world's population. Four major religions of the world—Hinduism, Buddhism, Sikhism, and Jainism—had their birth on this ancient land. People of other religions of the world, including Christians, Muslims, and Jews, have also lived on the subcontinent for centuries, which is solid proof of successful diversity. The book introduces readers to the rich cultural history, different religions, arts and architecture, social and political organizations, literature, science, and other aspects of a remarkable people and unique land.

The book is divided into three parts, and the first two parts are devoted to India. Part 1 deals with the physical and cultural background of India, encompassing land, climate, agriculture, people, religion, architecture, and the society. Part 2 covers the prehistory and early history of India, the medieval period dominated by Muslim rule, the history of the state of Bengal, rising Maratha power, and the impact of Europeans' rule in India. There is a special chapter on the making of modern India that discusses the rise of nationalism; the role of Mahatma Gandhi in gaining independence for India from British rule; the introduction of railways; Indian dress; music, dance, drama, and cinema; the partition of India in 1947; and economic development.

Part 3 of this atlas has short chapters on the other countries of the Indian subcontinent, including Bangladesh, Bhutan, Nepal, Pakistan, and Sri Lanka. There are a few chapters on regions of India also, such as the Northwest, the Northeast, and Central India. It includes a glossary of Indian names and words; a bibliography on different subjects; a gazetteer; a list of contributors; an index; and a chronological table of the cultural, economic, and political history of India. There are more than 250 beautiful illustrations and 36 color maps to support the text. It is difficult to write a book about the Indian subcontinent in 240 pages, but Johnson has done a remarkable job of introducing India and other South Asian countries in brief to readers. *Cultural Atlas of India* is an excellent addition to the literature and is recommended for all types of libraries.—**Ravindra Nath Sharma**

57. Kamachi, Noriko. **Culture and Customs of Japan.** Westport, Conn., Greenwood Press, 1999. 187p. illus. maps. index. (Culture and Customs of Asia). $45.00. ISBN 0-313-30197-2.

For years, most Japanese leaving the country for a long trip somehow ended up with a copy of Nippon Steel's *Nippon: The Land and Its People*. Now in its 20th edition, it continues to answer a variety of typical questions about Japanese history and culture with facing English and Japanese texts. However, as Japan became more of an economic powerhouse, a number of popular handbooks to understanding Japan for Americans emerged, some by writers whose Japanese knowledge was limited to brief visits and thus were full of whimsical impressions and factual errors. To counter this, "experts" were brought in to create newer guides. *Culture and Customs of Japan* is another example of this trend, written by University of Michigan, Dearborn, professor Noriko Kamachi. The book, although written by a historian, is not an academic one from both a positive angle (in that it is very readable) and a more critical one (there are few footnotes and the four pages of suggested readings are neither descriptive nor evaluative). Indeed, the table of contents reflects the series' aim of introducing Asian culture (religion; literature; art; housing; food; clothing; women, marriage, and family; festivals; entertainment; and social customs) to general Western audiences. From this perspective it could be seen as a cultural counterpart to the CIA country handbook, especially as Kamachi largely relegates post-war political Japan to three pages in the historical introduction. From the perspective of a ready-reference work, *The Kodansha Encyclopedia of Japan* (see ARBA 84, entry 305) or *Japan: An Illustrated Encyclopedia* (see ARBA 94, entry 115) are strongly suggested. Komachi's selection of topics and explanations are a good, readable (junior high and above) introduction to the vanishing world of Japanese traditional culture. If Greenwood comes out with a 2d edition, the editor should not to be afraid of the political aspects and perhaps should choose a less stereotypical cover photograph than the current one of a woman in kimono and bamboo umbrella.—**Andrew B. Wertheimer**

AUSTRALIA AND THE PACIFIC AREA

58. Banting, Erinn. **Australia: The Culture.** New York, Crabtree, 2003. 32p. illus. index. (Lands, Peoples, and Cultures Series). $22.60; $7.95pa. ISBN 0-7787-9345-1; 0-7787-9713-9pa.

59. Banting, Erinn. **Australia: The Land.** New York, Crabtree, 2003. 32p. illus. maps. index. (Lands, Peoples, and Cultures Series). $22.60; $7.95pa. ISBN 0-7787-9343-5; 0-7787-9711-2pa.

60. Banting, Erinn. **Australia: The People.** New York, Crabtree, 2003. 32p. illus. index. (Lands, Peoples, and Cultures Series). $22.60; $7.95pa. ISBN 0-7787-9344-3; 0-7787-9712-0pa.

These three volumes are designed with elementary-age children in mind. The books provide concise, general information and are filled with colorful photographs and illustrations. The first volume addresses the culture of Australians, beginning with the Aboriginals and continuing on with the many cultures that live there now, including the original British settlers, Europeans, Asians, and those from the Middle East. The book discusses how this mix of many cultures has shaped the religious practices, the holidays, the language, and the arts in Australia. *Australia: The Land* discusses the evolution of how Australia was formed two million years ago. It looks at the various wildlife, weather patterns, and types of crops grown on the continent. Special sections discuss the famous Australian outback and the Great Barrier Reef. The final volume, *Australia: The People*, discusses the history of the people of Australia as well as how they live today, the sports of the country, and families and schools.

The information in these three volumes is very general. The hardback price of $22.60 per volume will be too steep for most school libraries that would be interested in these volumes. At

$7.95 for each paperback volume, however, those needing this type of information should be able to easily afford this 3-volume set.—**Shannon Graff Hysell**

61.   Nickles, Greg. **Philippines: The Culture.** New York, Crabtree, 2002. 32p. illus. index. (A Bobbie Kalman Book: The Lands, Peoples, and Cultures Series). $15.45 reinforced library binding; $7.16pa. ISBN 0-7787-9354-0 reinforced library binding; 0-7787-9722-8pa.

62.   Nickles, Greg. **Philippines: The Land.** New York, Crabtree, 2002. 32p. illus. maps. index. (A Bobbie Kalman Book: The Lands, Peoples, and Cultures Series). $15.45 reinforced library binding; $7.16pa. ISBN 0-7787-9352-4 reinforced library binding; 0-7787-9720-1pa.

63.   Nickles, Greg. **Philippines: The People.** New York, Crabtree, 2002. 32p. illus. index. (A Bobbie Kalman Book: The Lands, Peoples, and Cultures Series). $15.45 reinforced library binding; $7.16pa. ISBN 0-7787-9353-2 reinforced library binding; 0-7787-9721-Xpa.
      This new set in Bobbie Kalman's The Lands, Peoples, and Cultures Series focuses on the more than 7,000 islands that comprise the Philippines. Following the same format as previous releases in the series, this set is organized into 3, 32-page volumes. *The Culture* volume explores the traditions and history of the many different groups that inhabit the Philippine islands. The language, customs, religions, holidays, and festivals of the Filipinos are covered along with Filipino art, music, dance, literature, and folklore. A Tagalog folktale about a carabao is even included. In *The Land* volume, information is provided on the Pacific archipelago's geography, climate, agriculture, natural resources, and wildlife. This volume also includes brief information about the Filipino people, including the Tagalog, Cebuano, Igorot, Manobo, and Negrito groups.
      The People volume discusses the diverse groups that inhabit the islands, each with their own history, culture, and language. A general history section covers the Filipinos' fight for independence from the Spanish, the Spanish-American War, and American rule and World War II. This volume expands *The Land* volume's coverage to discuss a few more Filipino groups, such as the Kalinga and Tausug groups. Daily life, education, sports, clothing, and cuisine are also covered. Each volume includes a table of contents, a glossary, an index, and several color photographs. These volumes can be very informative for young readers, but teachers and librarians should keep in mind that the material is very brief and basic. If a student wishes to explore a specific topic they will need to supplement these volumes with other references.—**Cari Ringelheim**

CANADA

64.   **Exploring Canada Series.** San Diego, Calif., Lucent Books/Gale Group, 2002. illus. maps. index. $27.45/volume.
      As the second largest country in the world in terms of geography, Canada spans many different geographical regions and has a diverse population. This series from Lucent Books is designed with middle to high school age students in mind in order to provide historical, geographical, and cultural information on the regions of Canada. To date, the series is comprised of six books covering Alberta, British Columbia, Manitoba, Ontario, Quebec, and Yukon Territory. Each volume is just over 100 pages in length and includes a page of facts, notes, a chronology, a further reading list, a list of works consulted, and an index. Black-and-white photographs and maps are provided as well. Each volume provides interesting sidebars that highlight historical facts or contemporary issues.

This set would be useful in middle school collections and children's collections in public libraries. At $27.45 a volume, however, the set will get quite expensive as it grows. Libraries will want to keep this in mind before committing to the set.—**Shannon Graff Hysell**

65. **Junior Worldmark Encyclopedia of the Canadian Provinces.** 2d ed. Timothy L. Gall and Susan Bevan Gall, eds. Farmington Hills, Mich., U*X*L/Gale, 1999. 254p. illus. maps. index. $45.00. ISBN 0-7876-3811-0.

The 2d edition of the *Junior Worldmark Encyclopedia of the Canadian Provinces* (see ARBA 98, entry 119, for a review of the 1st edition) describes in detail the 10 provinces and 3 territories that make up Canada. Each province or territory is listed alphabetically in the book and is described in about 15 pages, including maps and photographs. There are data provided on 40 categories of interest, including location and size, topography, climate, plants and animals, population, languages, history, local government, industry, agriculture, commerce, housing, education, libraries and museums, and a bibliography listing books and Websites. Introductory information provided for each territory or province includes its name; nickname; capital; date it entered the confederation; time zone; and state motto, coat of arms, flag, floral emblem, tartan, mammal, provincial bird, tree, and stone. A glossary, list of abbreviations, and index conclude the volume. This work is designed mainly for middle and high school students.—**Shannon Graff Hysell**

EUROPE

66. Banting, Erinn. **Ireland: The Culture.** New York, Crabtree, 2002. 32p. illus. index. (A Bobbie Kalman Book: The Lands, Peoples, and Cultures Series). $15.45 reinforced library binding; $7.16pa. ISBN 0-7787-9351-6 reinforced library binding; 0-7787-9719-8pa.

67. Banting, Erinn. **Ireland: The Land.** New York, Crabtree, 2002. 32p. illus. maps. index. (A Bobbie Kalman Book: The Lands, Peoples, and Cultures Series). $15.45 reinforced library binding; $7.16pa. ISBN 0-7787-9349-4 reinforced library binding; 0-7787-9717-1pa.

68. Banting, Erinn. **Ireland: The People.** New York, Crabtree, 2002. 32p. illus. index. (A Bobbie Kalman Book: The Lands, Peoples, and Cultures Series). $15.45 reinforced library binding; $7.16pa. ISBN 0-7787-9350-8 reinforced library binding; 0-7787-9718-Xpa.

Part of an ongoing series developed by Bobbie Kalman, these three volumes are designed to introduce upper elementary-aged students to the culture, land, and people of Ireland. In *The Culture* volume, young readers can learn about Celtic myths, Druidism, Saint Patrick's Day, Claddagh rings, and James Joyce. This volume even includes "Patrick and the Leprechaun," a traditional Irish folktale. *The Land* volume covers Ireland's geography, such as its mountains, rivers and *loughs* (lakes), islands, and major cities, as well as Ireland's economy and commerce (i.e., tourism, Waterford crystal, and wool markets) and wildlife.

The third volume in this set, *The People*, discusses the turbulent history of the Irish, from the Celts and the Vikings through the country's struggle for independence. Topics such as the Great Famine, the Anglo-Irish War, and Bloody Sunday are included. This volume also covers daily life in Ireland's cities and countryside, Irish cuisine, sports, and education. Multiple color photographs, a glossary, and an index are included in each volume. Obviously, with such limited space (each volume is only 32 pages) and so many topics, these volumes only provide a brief introduction to Ireland. They are not extensive enough to provide any in-depth coverage, so students will need to supplement them with others works if they want to learn more about specific topics.—**Cari Ringelheim**

69.   Milner-Gulland, Robin, and Nikolai Dejevsky. **Cultural Atlas of Russia and the Former Soviet Union.** rev. ed. New York, Checkmark Books/Facts on File, 1998. 240p. illus. maps. index. $50.00. ISBN 0-8160-3815-5.

The 1st edition of this atlas was published in 1989, and this revised edition supplements and complements some information covered previously, especially in such areas as religion (e.g., millennium of official conversion to Christianity that took place in 988 C.E.). There is an updated section on Josef Stalin's regime, new information on independent republics, and new entries in the bibliography. Part 3, "Regions and Countries of the Former Soviet Union," briefly covers significant changes. In examining the section on Ukraine, this reviewer found, unfortunately, that the information is too brief to be of substantial assistance to the reader, and occasionally there are some errors. For example, the population of Ukraine is not "over 51 million" but more than 52 million. There are several minorities in Ukraine but not "more than a hundred nationalities," and the information on Ukrainian industry and agriculture is not adequate. There is nothing about Ukrainian history or culture. In general, the atlas has good illustrations, the bibliography is adequate for the uninitiated, and the book, produced by Facts on File in Great Britain, is printed on high-quality paper.—**Bohdan S. Wynar**

70.   **Peoples of Europe.** Tarrytown, N.Y., Marshall Cavendish, 2003. 11v. illus. maps. index. $329.95/set. ISBN 0-7614-7378-5.

These volumes are targeted at the middle school level and describe the 44 European nations, including how they are different and how they are similar. The profiles introduce each country by highlighting its geography, history, religions, and life-style information (language, health conditions, cuisine, family life, the arts, music, and social customs). The narrative also describes the nation's current political situation. Each chapter has a gazetteer of demographic statistics, major cities, languages, currency, and so on. A useful feature is the historical timeline covering major events in each country's history. Although the sections are short, as appropriate to the target audience, a substantive amount of information is provided. These sketches portray the individual flavor of each country and its impact on life today. For example, the reader learns that in the 1500s the Italians invented the musical notation we still use today and that Jan Van Eyck of Belgium invented oil painting in the 1400s.

Each volume has a glossary and a bibliography for further reading for each country. The set concludes with a general index as well as specialized indexes by biographical names, geography, arts, music, festivals, food, people and culture, religions, and sports. There is also a pronunciation guide and a list of National Days.

This is a useful reference to whet the appetite of young students of European history and instill an appreciation for the many contributions these countries have made to the world's culture. [R: SLJ, April 03, p. 100]—**Adrienne Antink Bien**

LATIN AMERICA AND THE CARIBBEAN

71.   Brown, Isabel Zakrzewski. **Culture and Customs of the Dominican Republic.** Westport, Conn., Greenwood Press, 1999. 198p. illus. maps. index. (Culture and Customs of Latin America and the Caribbean). $45.00. ISBN 0-313-30314-2.

Greenwood launched the Culture and Customs of Latin America and the Caribbean series in 1998 with the purpose of documenting the unique histories and cultural practices of countries in the region. In the series foreword, series editor Peter Standish refers to global homogenization of culture that has become prevalent in our world and promotes these volumes as tools for understanding "the sensibilities of members of other cultures" (p. xii). Brown's volume on the Dominican Republic offers an overview of the country's history and culture, and offers rich detail on many of the everyday practices, habits, and customs that are uniquely Dominican.

This volume on the Dominican Republic follows the standard format for the series: a general overview of the country's history and thematic chapters on religion, social customs, media and cinema, literature, performing arts, and fine arts. The book includes a brief chronology of Dominican history from pre-Columbian times to 1996 that seems quite minimal when compared to those included in other volumes in this series. Each chapter contains endnotes, and the extensive bibliography reflects the broad corpus of English-and Spanish-language resources Brown consulted in preparing this work. An index is also included. Unlike other volumes in this series, there is no glossary of terms unique to the Dominican Republic or Dominican Spanish, despite the fact that Brown frequently refers to and defines such terms throughout the text. Most of these terms are not in the index, and a glossary would enhance the usefulness of the book as a reference tool.

Brown carries out her main task of synthesizing and summarizing a great deal of scholarship on the Dominican Republic in a clear and interesting manner. She is clearly strongest when writing about Dominican literature, and this chapter provides an excellent overview of the topic. Her chapters on social customs and the arts are also thorough and filled with many interesting insights and details. Brown's coverage of modern history is uneven at times, and can present an overly simplistic picture of the complicated political development the Dominican Republic experienced in the late twentieth century. There is also far too little attention paid to Dominicans living abroad—not just in New York but throughout the world—given how important this diaspora has been to the country's economic and cultural development. Aside from these omissions, the volume is a useful and informative resource appropriate for the general reader, and a source of many unique and interesting details for the more specialized researcher.—**Pamela M. Graham**

72.   Castillo-Feliú, Guillermo I. **Culture and Customs of Chile.** Westport, Conn., Greenwood Press, 2000. 168p. illus. maps. index. (Culture and Customs of Latin America and the Caribbean). $45.00. ISBN 0-313-30783-0.

This overview of specific aspects of Chile's culture, from colonial times to the present, is preceded by a lengthy chapter entitled "Context" that summarizes its history and discusses its geography, demography, ethnic groups, and other topics. Chapters devoted to religion, social customs, broadcasting and print media, literature, the performing arts, and art and architecture follow. Supplementary material includes a historical chronology of Chile, a glossary of Chilean Spanish terms, and a two-page bibliography. A good index facilitates access to the text. This well-written survey can be used either as a reference source or by general readers seeking to increase their overall knowledge of Chile. It would be a good addition to any library developing a collection that includes Latin American countries or are generally seeking to expand its holdings related to the international scene.—**Ann Hartness**

73.   Foster, David William, Melissa Fitch Lockhart, and Darrell B. Lockhart. **Culture and Customs of Argentina.** Westport, Conn., Greenwood Press, 1998. 173p. illus. index. (Culture and Customs of Latin America and the Caribbean). $45.00. ISBN 0-313-30319-3.

This debut volume of a new series is a thoughtful, in-depth examination of Argentina's culture. It considers the country's social customs, media, literature, cinema, and performing and visual arts within the context of the history, politics, and religion that shaped them. Two major influences discussed are immigration and military regimes.

The influence of the political climate is woven throughout each of the eight topical sections. Chapters on the arts discuss important authors, artists, and performers. Critical analysis of specific works is given especially in the case of films and works of fiction, which are analyzed in terms of their political commentary. Traditional visual arts are covered along with nontraditional subjects, such as the Silhouettes movement in which anonymous artists have painted outlines of the bodies of Los Desaparecidos (the "disappeared"). There is a comprehensive history of Argentine newspapers and radios, which examines the influences of the Catholic Church and the political regimes in power in specific time periods. Immigration is identified as having had a major impact on religious tolerance, social customs, food, and sports and is considered by the authors to be a primary cause of the Argentine "identity crisis."

This first volume in the series succeeds in accomplishing the stated goal of helping readers understand the factors that have shaped Argentina's culture. It should be noted that the book is narrowly focused, dealing with events that occurred after the country became independent, and may not be useful to those needing a basic source on Argentina. For example, except for a brief chronology, there is no information about the indigenous peoples or the Indian Wars.

The vocabulary used and concepts presented are geared toward post-secondary students. The subject index does not facilitate finding information quickly. Public and school libraries will be better served with standard sources such as *Worldmark Encyclopedia of Nations* (Gale, 1999) and the *Worldmark Encyclopedia of World Cultures* (see entry 127) or *Culturgrams: The Nations Around Us* (see entry 41).—**Marlene M. Kuhl**

74.   Handelsman, Michael. **Culture and Customs of Ecuador.** Westport, Conn., Greenwood Press, 2000. 153p. illus. maps. index. (Culture and Customs of Latin America and the Caribbean). $45.00. ISBN 0-313-30244-8.

Culture and Customs of Ecuador, part of Greenwood Press's Culture and Customs of Latin America and the Caribbean series, explores the diverse characteristics of this country that make it distinct from the rest of Latin America. The author begins with an introduction and chronology of Ecuador's history. The remainder of the book is divided into chapters discussing such topics as religion, social customs, media, cinema, literature, performing arts, and art and architecture. Each topic is covered fairly briefly, with the main points stressing the uniqueness of the country. Throughout the text there are black-and-white photographs of the country's citizens and geographical sites. The book concludes with a glossary, short bibliography, and index.

The writing and information presented in this book make it appropriate for middle school and high school students. As with the other works in this series, this volume will be valuable to school libraries looking to supplement their reference materials in area studies and cultural studies. —**Shannon Graff Hysell**

75.   Helmuth, Chalene. **Culture and Customs of Costa Rica.** Westport, Conn., Greenwood Press, 2000. 134p. illus. maps. index. (Culture and Customs of Latin America and the Caribbean). $45.00. ISBN 0-313-30492-0.

Costa Rica stands apart from other Latin American nations because of its democratic politics, economic stability, and progressive social programs. Aside from this, it is also considered a country rich in tradition and Latin American culture. The work, part of the Culture and Customs of Latin America and the Caribbean series from Greenwood Press, presents information on Costa Rica's social reform, religion, social customs, broadcasting and print media, literature, performing arts, and art. The chapters cover each topic briefly, without going into great detail about the history behind the subject. Each concludes with a useful reference section. The appendixes provide Websites featuring information about Costa Rica; results of presidential elections; and a statistical overview of the country, including currency, language, size, and population, to name a few. There is a four-page glossary that translates many Spanish words, a selected bibliography, and an index that conclude the work. This volume, as with the others in the series, are appropriate for middle and high school libraries looking to expand their international and cultural collections.—**Shannon Graff Hysell**

76. **Latin America, History and Culture: An Encyclopedia for Students.** Barbara A. Tenenbaum, ed. Farmington Hills, Mich., Charles Scribner's Sons/Gale Group, 1999. 4v. illus. maps. index. $350.00/set. ISBN 0-684-80576-6.

This encyclopedia, culled from the 5,300-entry *Encyclopedia of Latin American History and Culture* (see ARBA 97, entry 349), has been adapted and rewritten for middle and secondary school students, and its content has been updated. Its 700 entries, focusing on Latin America's past and present through people, places, events, and broad themes, are distributed among four volumes. They are enhanced with more than 200 photographs, maps, charts, and graphs, and an 8-page color insert in each of the volumes. It is arranged in alphabetic order. There are entries about each country and many cities; entries on topics related to current events (Indian policy, human rights); historical and cultural entries (Mexican Revolution, Football War, pre-Columbian art, samba); biographical entries; and those devoted to broad themes (agriculture, music, and dance). Geographical scope includes Mexico, Central America, South America, and all of the Caribbean islands. Each volume repeats a timeline for Latin America and the excellent index. The entries are well written in language appropriate for the targeted grade levels, and they are interesting and thorough in their coverage. This excellent source will meet the needs of students and of many adults seeking basic, accurate information about Latin America. This set is highly recommended for school and public libraries, and for libraries of universities that train teachers. [R: BR, Nov/Dec 2000, p. 79]—**Ann Hartness**

77. Williams, Raymond Leslie, and Kevin G. Guerrieri. **Culture and Customs of Colombia.** Westport, Conn., Greenwood Press, 1999. 148p. illus. maps. index. (Culture and Customs of Latin America and the Caribbean). $45.00. ISBN 0-313-30405-X.

This reference is part of a series on Latin American countries and provides a broad introduction to Colombian culture for the general reader. The authors concisely outline Colombian geography, history, religion, social customs, television, radio, newspapers, and arts (including literature, theater, music, cinema, photography, and architecture). The narrative demonstrates the authors' premise that Colombia is unique in Latin America with its extreme regionalism, its deeply founded traditionalism, an ingrained presence of the Catholic Church in daily life, and the country's political institutions, which surpass those of other South American nations. Features include an historical chronology, chapter notes, a glossary, a bibliography, and an index. The text is well written and effectively projects the authors' appreciation and affection for Colombia, its history, its literature, and its culture.—**Adrienne Antink Bien**

MIDDLE EAST

78. Black, Carolyn. **Pakistan: The Culture.** New York, Crabtree, 2003. 32p. illus. index. (Lands, Peoples, and Cultures Series). $22.60; $7.95pa. ISBN 0-7787-9348-6; 0-7787-9716-3pa.

79. Black, Carolyn. **Pakistan: The Land.** New York, Crabtree, 2003. 32p. illus. maps. index. (Lands, Peoples, and Cultures Series). $22.60; $7.95pa. ISBN 0-7787-9346-X; 0-7787-9714-7pa.

80. Black, Carolyn. **Pakistan: The People.** New York, Crabtree, 2003. 32p. illus. index. (Lands, Peoples, and Cultures Series). $22.60; $7.75pa. ISBN 0-7787-9347-8; 0-7787-9715-5pa.

The Lands, Peoples, and Cultures Series is designed with elementary-aged children in mind. The books in this 3-volume set on Pakistan are each 32 pages in length and each has a small index to its volume. The first volume in this series focuses on the culture of the people of Pakistan. It focuses a lot on the Muslim religion and the practices of its followers. Also discussed briefly are family traditions, literature and poetry, music, and storytelling in the country. The second volume discusses the climate and land of the region, city life, transportation, and plant and animal life. The final volume discusses the nationality of the people, their education, recreational life, food, and fashion. The colorful photographs, many of which include people in everyday settings add greatly to these volumes. The information is scant but will appeal to young readers and will be useful in school libraries.—**Shannon Graff Hysell**

OCEANIA

81.   Austin, Mary C., and Esther C. Jenkins, with Carol A. Jenkins. **Literature for Children and Young Adults About Oceania: Analysis and Annotated Bibliography with Additional Readings for Adults.** Westport, Conn., Greenwood Press, 1996. 326p. index. (Bibliographies and Indexes in World Literature, no.49). $69.50. ISBN 0-313-26643-3.

This bibliography of books for youth about Oceania is a niche publication. Yet Austin and the Jenkinses tune in so richly to the culture of the area that it is a treat for the librarian or teacher wishing to better understand and serve students who have immigrated to the United States from the islands of the Pacific, or who live there yet.

The introduction briefly describes the general geographic area of Oceania and tells the story of the movement of peoples. Then the authors break their material into three geographic sections: Australia; New Zealand; and the large island world called Melanesia, Micronesia, and Polynesia. They open for educators the indigenous literature characteristic of each area: hero tales, monster tales, numbskull tales, stories of unusual or little people, and so on. They provide, in each section, an annotated bibliography of books for children and young adults that includes information about folk, contemporary, and nonfiction literature. The authors include a list of recurring motifs and a bibliography for adults. Authors of the materials for youth are, for the most part, persons with Western names, but they draw, with the exception of clearly contemporary stories, from the native oral traditions.

District and regional libraries serving students of this background should make a copy available to their libraries. They should, in turn, inform their classroom teaching staffs of this superb overview. [R: Choice, June 96, pp. 1607-08]—**Edna M. Boardman**

3 Economics and Business

GENERAL WORKS

Biography

82. **Business Leaders for Students.** Sheila M. Dow, ed. Farmington Hills, Mich., Gale, 1999. 914p. illus. index. $95.00. ISBN 0-7876-2935-9. ISSN 1520-9296.

The purpose of this new book in Gale's popular line of business products for students is "to provide readers with a comprehensive resource of business biographies, giving them easy access to information on past and resent business leaders." This goal is met with 248 alphabetically arranged, engaging entries of historical and popular business leaders. It is, of course, impossible to be comprehensive in one volume. The advisory board of five teachers and librarians of young adults from diverse geographic locations did an excellent job of selecting the leaders for inclusion. The first entry is illustrative of the selections—Scott Adams, creator of the *Dilbert* comic strip. Historical figures such as Alexander Graham Bell, Benjamin Franklin, and Samuel Morse balance modern business leaders like Bill Gates, Charles Schwab, and Ted Turner. Many different areas of business are included, from food processing (e.g., Colonel Sanders, Oscar Mayer, Will Kellogg) to cosmetics (e.g., Mary Kay, Estée Lauder) to entertainment (e.g., Jane Fonda, George Lucas, Michael Jordan). Minority leaders are well represented with businesspeople such as Wally Amos, Akio Morita, and Barbara Proctor.

The entries are 3 to 4 pages in length, usually with a black-and-white photograph. Each begins with a one-paragraph overview, including the leader's major contributions to business, industry, and society. Next comes a summary of their personal life, with family history, vital statistics, education, affiliations, and awards, among other items. The section on career details focuses on career highlights and often reports their management style, business philosophy, or development of a product. The final sections are titled "Social and Economic Impact," which contains more in-depth analysis, and "Sources of Information," which lists mailing addresses and Websites. A basic bibliography provides suggested readings in monographs, periodicals, and databases. The separately boxed chronology features an easy-to-read list of major dates in the leader's life.

A master index provides easy access to business leaders, companies, and industries. This book is fun to peruse and stop off at any stimulating name. Its value as a basic reference tool for students seeking quick data on business leaders is great. This one volume will be much easier to use than the traditional biographical research tools and it is suited for high school and undergraduate students as well as public library patrons. [R: BR, Sept/Oct 99, p. 65; SLJ, Aug 99, p. 182]—**Georgia Briscoe**

83.   Carey, Charles W., Jr. **American Inventors, Entrepreneurs, and Business Visionaries.** New York, Facts on File, 2002. 410p. illus. index. (American Biographies). $65.00. ISBN 0-8160-4559-3.

This volume contains 264 biographical entries in alphabetic order, each 800 to 1,500 words with 2 to 5 "Further Reading" sources on 280 individuals. There are 16 double entries (e.g., the Duryea Brothers, Hugh and Christie Hefner). Included are "people from all categories of American life"; some are lesser known but interesting people who made contributions in new and imaginative ways. Their contributions include a corn refining machine (1715), the octant (1731), the cotton gin (1793), a paper bag machine, steel, steel plow, automobiles, linotype and adding machines, peanut butter, AOL, Ben and Jerry's ice cream, and the disposable diaper. Included are entrepreneurs in television production (Oprah Winfrey), conglomerates, organized crime, soap, ladies' hats, prostitution, and the slave trade. Among the well-known names are Henry Flagler, Jay Gould, Pinkerton, Pullman, Vanderbilt, Westinghouse (railroads); Eastman, Land (photography); Ray Kroc (fast foods); Morgan, Hetty Green, Michael Milken (finance); du Pont, Frasch, Hall (chemicals); Case, Gates, Hollerith, Wang, Wozniak, Jobs (computers); Field, Walton, Ward (mercantile activity); and Whitney (agriculture). This fun-to-read source will add spice for economics and business classes. Appendixes include entries by 53 invention/business types and by year of invention. A 7,000-word introduction weaves most of the entries into a historical narrative and an excellent index concludes the volume.—**Richard A. Miller**

84.   **Leading American Businesses: Profiles of Major American Companies and the People Who Made Them Important.** Farmington Hills, Mich., U*X*L/Gale, 2003. 3v. illus. index. $135.00/set. ISBN 0-7876-5428-0.

Leading American Businesses: Profiles of Major American Companies and the People Who Made Them Important is intended for use by middle school students, although nothing in the volumes themselves makes that clear. The editors chose 45 of "today's most successful and influential corporations" representing "the best of the energized, creative spirit that has shaped the American economy for more than 165 years." All three volumes have the same cover, featuring pictures of Oprah Winfrey, Bill Gates, and Henry Ford. Each volume begins with the same "Words to Know" (from *acquisition* to *wholesale*) and ends with the same cumulative index. Each entry includes a narrative article about the business, relevant sidebars, and photographs, as well as a timeline.

Among the 45 businesses chosen are standard industrial giants like Boeing and General Electric and General Motors. However, the majority of the entries deal with companies like Ben & Jerry's Ice Cream, Eddie Bauer, The Gap, Inc., Levi Strauss & Company, and Dream Works SKG (Steven Spielberg's studio), no doubt chosen to pique the interest of young consumers.

While these volumes are attractive and well researched, some of the information will rapidly become outdated. As an early introduction to American capitalism and economy, *Leading American Businesses: Profiles of Major American Companies and the People Who Made Them Important* serves a useful purpose; however, the degree to which these volumes fit the interests and needs of its target readers is perhaps debatable.—**Kay O. Cornelius**

85.   Logan, Rochelle, and Julie Halverstadt. **100 Most Popular Business Leaders for Young Adults: Biographical Sketches and Professional Paths.** Westport, Conn., Libraries Unlimited/Greenwood Publishing Group, 2002. 419p. illus. index. (Profiles and Pathways Series). $60.00. ISBN 1-56308-799-5.

There are 100 popular business leaders, many of them household names, included in this biographical reference source. Successful people from television, finance, Internet start-up companies, beauty and modeling businesses, and retail are among the interesting fields covered. The inclusion of unusual entrepreneurs such as Steven Jobs, Spike Lee, Laura Ashley, Paul Newman, Eileen Ford, and Quincy Jones, as well as the more traditional names such as Bill Gates and Donald Trump indicates how useful this book is. Each businessperson's picture, career highlights, important contributions, career path, and key dates are given. Each entry also includes advice from the person, an inspiring quote, and suggested further readings.

Clearly written, this book should be useful for all elementary and high school libraries as well as the children's department of public libraries. Another book in the series, *100 Most Popular Scientists for Young Adults* (see entry 460), might also be another useful addition.—**Carol D. Henry**

86. Sherrow, Victoria. **A to Z of American Women Business Leaders and Entrepreneurs.** New York, Facts on File, 2002. 252p. illus. index. (A to Z of Women). $44.00. ISBN 0-8160-4556-9.

This is a directory of American women from the seventeenth century to the present who have achieved outstanding success as business leaders or entrepreneurs. The categories of women who fit these parameters have changed over the centuries. Women who reached the top in the colonial period came from the ranks of innkeepers, merchants, and printers. By the nineteenth century, many of the women who excelled were factory owners, landowners, or dressmakers. The top women achievers in today's society are equally varied: financiers, founders of companies, and corporate executives. The sheer number of American businesswomen who have reached the top levels of success over the years means that the author has had to be very selective in her inclusions. The reference work includes diverse ethnic groups and fields of endeavor as well as women who overcame major obstacles in order to succeed. Many entries are one to two pages in length. Each entry is followed by a "Further Reading" bibliography. A table of contents and an introduction (a very well-developed, 10-page survey of American women in the workplace from the colonial period to the present) precede the biographical profiles. A list of "Recommended Sources," a list of entries by field, a list of entries by century or decade of birth, and a general index complete the work. A list of entries by state or country of birth and a list of entries by state or states where each woman made her accomplishments would be interesting additions to the biography.

Some of the material is available in other resources; however, this reference source brings together well-researched, readable, and lively information about the women as business leaders. The work complements both women's studies and history of American business collections. As such, this work should be found in all large and mid-sized academic libraries. Large and mid-sized public libraries should likewise acquire it.—**Dene L. Clark**

Directories

87. **Peterson's Summer Opportunities for Kids and Teenagers 1996.** 13th ed. Princeton, N.J., Peterson's Guides, 1996. 1241p. illus. index. $24.95pa. ISBN 1-56079-496-8. ISSN 0894-9417.

Thousands of sports, art, travel, and academic programs and camps that theoretically can enhance a child's development are profiled here. Some of these programs make jobs or financial aid available. Extensive indexing and tables will help users select programs that will meet their criteria, whether these be geographic, religious, special need (e.g., disabled), or residential. One criterion that is important to parents but that is not shown in the tables or indexes is price range; one must consult the individual profiles for this information. Prices vary enormously but depend largely on the length of the programs, which range from a few days to a couple of months. All programs receive brief descriptions covering interests, activities, contact information, hours, eligibility, and the like. Some 230 programs have longer 2-page descriptions written by their directors.

The book does not evaluate or rate these programs but tells users how to do so. Although parents are told to ask about American Camping Association accreditation, the book does not tell whether or not the camps included have this accreditation. (The American Camping Association has its own annual directory, *The Guide to Accredited Camps* [see ARBA 96, entry 811], which lists more than 2,000 camps.) *Peterson's* is a useful directory that will help parents find enriching experiences for their children. Information on summer programs is also available via the Internet at http://www.petersons.com. The print directory is not complete, however, and larger libraries may wish to supplement it with other reasonably priced directories.—**Susan V. McKimm**

Handbooks and Yearbooks

88.   **Economics.** Danbury, Conn., Grolier, 2000. 6v. illus. index. $319.00/set. ISBN 0-7172-9492-7.

The world of economics is presented in this six-volume set, which is designed for use by high school students. The volumes are divided as follows: "Money, Banking, and Finance"; "Business Operations"; "The Citizen and the Economy"; "The U.S. Economy and the World"; "Economic Theory"; and "Economic History."

Each volume, with the exception of "Economic Theory," contains a series of detailed chapters with detailed coverage of specific aspects of the volume's subject. For example, "Money, Banking, and Finance" includes chapters on banks and banking, inflation and deflation, personal finance, and the stock market. "Economic Theory" presents shorter A to Z articles rather than the lengthier chapters of the other volumes. Names of contributors are placed at the beginning of each volume rather than at the end of each chapter. Every volume has an index to the complete set, a glossary, and a bibliography of books and Websites. Cross-references to related articles are included. *Economics* is copiously illustrated and provides charts and diagrams. Chapters are written clearly and provide a helpful introduction on various aspects of the economy to young adults. In addition to its intended audience, this work should be useful to people of all ages who wish to learn more about certain aspects of economics and the world economy. Those looking for concise definitions of terms, such as "elasticity," "monetarism," and "privatization," will find them here. "Economic History" provides those new to the field with an overview of events and key people from ancient times to the present day. This work is recommended primarily to young adult collections in public and school libraries. [R: SLJ, Nov 2000, pp. 88-90; BR, Jan/Feb 01, p. 82]—**Lucy Heckman**

FINANCE AND BANKING

89.   Allen, Larry. **Encyclopedia of Money.** Santa Barbara, Calif., ABC-CLIO, 1999. 328p. illus. index. $75.00. ISBN 1-57607-037-9.

Written for the general reader rather than for the scholar, this compilation of some 300 brief essays (500 to 1,000 words in length) presents a variety of historical information regarding important monetary experiences that have influenced the evolution of money and banking. Although the author indicates an intent not to dwell on proving or disproving any specific theories of monetary economics, it is evident that certain exceptions prove the rule. Likewise, theories are brought into discussion only when they result in bringing some order out of chaos. In essence, the guiding principle is identification of the common characteristics that are shared within and between various monetary systems.

The work opens with an alphabetic list of entries, followed by a brief preface and introduction. Some entries include illustrations and all include cross-references and a brief bibliography of resources. A full bibliography and index supplement the main text.

To trained economists, this work might prove too vague and unrewarding. However, to the general reader, armchair historian, and seeker of curious facts, the work should be quite fulfilling. High school, public, and college library users might benefit from the clarity of discussions. [R: BL, 15 Nov 99, pp. 649-52]—**Edmund F. SantaVicca**

LABOR

General Works

90. **Career Discovery Encyclopedia.** Holli Cosgrove, ed. Chicago, J. G. Ferguson Publishing, 1997. 6v. illus. index. $129.95/set. ISBN 0-89434-184-7.

More than 500 occupations are described in this 6-volume set for upper elementary and middle school children. Each entry is two pages in length and includes a description of the work, training needed, salaries, demand, addresses to write for more information, and a picture of a person engaged in the occupation. Suggestions (such as potential auditors volunteering to be treasurer for a school club) are given for curious children who wish to further understand the skills and qualities needed for an occupation. Cross-references are displayed in a circle at the beginning of each article and invite the child to browse the volumes. Of use to librarians and teachers are the indexes —especially the general index and the index to skills groupings, which list occupations under such headings as "people skills" or "organizational skills."

The information is usually clearly and uniformly presented. Exceptions to this appear in the category "Outlook," which tells the reader, in a phrase, about the future. "Average," "About as Fast as the Average," and "Faster Than the Average" are rankings not explained, neither in the preface nor in specific articles. The authors also vary in describing salaries—some state the year(s) in which the salary is based; some do not. Although librarians will know to check the publishing date for a clue, most children will not. It is refreshing not to find this set a regurgitation of the *Occupational Outlook Handbook* (see ARBA 2001, entry 197), yet one wonders what the sources of the information are: government, industry, or personal experience? In general, this is a worthy set, with an engaging format and interesting descriptions; however, these aspects should be considered in the next edition.—**Juleigh Muirhead Clark**

91. **Encyclopedia of Careers and Vocational Guidance.** 10th ed. Chicago, J. G. Ferguson Publishing, 1997. 4v. illus. index. $149.95/set. ISBN 0-89434-170-7.

92. **Encyclopedia of Careers and Vocational Guidance.** 2d ed. [CD-ROM]. Chicago, J. G. Ferguson Publishing, 1997. Minimum system requirements (Windows version): IBM or compatible 386. Double-speed ISO 9660-compatible CD-ROM drive. Windows 3.1. 8MB RAM. 10MB hard disk space. SVGA monitor and graphics card. Microsoft-compatible mouse. Minimum system requirements (Macintosh version): MacOS 7.0. Double-speed ISO 9660 CD-ROM drive. Foreign File Access extension. 8MB RAM. 10MB hard disk space. 640 x 480 pixels color monitor.

Macintosh mouse or pointing device. $199.95 (single user); $299.95 (2-8 users); $399.95 (9+ users). ISBN 0-89434-171-5 (single user); 0-89434-172-3 (2-8 users); 0-89434-173-1 (9+ users).

Encyclopedia of Careers and Vocational Guidance (ECVG) continues to be one of the standard tools for libraries in the area of career development. This 10th edition continues the topical arrangement first tried in the previous edition (see ARBA 94, entry 386). In this format, volume 1 surveys 67 major industries, such as accounting, automotives, energy, hospitality, public relations, and toys and games. The remaining 3 volumes comprise alphabetic listings of individual jobs within industries; for example, the information services industry profile links to job descriptions for archivists, database administrators, indexers, librarians, library media specialists, and library technicians. In addition to the industry profiles, volume 1 includes 2 appendixes, 1 on career resources and associations for individuals with disabilities, the other focusing on internships, apprenticeships, and training programs.

The industry profiles lead off with an industry overview, including history and development, followed by a description of the industry's structure, the various careers within the industry, employment opportunities, and the industry outlook. A list of sources of additional information and links to related articles complete each industry section. The job profiles found in volumes 2 through 4 lead off with a paragraph-length description of each job, then provide a history of the job; describe the nature of the work; its requirements; opportunities for experience and exploration; methods of entering the profession; paths for advancement; employment outlook; entry-level, average, and high earnings; and conditions of work. As with the industry overviews, the job entries conclude with a list of sources of additional information and links to related articles. For example, the "librarians" entry lists (with their respective Website addresses) the American Library Association, the Special Libraries Association, the American Association of Law Libraries, and the Music Library Association as information sources.

For those libraries that can afford its higher cost, the 2d edition of the CD-ROM version of the ECVG offers additional text as well as enhanced searching capability. A database of 152 military careers put together by the U.S. Department of Defense describes each job's background, what activities are involved, work environment, and other useful information. Search capabilities include searching by interest and ability; training or education requirements; school subject (e.g., biology, mathematics); and numerous other fields. The CD-ROM version not only supports full printing options but also offers a letter-writing function that allows users to create and print a personalized letter of inquiry to any association or agency listed in the ECVG.

The information in the encyclopedia is thorough, reliable, and current. Whether in print or electronic format, it remains an important resource for school, academic, and public libraries.—**G. Kim Dority**

93. **VGM's Careers Encyclopedia: A Concise, Up-to-Date Reference for Students, Parents, & Guidance Counselors.** 4th ed. By the Editors of VGM Career Horizons. Lincolnwood, Ill., VGM Career Horizons/National Textbook, 1997. 456p. index. $39.95. ISBN 0-8442-4525-9.

This career encyclopedia provides detailed information on approximately 200 of the most popular jobs in the United States today. The jobs, ranging from blue collar to professional, appear in alphabetic order. The table of contents is an alphabetic list as well. The index consists of a keyword list, and it includes association names as well as numerous cross-references and *see also* references. Each occupational entry follows a uniform pattern, describing "The Job"; "Places of Employment and Working Conditions"; "Qualifications, Education, and Training"; "Potential and Advancement"; "Income"; and "Additional Sources of Information." The entries for many occupations list related jobs. The editors use such phrases as "strong demand," "average growth," or "little growth" to describe the job outlook for each occupation through the year 2005.

Public and academic libraries of all sizes require current information about occupations and the educational requirements for those occupations. Guidance counselors in secondary and academic institutions likewise need such basic material. *VGM's Careers Encyclopedia* is a basic, one-volume source eminently suitable for high school and junior college students seeking career advice. Libraries and schools with limited budgets will find this title to be current and authoritative. Academic libraries and public libraries serving a medium-sized or larger clientele should consider the four-volume *Encyclopedia of Careers and Vocational Guidance* (see entries 91 and 92), a much more comprehensive source. Libraries that can afford to duplicate holdings should also consider the *Occupational Outlook Handbook* (see ARBA 2001, entry 197).—**Dene L. Clark**

Career Guides

94.   **Career Exploration on the Internet: A Student's Guide to More Than 300 Web Sites!** Elizabeth H. Oakes, ed. Chicago, Ferguson, 1998. 208p. index. $15.95pa. ISBN 0-89434-240-1.

The Internet is transforming many facets of life. Its impact on the job search is dramatic for those in business, technical, and professional fields. This volume is a comprehensive narrative directory opening abundant information resources for anyone with access to the World Wide Web. Throughout the book, sites are listed and given helpful annotations that include scope, approach, and deficiencies where they exist.

Aimed primarily at the student or newly graduated job-seeker, these resources are most helpful for the job search, with chapters on how to find out about companies, nonprofit and public organizations, and international careers. Volunteer, internship, and summer job information and listings are covered also. Employment agencies, professional recruiting firms, and professional associations, as well as Websites of individual companies, are listed.

The opening chapters focus on sites for career exploration—sources of information on various fields and occupations. Some sites, frequently academic, offer self-assessment tools as well as occupational information. Clearinghouse sites are offered as "headquarters" for searching for career information. An individual's decision-making process may be made more difficult by such an abundance of information.

This guide assumes the reader is computer-proficient, particularly with the Internet. The style is lively and fast-paced, muck like where the listings lead. The only problem is that this means of job searching takes time and effort and diligence is clearly provided. This volume and others like it are essential tools for libraries and career centers. Anything in this venue will be outdated the minute after it is written, much less published, but the key resources and links will most likely linger even after newer and better sites come online. Thus, it provides an excellent base. [R: BR, Nov/Dec 98, p. 66]—**Barbara Conroy**

95.   **Career Opportunities in Television, Cable, Video, and Multimedia.** 4th ed. New York, Checkmark Books/Facts on File, 1999. 274p. illus. index. $35.00; $18.95pa. ISBN 0-8160-3940-2; 0-8160-3941-0pa.

This book offers coverage of a wide variety of career opportunities in the popular and expanding fields of broadcasting (radio aside), video technologies, and multimedia production of entertainment and information resources. It is an update of the 3d edition published nine years ago under the title *Career Opportunities in Television, Cable, and Video*. Nine years is a long time in these fields, and an update is welcome. The industry has expanded, and job responsibilities and titles reflect this. The whole new area of multimedia, including its Web aspects, has been added.

The introductory overview that precedes each section has been significantly updated to reflect changes in the field, new terminology, and to bring the numerous and varied statistics up-to-date.

Well organized and well laid out with better typography than the 3d edition, the material is basically divided into a television broadcasting and a cable, video, and media section. Within each of these two areas, the book is arranged by job function within a few broad areas of expertise. Each includes a job description, salary range, the education and skills required or expected, and information on unions. Within each of the two areas the book offers broad coverage of job opportunities. Nontechnical jobs as they relate to the electronic media industry are covered.

The television section is divided up by function within the areas of management, programming, production, engineering, performance, advertising, and news reporting. The functions are listed alphabetically within each area and are also included in the subject index at the back. In the 2d section, the functions or areas of competency are organized more under subject areas in which cable, video, and multimedia are used. Employment in private industry, government, the health field, the education field, commercial technical products, training, and producing (e.g., managing, engineering, programming, writing) are specified, and specific areas of competency are then arranged under each.

This guide is highly recommended for both public and academic libraries. Readers should find it comprehensive, readable, and a good place to start in seeking vocational information in electronic media production.—**Florence W. Jones**

96.   **Careers in Focus: Earth Science.** Chicago, Ferguson, 2002. 186p. index. $14.95. ISBN 0-89434-409-9.

97.   **Careers in Focus: Geriatric Care.** Chicago, Ferguson, 2002. 188p. index. $14.95. ISBN 0-89434-411-0.

Ferguson's Careers in Focus series takes an in-depth look at the careers offered in several specific fields. The two fields featured in the works reviewed are geriatric care and earth science. The books begin with an overview of the field. For example, in *Geriatric Care* the introduction discusses exactly who the geriatric population is, why these careers are in demand right now, and the skills needed to work with this segment of the population. The introduction of *Earth Science* focuses mainly on what studies earth sciences use, the employment outlook for the future, and where this type of work can be found.

The layout of each work is identical. For each volume about 20 careers are discussed thoroughly and listed in individual chapters. For each career option a description of the job is given (including a typical work day), educational requirements are given (for high school, postsecondary training, and certification and training), tips for exploring if this job is a good choice for the reader, who employs this type of professional, how to get started in the career, advancement, typical earnings, work environment, and job outlook. Each chapter ends with a list of agencies or organizations to contact for further information (listing address, telephone number, and e-mail and Website addresses). The works conclude with a short list of additional related careers and an index.

These works would be most useful in high school and public libraries that have patrons looking for possible career options. They are very elementary in scope so further research will be necessary, but they will provide a good starting point for interested young people.—**Shannon Graff Hysell**

98.   Echaore-McDavid, Susan. **Career Opportunities in Law Enforcement, Security, and Protective Services.** New York, Checkmark Books/Facts on File, 2000. 239p. index. (Career Opportunities). $35.00. ISBN 0-8160-3955-0.

This vocational guidance aid covering occupations in law enforcement and related fields will make a useful addition to career-planning collections. The main body of the work is divided into 12 sections ranging from police work, forensic investigation, private investigations, and computer security to construction inspectors and aviation security. The 70 jobs profiled range from the obvious, such as police officer or sheriff's deputy, to the more unexpected (e.g., locksmith, food inspector, plumbing inspector, lifeguard).

Individual entries provide duties, salary range, prospects, advancement, career ladder, education and training, skills, entry tips, and unions or associations. Each entry is about two 11-by-8 ½-pages in length, with 1 or 2 slightly longer (e.g., fire fighter, security guard). All entries start with a brief summary, with more detailed text of expanded information below. The entries give a good description and idea of what occupations are about.

The clear introductory materials outline how to use the book, give sources, and make suggestions for following up interesting prospects. In addition to contents and index, there are 10 appendixes providing a variety of useful information, including Internet resources, state and federal employers and certification agencies, occupational groups, colleges and universities, a bibliography, and a glossary. The educational institutions, however, only cover those offering programs related to fields where formal training is not widely available. This book is a thorough and useful career guide that is well worth considering for employment collections. [R: LJ, 15 Mar 2000, p. 70; RUSQ, Sept 2000, p. 402]—**Nigel Tappin**

99.   Field, Shelly. **Career Opportunities in Casinos and Casino Hotels.** New York, Checkmark Books/Facts on File, 2000. 268p. index. (Career Opportunities Series). $45.00; $18.95pa. ISBN 0-8160-4122-9; 0-8160-4123-7pa.

The growing career opportunities in the casino and casino hotels industry are illustrated in this comprehensive guide. More than 90 occupations are covered within 10 general employment sections. These sections cover not only careers on the gaming floor, but also administration and management, security and surveillance, entertainment, hotel management, and food and beverage services.

Each two-page entry begins with a career profile, including salary range, employment prospects, and prerequisites. A career ladder showing the normal progression within that career also appears at the beginning of each entry. For example, a credit manager begins as a credit clerk shift supervisor and could move up to casino credit supervisor or director of casino credit. The main text describes each position in detail covering salaries; employment prospects; advancement prospects; education and training; desired experience, skills, and personality traits; unions and associations; and tips for entry, such as taking classes, relocating, or attending job fairs.

The book concludes with a series of useful appendixes listing gaming academies and dealer schools, college programs, and trade associations and unions. There is also a directory of casinos and cruise lines, gaming conferences and expositions, seminars and workshops, and gaming industry Websites. This well-written and organized book is recommended for public libraries and academic libraries where there is particular interest in the gaming industry or hotel and restaurant management.—**Erin C. Daix**

100.   Field, Shelly. **Career Opportunities in Health Care.** 2d ed. New York, Facts on File, 2002. 243p. index. $44.50. ISBN 0-8160-4816-9.

This guide provides a good starting place for researching careers in the health industry. The 80 brief, easy-to-understand commentaries span those requiring little formal education (e.g., medical clerk, food service worker) to those that require advanced degrees (e.g., physicians, dentists). Each two-page entry furnishes a career profile, description of work, employment and advancement prospects, salaries, needed education and training, and suggested skills and personality types that would—college catalogs, books, magazines, and media programs. Some information was elicited through questionnaires and interviews of those working in the fields. The author also acknowledges friends and business acquaintances for providing data. Although potentially accurate, this causes the guide to pale by comparison to the authoritative details provided by the U.S. Department of Labor's *Occupational Outlook Handbook* (OOH: 2000-2001 ed.; see ARBA 2001, entry 197). The OOH also has broader coverage, supplying information on more than 250 careers in many diverse fields.

A few details are overlooked or misrepresented. Many occupations within the health care industry require state licensure. This important requirement is often noted (dental hygienist, pharmacist, physical therapist), but inexplicably excluded in the case of optometrists and registered nurses. It also seems that the employment prospects for nurses should be considered "excellent" rather than "good" given the current documented national nursing shortage and increased hiring and education initiatives.

This guide deserves a place on a guidance or career counselor's shelf. It is a good source for the beginning stages of research, but not reliable or comprehensive enough to use for a final career decision.—**Susan K. Setterlund**

101. Field, Shelly. **Career Opportunities in the Music Industry.** 4th ed. New York, Checkmark Books/Facts on File, 2000. 280p. index. (Career Opportunities Series). $45.00; $18.95pa. ISBN 0-8160-4083-4; 0-8160-4084-2pa.

The 4th edition of *Career Opportunities in the Music Industry* gives information about 86 jobs in all aspects of the music industry, including such diverse positions as artist relations and development representative, sound technician, piano tuner, opera singer, or nightclub manager. Each entry gives alternative titles, a career ladder that illustrates a normal job progression, a position description, salary ranges, employment and advancement prospects, and minimum education and training required. Entries also contain helpful advice on desired experience, skills, and personality traits; the best geographic location to find a job; valuable unions and associations; and tips for entry. These tips include suggestions on where to look for jobs (i.e., classified ads), if internships are available, and how and where to market businesses. These are particularly helpful, especially when considering that over 80 percent of the jobs described are listed as having either poor or fair job entry prospects.

There are 11 appendixes that include information such as the names and addresses of colleges and universities that offer degrees in related fields, relevant unions and associations, record companies and distributors, booking agencies, music publishers, and entertainment industry attorneys and law firms. There is also a bibliography that includes publications as recent as 1999. The major omission from this work is information regarding the use of the Internet for job searching. Although the appendix that lists unions and associations includes e-mail and homepage addresses, there could be more information throughout the book on how to take advantage of this medium. Overall, however, the book is informative and should be helpful for anyone exploring a career in the music industry. [R: LJ, 1 Sept 2000, pp. 192-194]—**Michele Russo**

102. Field, Shelly. **Career Opportunities in the Sports Industry.** 2d ed. New York, Checkmark Books/Facts on File, 1999. 280p. index. $18.95. ISBN 0-8160-3794-9.

Essential information on career opportunities in most aspects of sports is detailed for professional athletes, sports teams, and for individual sports such as boxing, wrestling, and horse racing. Positions in sports business and administration, coaching and education, officiating, sports journalism, recreation and fitness, sports medicine, and wholesaling and retailing are also described. Even though comprehensive, there are gaps, such as the position of team psychologist and the sport of auto racing.

Entries give a brief overview of the position and then expand that brief information into a longer narrative of two to three pages. Each entry describes the nature of the position together with its salary range and the employment and advancement prospects that can be anticipated. Strategic tips for entering the position are given. Entries also detail the characteristics, experience, and training required. Information about relevant unions and associations is included.

Helpful appendixes supplement the directory. One lists academic degree programs for sports administration and physical education. Sponsors of relevant workshops, seminars, and symposiums are cited in another. Leagues, associations, and unions offer contact points for information and a diligent job search. Listings of promoters and cable/network television sports departments will be helpful for the more specialized seeker.

This update of the 1991 edition evidences the rise in sports interest and participation. The field is, in many ways, informal and the diversity of titles and positions pronounced. This volume presents a useful framework for viewing scope and possibility. The approach is somewhat promotional, blending pragmatic information with enthusiasm for the field. The information has been gathered from interviews, questionnaires, and publications, so it is largely informal.—**Barbara Conroy**

103. Field, Shelly. **Career Opportunities in Theater and the Performing Arts.** 2d ed. New York, Checkmark Books/Facts on File, 1999. 257p. index. $35.00; $18.95pa. ISBN 0-8160-3798-1; 0-8160-3799-Xpa.

Although this book was written for "the many thousands of people who aspire to work in theater and other performing arts," it is very basic and would probably not be useful beyond the high school level. It is divided into nine sections according to type of career, such as performing artist or educator. Within each section are descriptions of individual careers (e.g., actor, playwright), which include duties, salary, employment prospects, prerequisites/preparation, advancement, unions/associations, and tips for entry into the career. Position descriptions are generally adequate, but information on education, skills, training, and experience is often vague and frequently states the obvious (e.g., dancers "need to be flexible, agile, and coordinated") .

There are several appendixes of varying usefulness. Useful are lists of educational opportunities in the performing arts and of theater and music companies that employ performing arts professionals. Less useful are a list of New York City-area theaters, a list of performing arts periodicals (not annotated), and a rather randomly selected bibliography. Although entries in the list give addresses and telephone numbers, it would have been helpful for the compiler to have included Website addresses, as many organizations and companies listed have excellent Websites that include e-mail addresses as well as information about auditions, educational programs, and job opportunities. In spite of its several flaws, this book covers an unusually wide range of careers, from secretarial to management, and may be appropriate for larger high school and public libraries or where there is particular interest in the performing arts.—**Gari-Anne Patzwald**

104. Fitch, Thomas. **Career Opportunities in Banking, Finance, and Insurance.** New York, Facts on File, 2002. 252p. index. (Career Opportunities Series). $49.50. ISBN 0-8160-4512-7.

This title, part of Facts on File's Career Opportunities Series, opens with a brief and interesting essay about the history of banking in the United States and a description of the typical organizational structures in banks, finance companies, investment and brokerage services, and insurance companies. The main section of this volume contains more than 80 job descriptions divided into 6 categories: banking, accounting/corporate finance, insurance, investment banking/securities, money management, and supervisory agencies. For each position, there is a brief career profile and career ladder, which indicates the location of the position within a typical career path. This is followed by more detailed discussions of the position, salary range (approximate for 2001), employment and advancement prospects, education and training needed, desirable intellectual and social skills, unions and professional associations, and tips for entry into the position.

The appendixes include a selective listing of colleges with programs supporting the professions covered in this book, but there is no indication of how these institutions were selected for inclusion. Other appendixes include a list of professional associations, professional certifications, periodicals, regulatory agencies, and Internet resources for career planning. A brief glossary and bibliography are also included.

The material for each position is clearly written and well organized. The cost is reasonable and having all related occupations in one concise volume is convenient. It should be noted, however, that for many of the occupations in this title, more detailed information can be found in the U.S. Department of Labor's *Occupational Outlook Handbook* (2000-2001 ed.; see ARBA 2001, entry 197). As such, purchase of *Career Opportunities in Banking, Finance, and Insurance* is not essential.—**Michele Russo**

105.   Guiley, Rosemary Ellen, and Janet Frick. **Career Opportunities for Writers.** 4th ed. New York, Facts on File, 2000. 244p. index. (Career Opportunities Series). $45.00. ISBN 0-8160-4143-1.

The 4th edition of *Career Opportunities for Writers* continues the Facts on File series designed to provide the best single source of information about jobs for all kinds of writers. Students considering a writing career will find information about entry-level jobs, while experienced writers desiring a career change can get specific information on possible employers. The book begins with an introductory essay on the outlook for employment for writers and other communicators. Individual chapters cover the mass media: newspapers and news services, magazines, television, and radio. Other chapters discuss book publishing; arts and entertainment; business communications and public relations; advertising; federal government; scholastic, academic, and nonprofit institutions and freelance services; and self-publishing. Each job listing has a quick-look heading listing the job's duties, salary range, employment prospects, and prerequisites, followed by complete information garnered from many sources, including interviews with present holders of similar positions.

The job descriptions are followed by four appendixes that list educational institutions offering undergraduate degrees in journalism and communication; useful Websites for writers; professional, industry, and trade associations and unions; and major trade periodicals. Also provided are a bibliography and an index.

Volumes like *Career Opportunities for Writers* will be most valuable to high school students and others in search of a career or seeking to make a career change. The volume is clearly written and easy to use. As with all such books, part of the material will soon be outdated, but for the foreseeable future, this volume contains much to recommend it as part of a collection of career guidance materials.—**Kay O. Cornelius**

106.   Parks, Peggy J. **The News Media.** San Diego, Calif., Lucent Books, 2002. 112p. illus. index. (Careers for the 21st Century). $27.45. ISBN 1-59018-205-7.

Geared toward young adults exploring career possibilities, this work examines various roles in news media. The chapters cover reporters, photojournalists, television anchors, broadcast producers, and radio announcers. Each chapter includes a description of the job, what a typical day is like, and skills needed. The appendixes include organizations to contact, lists of works for further reading, and a list of works consulted.

Although the intention is to keep this at the age-appropriate level, coverage of possible media careers is superficial. The news media offers a wider variety of jobs well beyond the five highlighted. The choice of jobs also seems to be based on a traditional view rather than examining the impact of the Web, digitization, and the trends in news media. There are several other sources, including the *Occupational Outlook Handbook* (2000-01 ed.; see ARBA 2001, entry 197), and a variety of Websites that offer better coverage of careers and would be better sources for career exploration.—**Joshua Cohen**

107. **Professional & Technical Careers: A Guide from World Book.** Chicago, World Book, 1998. 496p. illus. index. $35.00. ISBN 0-7166-3311-6.

Professional and Technical Careers contains more than 600 careers described in terms appropriate for an international adolescent audience. Colorful, friendly, cartoon-like pictures illustrate the introductory section on career planning. In the chapter entitled "What Is Work?" the differences between paid employment, self-employment, volunteer work, and unemployment are described, as well as practical information to help the student understand the implications for mental and physical health, gender, age, personality, and appearance.

The main body of text is an alphabetic guide to specific careers. It begins with a guide to using the book, which is followed by a general subject index. The student can review the list of careers arranged topically, with headings such as "Outdoor/Active," "Artistic/Creative," or "Service and Sales." The articles are usually one page in length, but sometimes as long as seven. The longer articles have profiles of individuals who do a particular job—for example, an Indian broadcaster, a Malaysian teacher, an Irish international aid worker, a Canadian writer. Usually, the educational requirements for the United States and the United Kingdom are listed. Highlighting the articles are color-coded boxes listing skills and personal qualities needed, school subjects a student should enjoy, and general advice to contact a relevant professional organization. To find out what this organization would be, the student must consult another source.

The final chapter of the book tells the reader where to go for further information in the reader's specific country. The U.S. section relies heavily on the *Occupational Outlook Handbook* (see ARBA 2001, entry 197), but also includes a list of state employment agencies. The most unique feature is how to get information on finding a job in a foreign country, such as the topic "Working in New Zealand for Foreign Nationals." An index concludes the book and will send the fledgling toy maker to the article on "Craftwork."

The articles are informative, and the international flavor is refreshing. Not only are adolescents learning about the world of work, they are also learning about work in the world. Pair this volume with the *Occupational Outlook Handbook* for specifics on work in the United States. [R: BL, July 98, p. 1908; SLJ, Nov 98, p. 158]—**Juleigh Muirhead Clark**

108. Sims-Bell, Barbara. **Career Opportunities in the Food and Beverage Industry.** 2d ed. New York, Facts on File, 2002. 223p. index. $49.50. ISBN 0-8160-4493-7.

A search of the OCLC database showed that there is nothing that approximates this work. The author of this book certainly knows the field. She started the Santa Barbara (California) Cooking School, and has been in the business for 25 years. She saw to the authenticity of the book by making onsite visits and doing interviews in each of the categories of the book. She also sent drafts of the manuscript to people in the businesses in order to make sure nothing had been omitted. The information is current and complete.

The book is also comprehensive. It has 14 categories and 78 separate descriptions. The scope is everything from the conventional baker, chef, and caterer careers to very diverse careers that are constantly emerging. Some of the more fascinating ones are wine steward, food bank manager, farm tour manager, winery publicist, restaurant supply buyer, kitchen designer, sports nutritionist, foods Webmaster, culinary food business editor, and food photographer. Within each entry, the author first does a career profile and then covers each part of the profile in depth. The entries include duties, alternate titles, salary range, employment prospects (the author is very honest about this), advancement prospects, best geographical locations, prerequisites (education and training), career ladder, and tips for entry.

At the end of the book there are four appendixes that give lists of culinary schools and academies, a bibliography of books, and lists of magazines and journals and culinary professional and trade organizations. There is a good index at the end of the book, but it is not hard for readers to find their way around the book. Looking at the table of contents gets readers where they want to be very quickly. This work is an excellent directory for any collection that deals with the world of food in even the most remote way.—**Lillian R. Mesner**

109.   Vogt, Peter. **Career Opportunities in the Fashion Industry.** New York, Facts on File, 2002. 224p. index. (Career Opportunities Series). $49.50. ISBN 0-8160-4616-6.

Titles in Facts on File's Career Opportunities Series are somewhat similar to the Department of Labor's *Occupational Outlook Handbook* (OOH) listings, but contain greater detail on individual careers. While the OOH may describe the outlook for purchasing managers (no matter what they might be purchasing), Vogt has entries such as "Merchandise Manager" and "Fashion Buyer" that note specifically how they relate to the fashion industry, such as buying for the future based on fabric samples or black-and-white drawings. The book covers 65 careers in 7 areas: textiles, production, retail, media, promotions, education, and miscellaneous. There is a wide range here, from entry-level positions with little training or education required (e.g., runway model, spreader, cashier, sewing machine operator) to professional (e.g., fabric librarian, costume designer, industrial engineer).

Each entry contains a brief career profile with duties, salary range, employment and advancement prospects, best geographical location, prerequisites (education, training, experience, special skills, and personality traits), and career ladder. These topics are fleshed out in two to three pages of text, with additional information on related unions and associations and tips for entry into this kind of position. Statements about salaries and prospects cite recent Department of Labor statistics. Appendixes listing college and other educational programs; professional and trade associations and unions; fashion and apparel periodicals (consumer and trade) and Websites; and a bibliography complete the book. There is a general index. Most reference collections in which there is a demand for career information will find this a useful addition. [R: LJ, 1 Feb 03, p. 79]—**Deborah V. Rollins**

110.   **Young Person's Occupational Outlook Handbook: Descriptions for America's Top 250 Jobs.** Indianapolis, Ind., JIST Works, 1996. 262p. illus. $19.95pa. ISBN 1-56370-201-0.

With the publication of the 22d edition (1996-97) of the *Occupational Outlook Handbook* (OOH), the U.S. Department of Labor, Bureau of Labor Statistics celebrates the 50th year in print of occupational outlook information. During those 50 years, schools, colleges, veterans' offices, guidance counselors, employment agencies, and community organizations have used this information to educate individuals about the world of work. The demand for such information has been so great that this government publication has been widely reprinted by private publishers. Some have published the identical source under the same title (Bernan Press and VGM Career Horizons, to name a couple). Others have reorganized the information and retitled their editions, such as *The Big Book of Jobs* from VGM Career Horizons (1996) and *America's Top 300 Jobs* from JIST Works (see ARBA 94, entry 276, and ARBA 91, entry 241). More recently, publishers have repackaged the handbook in a variety of formats (a slide series, a video, microcomputer versions, multimedia editions on CD-ROM, and hypertext translations available on the Internet).

Occasionally, the repackaging is designed to target a specific audience. The *Young Person's Occupational Outlook Handbook* is one such republication. While not so stated, its content, format, and length appear to be crafted for young adolescents. Cartoonlike illustrations on the cover and first page of each section will appeal to preteens, but the vocabulary, differing little from the government source, rules out a younger audience. Each one-page entry includes a clarified version of the Department of Labor's job description, working conditions, and list of related occupations, but for only 250 jobs. While the title implies that these are the top jobs, there is no rating of the occupations or substantiation for this claim. Simple black-and-white graphics for the categories of earnings, education and training, and outlook add little to the information. The user must turn to the inside back cover for an explanation of the ratings.

Other attempts to add value are interesting, but not always informative. A large portion of each page is made up of a box labeled "Something Extra," which provides interesting facts, occasionally vaguely related to the job. For instance, a discussion of the discovery of gold is added to the entry for mining engineers. An account of early attempts at flight seems better suited to pilots than flight attendants. The "Subjects to Study" is a nice link from school to work, but inconsistencies in subjects abound. What is listed as "social sciences" on one page, is "social science" on the opposing page. Both "physics" and "physical science" appear in the same list. This lack of attention to detail carries over into the text as well. Several job descriptions lack uniform style, and "complishments" rather than "accomplishments" appears on page 89. The paper cover and glued binding will not hold up to frequent copying any better than the original OOH.

While young people may appreciate the abbreviated format of the *Young Person's Occupational Outlook Handbook*, it refers readers to OOH for more information. Parents, teachers, and counselors dedicated to helping adolescents explore career possibilities may prefer the original. Middle school libraries may want to offer both to their students. [R: BR, Nov/Dec 96, p. 47]—**Debra S. Van Tassel**

4   Education

ELEMENTARY AND SECONDARY EDUCATION

111.   Beck, Peggy. **GlobaLinks: Resources for World Studies, Grades K-8.** Worthington, Ohio, Linworth, 2002. 148p. index. $39.95pa. ISBN 1-58683-040-6.

Although resources are numerous and readily available, Americans are often accused of being provincial and out of touch with the rest of the world. Beck's bibliography promotes a more global, multicultural, and diverse view of the world. The book is divided into three areas: print and nonprint, Websites, and key pal/pen pal projects. These areas are further divided into a wide range of subjects that fit under the umbrella of "World Studies."

Each alphabetically arranged entry includes complete bibliographic information plus the ISBN and a suggested age range for which the item is best suited. Websites obviously include their URLs. The author's strength, however, lies not only in her selections, but also in her consistently high-quality annotations. The mention of the occasional quirky bits of information is apparent proof that Beck has reviewed each of the sources included in the bibliography. True to a librarian's heart, almost 35 pages (out of 148) are devoted to indexes—Website title, author/illustrator, title, and subject. This compilation is highly recommended for the professional collection of young adult sections and school media centers. [R: BR, Mar/April 02, p. 70; SLJ, Mar 02, p. 263]—**Phillip P. Powell**

HIGHER EDUCATION

General Works

Directories

112.   **Barron's Best Buys in College Education.** 5th ed. By Lucia Solórzano. Hauppauge, N.Y., Barron's Educational Series, 1998. 716p. index. $14.95pa. ISBN 0-7641-0430-6.

Like the many other Barron's publications, this is a source filled with information for the prospective college freshman. *Barron's Best Buys in College Education* is almost solid text, but it is not overwhelming in its presentation.

There is a relatively brief introduction prior to the main section where the reader will find the descriptions and discussions of the nearly 300 schools included. A brief discussion of the selection process is presented, with two common qualities pervading—good value and high, but not necessarily unattainable, academic standards. These are colleges that are not always well known nationally, but often have solid regional reputations. Most information is gathered either from other Barron's publications or by the use of questionnaires. Besides statistical information, student opinions are weighed heavily. Finally, the introduction concludes with an explanation of each segment within a given entry.

The arrangement is alphabetic by state then by institution. The colleges included are public and private, large and small. Following the heading of the college name and its address is a box containing standard statistical information, including enrollment, average SAT scores, student/faculty ratio, and tuition. What follows is a much lengthier, more anecdotal, description of the college. Having some knowledge of at least a couple of the colleges listed, the reviewer found that these portions were both entertaining and accurate on most accounts. Although most narratives were positive, they did not fail to include some of the downsides of these colleges when appropriate. This offering from Barron's Educational is recommended for high school and public library collections. —**Phillip P. Powell**

113.   **Peterson's Colleges with Programs for Students with Learning Disabilities or Attention Deficit Disorders.** 5th ed. Princeton, N.J., Peterson's Guides, 1997. 663p. index. $32.95pa. ISBN 1-56079-853-X.

This directory includes information from more than 1,000 accredited 2-year and 4-year colleges that provide comprehensive and special services for those students having learning disabilities (LD) and attention deficit disorders (ADD). This edition reflects a name change from the previous edition, which was entitled *Peterson's Colleges with Programs for Students with Learning Disabilities* (see ARBA 96, entry 341) and the inclusion of more than 200 more programs. There are sections in the directory that include sample letters of inquiry, a "Personal Summary Chart" to assist the student in listing features of a school's services, and an "Information Resources" list of organizations that are related to LD and ADD. A "Quick-Reference Chart" is provided to aid in identifying whether a school provides comprehensive or special services, is a two-or four-year college, or charges a special fee. The arrangement is alphabetic by state, then college, with the page number provided to the college's entry.

Each comprehensive and special services college entry has two main sections: "Learning Disabilities Program or Services Information" and "General College Information." The comprehensive sections provide an additional checklist summary chart. Under the LD section there is a summary of the history of the LD program or services offered, the number of students served, the number of staff members, the amount of special fees charged, application and admission requirements, and what specific services are provided. Specific services include information on what is provided at the school; diagnostic testing, tutoring, remediation, advising, special courses, counseling, and auxiliary aids (taped textbooks, tape recorders, calculators, notetakers). The general college information summary provides an enrollment profile, graduation requirements, number of computers on campus, expenses and financial aid information, and the name of a contact person. The directory includes an alphabetic index listing of all colleges and universities, with those having comprehensive programs listed in bold typeface.

A compact disk is included that provides several useful academic options. Useful features include the ability to customize college selection based on several categories (majors, region and state, LD services, costs, entrance difficulty, and type of institution). Also, there is the ability to create a comparison chart for up to four institutions at a time, the ability to print checklists of needed items for each college, and the ability to customize letters of inquiry.

This is a useful directory for those persons considering colleges that will provide services or programs that are sensitive to the needs of students with LD or ADD. It is an important source for all libraries.—**Jan Squire Whitfield**

114.   **Peterson's Guide to Four-Year Colleges 1999 (with CD-ROM).** 29th ed. Princeton, N.J., Peterson's Guides, 1998. 3258p. illus. index. $24.95pa. Minimum system requirements (Windows version): IBM or compatible 486. Double-speed CD-ROM drive. 8MB RAM. Color monitor. Minimum system requirements (Macintosh version): 68030 processor with System 7.1. Double-speed CD-ROM drive. 8MB RAM. Color monitor. ISBN 1-56079-987-0. ISSN 0894-9336.

Peterson's Guide to Four-Year Colleges 1999 continues as a pace-setting access tool for information on predominantly undergraduate colleges. The prefatory material is extremely helpful. This section contains such concisely written sections as "Considering College Quality," "How to Make a List of Appropriate Colleges," "Surviving Standardized Tests," "Preparing to Get Admitted," "Financial Aid," and "Using the Internet in Your College Search." There are 4 quick-reference college search indexes that will facilitate the process: a state-by-state summary table index, an entrance difficulty index, a cost ranges index, and a majors index. There is a separate section on the military and higher education.

The main section comprises college profiles of approximately 2,000 institutions. Each profile covers such information as indicators of quality, profile of undergraduates, academic programs, majors, library resources, computing, college life, housing, athletics, career planning, expenses, financial aid, and application procedures. This section is followed by a collection of more extensive profiles of 1,000 universities that elected to furnish such information. The print guide is accompanied by a CD-ROM, which enables users to link to the Peterson's homepage, where they may explore such topics as colleges and universities, graduate programs, study abroad, summer camp, private schools, 5,000 company profiles, and executive education programs (Bricker's database). Meticulously edited and imaginatively formatted, this volume is an exemplary reference resource. This CD-ROM is recommended with great enthusiasm for all types of libraries.—**Arthur P. Young**

115.   **Peterson's Honors Programs: The Only Guide to Honors Programs at More Than 350 Colleges and Universities Across the Country.** By Joan Digby. Princeton, N.J., Peterson's Guides, 1997. 436p. index. $21.95pa. ISBN 1-56079-851-3.

Students seeking a directory of honors programs at colleges and universities in the United States will find this to be the only one currently available. Checking the catalogs shows that the last one compiled by the same organization, the National Collegiate Honors Council, was in 1967.

Formatted like other Peterson's guides, this book has a major difference. Because of the comparative brevity of the book, the print is substantially larger than in most other Peterson guides. This guide contains a large amount of introductory material with the most important portion being the introduction. The reader is given explanations for the compilation of the book followed by sections that define honors programs. The final section includes an explanation of symbols used within each entry. The symbols are simple, but the explanation is helpful. Following the introduction are segments whose purpose and benefits this reviewer finds questionable. Included are profiles of honors program alumni and essays discussing honors from several points of view. Although providing additional detail and a new spin for the reader, the essays have a repetitious quality. Many of the same ideas have been put forth previously in the introduction. Finally, the "Honors Snapshots" serve little purpose.

Each entry, arranged alphabetically by institution name, contains all or some of the following information: program descriptions, participation requirements, admission information, scholarship availability, living expenses, tuition, the campus, and who to contact. Much of it is standard information designed for a specific audience. Examination of several college Websites shows that text was often lifted directly from what a college itself had written about its honors program. This directory will be particularly suited for secondary school libraries and public libraries. [R: BL, 1 Feb 98, p. 940]—**Phillip P. Powell**

Handbooks and Yearbooks

116. **The Princeton Review Student Advantage Guide to Visiting College Campuses.** 1997 ed. By Janet Spencer and Sandra Maleson. New York, Princeton Review/Random House, 1996. 367p. maps. index. $20.00pa. ISBN 0-679-77852-7.

This guide is intended as an aid to prospective students and their parents planning to visit colleges and universities of interest. Approximately 250 schools in 50 states, mostly private institutions with some state universities, are included. For some states, not a single school is listed, and no criteria are given for the selection of the institutions discussed. This is strictly a guidebook for reaching the school and for short stays in the area. No information on curricula, notable faculty, or strengths or weaknesses of the educational programs is given.

Entries are arranged under state and are accompanied by a small state road map. Each entry provides the address, telephone number, and location and hours of the admissions office, as well as a vacation schedule of the school. A sidebar contains specifics on campus tours, interviews, class visits, and overnight dormitory stays. Supplementary paragraphs briefly describe transportation to the institution, directions, a few hotels or motels nearby, and local attractions. Once again, no criteria for inclusion are given. Two appendixes provide regional mileage matrices and college calendars. A short introduction suggests points to consider during observations and questions to ask officials and students.

This compilation should be useful to the audience for whom it is intended—private preparatory schools and large public high school collections. High school counselors may also find it helpful.—**Shirley L. Hopkinson**

Financial Aid

117. Clark, Andy, and Amy Clark. Breslow, Karen, ed. **Athletic Scholarships: Thousands of Grants—and over $400 Million—for College-Bound Athletes.** 4th ed. New York, Checkmark Books/Facts on File, 2000. 338p. index. $35.00. ISBN 0-8160-4308-6.

This book could be worth thousands of dollars to the right readers. High school students (of both sexes) with athletic ability and adequate grades can obtain substantial college and university scholarships if they know how and where to apply. *Athletic Scholarships* will provide them with the necessary guidance.

The introduction leads readers through the application process and includes suggestions on how to prepare résumés, how to write letters (samples provided), and, most importantly, how to make the best impression on coaches and recruiters. Next, there are state-by-state listings of the institutions, which show what scholarships are available and provide directory information. The last part lists the academic institutions by sport, which is particularly useful when a sport is less common, such as badminton, racquetball, or riflery.

The fact that this book is in its 4th edition is strong evidence of its intrinsic value. It also has clear typeface, a sturdy binding, and a reasonable price.—**Samuel Rothstein**

118. **College Costs & Financial Aid Handbook 1998.** 18th ed. By the College Scholarship Service New York, College Entrance Examination Board, 1997. 334p. $17.95pa. ISBN 0-87447-562-7.

The 1998 edition of *College Costs & Financial Aid Handbook* is designed for parents and students who seek information on college costs and financial aid. It is useful not only for high school seniors and juniors, but also for parents. Because of the increasing cost of higher education in the United States, students and their parents need a guide that explains how, when, and where to apply for meeting college costs. The book provides step-by-step advice on applying for financial aid and gives strategies for planning to pay for college. Question and answer sections for each step are helpful features that the book provides. In addition, there are tables for student expenses and parent's contributions, sample cases and worksheets of three students, and a glossary section that lists important terms. If the book included a checklist for the financial aid process and a calendar, it would be more helpful for users.

After readers become familiar with financial aid plans, the book guides them to lists of individual college costs. There are 18 categories of up-to-date costs and financial aid information provided here for 3,100 colleges. Other useful features that set this book apart from similar ones are indexes for colleges that offer academic, music or drama, or art scholarships; colleges that offer athletic scholarships; colleges that offer tuition and fee waivers and special tuition payment plans; and an alphabetic list of colleges. The handbook is a useful guide that every high school and college library should keep in its reference room.—**Sung Ok Kim**

119. **College Financial Aid: The Best Resources to Help You Find the Money.** Issaquah, Wash., Resource Pathways; distr., Ashland, Ohio, Bookmasters, 1997. 266p. index. (College Information Series). $24.95pa. ISBN 0-9653424-5-X.

In this information age, with so much information on college financial aid available in libraries, in bookstores, and on Internet Websites, it is hard to determine which information sources are most useful. This book lists and reviews about 150 resources in various media. The reviews are arranged by the type of media, including print resources, Internet Websites, software resources, videotape resources, and commercial online services. The editors attempt to cover up-to-date materials and to provide current information on availability. An overall star rating system (1 to 4 stars) within each media section ranks the resources, and the best resources are listed first.

Each review provides detailed information on where to buy or how to access each resource, including ISBN numbers for obscure print media, direct order numbers for publishers, and URL addresses for sites on the Internet. Appendixes at the end of the guidebook address frequently asked questions and define special terms and acronyms. Indexes to all resources reviewed are provided, either by title, by author, or by publisher. No comprehensive or broad subject index is provided, but "Index for Steps in the Financial Aid Process" and "Index for Privately Funded Scholarships," which are intended for browsing, substitute fairly well for this omission. The book is recommended for high school libraries, college libraries, and public libraries. It is also recommended for home purchase.—**Vera Gao**

120. **The Financial Aid Book: The Insider's Guide to Private Scholarships, Grants, and Fellowships.** 2d ed. Compiled by Student Financial Services. Seattle, Wash., Perpetual Press; distr., Chicago, Independent Publishers Group, 1996. 537p. index. $19.95pa. ISBN 1-881199-30-4.

This eye-catching book is a directory for introducing students to private scholarships, grants, and fellowships. Because of the increasing cost of higher education in the United States, any amount of financial aid would be helpful for most students, yet many of them do not know that private scholarships other than state and federal grants and loans are available. This reliable guide provides 3,500 sources of funds: 2,700 sources for scholarships and grants; 200 sources for student loans; and 600 sources for fellowships, internships, and research opportunities. It also provides the most accurate and up-to-date information available, owing to the Student Financial Services research team that investigated scholarship offerings and interviewed financial aid experts.

Each entry gives exact names, addresses, telephone and fax numbers, college majors or interests, amount of scholarship, number of scholarships, application deadline, and eligibility criteria. Good features of the directory include a comprehensive indexing system in six different groups of categories; special tips from financial aid experts that increase the chances to apply; and four steps of the application process, including sample letters of request and sample essays for applicants. This scholarship directory makes the application complete, without help from any other references. It is recommended to all levels of libraries, including school, college, research, and public.—**Sung Ok Kim**

121.   **Peterson's Sports Scholarships & College Athletic Programs.** 3d ed. Princeton, N.J., Peterson's Guides, 1998. 865p. index. $24.95pa. ISBN 1-56079-830-0. ISSN 1069-1383.

This guide to scholarships and financial aid for athletes at 1,700 higher education institutions in the United States is a must for college-bound high school athletes. The primary entries are organized alphabetically by college name, rather than by state. Listings include contact information (including e-mail address and fax number) of the athletic department, facilities, administrators, scholarships, and the names and telephone numbers of coaches for each sport for that year. One-quarter of the entries reflect four-year schools that do not award scholarships, but do offer aid packages. Users must follow a complex series of steps in the two indexes—men's sports and women's sports—to determine which schools actually offer scholarships. Under a particular sport, users select the association or division affiliation of the school, followed by the state, and finally arrive at the schools that award scholarships in that sport. In this way the directory provides two primary access points to scholarship information: alphabetic by college name and by male or female sport.

The introductory material includes several concise and helpful articles. The most informative, "Financing Your College Education," by Stephen and Howard Figler, summarizes the pros, cons, and how-tos of athletic scholarships in five pages. Other topics include motivational words by popular college coaches, advice to international athletes, and "Keeping Your Balance" by Derrick Harmon, former Cornell University football player and San Francisco 49er. This directory is highly recommended for high school, public, and academic libraries in areas with active high school athletic programs.—**Anne C. Moore**

122.   Schlachter, Gail Ann, and R. David Weber. **High School Senior's Guide to Merit and Other No-Need Funding 2000-2002.** El Dorado Hills, Calif., Reference Service Press, 2000. 400p. index. $27.95. ISBN 0-918276-87-X.

Written for the many high school seniors whose family income is too high to meet financial need-based scholarship requirements, but who lack sufficient funds to pay for a college education (and for the counselors and librarians serving them), this excellent directory contains a wealth of information about possible sources of support. Over 1,100 entries organized into 4 categories—sciences, social sciences, humanities, and any subject area—constitute the major section of this book, providing a great deal of information (including purpose, eligibility, deadlines, address, e-mail, and Website location) about each award-granting program. There are also two other useful sections, one about sources of information on educational benefits organized by state and another about other literature and Websites where additional information is available. All three sections are clearly formatted and easy to use, but should users wish to search using indexes, there are six excellent ones: program title, sponsoring organization, residency, tenability, subject, and calendar.

All in all, Schlachter and Weber have done an exemplary job of organizing an enormous amount of information that could be priceless to all students who believe they may not have the financial means to go to college. It belongs in all libraries patronized by them and those who care about their futures.—**G. Douglas Meyers**

123.   Sponholz, Joseph. **Winning Athletic Scholarships: Guaranteeing Your Academic Eligibility for College Sports Scholarships.** 1998 ed. New York, Princeton Review/Random House, 1997. 177p. $18.00pa. ISBN 0-679-77879-9.

This book is a helpful guide for young people who are talented enough to be considering athletic scholarships to college. During the last few years, controversy about the place of student athletes at colleges and universities has erupted around the country. Athletes are often ill-prepared for the life of a student athlete, both emotionally and academically. This book will go a long way toward rectifying that.

Chapters in the work define the major organization that oversees college athletics (the National Collegiate Athletic Association [NCAA]), eligibility requirements, and recruiting. Chapters on "The Real Story" give advice from top NCAA coaches about how they view recruits and recruiting. A chapter on the SAT tests includes not only advice but a practice test as well. Appendixes consist of 45 pages, listing various athletic scholarships around the nation. A list of team names rounds out a useful reference work that is appropriate for school and public libraries. As the author makes clear, there is very much at stake in NCAA athletics for both the schools and their prospective student-athletes. This book will help both immensely.—**Bob Craigmile**

INTERNATIONAL EXCHANGE PROGRAMS AND OPPORTUNITIES

124.   **Yale Daily News** Guide to Summer Programs 2000. By Sara Schwebel and the staff of the *Yale Daily News*. New York, Kaplan Books/Kaplan Educational Centers and Simon & Schuster Trade Paperbacks, 1999. 378p. illus. index. $22.00pa. ISBN 0-684-84213-0.

The idea behind this book for high school students is that if they do something interesting with their summer, they will learn something, have fun, and look good on college applications. Useful advice about the merits of a summer experience, the application and interview process, and how to decide which one is appropriate form the first two chapters. The directory of over 500 programs is arranged into chapters that cover seven broad categories of academic, study abroad, community service, outdoor adventure, athletic, arts, and leadership offerings. Traditional summer camps are not included for the most part.

Each section starts off with information on what to expect and how to make it work. For instance, there are hints on how to audition on tape or in person for performing arts programs, and warnings about the physical demands required in many community service programs. Black-and-white photos throughout show students engaged in various activities, and quotations from student participants are highlighted in numerous sidebars; both serve to pique the reader's interest. Individual entries give the program's address, e-mail, URL, program name, location, subject areas, description, dates, duration, and cost. There are also data about financial aid, academic credit, eligibility requirements, application process and deadline, and the average number of applicants and participants. Some families might want to know how long a program has been operating, so perhaps a starting year could be included in future editions. A final chapter notes how to make the college connection from a summer program, be it obtaining letters of recommendation or listening to counselors' advice.

There are five indexes by name of organization, by subject, by cost (some no-cost programs are included), by location (international and U.S.), and by duration. Unfortunately, only the organization name index gives page numbers, so it must always be consulted after using one of the other indexes to find the program listing. There are a couple of caveats for using this directory. The author does not state criteria for inclusion, and although many of the names are certainly familiar (e.g., Amigos de las Americas, National Outdoor Leadership School, Rhode Island School of Design), others may not be. Also, users should be aware that hundreds of worthwhile programs are omitted from the directory (e.g., Bates Dance Festival and the University of Maine Pulp and Paper Foundation's Introduction to Engineering). *Peterson's International Directory of Summer Opportunities for Kids and Teenagers* (Peterson's, 1999), the National Association for Gifted Children (www.nagc.org), and even a Yahoo! search for K-12 summer programs could be used to supplement the information here. Nevertheless, this is a good, inexpensive guide to get high school students started and will be used in any public or school library where it finds a home.—**Deborah V. Rollins**

VOCATIONAL AND CONTINUING EDUCATION

125.   **Ferguson's Guide to Apprenticeship Programs.** 2d ed. Elizabeth H. Oakes, ed. Chicago, Ferguson, 1998. 2v. illus. index. $89.95/set. ISBN 0-89434-243-6.

This 2-volume set, now in its 2d edition, will be invaluable to students looking for career options that will let them earn money while learning marketable skills from experts in their field. This expanded and revised resource provides information on more than 7,500 programs in 52 job categories. It will be useful for those high school graduates who do not go on to college. It will also be handy for adults facing layoffs or looking for alternative career paths. A helpful introduction explains apprenticeship programs and how to use this reference source to locate fields ranging from agricultural workers to midwives and writers.

Although this book is not a listing of every available apprenticeship and on-the-job training program, it is an excellent place to start, and it also provides many different ways to find further information. The set is divided into four parts. Section 1 lists programs in 52 job categories. Section 2 provides programs for individuals who meet certain eligibility requirements. Section 3 lists job centers and vocational schools with on-the-job training or apprenticeship programs; preparatory programs; and the offices for local, state, and federal job training programs. Section 4 includes a glossary, career resources on the Internet, a selected list of occupational titles taken from the *Dictionary of Occupational Titles* (DOT), a job index, and a state index. This guide is highly recommended for high school, public, community college, academic, and special libraries serving young adults looking for careers. [R: BL, 15 Nov 98, p. 610]—**Diane J. Turner**

126.   Phifer, Paul. **College Majors and Careers: A Resource Guide for Effective Life Planning.** 3d ed. Chicago, J. G. Ferguson Publishing, 1997. 188p. index. $14.95. ISBN 0-89434-179-0.

This work functions as a basic introduction and guide to choosing academic fields of study and future careers. Accordingly, the major portion of text is given over to profiling 61 college majors or fields of study. Each profile opens with a 100-word scope statement of the discipline, followed by a list of related occupations (with an indication of educational level needed for that occupation). Discussions of related avocational and leisure-time activities, related skills, values and personal attributes often associated with this area, sources for further exploration, and a list of related organizations complete the profile. Following this is another large section that provides explanations and exercises for self-discovery, to assist in choosing a suitable field for study and career.

These two major sections are prefaced by an introduction, a guide to using the text, and an explanation of who might profit most from the information contained therein. Appendixes include descriptions of selected occupations, skill statements, definitions of values and personal attributes, publishers, a list of college majors and related high school courses, and a table indicating the number of degrees awarded by fields. Comprehensive indexes, by major and by occupation, complete the volume.

This guide is highly recommended for high school libraries and counselors and in similar academic settings where students need access to such information. The book is intelligible and well organized.—**Edmund F. SantaVicca**

Ethnic Studies and Anthropology

ANTHROPOLOGY AND ETHNOLOGY

127. **Junior Worldmark Encyclopedia of World Cultures.** Jane Hoehner, ed. Farmington Hills, Mich., Gale, 1999. 9v. illus. maps. index. $225.00/set. ISBN 0-7876-1756-X.

This new encyclopedia is modeled after *Junior Worldmark Encyclopedia of the Nations* (see entry 127). Although the information contained in its predecessor is general in scope, this work focuses on the culture of 295 ethnic groups outside of the United States. It is designed for use by upper elementary students; however, it is suitable for readers of all ages because it contains much information that may not be readily available elsewhere.

The format is attractive. The type is easy to read and there are black-and-white illustrations, including location maps. There are a reader's guide and a cumulative table of contents at the beginning of each volume, a glossary, and a cumulative index at the end of each. The arrangement is alphabetic by country and is continuous in the nine volumes. Within each chapter, cultural groups are treated individually. Information about each group follows the same pattern in 20 subheadings, which include language, religion, holidays, living conditions, and a bibliography. An interesting feature is the inclusion of ethnic recipes.

Political problems and ethnic conflicts are addressed only briefly under social problems. A critical omission, in the light of current events, is the lack of inclusion of Yugoslavia and its ethnic groups. However, Bosnia-Herzegovina and Croatia are included. It is hoped that the former omission will be rectified in subsequent editions.

This set is recommended as a worthwhile addition to a children's library collection or a supplement to social studies classes. If budgetary restrictions necessitate a choice between this set and its predecessor, one would probably choose the earlier work, although each deserves consideration. [R: BL, June 99, pp. 1881-1882; SLJ, Feb 99, p. 136; RUSQ, Fall 99, p. 95]—**Patricia A. Eskoz**

128. **Peoples of the World: Customs and Cultures.** Amiram Gonen and Barbara P. Sutnick, eds. Danbury, Conn., Grolier, 1998. 10v. illus. maps. index. $289.00/set. ISBN 0-7172-9236-3.

The stated goal of this set is to promote understanding of "how our global neighbors live and think," particularly among students in middle and high school. With this noble purpose and the current dearth of information on the subject for young people, the set is, at first glance, promising. However, potential buyers and users should be cautioned about its shortcomings before they make a purchase.

The text covers some 1,200 cultures (i.e., ethnic groups and nations) currently in existence around the world. Each group is described in terms of who they are, where they live, and where they come from. Information is also given about the size of the population, its history, role as a minority or majority, political and economic status, religion, language, and culture. Color photographs, drawings, and 280 maps accompany many of the articles. In addition, there is a brief glossary and index. All this is fine, but a closer look at the work's content reveals significant problems.

The most disturbing problem with this set is its misrepresentation of peoples through photographs. A student using this set might come away with the impression that Dutch women walk about the streets of Holland wearing wooden shoes, ankle-length dresses, shawls, and pointed caps. Although for some countries or groups (e.g., England, Russia) contemporary images are provided, for others (e.g., Germany, Mexico, Japan) the images are decidedly dated. And photograph captions and text do not always clarify this issue. For example, the article on Mongolia depicts the traditional nomadic way of life and animal husbandry practices of the people, but fails to mention that most Mongolians today are urban dwellers and that there are industries in the country apart from livestock. Other generalities and a lack of detail in the text can also mislead readers. The famine in Ukraine during the 1930s that was artificially induced by the Soviet regime is described simply as "a hunger" that occurred in that country. Coverage of other groups is too brief to inform (e.g., for the Laz of Turkey we are given only a two-line entry).

Some 20 pages of glossary and index are repeated in each of the 10 volumes, which seems a waste, especially when one considers the content of these features. For instance, "yurt" (the traditional home of Mongolian nomads) does not appear in the glossary or index, although a drawing of a yurt does appear with the entry on Mongolia and in its caption. A more detailed glossary and index could have easily been included with only one of the volumes at the expense of repetition. If the editors had made the effort to develop these features, they would have used their pages more effectively.

With these rather serious flaws, this set should never be used as a single, authoritative reference. However, if used in conjunction with other more accurate or detailed sources, it could provide a good starting point. [R: BL, 1 Oct 98, p. 366]—**Barbara Ittner**

129.   **Worldmark Encyclopedia of Cultures and Daily Life.** Timothy L. Gall, ed. Detroit, Gale, 1997. 4v. illus. maps. index. $299.00/set. ISBN 0-7876-0552-2.

This set covers more than 500 cultural groups in 4 volumes: Africa; Americas; Asia and Oceania; and Europe. The overall format is attractive, logical, and easy to use and parallels organization of its companion set, *The Worldmark Encyclopedia of the Nations* (see ARBA 2002, entry 85). Articles begin with a primary location map and a photograph of the people. Although all maps and photographs are black and white and lack appeal, they provide good information about the culture. Each article follows a standard 20-heading outline, with a focus on traditions, living conditions, and personalities of cultural groups today. The consistency in format adds to the ease of use of the set. Topics in the outlines include a general introduction, with historical information about the culture, language, folklore, religion, food, clothing, education, and other subjects about everyday life in today's world. A bibliography lists benchmark publications about the culture. A glossary of terms and a comprehensive index appear at the end of each volume. The breadth of coverage and the affordable cost (under $300) make this set a recommended purchase for school and public libraries. [R: SLJ, Aug 98, p. 190]—**Lynda Welborn**

ETHNIC STUDIES

General Works

130.   **Peoples of the Americas.** Tarrytown, N.Y., Marshall Cavendish, 1999. 11v. illus. maps. index. $329.95/set. ISBN 0-7614-7050-6.

Dense with facts, this compact multivolume geography and demography of the Americas is a meditation on survival. The nature of our land and its resources, who came first, what has been our social history, and where are we now are all told in scholarly paragraphs at the junior high school reading level. Topics include ethnic foods and folk celebrations, traditional patterns, education, and urban industrialization. But the authors neglect to discuss our debt to European intellectual civilization, which influenced American modernism with arts and sciences made public in museums, concert halls, theaters, libraries, engineering, government, and the law. Most pages have old prints of scenes of former generations or modern-day candid photographs. The indexes are effective and the glossaries are rudimentary. The maps, sidebars, and timelines are essential. Further study is facilitated by the bibliographies and text. Besides helping junior high school students, this work could be informative and interesting for American history and sociology enthusiasts.—**Elizabeth L. Anderson**

131.   **U*X*L Multicultural CD: A Comprehensive Resource on African Americans, Hispanic Americans, and Native North Americans.** [CD-ROM]. Detroit, U*X*L/Gale, 1997. Minimum system requirements: IBM or compatible 286 (386 or higher recommended). ISO 9660-compatible CD-ROM drive with MS-DOS CD-ROM Extensions 2.1 (double-speed or faster recommended). DOS 3.3. 640K RAM. 10MB hard disk space. VGA monitor and graphics card. Mouse (optional). Printer (optional). $325.00/stand-alone version. ISBN 0-7876-1285-5. (Also available in Macintosh version.)

In the past, current history and social studies textbooks have focused on the lives of the controlling figures and events in North American history. Often these are one-sided presentations because the history of the North American continent is not one story but actually a collection of stories of the different peoples inhabiting the area. The *U*X*L Multicultural CD* was developed to overcome this limitation by giving students and teachers a more complete picture of North American history and culture in presenting the stories of African Americans, Hispanic Americans, and Native North Americans. Although primarily targeting the younger student in grades 5 and up, this CD-ROM resource is an excellent addition to any multicultural collection, including those at the undergraduate level. It offers fast, easy access to a wide variety of information on North America's largest and most often studied ethnic groups.

The disc explores diverse subject areas. Its 3,400 entries cover historical and current events, prominent figures, and cultural aspects of the daily life of the three ethnic groups. The work offers biographies on more than 500 prominent individuals, both living and deceased, who have made significant contributions. The CD-ROM also includes more than 900 photographs, illustrations, and maps, as well as a glossary. A special feature of the disc is an option to create a timeline. The timeline examines the social, cultural, political, economic, and educational impact of the groups, spanning from prehistory to modern times. The teacher's guide that is provided is designed to suggest creative, interactive activities for further support of the in-depth use of the CD-ROM.

With help from the user's manual, the software is easy to install. The disc is available in both DOS and Macintosh formats. There are search options for both simple and complex assignments. Students can select a subject, period, person, or issue to quickly retrieve information that can be printed or saved to a disk for use outside the library. The user's manual also provides an index or list of subject terms divided by ethnic group as a word list. Detailed on-screen help is available from most screens simply by selecting the Help button with the mouse. The Help screen that appears gives help for the operation that is currently in use. There are two additional features of the Help button that are extremely useful. Selection of the Tutorial button at the bottom of any Help screen brings up a tutorial that shows a few sample searches. Selection of the Navigation button, which is also at the bottom of any Help screen, brings up a summary of the navigation options available in the program.

U*X*L Multicultural CD furnishes a diverse and dynamic approach to multiculturalism not afforded in standard history or social studies texts. It is recommended for any multicultural collection. [R: RBB, 15 May 97, p. 1610]—**Judith A. Valdez**

African Americans

132. **The African American Encyclopedia Supplement.** Kibibi Voloria Mack, ed. North Bellmore, N.Y., Marshall Cavendish, 1997. 2v. illus. index. $149.95/set. ISBN 0-7614-0563-1.

These 2 volumes are an alphabetically arranged supplement to the 1993, 6-volume set of the same title (see ARBA 94, entry 402). Reviews of the original set, although generally lacking critical analysis, welcomed the new reference tool. The supplement with its 505 additional entries (71 are updates) will also be welcomed. Its format follows that of the original: mostly short, unsigned articles with a scattering of longer pieces (usually signed and sometimes with a bibliography) and many black-and-white photographs. Following the articles are an African American timeline from 1619 to 1996; an annotated, classified bibliography; an annotated filmography of feature films and documentaries; a list of the "100 Most Profitable Black-Owned Businesses, 1995"; lists of black achievements in various sports; a list of African Americans by profession; and a detailed, comprehensive index to the whole 8 volumes.

Generally accurate in detail, there are only a few errors (e.g., sociologist Guy B. Johnson was white, not black). The greater danger lies in its avoidance of controversy and complexity (e.g., *Ebony* is praised, but the entry does not mention the charges of its elitism) and in what the encyclopedia omits (e.g., in spite of its emphasis on popular culture, it gives insignificant coverage to two of African America's most significant contributions to world culture, blues and gospel).

This encyclopedia lacks the grandeur and scholarly depth of the recent *Encyclopedia of African-American Culture and History* (see ARBA 97, entry 331). Also its contributors, unlike the editor of the aforementioned title, are not the academic stars of African American studies. This supplement is easy reading, is attractively laid out, and has good-quality reproductions. The encyclopedia is designed for use by students from middle school through lower-level undergraduates. —**Fred J. Hay**

133. **African American Voices.** Deborah Gillan Straub, ed. Detroit, U*X*L/Gale, 1996. 2v. illus. index. $55.00/set. ISBN 0-8103-9497-9.

This work consists of a collection of excerpted speeches delivered by African American civil rights activists, religious leaders, educators, feminists, abolitionists, politicians, writers, and other key figures who have changed the course of history by speaking out on a variety of issues. Here the reader will find the words of Frederick Douglass, Henry Highland Garnet, Mary McLeod Bethune, Rita Dove, Alex Haley, Stokely Carmichael, Eldridge Cleaver, Roy Wilkins, Ben Carson, Fannie Lou Hamer, Marcus Garvey, Martin Luther King Jr., Thurgood Marshall, Adam Clayton Powell Jr., and more. Speech topics include abolition, arts and literature, black nationalism, black power, childhood and family, civil rights, discrimination, education, employment, family history, black history, Jim Crow laws, lynching, militancy, poverty, religion, slavery, violence, voting rights, and more.

Divided into two volumes for easy handling, the entries are arranged in alphabetic order by speaker. Each entry begins with introductory material, including a biographical sketch of the speaker and the historical context of the speech that follows. Sidebars expand on topics mentioned within the entries. A listing of sources provides bibliographic information on books, periodicals, and other sources for additional information related to the speech. Words and phrases that might be unfamiliar to the reader are defined in the lower margin of the page on which they appear. Additional features of the work are more than 90 black-and-white photographs and illustrations, a subject index, a listing of speeches by major topics, and a timeline. Highlighted headings, wide margins, and generous typeface size further enhance the work and its accessibility.—**Dana McDougald**

Biography

134. **African American Biography, Volume 5.** By Judson Knight. Lawrence W. Baker, ed. Farmington Hills, Mich., U*X*L/Gale, 1999. 255p. illus. index. $39.00. ISBN 0-7876-3562-6. ISSN 1522-2934.

The 5th volume of the *African American Biography* continues as an excellent source for middle school and junior high school students. This new volume includes 40 biographies; 22 are new and 18 are updates from earlier profiles. The new biographies include historical figures such as Cinque and the Delaney sisters; sports heroes such as Tiger Woods, Dominique Dawes, and Venus Williams; entertainers; political leaders; and authors. Each biography includes a picture of photo, a readable narrative that also includes controversial aspects of the person's life, a quotation summarizing their philosophy, and a short bibliography. The bibliographies consist of Web pages, books, and popular magazines. Special features include extensive cross-references and a timeline of significant African American events from 1731 through 1998. Some of the terms in the glossary are curious (e.g., Halley's Comet, Soviet Union, and Yoga). There is a comprehensive list of all entries indicating volume and page number. Also included is a general bibliography of books and magazines. This series is not as comprehensive as other Gale publications, such as *Reference Library of Black America* (94th ed., 1994), *Notable Black American Women* (see entry 136), and *Who's Who Among African Americans* (14th ed.; see ARBA 2003, entry 313). This volume is highly recommended for school and public libraries.—**Karen Y. Stabler**

135. Engelbert, Phyllis. **African American Biography, Volume 6.** Farmington Hills, Mich., U*X*L/Gale, 2000. 289p. illus. index. (African American Reference Library Series). $42.00. ISBN 0-7876-3563-4.

This is the 6th volume of an ongoing series (see entry 134, for a review of volume 5). This volume presents biographies of 20 notable African Americans and updates 10 profiles from previous volumes. Included are African Americans from a variety of fields of endeavor, such as Clive O. Callender (surgeon), Joyce Dixon (social worker), Father Divine (religious leader and social activist), T. Thomas Fortune (journalist), and Elijah McCoy (inventor).

Each entry consists of at least one photograph on the biographee, personal and career information, and sources for further reading. Some entries include a sidebar with additional information of special interest. Volume 6 also features a list of biographees, under their field of endeavor, who have been profiled in all six volumes. A comprehensive index covers all six volumes. Wide margins, boldfaced headings, and generous type size provide a comfortable reading experience. [R: BR, Sept/Oct 2000, p. 62]—**Dana McDougald**

136.   **Notable Black American Women, Book II.** Jessie Carney Smith, ed. Detroit, Gale, 1996. 775p. illus. index. $75.00. ISBN 0-8103-9177-5.

As in the case of the 1st volume, *Notable Black American Women, Book II* focuses on the most famous and important African American women. This 2d book features more than 300 additional women, 100 of whom are historic, and the remaining 200 more contemporary. The selection is diverse, with inclusions from all geographic areas and all professional categories. Information on the individuals profiled has been collected from printed sources and the entrants and their descendants.

Each entry includes the name of the individual, birth and death dates, occupation, and a biographical sketch ranging from somewhat brief (in cases where less information is available) to extensive for better-known black women. In many cases, a black-and-white photograph is also provided. Wherever possible, the editor has supplied a list of primary sources, archival materials and where they are located, and listings of any special collections available concerning the individuals. The second volume has also added two useful features: a list of all the living biographees' addresses and a geographic index including birthplace and residence. Also provided is a detailed subject index.

The title under review is an important source of information for both historic and contemporary black women. One can learn about Alice of Dunk's Ferry (ca.1686-1802), an oral historian and slave; Mollie Ernestine Dunlap (1898-1977), a well-respected librarian and editor; and even Willie Mae (Big Mama) Thornton (1926-1984), who, of course, is a musician, blues singer, and songwriter familiar to many. The biographies are clearly written and detailed, but not overly long. In most cases, the bibliographies included provide useful sources for additional information. This work is highly recommended for all libraries, and especially for larger academic and public collections. It would also be a useful addition for secondary school libraries where information on African American women is sometimes hard to find. [R: Choice, June 96, p. 1621; RBB, 15 Feb 96, p. 1040]—**Robert L. Wick**

Handbooks and Yearbooks

137.   Torres-Saillant, Silvio, and Ramona Hernández. **The Dominican Americans.** Westport, Conn., Greenwood Press, 1998. 184p. illus. index. (The New Americans). $39.95. ISBN 0-313-29839-4.

During the 1930 to 1961 dictatorship of Trujillo, the Dominican Republic's population increased from 900,000 to 3,000,000. During recent decades, the United States has supported Western-leaning but unpopular dictators of this island by allowing entry visas to revolutionaries. These dictators have taken international loans and accepted global corporations but neither have increased the incomes of the poorer class—the majority of the population. Since the 1970s as many as 20,000 uneducated people migrate each year, usually to New York City. Because the United States has changed economically from industrial to service oriented, low-level jobs are not common and when found are low paying. The 1990s cutoff of welfare money is parallel to youth being attracted to the drug culture. Some Dominicans write and create music and art but Latin American professional organizations have been slow to acknowledge this. This story is clearly and coherent told by two Dominican Americans, emphasizing gender, race, and class issues. Although religion, health, and family perspectives might be the genesis of a solution, they are not developed; instead social determinism has precedence. Education, work, and political muscle are believed to be the paths to rectitude of dire circumstances. The prevalence of poverty around the world and the problem of how to curtail it, say nothing of escape it, make this book valuable. Self-respect and validation from neighbors and communities are well supported by these writers and their data. The bibliography, created by a separate scholar, is a treasure in itself.—**Elizabeth L. Anderson**

Africans

138. **African Biography.** Virginia Curtin Knight, ed. Detroit, U*X*L/Gale, 1998. 3v. illus. maps. index. $84.00/set. ISBN 0-7876-2823-9.

Aimed at middle school students and older, this 3-volume work contains biographical entries on 75 notable Africans who lived from 1182 to modern times. Alphabetically arranged by biographical subject, the volumes include essays on individuals ranging from South African President Nelson Mandela to Nobel Laureate in literature Nadine Gordimer to the late Ethiopian Emperor Haile Selassie. Other entries describe lesser-known people who have achieved distinction as labor leaders, musicians, or religious figures, to name only a few fields. The entries contain more than 150 illustrations and maps, sidebar information related to the individual, and a bibliography. In addition, the volumes include a glossary, a timeline of significant events in African history, and name and subject indexes. *African Biography* is an excellent reference source: well written, nicely designed, and usefully organized. The editor deserves particular praise for resisting the pressures of politically correct publishing: the work does not omit critical material on some frequently praised individuals, includes notable white Africans, and covers the underreported topic of Arab slave trading. One note of criticism: The authors of these fine essays should have been included in each entry.—**Donald Altschiller**

139. **Nations of Africa.** By the Diagram Group. New York, Facts on File, 1997. 112p. illus. maps. index. (Peoples of Africa). $19.95; $95.00/set. ISBN 0-8160-3488-5; 0-8160-3482-6/set.

140. **Peoples of Central Africa.** By the Diagram Group. New York, Facts on File, 1997. 112p. illus. maps. index. (Peoples of Africa). $19.95; $95.00/set. ISBN 0-8160-3486-9; 0-8160-3482-6/set.

141. **Peoples of East Africa.** By the Diagram Group. New York, Facts on File, 1997. 112p. illus. maps. index. (Peoples of Africa). $19.95; $95.00/set. ISBN 0-8160-3484-2; 0-8160-3482-6/set.

142. **Peoples of North Africa.** By the Diagram Group. New York, Facts on File, 1997. 112p. illus. maps. index. (Peoples of Africa). $19.95; $95.00/set. ISBN 0-8160-3483-4; 0-8160-3482-6/set.

143. **Peoples of Southern Africa.** By the Diagram Group. New York, Facts on File, 1997. 112p. illus. maps. index. (Peoples of Africa). $19.95; $95.00/set. ISBN 0-8160-3487-7; 0-8160-3482-6/set.

144. **Peoples of West Africa.** By the Diagram Group. New York, Facts on File, 1997. 112p. illus. maps. index. (Peoples of Africa). $19.95; $95.00/set. ISBN 0-8160-3485-0; 0-8160-3482-6/set.

This set was created specifically for middle and high school students. Peoples of Africa presents the different cultures and traditions of the major ethnic groups. Each volume presents information on history (including timelines), language, way of life, social structure, culture, and religion, putting it in the context of the particular group's environment—land, climate, vegetation, and wildlife. Special features on cultural and political topics are included, as are a chronology and pictorial history of the region, a glossary, and a language tree.

Facts on File is usually consistent in its published books. However, this set falls flat. Even though the information is current and the topics included are important, the lack of photographs and color illustrations is noticeable. The color (or lack of) is in black, rust, and gray tones, somewhat reminiscent of the early rotogravures. For example, when the wildlife and vegetation of each area are shown, only the names are given. There is no way for the reader to know the colors. If research by students includes the reproduction of specific animals and vegetation, another book will need to be used. The *Nations of Africa* volume shows flags, but once again without color. The color key is at the bottom of the picture. Also, indigenous words (e.g., Mahdi, shari'a) are used without pronunciation guides, which would cause difficulty for students giving an oral report.

When doing serious research, students today like to use books that are pleasing to the eye. These books certainly would provide all the information needed for any report about Africa. However, students would not gravitate toward these readily due to the blandness of the illustrations. The price of $95 for a 6-volume set is not too much money considering the information found in these books, but a better choice may be the Enchantment of the World series (Childrens Press, 1982-), with useful information as well as illustrations and photographs, so that students can get a feel for the continent of Africa.—**Barbara B. Goldstein**

145. **Peoples of Africa.** Tarrytown, N.Y., Marshall Cavendish, 2000. 11v. illus. maps. index. $329.95/set. ISBN 0-7614-7158-8.

Divided into 11 books, this reference begins with an introductory essay giving a general overview of African history. The series proceeds with individual entries focusing on each country's history, political evolution, cultural development, and geographic distinctions. Each nation is showcased with an article illustrating its uniqueness and connects the reader to the people of that geographical entity by providing information on the economy, music, dance, arts, cuisine, religion, language, and daily activities of the populace. Maps, photographs, timelines, sidebars, and even recipes highlight each country's contributions to the world's experience. The diversity of the region is portrayed and the reader is readily engaged.

Readers learn many interesting insights into the continent. For example, only 42 percent of the Angolan population is literate. Burkina Faso has an international reputation for its Pan-African film festival. And, Ceuta was the first European colony in Africa and is still governed as a territory by Spain.

Features include a glossary of definitions for the key concepts covered in each volume. There is a comprehensive index by general topic as well as additional indexes by individuals, national holidays, geographic features, arts, festivals, food, religion, and sports. Referrals for further reading are also given. This set is a well-written secondary education resource for a little-understood and under-appreciated part of the world.—**Adrienne Antink Bien**

Arab Americans

146. **Arab American Biography.** Loretta Hall and Bridget K. Hall, eds. Farmington Hills, Mich., U*X*L/Gale, 1999. 2v. illus. index. $63.00/set. ISBN 0-7876-2953-7.

Defining an Arab American as an individual who traces his or her ancestry to 1 or more nations belonging to the League of Arab States, this 2-volume set profiles 75 persons who have made noteworthy achievements in a variety of fields, including politics, business, entertainment, science, and religion. Each entry includes date and place of birth (most of the individuals are currently alive), a narrative biographical description, often a black-and-white photograph, and a bibliography. Frequent sidebars provide interesting facts related to the individual. Each of the two volumes includes a table of contents, indexes by occupation and country of ancestry, and a cumulative alphabetic index for names and subjects.

Like some other ethnic reference publications, the criterion for inclusion is the individual's ancestry, not necessarily a professed commitment or involvement in the culture of his or her heritage. While many essays in this volume do describe individuals with strong Lebanese or other Arab background, some entries (such as race car driver Bobby Rahall, football star Doug Flutie, or high school teacher-turned-astronaut Christa McAuliffe) reveal little information pertinent to a student consulting a specialized reference work on Arab Americans. A future revised edition would be better as a 1-volume work, limited to individuals who were genuinely shaped by their ethnic background. The elementary level of the glossary and timeline demonstrate that this work is aimed—like other volumes in the U*X*L imprint of the Gale Group—at students in grades 5 and up. [R: BR, Nov/Dec 99, p. 71; RUSQ, Fall 99, p. 86]—**Donald Altschiller**

147.   **Arab American Encyclopedia.** Anan Ameri and Dawn Ramey, eds. Farmington Hills, Mich., U*X*L/Gale, 2000. 310p. illus. index. $42.00. ISBN 0-7876-2952-9.

148.   **Arab American Voices.** By Loretta Hall. Farmington Hills, Mich., U*X*L/Gale, 2000. 233p. illus. index. $42.00. ISBN 0-7876-2956-1.

The publication of these two titles completes U*X*L's Arab American Reference Library series, whose focus is Americans whose ancestry can be traced to one of the 21 Arab countries that are members of the League of Arab States. Each book in the series, which began with the publication of *Arab American Biography* (see entry 146), is designed as a unique title even though a cumulative index is available if the three parts of the series are purchased as a set.

Arab American Encyclopedia was compiled by the Arab American Center for Economic and Social Services (ACCESS). The encyclopedia is divided into 19 sections focusing on such diverse topics as health and environmental issues, family and gender roles, and literature. Also used are sidebars, a timeline, and a glossary to supplement the text. The glossary, though, is short on necessary details such as the differences between the Shi'a and the Sunni Muslims. Bibliographic citations for further research are included both at the end of each section and in a short three-page bibliography. Many of the items suggested for further research are published by academic presses and seem much too advanced for the target audience of middle to high school students. The outstanding index that concludes the book is much more detailed than is usually evident in a work aimed at school-age children.

Arab American Voices is a compilation of 27 previously published primary sources, some of them excerpted, that are arranged into several sections. Each of these sections begins with an overview of the topic to provide context and concludes with bibliographic citations for further research. Libraries interested in this title might also want to consider the *Gale Encyclopedia of Multicultural America: Primary Documents* (see ARBA 2001, entry 271). The books in the Arab American Reference Library series are all recommended for public and school libraries. These titles fill a niche that has long been neglected in juvenile reference sources. [R: BL, July 2000, p. 2055; SLJ, Aug 2000, p. 127; BR, Sept/Oct 2000, p. 71]—**John R. Burch Jr.**

Asian Americans

149.   Do, Hien Duc. **The Vietnamese Americans.** Westport, Conn., Greenwood Press, 1999. 148p. illus. index. (The New Americans). $39.95. ISBN 0-313-29780-0.

The Vietnamese American issues the author treats are elders who would rather be back home; the first generation who find good in both cultures commercializing their folk festivals, trying to learn English to fulfill their and our values of health, prosperity, and happiness; and the next generation who are integrating, or quite to the contrary have neither Vietnamese nor American acculturation, and become frightening delinquents. The author's social science doctorate prepares him to analyze and make conclusions based on wide reading, interviews, and observations in southern California.

Although federal and nongovernmental organization's money have brought over two million Vietnamese refugees stranded by war, Americans, whose ethnic migrations centuries or decades earlier, have not welcomed them. Basic networks of an integrated work place and education established in the United States—by those earlier refugees—do sustain new populations. The author believes America is now a mosaic, not a melting pot. The work includes minimal black-and-white pictures, a good bibliography, and an index. There are no maps or sidebars. —**Elizabeth L. Anderson**

150.   Hurh, Won Moo. **The Korean Americans.** Westport, Conn., Greenwood Press, 1998. 190p. illus. maps. index. (The New Americans). $39.95. ISBN 0-313-29741-X.

This is not a reference book in the strictest sense of the word, rather it is a sociological and cultural survey of Korean Americans. Although the Library of Congress classifies it as history, only part 2 is concerned with the historical overview of Korean immigration to the United States.

This title is part of the publisher's The New Americans series and is "designed for high school and general readers who want to learn more about their new neighbors" (p. xiv). It is also suitable for undergraduate college students. The author is a professor of sociology at Western Illinois University who has written extensively on Korean Americans, ethnic and race relations, and comparative sociology. In 1984 he published *Korean Immigrants in America.* Hurh is a well-established and respected researcher and author in Korean American studies.

Part 1 introduces the reader to the Korean cultural heritage. Part 2 is a historical overview of Korean immigration to the United States. Part 3 is the longest section, examining Korean American adaptation and adjustment to American society. Part 4 emphasizes "Unique Characteristics of Korean Americans and Their Impact on American Society." The appendix lists "Notable Korean Americans" in $3\frac{1}{2}$ pages. Sections containing references and further reading, both unannotated, follow. There are 11 black-and-white photographs and one map as well as statistical tables and figures. Some of the statistics are rather dated, and many of the photographs and statistics emphasize the Korean American experience in Chicago. Special features include an emphasis on the uniqueness of Korean Americans in comparison with other Asian Americans and other minority groups, plus the effective use of personal narratives throughout the text.

Hurh's book successfully summarizes important historical, socioeconomic, and cultural information about Korean Americans in an authoritative manner and in an easy-to-read style. Thus it is a valuable and needed addition to current Korean American studies.—**Marshall E. Nunn**

151.   Ng, Franklin. **The Taiwanese Americans.** Westport, Conn., Greenwood Press, 1998. 163p. illus. maps. index. (The New Americans). $39.95. ISBN 0-313-29762-2.

Chinese Americans are the largest Asian American group, only slightly outnumbering Filipino Americans. Taiwanese Americans are the second largest subgroup of Chinese Americans, following in size immigrants from mainland China and outpacing those from Hong Kong and Singapore. These figures add more importance to this book because it is the first one published on Taiwanese Americans. It is another title in The New Americans series, which is "designed for high school and general readers" (p. x). It focuses on community organization, information networks, religion, culture, and the nature of the second generation. Even though it does provide helpful historical background information, its main emphasis is on the cultural and sociological aspects of Taiwanese American life.

The author covers his subject in 4 parts. The introduction gives basic background information on Taiwan's land, people, language, religion, and history. "Coming to America" discusses early Chinese and Taiwanese immigration, composition of the new immigrants, and family and youth patterns. "Living in America" is concerned with associations, newspapers and the media, religion, and festivals. The last part, "An Evolving Taiwanese American Identity," gives valuable information on conflicts with mainlanders, politics in Taiwan, the second generation, intergroup relations, and Taiwanese Americans' "complex and evolving identity" (p. 126). Black-and-white photographs illustrate scenes from contemporary cultural life and activities. Two appendixes profile biographies of six successful Taiwanese Americans and provide eleven statistical immigration tables. There is also an unannotated bibliography that includes Internet Websites.

Ng is a professor of anthropology at California State University, Fresno, and has authored and edited several notable books on Asian American studies, including *The Asian American Encyclopedia* (see ARBA 96, entry 394) and *Chinese American Struggle for Equality* (Rourke, 1992). He writes with clarity and authority, and this book, although not strictly a reference work, belongs in all libraries. [R: SLJ, Nov 98, p. 141]—**Marshall E. Nunn**

152.   Posadas, Barbara M. **The Filipino Americans.** Westport, Conn., Greenwood Press, 1999. 190p. illus. maps. index. (The New Americans). $39.95. ISBN 0-313-29742-8.

Historically, Filipino Americans have been known as an invisible minority, and there has been a real need for a comprehensive, up-to-date, reliable guide to their immigrant experience. Posadas' book admirably fills this need. Even though the books in the New Americans series are designed for high school and general readers, they are quite valuable for college students and teachers as well.

The book is tightly and logically organized into two parts and nine chapters. Its emphasis is on immigration, particularly after 1965; social and cultural issues, including values, customs, and economic and political power; identity in a multicultural society; contemporary issues for adults and elders; and the future of Filipino immigration.

A map, 5 statistical tables detailing Filipino immigration from 1920 to the present, and 18 black-and-white photographs effectively supplement the text. There are two appendixes: "Filipinos in the U.S. Census, 1910-2000" and "Notable Filipino Americans" (with eight short biographies). A glossary of cultural and immigration-related terms; a bibliography of films, videos, and distributors; and an unannotated bibliography of books and articles are also included. This is a survey but more information on certain aspects or the subject, especially on Filipinos in Alaska and Hawaii, would be helpful.

With this book, Posadas has established herself as the leading authority on Filipino Americans. She is eminently qualified as a professor of history at Northern Illinois University, as a member of the editorial boards of *Amerasia* and the *Journal of American Ethnic History*, and as the director of the Filipino National Historical Society.—**Marshall E. Nunn**

153.   Tong, Benson. **The Chinese Americans.** Westport, Conn., Greenwood Press, 2000. 248p. illus. index. (The New Americans Series). $39.95. ISBN 0-313-30544-7. ISSN 1092-6364.

The Chinese were the first Asians to arrive on America's shores in the 1780s. Historically, Chinese Americans have been the largest and most prominent Asian American group; however, the 2000 U.S. census will most likely show that they are now slightly outnumbered by Filipino Americans. This new and authoritative treatment of their immigrant experience deserves our serious consideration.

This volume is part of Greenwood Press's New Americans Series. The series foreword states that "these volumes are designed for high school students and general readers"; however, this particular volume's sophisticated style and treatment make it more appropriate for college students and teachers as well as the educated reader.

In chapter 1 the author provides the necessary background information on Chinese culture and society during the late Qing Dynasty (1644-1912). His discussion of Chinese geography, language, society, philosophy and religion, politics, and dynastic history places Chinese American immigration in a suitable context. The next 5 chapters consider the Chinese American experience chronologically, with coverage emphasizing post-1945 developments.

Within each chapter the author identifies and explores major social and economic themes rather than giving a straightforward historical narrative. He is particularly good on the role of women, labor, and economic issues, and on U.S. immigration legislation and anti-Asian laws. In chapter 7, Tong discusses the arts and Chinese Americans, including such topics as their images in film, fiction, poetry, theater, television, documentaries, visual arts, and music. His insights on feminist perspectives are especially helpful. Chapter 8, "Chinese American Families and Identities," concludes the main body of the work. Here are valuable sections on gangs and juvenile delinquency, gay men and lesbians, and interracial marriage. An appendix, "Noted Chinese Americans," concludes the work. It contains 15 short biographies of prominent contemporary figures, such as March Fong Eu, Maxine Hong Kingston, Maya Lin, Gary Locke, Yo-Yo Ma, and I. M. Pei.

The work is heavily documented with extensive chapter notes and a selected unannotated bibliography. There are no Internet Website citations in either of these sections. There are 14 black-and-white photographs, which are interesting but of average quality.—**Marshall E. Nunn**

Hispanic Americans

154.   **Dictionary of Hispanic Biography.** Joseph C. Tardiff and L. Mpho Mabunda, eds. Detroit, Gale, 1996. 1011p. illus. index. $120.00. ISBN 0-8103-8302-0.

The *Dictionary of Hispanic Biography* (DHB) is a much-needed, single-volume source for information concerning Hispanic individuals from the past and present. With more than 450 entries, this dictionary is among the largest biographical sources available. The only other source that comes to mind that provides a larger list of names is the *National Directory of Latin Americanists* (see ARBA 87, entry 139), which includes not only Hispanics but also individuals who are scholars in Hispanic studies. Other such works as *Champions of Change: Biographies of Famous Hispanic Americans* and *The Hispanic 100* (see ARBA 96, entry 408) provide a much smaller listing and concentrate on Hispanics living in the United States.

DHB profiles Hispanic men and women who lived from the fifteenth century to the present, and covers all endeavors from art, business, education, and entertainment to journalism, politics, religion, science, sports, and activism. Approximately 70 percent of the individuals listed are contemporary. Each entry provides an in-depth biographical sketch (usually from 300 to 700 words), along with lists of the sources used to obtain the information. Many of the entries have black-and-white photographs. Indexes include an occupation index, a nationality/ethnicity index, and a subject index.

DHB appears to be well balanced in that most of the Hispanics who come to mind are listed; the compilation seems very satisfactory. The editors contend that their original list contained more than 700 names, and was carefully cut down to the 450-plus notable Hispanics chosen for inclusion. This work is recommended for all libraries. While it is essential for all larger academic and public libraries, one hopes that smaller public and school libraries will also consider DHB as an important reference tool for students. [R: LJ, Feb 96, p. 142; RBB, 15 Mar 96, p. 1312]—**Robert L. Wick**

155.   Gonzalez-Pando, Miguel. **The Cuban Americans.** Westport, Conn., Greenwood Press, 1998. 185p. illus. index. (The New Americans). $39.95. ISBN 0-313-29824-6.

The New Americans series from Greenwood Press seeks to introduce new, post-1965 immigrants to a general readership, examining the migration and settlement processes of different national groups. Gonzalez-Pando's volume, *The Cuban Americans*, provides a readable and rich narrative of the experience of immigrants from this Caribbean nation. Although the author's own political leanings inevitably surface throughout the text, the book offers a good basic introduction to the study of Cuban immigrants in the United States.

Following the general format designed by the series editor, the author provides an overview of the genesis of Cuban immigration; a period account of the development of the Cuban American community in South Florida; and thematic chapters on economic achievements, cultural and national identity politics, and the development of involvement in more formal political participation. The book's appendix contains an annotated listing of notable Cuban Americans, a chronology of Cuban immigration, a brief set of statistics, and a short bibliography.

The greatest strength of this work is the frequent integration of oral histories into the narrative, allowing the voices of Cuban immigrants to speak for themselves. However, the author has drawn primarily from interviews with prominent and powerful Cuban Americans, and seems to offer little material from ordinary Cubans whose experiences may be more representative of this group's experience. The chapters on cultural and national identity and on politics are impressively balanced and provide original insight into the complex experience of Cuban Americans, countering prevailing simplistic stereotypes of this group's conservative politics.

Although the author notes that the Cuban American community has become increasingly diverse in its racial and class composition, it would have been useful to develop this theme more fully. The statistical information provided is minimal, especially when compared to other volumes in the New Americans series. More data on the educational, economic, and racial profile of the Cuban American community would enhance this book's usefulness as a general reference and facilitate comparison with the experiences of other national immigrant groups. The author also focuses almost exclusively on Miami. Although this is clearly the heart of Cuban American settlement in the United States, other major centers of residence such as Union City, New Jersey, warrant more coverage.

Despite these shortcomings, *The Cuban Americans* fills a gap in the extensive scholarship on Cubans in the United States by providing an informative text appropriate for secondary school and general audiences. This volume should go far in fulfilling the series' goals of introducing and increasing understanding of the United States' newest immigrant groups. [R: BR, Nov/Dec 98, p. 80; SLJ, Oct 98, p. 154; VOYA, Dec 98, p. 380]—**Pamela M. Graham**

156.   **Hispanic American Chronology.** Nicholàs Kanellos and Bryan Ryan, eds. Detroit, U*X*L/Gale, 1996. 195p. illus. maps. index. $29.00. ISBN 0-8103-9826-5.

Hispanic American Chronology offers readers a concise narrative of important events concerning Hispanics in the Americas. The chronology is arranged by year and then by month and day. The reference encapsulates the principal social, political, economic, cultural, and educational contributions of Hispanic Americans. The entries are brief and lack the type of detail that would have made this volume truly worthwhile. It seems that the only purpose and use of the chronology is to verify dates of important events, although the information provided can be obtained from any encyclopedia. However, there are many illustrations, maps, and photographs to supplement the entries. This book can only be recommended for public libraries, primary/secondary school libraries, or for classrooms that serve Hispanic students. [R: BR, Sept/Oct 96, p. 54; SLJ, Nov 96, p. 138]—**Dario J. Villa**

157.   Meier, Matt S., with Conchita Franco Serri and Richard A. Garcia. **Notable Latino Americans: A Biographical Dictionary.** Westport, Conn., Greenwood Press, 1997. 431p. illus. index. $65.00. ISBN 0-313-29105-5.

Over the last several years, a number of reference works have been published focusing on the Hispanic American community in the United States. Meier, an author of several books on Chicano ethnic studies and history, has compiled a biographical dictionary of 127 Latinos from all walks of life who have made a significant contribution in their respective fields. Sports figures (Jose Conseco), politicians (Lincoln Diaz-Balart), entertainers (Gloria Estefan), performing artists (Jose Limon), and other luminaries are given three-page entries on their personal and professional lives. The emphasis always includes the struggles or prejudices these people faced in becoming ultimately positive role models for contemporary Latino youth.

The writing style is more simplistic than that of entries appearing in *Notable Hispanic American Women* (see ARBA 94, entry 962), but is usually more detailed than biographical entries published in *The Latino Encyclopedia* (see ARBA 97, entry 337). There is approximately an 80 percent overlap in coverage with these two reference works alone. An appendix, which is arranged by professionals in the field, is a good ready reference source for determining which Latinos were dancers, artists, lawyers, etc. This work is a reasonably good choice for school, public, and community college libraries. [R: LJ, 15 April 97, p. 70]—**Judith A. Valdez**

Indians of North America

Atlases

158.   Waldman, Carl. Illustrated by Molly Braun. **Atlas of the North American Indian.** rev. ed. New York, Facts on File, 2000. 385p. illus. maps. index. (Facts on File Library of American History). $45.00; $21.95pa. ISBN 0-8160-3974-7; 0-8160-3975-5pa.

Originally published in 1985 (see ARBA 86, entry 380) this revised edition is 109 pages longer. The arrangement remains the same as the prior edition—seven chapters from Paleo-Indians to contemporary Indians. Most of the sections have a few added or revised paragraphs. For example, in the chapter dealing with Paleo-Indians, Waldman added a section addressing a seaborne migration theory that is slowly gaining acceptance among North American archaeologists. As in the previous edition, it remains true that there is significantly more text than maps for an atlas, but there are 14 new maps. One of the improvements of this edition is that the maps are now black and white rather than several shades of brown. In most cases, revision involves a new map related to a new section, such as the material and map for the Poverty Point complex in the lower Mississippi River Valley or the material and map related to pre-contact trade in North America. The chronology has substantial new entries for 1985-1998. There are several entries for 1999, including one for the creation of Nunavut as a new Canadian territory for the Inuit people. There is also a single entry for 2000 (the issuance of the Sacajawea dollar coin). The contemporary Indians chapter, as expected, contains the most new material with a long section on Indian gaming, and one on "Indian Country" and what that term does and does not mean. This revised edition is a worthwhile purchase even if readers do have the original edition. [R: SLJ, Aug 2000, p. 136; BL, 1 Sept 2000, p. 172; VOYA, Oct 2000, p. 300; BR, Nov/Dec 2000, p. 74]—**G. Edward Evans**

Biography

159.   **Native North American Biography.** Sharon Malinowski and Simon Glickman, eds. Detroit, U*X*L/Gale, 1996. 2v. illus. index. $55.00/set. ISBN 0-8103-9821-4.

Intended for middle and high school students, this work does not pretend to the coverage of other references such as Duane Champagne's *The Native North American Almanac* (see ARBA 95, entry 439). However, it usefully profiles 112 Native North Americans from the United States and Canada, both living and deceased. The result is enjoyably browseable. Written in a somewhat journalistic style and objective in tone, the work only rarely includes controversial evaluations.

The contents are alphabetically ordered, with portraits accompanying most entries, and a list of sources at the end of each. It must have been difficult to decide what prominent Native Americans should not be included: One might have welcomed such personalities as the anthropologists Francis La Flesche (Osage) and Edward Dozier (Tewa), the painters Fritz Scholder (Luiseño) and Harry Fonseca (Maidu), and the poets Wendy Rose (Hopi/Miwok) and Simon Ortiz (Laguna).

The front of each volume has an index by tribal groups/nations that runs into problems of terminology. Thus, the entry on Charles Alex Eastman identifies him as "Santee Sioux writer," but he is indexed only under "Dakota," while Amos Bad Heart Bull, "Oglala Sioux artist," is indexed only under "Lakota"; there is an index entry "Sioux," but no cross-referencing. Each volume ends with another index by field of endeavor, such as art, dance, or education. A more complete index—including the variant name forms for many of the personalities who are profiled—would have been useful. [R: BR, May/June 96, p. 45; SLJ, Aug 96, p. 182; VOYA, Aug 96, p. 190]—**William Bright**

Dictionaries and Encyclopedias

160.   **Native Americans.** Danbury, Conn., Grolier, 2000. 10v. illus. index. $325.00/set. ISBN 0-7172-9395-5.

Native Americans is a 10-volume set aimed at students ages 10 to 15 and designed to cover the background, anthropology, and archaeology of Indian tribes on the North American continent. Each sle nder, 80-page volume is arranged alphabetically by subject. All include the same "A-Z of Indian Tribes" list, containing thumbnail sketches of 96 tribal groups, and an index covering the entire set. Index entries treated in that particular volume are in bold typeface.

Each volume's colorful cover features an arresting portrait or image that, while otherwise unidentified, appears somewhere in the volume. *Native Americans* has many full-color illustrations, along with diagrams, maps, charts, sidebars, and cross-reference boxes. Information about the history and culture of particular tribes is supplemented with discussions of social issues and profiles of modern Native American leaders.

Native Americans contains material not usually found in such encyclopedias for this age group. Several lesser-known tribes are included and details are offered about subjects like basketmaking, human sacrifice, and weaponry. Yet, as a complete reference, it has several drawbacks. It claims to be all-inclusive, yet inexplicably omits the Cherokee tribe from the "A-Z of Native American Tribes" list that includes obscure groups like the Hidatsa, Ingalik, and Kutenai. While the index shows Cherokee-related topics appearing in 6 of the 10 volumes, the tribe itself lacks a separate article.

These volumes lend themselves well to browsing, but are not efficient for the student in search of specific information. For example, the index shows that "shamanism" appears in all 10 volumes. The index entries for "Spain and the Spanish conquest" are complex and bewildering, and "Gathering," "Hunter-gatherers," and "Hunting" seem to be somewhat repetitious topics. Some articles end so suddenly as to appear inconclusive. Quite often, words like "palisaded townships" and "wickiup" are used without definition. Also, some material appears to be unsuitable for the target age group. *Native Americans* has much to commend it, but perhaps it should be considered as a supplementary work on the subject rather than a collection's only such reference. [R: BL, Jan 2000, p. 978; SLJ, May 2000, p. 90; BR, May/June 2000, p. 76]—**Kay O. Cornelius**

161.   **Scholastic Encyclopedia of the North American Indian.** By James Ciment, with Ronald LaFrance. New York, Scholastic, 1996. 224p. illus. maps. index. $17.95. ISBN 0-590-22790-4.

Scholastic Encyclopedia of the North American Indian includes information concerning 143 groups of American Indians in alphabetic order, but it is not an ordinary encyclopedia. In his introduction, Ronald LaFrance, a Ph.D. and an Iroquois, states that there is no single Indian culture and that Indian tribes are as different from one another as the Spanish are from the French or the English from the Dutch. Indian tribes are portrayed in three time frames: past, present, and future. This work seeks to avoid creating new stereotypes or reinforcing old ones.

Information about each of the listed tribes includes its language family, lifeways, location, and its own name for the tribe. Sidebars on each page contain further information about specific members of the tribe, past or present, and aspects of the tribe's life. Many photographs and drawings are used throughout the book. Helpful end material includes a timeline; list of museums and resources; and maps showing regions and peoples, language families, forced migrations, and the loss of land. Topics printed in red in the subject index show the best place to look for specific information.

This volume lends itself more to browsing than to finding facts quickly. No subject heading is provided for "Delaware," and a student must go to four entries to get complete information about "Shawnee." Users should be aware that bias toward the Indian occasionally distorts historical fact, and some of the terms and language seem beyond upper elementary level. However, despite its shortcomings, *Scholastic Encyclopedia of the North American Indian* offers a lot of information at a reasonable price.—**Kay O. Cornelius**

162.   **U*X*L Encyclopedia of Native American Tribes.** Sharon Malinowski, Anna Sheets, and Linda Schmittroth, eds. Farmington Hills, Mich., U*X*L/Gale, 1999. 4v. illus. maps. $99.00/set. ISBN 0-7876-2838-7.

This encyclopedia, written at a 5th grade reading level, contains entries on 80 Native American tribes, confederacies, or groups. The entries are divided into 10 sections in 4 volumes: The Northeast and Southeast; The Great Basin and Southwest; The Arctic, Subarctic, Great Plains, and Plateau; and California and the Pacific Northwest. Each section begins with an essay that introduces the area's history and shared cultural experiences. The entries for individual groups follow. Each begins with basic information, such as name, location, population, language family, and group affiliations. This is followed by specific topics, such as history, language, religion, government, and arts. Suggestions for further reading conclude each entry.

One problem with this title is that there are simply not enough tribal entries. For example, the Southeast includes six tribal entries: Caddo, Cherokee, Chickasaw, Choctaw, Creek, and Seminole. On the map entitled "Historic Locations of U.S. Native Groups," there are 10 tribes in Georgia alone. Six is not representative of the region as a whole.

"Moundbuilders" is an extremely curious entry considering it combines 4 distinctively different cultures, dating from 1500 to 1751 B.C.E., into 1 group. The Creeks and Cherokees had much more in common than these four groups but they certainly merit separate entries. The Mississippian Culture also extended further west than Arkansas. Some of the finest examples of Mississippian shell engravings come from the Spiro Mound Group in Eastern Oklahoma. Readers interested in the moundbuilders would be better served by *Archaeology of Prehistoric Native America: An Encyclopedia* (see ARBA 99, entry 443).

Sections entitled "Words to Know" and "Timeline" are included, along with many maps and pictures that supplement the text nicely. Each volume also contains a complete bibliography of books, periodicals, Websites, and CD-ROMs. The volumes uses continuous pagination and each contains the index for the entire set.

Future editions of this work are planned to expand on the number of Native American groups profiled. Rather than wait and buy each subsequent edition, interested individuals should just purchase *The Gale Encyclopedia of Native American Tribes* (see ARBA 99, entry 389). It shares both general format and two editors with this volume. It also contains nearly 400 tribal entries in much more detail. [R: BR, Nov/Dec 99, pp. 79-80]—**John R. Burch Jr.**

Handbooks and Yearbooks

163.   Carrasco, Davíd, with Scott Sessions. **Daily Life of the Aztecs: People of the Sun and Earth.** Westport, Conn., Greenwood Press, 1998. 282p. illus. maps. index. (The Greenwood Press "Daily Life Through History" Series). $45.00. ISBN 0-313-29558-1.

Carrasco, director of the Moses Mesoamerican Archive and professor of history of religions at Princeton University, and Sessions, doctoral candidate in the department of religion at Princeton University, have combined their talents to present this overview of pre-Columbian Aztec culture that reflects the latest scholarship while remaining accessible to lay readers. It provides a glimpse of Aztec life that is often overlooked in texts that tend to dwell on subjects such as ritualistic human sacrifice and cannibalism. These subjects are also included in this book but are examined in context with their role in society as a whole.

The first two chapters are designed as an introduction to the geography and cosmology of the Aztec world. Chapter 3 focuses on life in the community in general. Three chapters focusing on education, societal dynamics, and aesthetics supplement it. Chapter 7 is extremely informative and focuses on human sacrifice and its role in Aztec religion. The authors carefully explain the role of priests and the function of sacrifice in an effort to dispel the stereotypical view of bloodthirsty priests that has dominated the literature on the subject. The 10th chapter focuses on the clash of cultures between the Aztecs and Spaniards that proved to be the end of the Aztec Empire. The 11th chapter serves as an epilogue, which examines the impact of the Aztecs on Mexican culture today. All of the chapters are greatly enhanced by the large number of pictures and photographs scattered throughout the text. The book also includes both an index and a selected bibliography. Especially noteworthy is a glossary, which includes a pronunciation guide for Nahuatl terms. This excellent book is recommended for public and academic libraries.—**John R. Burch Jr.**

Jews

164.   Burstein, Chaya M. **A Kid's Catalog of Israel.** rev. ed. Philadelphia, Jewish Publication Society, 1998. 279p. illus. maps. index. $16.95pa. ISBN 0-8276-0651-6.

First published in 1988, the revised edition of *A Kid's Catalog of Israel* provides an overview of the land and its cultures and peoples. Israel is a young country with an ancient history and a diverse population. The 17 chapters of this book are a trip through time and the land. They point out historical sites, geographic features, and wildlife. Interviews with Arab and Jewish adults and children provide a personal connection between readers and their Israeli peers. Maps, quizzes, games, songs, stories, recipes, and craft projects offer opportunities for hands-on activities that increase understanding of the country and its rich heritage. Although this is a children's book, adults will enjoy it. The reading level is appropriate for ages 10 and up. It is an excellent source of projects for classes, youth groups, and families. *A Kid's Catalog of Israel* is recommended for school, synagogue, and public libraries. Families with young children will want it for their homes as well.—**Barbara M. Bibel**

6 Geography

GENERAL WORKS

Atlases

United States

165.   **The National Atlas of the United States of America. http://www.nationalatlas.gov.** [Website]. 2002. Free. Date reviewed: Oct 2002.

This ambitious, largely Web-based resource is an update of the print *National Atlas of the United States* (U.S. Geological Survey, 1970). The original book lived out the limitations of a print national atlas in that it was large and colorful (and therefore expensive) but contained quickly dated thematic content. The new *Atlas*, begun in 1997, is issued not as a book but as a coordinated ongoing program. Umbrellaed under the one URL, the varied components range from entirely digital to print format. The scope of the project is broader, as are the audience and the variety and utility of output. In spite of this it manages to stick to its stated purpose of providing a "reliable summary of national-scale geographical information," while also furnishing links to more detailed sources of information on many topics.

The *Atlas* consists of five major components: an interactive map engine, several multimedia maps, a data warehouse, printed maps, and printable maps. The interactive map engine allows the user to zoom in and pan around a map of the United States, adding themes of information from a long list ranging from agriculture to population characteristics to hazardous waste. The seven multimedia maps depict somewhat random topics, including animations of U.S. geology over 2.6 billion years, avian cholera, volcanoes, and 2,000 incidents of West Nile virus. To view all seven animations it is necessary to download and install the viewing plug-ins Shockwave, Flash Player, and QuickTime Player. The Data Warehouse is intended for researchers who can utilize data files that underlie many of the thematic maps. Most files are only usable in GIS software packages. A few others are in .dbf format, usable in a number of database programs. Since 1970 update maps of the *National Atlas* have been published and sold as looseleaf sheets. The "Printed Maps" page provides ordering information for dozens of these sheets and provides a link to scanned images of the entire original atlas. The "Printable Maps" section presently provides reduced versions of West Nile Virus and President Election maps, ready to print on standard color printers.

The drawbacks to online maps in general are the limitations of bandwidth and screen size. Viewing graphics on the Internet requires good access speed, and the small viewing window makes map analysis difficult over a large area. Print output is limited to whatever options the end user possesses, which is almost always of lower quality than a professionally published map. Overall, the site is strong in content with some room for improvement on navigability. Since 20 federal agencies and 1 private partner provide the content, each component possesses a different arrangement and logic. It is an enjoyable tool if one takes a few minutes to become acquainted with atlas content and navigation. This site is recommended both as a resource and as a pointer to further resources for the upper elementary to graduate levels.—**Kathleen Weessies**

166. **National Geographic United States Atlas for Young Explorers.** Washington, D.C., National Geographic Society, 1999. 176p. illus. maps. index. $24.95. ISBN 0-7922-7115-7.

Both the *National Geographic Beginner's World Atlas* (for children ages 5 to 8) and the *National Geographic United States Atlas for Young Explorers* (for children ages 8 to 12) are excellent atlases designed specifically for use by young people and families. The atlases are the most recent addition to a children's series begun by the National Geographic Society in 1998 with *National Geographic World Atlas for Young Explorers.*

The *Beginner's World Atlas* focuses on the seven continents. There is an introductory chapter called "Understanding Your World," which provides age-appropriate explanations about maps and mapmaking as well as vivid illustrations portraying the physical world map, physical world map symbols, and the political world map. Completing the introduction are two pages describing "what this atlas will teach you." The seven sections that follow describe each of the seven continents. A young child introduces each continent and a scenic vista portrays a beautiful part of the landscape. The section called "The Land" describes major land regions, waterways, climate, plants, and animals in brief, fact-filled text. Another division, "The People," tells about various countries, cities, native peoples, languages, and products for each continent.

Accompanying the large-format, easy-to-read maps are more than 100 color photographs with great appeal to young children. A page of world facts, a glossary, and an index complete the atlas. The *United States Atlas for Young Explorers* combines beautiful photographs, two-dimensional maps, and information presented in colorful, fact-filled pages. Two introductory pages explain how to use the atlas and show that the United States has been divided into five regions. The following two sections contain in-depth information about the physical and political U.S. areas. These pages have excellent maps, beautiful photographs, and clear and brief explanations—all with the younger student in mind. Another brief section has a map and information about our nation's capital. The main portion of the atlas is devoted to each of the five regions of the United States. A panoramic photograph with a list of the states in the margin introduces each region. A physical map of the area is followed by clear and concise descriptions and photographs of the region. To complete the regional coverage, each state is portrayed with a map, fact capsules, and a brief summary. Completing the atlas are several pages covering the U.S. territories, facts and figures, a glossary of terms, abbreviations and Websites, and a comprehensive index.

National Geographic's high standards are evident throughout both volumes. Their world-renowned quality and accuracy are further validated by a collaboration of education consultants and geographers. Both atlases should be on every shelf at home as well as school and public libraries.—**Mary L. Trenerry**

167. **Rand McNally Children's Millennium Atlas of the United States.** Skokie, Ill., Rand McNally, 2000. 109p. illus. maps. index. $16.95. ISBN 0-528-84204-8.

Aimed at children aged 8 to 12, these atlases are richly illustrated and fun to read. Both provide brightly colored and easy-to-read maps. Color photographs illustrate the history and culture of various regions. The main maps show principal cities, highest peaks, rivers, and other features. Both works also include an index to major places.

The world atlas is arranged by continent, with a full chapter devoted to each of the seven continents. There is also a millennium timeline and an introduction to the basics of maps and cartography. Along with political maps there are also physical maps and thematic maps for populations, climates, and economies. A guide to each country's flag along with information on size, population, and capital cities and a glossary are also included.

The U.S. atlas opens with a map illustrating what life was like in the area now known as the United States of America in the year 1000. Next, individual state maps denote major cities, lakes, rivers, highest peaks, and national parks. Each of these maps is accompanied by various information about the state, including a historical timeline and a sidebar illustrating the state's flag, bird, flower, and much more.

Both works are educational and entertaining for children and adults. While larger atlases will provide more in-depth information, these works provide basic informational data for a reasonable price. They will be very appealing to young learners and a good addition to juvenile reference collections.—**Cari Ringelheim**

International

168.   **Answer Atlas.** Skokie, Ill., Rand McNally, 1996. 176p. illus. maps. index. $12.95pa. ISBN 0-528-83872-5.

The *Answer Atlas* is a unique volume combining an answer section with an up-to-date map section. The 50-page answer section includes 2 main parts. The 1st part contains more than 130 intriguing questions, such as "Where in South America could you find places in which no rainfall has ever been recorded?" and "Is Venice, Italy really sinking?" Answers accompany the questions. The 2d part is entitled "World Superlatives, Facts and Rankings" and includes 30 pages that readers will find useful when trying to locate statistics and interesting information on such topics as the universe and solar system; the Earth; continents and islands; mountains, volcanoes, and earthquakes; oceans and lakes; rivers; climate and weather; population; the world's most populous cities; and countries and flags.

The remaining two-thirds of the *Answer Atlas* features maps from *Goode's World Atlas* (19th ed.; Rand McNally, 1995). General maps are organized by continents and further break down into countries or groups of countries on one-and two-page spreads. Others include physical, political, population, precipitation, and demographic maps. Special pages are inserted with information on current topics, such as urbanization in North America and the destruction of the rain forest.

A short glossary and an index of approximately 5,000 entries are appended to the main text. This medium-sized atlas ($8\frac{1}{2}$ x 11 inches) with softbound cover is a fine introductory atlas for home or school use. —**Vik Brown**

169.   **Children's Illustrated Atlas.** 1997 ed. Chicago, World Book, 1997. 288p. illus. maps. index. $29.95. ISBN 0-7166-4033-3.

Children's Illustrated Atlas is a clearly and simply written atlas intended for use by young, elementary-age children. The moderately oversized (9 by 14 inches) volume presents an overview of the Earth, with brief text that is enhanced by more than 400 color illustrations and 250 color photographs. Cartoon characters are introduced in the first section, "You and Your World," and serve as tour guides to enliven the explanatory material introducing students to basic map skills and terminology. More than 100 basic maps are interspersed throughout the book.

The majority of this volume is divided into 15 sections, each introducing a major region of the world. Each section begins with a welcome page and then presents colorful two-page spreads acquainting the students with the countries in the region, the land, plants and animals, growing and making (farming and manufacturing), people and how they live, the cities, and occasionally special sections such as "Through Europe by Truck."

Young students will enjoy this introductory atlas. A simple index and a pronouncing gazetteer are included. This atlas is fine for home or elementary school use.—**Vik Brown**

170. **DK Student Atlas.** New York, DK Publishing, 1998. 160p. illus. maps. index. $19.95. ISBN 0-7894-2399-5.

An excellent atlas for adults as well as students, this volume opens with an outstanding 24 pages that would be most helpful to anyone who is not familiar with atlases. Divided into 2 sections, "Learning Map Skills" and "The World," the book covers such topics as how maps are made, how to read them, how to use this particular atlas, the earth's structure, climates and life zones, and borders and boundaries. After this introductory material, the actual atlas opens with an excellent flat map of the world with all the nations, seas, and oceans clearly delineated. Each area of the world is then covered in separate sections, with larger continents broken down further into specific geographic areas. Each area covered contains a map of that area and various other thematic maps that represent such data as population concentrations, climate, food production, or other subjects deemed pertinent. Along with the maps are various bits of factual information, photographs, and charts. The front inside cover provides a key to regional maps and a map of the continents; those at the back display flags of the various nations.

Although necessity demands rather small print in many instances, the labeling of the maps and the layout of the pages is clear and user-friendly. A brief examination of the index found it to be accurate. Students should find most anything they need from an atlas in this well-thought-out resource, and educators will find the front matter to be an excellent guide for teaching students how to use atlases in general. This resource is recommended for all school and public libraries. [R: BL, 1 Sept 98, p. 153; SLJ, Nov 98, p. 159]—**Jo Anne H. Ricca**

171. **Dorling Kindersley Children's Atlas.** updated ed. New York, DK Publishing, 2000. 176p. illus. maps. index. $24.95. ISBN 0-7894-5845-4.

This newly updated edition of the popular *Dorling Kindersley Children's Atlas* features more than just detailed maps; it gives an overview of the geography, vegetation, and climate of the Earth in easy-to-understand terms that children will relate to. A team of 20 cartographers and researchers created this atlas with the latest cartographic information and digital technology. The resource begins with a 12-page introduction to the Earth as a whole, discussing the Earth in space, landscapes, climate, people's relationship to the planet, and a guide to using the atlas. Because the clientele is based in the United States there is a special section on North America, which covers North America's physical traits, environment, history, people, and politics. Following this the seven regions of the world are featured: North America, Central and South America, Europe, Africa, North and West Asia, South and East Asia, and Australasia and Oceania. For each region the major countries are featured and information on their climate, history, industry, and people are provided. The photographs and maps are beautiful (typical of DK Publishing) but the information is scattered and inconsistent. A glossary of terms and an index conclude the volume.

This atlas will be popular in elementary and middle school libraries as well as public libraries children's reference collections. At only $24.95 there is a lot of valuable information provided along with the excellent maps.—**Shannon Graff Hysell**

172. **Dorling Kindersley Concise Atlas of the World.** New York, DK Publishing, 2001. 350p. illus. maps. index. $29.95. ISBN 0-7894-8002-6.

If indeed the primary function of a world atlas is to help pinpoint places on the globe, then most atlases published today do this well. The *Dorling Kindersley Concise Atlas of the World* does a good job for the money, perhaps the only reason for selecting the concise edition, as it is an up-date of its parent, the *DK World Atlas* (see ARBA 2001, entry 328). Easy access to the contents of this 34-centimeter volume arranged by continent is assured through map and flag keys printed on the endpapers. Main-entry maps on each slick and colorful page are surrounded by a repeated se-ries of diminutive satellite-like, "at-a-glance" facts, diagrams, and photographs. These thumbnail color photographs help to illustrate a country's physical and cultural characteristics and serve as little windows into lands near and far. Some atlases you consult; this atlas, with its straightforward prose, you can pour over or peruse. [R: LJ, 15 Sept 01, p. 69]—**Anthony F. Verdesca Jr.**

173. **Dorling Kindersley World Atlas.** 3d ed. New York, DK Publishing, 2000. 354p. illus. maps. index. $50.00. ISBN 0-7894-5962-0.

This atlas portrays each continent, and the countries within that landmass, as an integrated whole with the interdependencies of its parts recognized. A profusion of narratives and illustra-tions tell the story of daily life as it varies across the globe. Brief political and economic summaries are given for every mapped area. In addition to landscape details and political boundaries, the an-notations provide insights as to cultural development, economic activity, and natural resources. Photographs are sprinkled throughout the volume and bring alive the depicted countries and re-gions. For example, when studying the section for eastern Canada, the reader not only notes the correct location of the Bay of Fundy, but also sees a photograph of the bay's shoreline at low tide and learns that the tides in this bay are among the highest in the world. All map place-names are in the native language of that country. Maps are also provided for the world's oceans.

The index-gazetteer offers additional background material. The geographic comparison ta-bles list data such as square miles, rainfall, gross national product, language usage, and so on. A thumbnail sketch is presented for each country, with population, religion, currency, literacy, and caloric consumption information. The names used on all 450 maps are listed alphabetically and identified by language and type of geographic feature. There is also a glossary of geography terms from abyssal plain to weathering. Maps are easy to find either through the comprehensive index, the table of contents, or the key to map pages. This reference goes beyond traditional expectations of an atlas. This is an eye-pleasing and user-friendly resource to better understand the world in which humans live, work, and travel.—**Adrienne Antink Bien**

174. **The Dorling Kindersley World Reference Atlas.** 2d ed. New York, DK Publishing, 1996. 731p. illus. maps. index. $49.95. ISBN 0-7894-1085-0.

The core of this publication is a country-by-country description of the 192 countries defined by the United Nations, with information for each organized into 18 topics: climate, transportation, tourism, people, politics, world affairs, chronology, aid, defense, economics, resources, environ-ment, media, crime, education, health, wealth, and world rankings. Abundant use of color, bar and pie graphs, colored landscapes, photographs of persons, and country maps summarize much of the information. Use of symbols and icons helps to visually locate information. Less detailed informa-tion is presented on 57 overseas territories and dependencies. In addition to three maps under each country, special map sections are devoted to world and continental maps and to global issues. An index-gazetteer of about 20,000 places completes the work.

Strong features include clear organization, graphic summaries of data, and concise relevant textual characterizations. The information is up-to-date and comparable from country to country and is effectively presented for quick location and easy comprehension. An intriguing feature is graphic depiction of world rankings of countries on eight variables, such as life expectancy, infant mortality, gross national product per capita, and literacy. Overall, this is a useful, graphic, colorful, information-packed, pointed basic reference handbook on countries of the world. Although desig-nated as an atlas, its 600 generally small maps, useful in combination with the other information for quick reference within the volume, are not a substitute for a larger, more detailed general reference atlas.—**Chauncy D. Harris**

175.   **Facts on File Children's Atlas.** updated ed. By David Wright and Jill Wright. New York, Facts on File, 2000. 96p. illus. maps. index. $18.95. ISBN 0-8160-4433-3.

This is an updated version of previous editions (see ARBA 99, entry 412; ARBA 94, entry 447; ARBA 92, entry 400; and ARBA 88, entry 455). The oversized volume has maintained the same organizational format of nine sections that include information on the planet Earth, continents and land areas, and quiz questions. Except for color enhancements and updated political boundaries, the maps are basically unchanged from the previous edition. Statistics have also been updated; however, much of the text is unchanged.

Each geographic area or topic is covered in a two-page spread. A large map, photographs, a fact box, entertaining quizzes, and brief text fill the two pages. Population, topography, culture, religion, and climate are mentioned in each section. End pages are illustrated with flags from various countries. An extensive index and answers to questions found throughout the book conclude the atlas. The volume is colorful and attractive but it does not provide in-depth information on the geographic areas. The volume is more of an introductory geography book than an atlas, and coverage is uneven. The United States gets six pages while the former Soviet Union is covered in two pages entitled, "Russia and Neighbors." A listing of the republics, their capitals, and populations would be helpful. Although an intended audience is not given, the amount of text and reading level would make it suitable for grades 3-6.—**Elaine Ezell**

176.   **Hammond Citation World Atlas.** Maplewood, N.J., Hammond, 1996. 328p. illus. maps. $19.95pa. ISBN 0-8437-1295-3.

The regional, national, and state political maps of the United States in this atlas are accompanied by smaller, full-color "Topography" (relief) maps and "Agriculture, Industry and Resources" (economic) maps. Also included are illustrations of flags; global locator maps; and indexes by cities and towns, by other features, and by counties in the United States. Some countries' and regions' entries contain maps of population distribution, vegetation, temperature, rainfall, time zones, and highways. The body of the atlas is preceded by 20 plates of world terrain maps.

The atlas' best features are that the political maps have clearly readable county, state, and provincial boundaries (helpful for family history researchers); that indexes are printed next to the maps, not at the end of the atlas; and that the indexes contain population figures (1990 census figures for the U.S. maps). Its disappointments are that all maps have been reduced so much that many captions for cities require a magnifying glass for reading; that its gutters (the inside margins between facing pages) are too wide for the easy reading of maps printed on two pages; and that a low percentage of the number of named cities and towns appearing on maps are not indexed. A study of its indexing coverage of Rhode Island found that only 62 percent of its cities and towns are indexed.

This atlas is not recommended for libraries, but it could be useful for the home libraries of patrons in need of readable county, state, and provincial boundaries, who would prefer not coming to the library to check the same in the *Rand McNally Commercial Atlas and Marketing Guide* (see ARBA 95, entry 326). It also could be a home aid for those interested in recent population figures not provided in almanacs.—**J. Carlyle Parker**

177.   **Illustrated Atlas.** Chicago, World Book, 2000. 288p. illus. maps. index. $29.00. ISBN 0-7166-4034-1.

This is a revised edition of the *Children's Illustrated Atlas* (see entry 169). It is also published under the title *Childcraft Picture Atlas*. The volume is printed in a 9-by-12 format and is slightly smaller than the previous version. Students are introduced to basic map skills; globes; scales; continents; and topography, water, and economic maps of the world in the first section. The volume is then divided into 16 geographic areas. For example, Europe is divided into western, northern, and eastern regions. For each division the user is welcomed to the region with the countries introduced and colorfully identified on a world map. Brief historical facts, flags of the nations, and current information and data are also given for the region. Each division has two-page spreads of the following topics: looking at the land, plants and animals, growing and making, and people and cities. Some regions also have special topics, such as an essay about the Great Wall in the information about China and eastern Asia. The extensive use of color maps, illustrations, and photographs makes this an appealing atlas to elementary students. A glossary and index conclude the volume.—**Elaine Ezell**

178. **Maps of the World.** Danbury, Conn., Grolier, 1997. 10v. illus. maps. index. $319.00/set. ISBN 0-7172-7662-7.

The commendable premise of this set of books is to introduce young students to the world of maps. Despite the publisher's claims that this is a comprehensive resource of world maps, the set will have limited value outside the United States because the information about other countries is too general to be of significant use. The 1st volume provides a clear, concise, and helpful overview of types of maps, definitions of terms found on maps, and intriguing "geofacts" about geographic features. This volume also includes a valuable 15-page resource unit on map skills that is reproduced in its entirety in volumes 3, 4, 8, 9, and 10. Volumes 2, 3, and 4 concentrate on political, physical, and cultural maps of the United States. Although these volumes include an abundance of data, they are not as useful as they could be because the data are inconsistent. A map showing the crime rate, for example, is based on 1993 figures, and a corresponding map on police officers is compiled from 1982 statistics.

Volumes 5, 6, and 7 provide political maps and accompanying descriptions of geographic, economic, and historical information for the rest of the world. Each of these 3 volumes includes the same comprehensive place index. Volume 5, which encompasses Africa and Asia, files the countries of the Middle East alphabetically with those of Asia. France, Germany, Russia, and the United Kingdom are the only countries that warrant a double-page spread in volume 6 (Australia and Europe), but 18 pages are dedicated to Canada in volume 7 (North and South America). The data for volumes 8, 9, and 10 are primarily based on 1996 estimates, but again contain inconsistencies. For example, both maps of world television and radio receivers are compiled from 1993 statistics, the world map of telephone ownership from 1994 estimates, and the map on newspapers from 1992 estimates. Volume 10, *U.S. and World History Atlas*, although illustrating key moments in world history accompanied by text summaries and arranged by date or theme, devotes the majority of its pages to the history of the United States. Perhaps this emphasis would not be a liability if the title of the set was not *Maps of the World*.—**Gail de Vos**

179. **Oxford Atlas of Exploration.** New York, Oxford University Press, 1997. 248p. illus. maps. index. $40.00. ISBN 0-19-521353-X.

Although humans have always been explorers, as documented by this superb atlas, their motives for exploration have varied widely over time. In pursuit of game, for example, prehistoric hunters ventured from Africa to Europe, arriving eventually in Australia some 50,000 years ago. And by way of the Ice Age land bridge, they crossed from Siberia to Alaska about 14,000 years ago and within a scant millennium stood at the tip of South America. More recent explorers have been prompted by both material and noble impulses. Whereas financial gain, for instance, drove those fifteenth-and sixteenth-century conquistadors such as Cortés in Mexico and Pizarro in Peru and all those gold-crazed pursuers of El Dorado, the love of knowledge was a more compelling force for the nineteenth-century explorations of Charles Darwin aboard the *Beagle* and Baron Von Humboldt in South America. The earliest written accounts of explorations dates from the fourth millennium B.C.E., and so this atlas begins with the ancient Egyptians, Phoenicians, and Greeks and moves swiftly across Asia, Africa, the Americas, the distant Pacific, and the polar icecaps. In the process, attention is drawn to figures such as Ptolemy, James Cook, and Carl Linné.

Replete with an abundance of colorful maps, drawings, and photographs as well as a biographical section highlighting the careers of explorers from Erik "The Red" to Marco Polo to Henry Stanley, a time chart of explorations around the globe, and a thorough index, this would be a worthwhile addition to high school and college reference collections. Although the cartography is not quite as sharp as that of *The Times Atlas of World Exploration* (see ARBA 92, entry 408), the narrative is as clear and precise. This work will appeal to students and interested patrons.—**John W. Storey**

180. **Scholastic Atlas of the World.** New York, Scholastic, 2001. 224p. illus. maps. index. $19.95. ISBN 0-439-08795-3.

This 1-volume children's atlas, aimed at grades 4 through 8, provides over 80 maps and hundreds of photographs in 2-page color layouts. Its goal is to present "information in a new and exciting way" by comparing data such as land area and time zones between the United States and other countries of the world. The atlas includes topographical maps, important cities, mountains, borders, simple essays about a country's culture and geography, and boxed highlights. A country index faces the contents page making for a quick reference guide. Approximately the first 30 pages of the atlas cover topics such as how to use the atlas, making maps, Earth in space, and weather and climate. This is followed by additional two-page spreads entitled "Countries of the World" and "The Physical World." The 11 sections are arranged by continent and oceanic region. A list of dependencies, a glossary, and an index complete the volume. Information is based on sources such as U.S. Census data and the CIA's *World Factbook* (see ARBA 2002, entry 91). Some identifying features, such as the Mississippi and Missouri Rivers (pp. 42-43) are difficult to read. The gutter swallows pieces of the maps, such as that of Stockholm on page 93. On pages 134 and 136, there is no explanation of the situation regarding Israel, the West Bank and Gaza, and the Golan Heights. These lessen the usefulness of the atlas at report time. This atlas is probably best for circulating collection rather than the reference atlas case. [R: BR, Mar/April 02, p. 62] —**Esther R. Sinofsky**

181. **World Almanac Atlas of the World.** Mahwah, N.J., World Almanac Books, 2002. 192p. maps. index. $18.95; $12.95pa. ISBN 0-8343-0117-2; 0-8343-0118-0pa.

The 192 maps in this atlas represent every continent, country, U.S. state, and Canadian province. The maps, even the smallest ones, are sharp and easy to read, although only major cities, towns, or waterways are shown. The scale of each map is given, and each map includes a visual scale for measuring distance. Insets feature information on the national capital; the country or state's flag; population; language; largest city; monetary unit; and locations of major cities, rivers, islands, or other important features.

The atlas is divided by major divisions of the world. After the introductory material, there is a world map followed by major sections on Asia and Oceania, Europe, Africa, South America, North America, the Polar Regions, and the United States. A full page is devoted to maps of major countries and each state of the United States, but maps for smaller countries are placed from two to five per page. Surprisingly, even pages with five maps look uncluttered because of the quality of the graphics. A two-page spread is devoted for the introductory maps of the continents, with thematic maps and graphs provided for each.

Introductory material for the atlas includes thematic maps, graphs, and tables of information based on the 2000 U.S. census. There are also maps, graphs, and tables of statistics that examine the growing world population and the latest trends in health and mortality. There are two indexes: a world index and an index of the U.S. states. This publication is a very easy-to-use atlas with maps that are sharp and clear. The largest and most detailed maps are those of the U.S. states. It is quite inexpensive and thus would be ideal for students and even home use.—**Dana McDougald**

182. **The World Book Atlas.** Chicago, World Book, 2000. 1v. (various paging). illus. maps. index. $49.00. ISBN 0-7166-2650-0.

The World Book Atlas is a large-size, general world atlas incorporating maps of the world and illustrative materials from Rand McNally and *Goode's World Atlas* (20th ed.; see ARBA 2001, entry 330). An introductory section contains articles and color photographs on oceans and mountains, rivers and streams, lakes and ponds, forests and grasslands, polar caps, and world time zones. There are also pages describing how to use the atlas and an index map and legend.

The main body of the atlas covers approximately 144 pages of maps, most of which are physical maps emphasizing terrain, landforms, and elevation. There are political maps of the world for each of the continents except for Antarctica. Map scales range from 1:2,500,000 to 1:30,000,000, and a bar scale with each map is expressed in both miles and kilometers. Another scale accompanying each map identifies in feet the meters all of the elevation and depth categories that appear on the map. The atlas appears to be up to date with recent name changes, such as Congo, Czech Republic, and Slovenia presented correctly. The majority of the maps are presented in double-paged spreads, which is problematic because the book does not lie flat enough to see the information on the inside without straining the binding.

The index includes approximately 54,000 names of places and geographical features that appear on the reference maps. Each name is followed by the name of the country or continent in which it is located, an alpha-numeric map reference key, and a page reference. All abbreviations used in the index are defined in the list of abbreviations at the beginning of the index.

This is a reasonably priced atlas that is quite adequate for searching world locations and would be a good choice for both school and home use. The binding is sturdy, the print is easy to read, and the maps are current. The extensive index, legends, and latitude and longitude grids make locating a place or geographical feature fast and easy.—**Dana McDougald**

Biography

183. **Explorers.** Englewood Cliffs, N.J., Salem Press, 1998. 2v. illus. maps. index. (Magill's Choice). $95.00. ISBN 0-89356-970-4.

This attractive, 2-volume set of 78 biographical essays on prominent explorers will serve as a first resource for students of exploration history. The explorers profiled range widely in time and accomplishments, from the mysterious Carthaginian seafarer Hanno (ca.520 B.C.E.) to American astronaut Sally Ride.

The short biographies were written by 65 academics. Despite this extraordinary authorial diversity, the essays follow strict rules and read consistently well, showing the strong hand of the editors (who are curiously left anonymous). Each biography starts with a brief abstract of the explorer's identity and history, followed by the main text divided into "early life," "life's work," and "impact." A short annotated bibliography is included after each profile, providing immediate reference to the primary historical sources. There are occasional portraits and photographs included in the essays, along with a few maps (of which the reader could use more).

The biographies are for the most part very well written. They do not follow any particular political or cultural formula. Asian explorers such as Cheng Ho and Hsüan-tsang are included with the traditional western Europeans, such as James Cook and Henry Hudson. Some pioneers not often thought of as explorers made the cut, including John Winthrop of Massachusetts and Stephen Austin of Texas. The editors were thoughtful enough to include Sacagawea as well as Meriwether Lewis and William Clark. For some reason, three pioneering aviators (Amelia Earhart, Charles Lindbergh, and Jacqueline Cochran) are considered explorers. They were heroes, of course, but they do not fit the prevailing model of participants in geographically based exploration. Their inclusion brings up the nagging and inevitable questions about who was *not* profiled. The aviators could have been replaced with, for example, Giovanni da Verrazano, Alexander von Humboldt, and Jim Bridger. The intrepid Antarctic explorers Robert Scott and Ernest Shackleton also deserved space. This set is recommended for all libraries, particularly those used by high school and undergraduate students.—**Mark A. Wilson**

184.   **Explorers and Discoverers, Volume 5: From Alexander the Great to Sally Ride.** Nancy Pear and Daniel B. Baker, eds. Detroit, U*X*L/Gale, 1997. 237p. illus. maps. index. $34.00. ISBN 0-7876-1990-6.

This volume is a supplement to the publisher's 4-volume original set (see ARBA 94, entry 463); reviews of this set commented on its focus on women and non-European explorers, who are frequently slighted in other works. The supplement features 30 biographies of men and women who have expanded the horizons of our world and universe. The people range chronologically from Fa-Hsien (ca.374-462), a Buddhist monk who made an epic 15-year journey to India, to Pedro de Alvarado (1485-1541), a Spanish conquistador, to Steve Fossett (1945-), a contemporary adventurer who has broken sailing and aviation records. Also included are two historic machines, the *Mir* space station and H.M.S. *Titanic*, as well as the National Geographic Society, the largest nonprofit scientific and educational institution in the world.

The alphabetically arranged, illustrated biographies average from five to seven pages in length. Maps provide geographic details of specific journeys. Additionally, 16 maps of major regions of the world lead off the volume, and a chronology of exploration by region, a list of explorers by date of birth, and an extensive cumulative index conclude the volume. The index is well designed. For example, one of the entries concerns Barry Clifford, a treasure hunter who discovered and salvaged a pirate vessel. A check of the index found an entry under *pirate* as well as *Clifford*, a valuable addition because a user of the volume might be interested in information about pirates but not know Clifford's name.

In telling of the exploits of a person, the editors include the reasons why the person chose to make a particular expedition and also give credit to those who accompanied him or her and contributed to the survival of the group. Entries are readable for the middle grades and up. The set and its supplement will greatly enrich the reference collection but will also be of interest to browsers.

Another good 1-volume work that examines the life and work of 12 explorers is William Scheller's *The World's Greatest Explorers* (Oliver Press, 1992). A volume to consider to support the use of this Gale set is *The Times Atlas of World Exploration: 300 Years of Exploring, Explorers, and Mapmaking* (HarperCollins, 1991). [R: BL, 15 Dec 98, p. 765]—**Vandelia L. VanMeter**

185.   **Explorers & Discoverers, Volume 6: From Alexander the Great to Sally Ride.** Nancy Pear and Daniel B. Baker, eds. Farmington Hills, Mich., U*X*L/Gale, 1998. 265p. illus. maps. index. $39.00. ISBN 0-7876-2946-4.

This additional volume to the *Explorers & Discoverers* set (see ARBA 96, entry 454, for a review of the original 4-volume set) features an additional 30 biographies of 19 men, 9 women, 1 facility, and 1 machine. Those chosen span a time period from approximately 1520 B.C.E. to the present. Except for one person, all individuals included are deceased. The men and women included were selected based on their contributions to human knowledge about the earth and its life-forms. The reader learns who these adventurers were, when and how they lived and traveled, and the significance and consequences of their discoveries. The introduction provides insight into the reasons that motivate people to enter the unknown, including information on what motivated 19 of those included in the volume.

Entries are alphabetically arranged and enhanced with extensive photographs, illustrations, and maps. The volume concludes with a cumulative chronology of exploration by region, a list of explorers by country of birth, and a cumulative index to volumes 1 through 6. Libraries holding the original series will want to expand the set with this additional volume.—**Elaine Ezell**

186.   **Explorers & Discoverers, Volume 7: From Alexander the Great to Sally Ride.** Nancy Pear, Daniel B. Baker, and Jane Hoehner, eds. Farmington Hills, Mich., U*X*L/Gale, 1999. 295p. illus. maps. index. $39.00. ISBN 0-7876-3681-9. ISSN 1522-9947.

The latest supplement to this set, volume 7, adds 30 biographies of men, women, and machines that have expanded our horizons. The 20 men, 8 women, 1 museum, and 1 ship newly inducted into the set include Thor Heyerdahl, Nearchus, Mel Fisher, John Bryon, Helen Thayer, and the National Air and Space Museum. Although they represent a time range from ancient to modern, they are mainly European or American. Arranged alphabetically, the entries focus on the motivation driving these explorers and discoverers and the journeys themselves. There is little information about family or early life. Sources are included for each entry. Entries do include items such as illustrations, maps, geographic details of journeys, and similar information. The volume begins with a section of 16 black-and-white maps of major world regions. The end sheets provide a general world map. The section on chronology and exploration covers all seven volumes by area explored. The index is cumulative. This is a nice supplement to upper elementary and middle school history classes. It brings to the forefront some figures who might otherwise be forgotten and will provide additional information for research. [R: BR, Nov/Dec 99, p. 72]—**Esther R. Sinofsky**

Dictionaries and Encyclopedias

187.   **The DK Geography of the World.** New York, DK Publishing, 1996. 304p. illus. maps. index. $39.95. ISBN 0-7894-1004-4.

Each of the six major sections of this work opens with a two-page spread showing the major physical features of a continent, followed by another spread that highlights the people of the region. Following spreads cover a country (or group of countries) with maps showing main physical and political features, and other maps that show the relation of the country to the continent, while photographs and descriptive paragraphs highlight features such as festivals, national foods, major industries, the economy, and other topics related to that nation or region. Fact boxes provide access to key facts. The United States is covered in four spreads, including one spread each on the western, central, and eastern states.

Through the thorough index, one may access, in addition to physical and political places, information on such varied topics as acid rain, cotton growing, debtor countries, and immigrants. The presentation on each spread is rather busy, but the attractive arrangement of photographs, drawings, and text introduces a wide variety of topics suitable for further research. The concise but clear explanation of the crisis in the former Yugoslavia attests to the currency of the coverage.

The work opens with general information about the physical and political world, and concludes with a reference section that highlights political systems, international organizations, world religions, world trade, and similar topics. A glossary, gazetteer, and index are included. Colors and printing are crisp, the binding is sewn, and the paper is of high quality.

This attractive, up-to-date atlas is suitable for elementary students. Another fine atlas that serves this same audience is *The Dillon Press Children's Atlas* (see ARBA 95, entry 476). [R: RBB, 1 Nov 96, pp. 534-36]—**Vandelia L. VanMeter**

188.   **The Grolier Student Library of Explorers and Exploration.** Danbury, Conn., Grolier, 1998. 10v. illus. maps. index. $299.00/set. ISBN 0-7172-9135-9.

This 10-volume set, geared toward young adults, tells about global exploration through narrative and historical accounts. The stories and biographies cover both well-and lesser-known explorers of land, sea, air, and outer space. They attempt to answer such questions as "Why did this person explore? What was the impact on the native population? On the natural environment?" Instruments and technology created to enhance and expand exploration are also discussed. Of particular note is the set's international focus. It provides information about the exploration of Asia, Africa, and the Middle East that truly supplements traditional history textbooks and general encyclopedia articles. The discussion of North America includes Canada, especially the search for the fabled Northwest Passage.

The first 4 volumes progress chronologically from prehistoric times to the Victorian Era. Volume 1 highlights the earliest explorers, for example, early humans, the ancient Egyptians, Greeks, Romans, and Persians, up to medieval Europe. Volume 2 continues with the "Golden Age" of Christopher Columbus, the Elizabethans, the Spanish, and the Portuguese. Volume 3 follows "Europe's Imperial Adventures" with tales of James Cook, North America, India and the Far East, and Russia's explorers. Volume 4 closes the chronology with coverage of Charles Darwin, the Northwest Passage, the hunt for Franklin, Australia, Tasmania, Antarctica, and the Russians. The next 5 volumes focus on specific geographic areas: Latin America, North America, Australasia and Asia, Africa and Arabia, and the polar regions. The topics range from the conquistadors, Jewish settlers, and quinine to the Great Plains, the Nile, West Africa, and both poles. Volume 10 looks at space and the ocean, including early flights with people on board, the Soyuz Program, *Apollo 13*, the *Challenger* disaster, and even the *Titanic*.

Each volume runs roughly 80 pages with a plethora of sidebars, maps, color illustrations, and a set index. The maps will be particularly helpful to students working on assignments to trace exploration routes. However, the blue used to indicate some routes sometimes is indistinguishable from the map background. The page layouts, typeface size, and abundant use of color will attract browsers as well as report writers. The set would probably be best for grades 5-10. [R: SLJ, Nov 98, p. 152]—**Esther R. Sinofsky**

Handbooks and Yearbooks

189.   **Historical Maps on File.** rev. ed. New York, Facts on File, 2002. 2v. maps. index. $330.00/set looseleaf w/binder. ISBN 0-8160-4600-X.

The revised edition of *Historical Maps on File* (see ARBA 85, entry 492, for a review of the original edition) increases the number of maps provided to more than 400, requiring 2 loose-leaf binder volumes. These new maps fill in the gap of coverage from 1982, where the original edition ended, through 2000. As with all the On File publications, the materials are easily reproducible and copyright free for classroom use. Like the original edition, a large portion of the work, approximately one-third, is devoted to the United States.

The maps are organized into nine sections: "Ancient Civilizations," "Medieval Europe," "Europe (from 1500 to 1815)," "Europe (from 1815 to the Present)," "The Untied States," "The Western Hemisphere," "Africa and the Middle East," "Asia," and "Australia and the Pacific Islands." Major political, military, and economic topics are displayed in the maps, such as the Punic Wars, the Holocaust, U.S. presidential elections, colonialism in Africa, and the Korean War. Interestingly, the Vietnam War is not covered. A lengthy index is provided at the end of volume 2.—**Cari Ringelheim**

190. **How Geography Affects the United States.** Westport, Conn., Greenwood Press, 2002. 5v. illus. maps. index. $199.95/set. ISBN 0-313-32250-3.

Each volume of this set begins with a table of contents, a short introduction, and two tables of statistical data about the states within the area. It explains its respective region with 6 to 10 chapters that focus on major geographic features within that region. For instance, the chapters of "The West" are "Columbia River," "Great Basin," "Hawaii," "Pacific Ocean," "Rocky Mountains," and "Sierra Nevada." End matter includes a page of sources from books and Websites, and an index from that particular volume. There is no comprehensive index of the set. To study the effects of hurricanes on the United States, for example, a student would need to examine three indexes from separate volumes.

Information is recent, from the destruction of the twin towers of the World Trade Center to the ongoing eruption of the next Hawaiian Island, Loihi. There are occasional errors of fact. On page 114 of "The Northeast" the map shows the Narrows of New York Bay between Staten Island and Brooklyn but the text says they are between Staten Island and Manhattan. Shrimp is described as the most important seafood product of the Gulf of Mexico, yet is not listed in the index of the appropriate volume (and the caption of the shrimp boat shown on page 54 is incorrect).

An effort is made to help students with pronunciation of unfamiliar words, such as the names of native tribes, often more than once in the same volume. It is unclear why a similar effort has been made with words such as religion, Virginia, or scientists. Surprisingly, help with pronunciation is not provided with Hawaiian words or Spanish words.

The flow of the text may be difficult to follow, especially for students. For example, in the "West," sections, in order, are "Salt Lake City," "Commerce," "Borax in Death Valley," "The Coming of the Railroad," and "The Great Basin and the Military," with no apparent thread connecting them. The text is often interrupted by "fast facts" (contained within both oval and oblong outlines), photographs, shaded ovals and oblongs of supplemental information. The glossy color photograph on the cover belies the rather plain interior. Photographs are all black and white.

At approximately $200 for just over 600 pages of text, this is not an inexpensive set of books. The plan for each of the volumes may have been overly ambitious. For instance, the "Northeast Region" deals with 11 states and Washington, D.C. The 120-page volume attempts to describe the geography, industry, transportation, significant individuals, cultures, environmental problems, and 400 years of history. These volumes can provide a broad introduction to the contained subject areas but much of the information seems disconnected.—**Craig A. Munsart**

191. **Junior State Maps on File.** New York, Facts on File, 2002. 1v. (various paging). maps. index. $185.00 looseleaf w/binder. ISBN 0-8160-4752-9.

In keeping with Facts on File's On File series, this title offers more than 400 reproducible state maps and fact sheets in a looseleaf, three-ring binder format for grades 4 through 10. The nine tabbed dividers teamed with the table of contents provide easy access to the maps. After a general section on the United States and its regions, the maps are arranged by geographic region: New England, Mid-Atlantic, Midwestern, Mountain and Prairie, Southern, Southwestern, and Western and Pacific. Five maps and a fact sheet are provided for each state: major cities, outline map, physical features, industry, agriculture, and state facts and flag. Printed on heavier paper stock, the crisp black-and-white sheets make excellent masters for photocopying supplemental instructional materials, creating overhead transparencies, or simply enhancing research reports. This is an excellent U.S. geography resource for school and public libraries that do not subscribe to the online version.—**Esther R. Sinofsky**

192.   **Mapping the World.** Danbury, Conn., Grolier, 2002. 8v. illus. maps. index. $239.00/set. ISBN 0-7172-5619-7.

Maps are often viewed as superficial pieces of paper that show where to make a left or right turn. In reality, they are an integration of technology and art that have played a critical role throughout history, both on Earth and beyond. Whether going on vacation or landing on the moon, maps are necessary, but they can be difficult to understand. Maps are the result of an often complex progression of data gathering, interpretation, and portrayal, which are the focus of this set.

Each of the 8, 48-page volumes contains front matter consisting of a table of contents, general information about the entire set, and an introduction to the particular volume. End matter contains a volume-specific glossary, a listing of further reading and Websites, and a comprehensive index for the entire set. Volume titles are "Ways of Mapping the World," "Observation and Measurement," "Maps for Travelers," "Navigation," "Mapping New Lands," "Mapping for Governments," "City Maps," and "Mapping for Today and Tomorrow." The many drawings and photographs in each volume are all in color. In many cases, an aerial photograph and map are drawn side-by-side to improve interpretation skills. The text incorporates both English and, in parentheses, SI or metric units. In the volume "Observation and Measurement," these two measurement systems are referred to as imperial and metric, respectively.

The greatest problem with this set is one that comes from the nature of the subject itself. The fact that a map results from an integration of so many processes means that a study of maps does not lend itself to alphabetic, encyclopedic entries or a neat, linear progression of study. To obtain maximum benefit, the user of this set will probably need to integrate information from multiple entries in the same volume or entries in several volumes. Cross-referencing between volumes is accomplished through the set index at the back of each volume and by marginal notations across the bottom of the left page.

Technological and mathematical applications addressed range from the logic of Eratosthenes to measure the Earth's circumference over 2,000 years ago to today's global positioning and geographic information systems. While not designed specifically as a history book, the maps and discussions of the Crusades (volume 2); Columbus, Magellan, and Captain James Cook's travels (volume 4); and explorations of Africa (volume 5) provide useful historical information.

The edition reviewed was published exclusively for the school and library market. While a primary-grade student may benefit from some of the illustrations, intermediate and middle school students and older would learn the most from the set. Mapping is a perpetual process. Today, satellites enable scientists to determine centimeter changes in sea level to fuel the debate over global warming or to determine minute elevation changes in Mt. Everest as the duel continues between plate tectonics and erosional forces. This set can provide students with a strong background into what mapping is and how the mapping process can be applied to a variety of interests (other than going on vacation). [R: SLJ, Nov 02, pp. 102-104]—**Craig A. Munsart**

193.   **Maps on File.** 2002-2003 ed. New York, Facts on File, 2002. 2v. maps. index. (Facts on File Library of World History). $250.00 looseleaf w/binder. ISBN 0-8160-5006-6.

194. **Outline Maps on File.** updated ed. New York, Facts on File, 2002. 1v. (various paging). maps. index. (Facts on File Library of World History). $185.00 looseleaf w/binder. ISBN 0-8160-4996-3.

This edition of *Maps on File* retains the clear, concise layout of previous editions (see ARBA 2002, entry 350, for a review of the 2001 edition, and ARBA 2002, entry 351, for a review of the online edition). This edition is presented in 2 volumes and features 500 reproducible maps that are ideally suited for middle and high school students writing reports or preparing presentations. Volume 1 provides country maps of the world's regions, including Africa, Asia, Australia and Oceania, Europe, North and Central America, South America, and the Canadian provinces. Each country map provides major cities, borders with neighboring nations, a scale in miles and kilometers, and names of major rivers and roads. The second volume provides detailed maps of the U.S. states as well as maps representing each country's demographics, natural resources, politics and military, education and social issues, and statistics.

Outline Maps is much like volume 1 of *Maps on File*, but without the map lables. Presented here are reproducible blank maps of countries and regions throughout the world. This set is ideal for teachers teaching a geography lesson or testing their students. A "Teacher's Guide" is provided at the back of the volume, which provides the answer key to all maps. Because the volume is presented in a looseleaf format with a three-ring binder, the "Teacher's Guide" can easily be removed from the volume.

These sets are an ideal addition to middle and high school libraries. Each map is reproducible, ensuring that the volume will be used frequently. Available for an additional $75.00 annually are the replacement maps for *Maps on File* that reflect changes within the past year.—**Shannon Graff Hysell**

195. **The Usborne Internet-Linked Encyclopedia of World Geography with Complete World Atlas.** By Gillian Doherty, Anna Claybourne, and Susanna Davidson. Tulsa, Okla., EDC Publishing, 2001. 400p. illus. maps. index. $39.95. ISBN 0-7945-0108-7.

In 22 chapters, this 1-volume encyclopedia of world geography covers the planet Earth; earthquakes and volcanoes; rivers and oceans; weather; climate; world ecosystems; people and the world; and peoples of North America, South America, Australasia and Oceania, Asia, Europe, and Africa. It also provides an atlas of the world; maps of those same regions (plus the Arctic and Antarctica); and a fact file, glossary, and map and general indexes. The lavishly illustrated two-page spreads use photographs and diagrams, a larger font, and fairly simple sentence structure, which makes this appropriate for upper-elementary grades and older. The maps were printed with the book gutter in mind and are readable across the two-page layout. Recommended Websites are generously sprinkled throughout the volume and may be accessed via the publisher-maintained Website that promises to regularly update the links. The book also indicates which images may be freely downloaded for class reports but not for any commercial purposes. An Internet-related help section includes safety tips for children and young adults who surf the Internet. The book reflects its British origins in references to the United States, such as the one on page 87 that equates the 1992 Los Angeles riots to heat rather than the jury decision in the Rodney King case. Most of this volume seems more suitable for browsing rather than reference. The essays are superficial, resembling expanded dictionary definitions rather than encyclopedia entries.—**Esther R. Sinofsky**

7 History

ARCHAEOLOGY

196.   Brier, Bob. **Encyclopedia of Mummies.** New York, Facts on File, 1998. 248p. illus. index. $35.00. ISBN 0-8160-3108-8.

From the lighthearted to the gruesome, *The Encyclopedia of Mummies* documents the fascination people have had with the dead since the beginning of civilization. The alphabetic listings begin with *Abbott and Costello Meet the Mummy* and go to Gaetano Zumbo, an Italian wax sculptor who often used human corpses as a base for his wax work. Entries run from a few sentences to many pages. Included are numerous photographs and drawings.

Brier has managed to collect more information into one slim volume than could be found elsewhere. Covering the ancient embalmer's art of Egypt to natural mummification in various parts of the world to a modern resurgence in the practice in the western United States, the author gives basic scientific information on the various processes. Ethical considerations are discussed as well. Detailing fact, fancy, and myth, Brier has included entries on such famous ancient mummies as Ramses II, III, V, and the Marquise of Tai as well as such famous modern ones as Napoleon, Lenin, and Eva Perón (Evita). Not just a "who was who," the book goes on to include information on how mummies have helped solve mysteries such as the ill-fated Franklin expedition of 1845 (the entire crew probably died of lead poisoning).

A whimsical appendix listing the mummy films is included. Another appendix details museum collections from around the world. An extensive bibliography of other sources and a detailed index follow. Although not recommended as a complete scholarly source, the *Encyclopedia of Mummies* is recommended as a fun, quick starting point for most middle and high school libraries. [R: Choice, July/Aug 98, p. 1825]—**Kevin W. Perizzolo**

AMERICAN HISTORY

General Works

197.   **American Civil War: Almanac.** By Kevin Hillstrom and Laurie Collier Hillstrom. Lawrence W. Baker, ed. Farmington Hills, Mich., U*X*L/Gale, 2000. 251p. illus. maps. index. $42.00. ISBN 0-7876-3823-4.

198.   **American Civil War: Biographies.** By Kevin Hillstrom and Laurie Collier Hillstrom. Lawrence W. Baker, ed. Farmington Hills, Mich., U*X*L/Gale, 2000. 2v. illus. index. $79.00/set. ISBN 0-7876-3821-8.

199.   **American Civil War: Primary Sources.** By Kevin Hillstrom and Laurie Collier Hillstrom. Lawrence W. Baker, ed. Farmington Hills, Mich., U*X*L/Gale, 2000. 176p. illus. index. $42.00. ISBN 0-7876-3824-2.

Tackling the American Civil War is always a daunting task because it is such a huge conflict and so much has been written on the subject. One of the latest contributions is U*X*L/Gale's American Civil War Reference Library to which these 4 volumes belong.

The *Almanac* provides a concise overview of the war, including its causes and the Reconstruction period. Two volumes of *Biographies* present 60 life stories of important Civil War people. The last volume, *Primary Sources*, contains 14 accounts of people who experienced various aspects of the war. The books are well designed, with a handy timeline in the front, numerous photographs, interesting sidebars, and suggests for further reading.

Because of its single-volume length, the almanac is a concise history of the war with few first-person accounts in the text. Although the major battles are briefly described, others such as the Crater are not even mentioned. Indexing glitches are also present: there are no entries for "casualties," "illness," or "disease" in the index, yet a sidebar dealing with these important subjects is on pages 182 to 183. There is also no index entry for "prisons" or "Andersonville," which are very important subjects that should be in any Civil War overview (although they are described in *Biographies*).

It is admirable to want to include lesser-known personalities in *Biographies*, such as Winslow Homer or Mary Boykin Chesnut, but with only 60 available slots it would have been more useful to include those who actually shaped the Civil War, such as George Armstrong Custer. *Primary Sources* would be better if there were less introductory material for each first-person narrative, with the authors getting to the narrative more quickly and making room for other accounts. For example, the section on Frank Holsinger contains seven pages of analysis and three pages of his eyewitness descriptions.

All this sniping aside, the American Civil War Reference Library does a good job of presenting the basic facts of the Civil War. It is a valuable resource for middle school and high school students, especially in libraries that have limited or outdated Civil War material. [R: BR, Sept/Oct 2000, pp. 66-67]—**Mark J. Crawford**

200.   **American Revolution: Almanac.** By Barbara Bigelow and Linda Schmittroth. Stacy A. McConnell, ed. Farmington Hills, Mich., U*X*L/Gale, 2000. 195p. illus. maps. index. (U*X*L American Revolution Reference Library). $149.00/set; $42.00/vol. ISBN 0-7876-3795-5.

201.   **American Revolution: Biographies.** By Linda Schmittroth and Mary Kay Rosteck. Stacy A. McConnell, ed. Farmington Hills, Mich., U*X*L/Gale, 2000. 2v. illus. index. (U*X*L American Revolution Reference Library). $149.00/set; $79.00/2-volume set. ISBN 0-7876-3792-0.

202.   **American Revolution: Primary Sources.** Linda Schmittroth, Lawrence W. Baker, and Stacy A. McConnell, eds. Farmington Hills, Mich., U*X*L/Gale, 2000. 264p. illus. index. (U*X*L American Revolution Reference Library). $149.00/set; $42.00/vol. ISBN 0-7876-3790-4.

Four volumes make up U*X*L's American Revolution Reference Library. The first volume, *American Revolution: Almanac*, presents an overview of the war. Its first chapters give information about the colonies, daily life during colonial times, and the political situation. Subsequent chapters detail the course of the rebellion as it built toward inevitable war and then follow the war itself, giving information on specific battles or political developments. Each chapter is followed by a bibliography of further sources, including Web sources.

The second and third volumes of the set are titled *American Revolution: Biographies*. In these volumes, both well-known and lesser-known players on the revolutionary stage are profiled. Information on Betsy Ross, Thomas Jefferson, Ethan Allen, and George III is presented here. The student can also find information on such unknown but fascinating characters as Simon Girty, an uneducated, rough frontiersman who acted as interpreter during negotiations with the Ohio Indian tribes as efforts were made to ensure their neutrality. There is also information on Mary Katherine Goddard, the printer and publisher of the *Maryland Journal* during the revolutionary years who was chosen by the Continental Congress to print the first copies of the Declaration of Independence containing the names of all the signers.

Excerpts from various pertinent contemporary documents, along with commentary, make up the fourth volume, *American Revolution: Primary Sources*. The Stamp Act, the Intolerable Acts, and the Declaration of Independence are all excerpted and discussed. Also included are excerpts from letters and speeches of the time. These are also from a mix of such luminaries as Benjamin Franklin and Thomas Paine and more ordinary Americans who left a record of their thoughts.

All four volumes are well illustrated with engravings of the period, maps, and portraits. Numerous sidebars sprinkled throughout the text give students a snapshot of a specific moment or theme. Preliminary material in each volume includes a timeline of the war and a glossary of terms. Also included is a section that presents ideas for class discussion. These themes and questions will also help an ambitious, independent student think more deeply on various topics.

Both general and specific questions can be addressed through the almanac. Students wanting an answer to a specific question can probably find it through the chronologically arranged chapters, or in the biographies. Those wishing for more in-depth information about a particular event can read one or several chapters. This would be a useful source for middle school libraries, particularly for its coverage of lesser-known participants in the American Revolution. [R: VOYA, Dec 2000, p. 373; SLJ, Nov 2000, pp. 87-88]—**Terry Ann Mood**

203. **Colonial America: Almanac.** By Peggy Saari. Julie L. Carnagie, ed. Farmington Hills, Mich., U*X*L/Gale, 2000. 2v. illus. index. (U*X*L Colonial America Reference Library Series). $185.00/set; $45.00/vol. ISBN 0-7876-3763-7.

204. **Colonial America: Biographies.** By Peggy Saari. Julie L. Carnagie, ed. Farmington Hills, Mich., U*X*L/Gale, 2000. 2v. illus. index. (U*X*L Colonial America Reference Library Series). $185.00/set; $79.00/2-volume set. ISBN 0-7876-3760-2.

205. **Colonial America: Primary Sources.** By Peggy Saari. Julie L. Carnagie, ed. Farmington Hills, Mich., U*X*L/Gale, 2000. 297p. illus. index. (U*X*L Colonial America Reference Library Series). $185.00/set; $45.00/vol. ISBN 0-7876-3766-1.

Middle school students are the target audience for this five-volume set on Colonial America. Two volumes titled *Almanac*, two titled *Biographies*, and one titled *Primary Sources* make up the set. All of the volumes are arranged attractively, are heavily illustrated, and have numerous sidebars interwoven into the main text, which present short bursts of information on specific topics. The format should appeal to the intended age group, who have grown up with hypertext and have become accustomed to jumping from one spot to another.

The two almanac volumes set the stage and place colonial times in context. Volume 1 contains chapters on such topics as Native Americans, Spanish exploration, and social and political issues. Volume 2 concentrates more on daily life in the colonies, with chapters on religion, family life, education, science and medicine, and arts and culture.

Biographies of both well-known and lesser-known people of the period are in the two biography volumes. As one might expect, John Rolfe is here, as are Powhaten and Pochahontas. Also included are Eliza Lucas Pinckney (a plantation manager in South Carolina who cultivated indigo), John Smibert (the first portrait painter in colonial America), and Catherine (Kateri) Tekakwitha (a Mohawk who was a Catholic nun and is now a candidate for sainthood).

Primary Sources, the final volume, gives young students a taste of what doing original research is like, presenting contemporary documents for them to read. To ease the process of reading often arcane language, support material accompanies each document. A section entitled "Things to remember when reading [name of document]" is included, as is a glossary of unusual words, and a section called "What Happened Next?" that leads the student forward in time.

Like its counterpart from U*X*L on the American Revolution (see entries 200, 201, and 202), this should satisfy both students wanting brief information on a specific topic and those willing to make a deeper exploration of the times and events that shaped Colonial America. [R: BL, July 2000, p. 2056; SLJ, Nov 2000, p. 96]—**Terry Ann Mood**

206.   Hanes, Sharon M., and Richard C. Hanes. **Great Depression and New Deal: Almanac.** Farmington Hills, Mich., U*X*L/Gale, 2003. 278p. illus. index. (U*X*L Great Depression and New Deal Reference Library). $55.00/vol.; $145.00/set. ISBN 0-7876-6588-9.

207.   Hanes, Sharon M., and Richard C. Hanes. **Great Depression and New Deal: Biographies.** Farmington Hills, Mich., U*X*L/Gale, 2003. 241p. illus. index. (U*X*L Great Depression and New Deal Reference Library). $55.00/vol.; $145.00/set. ISBN 0-7876-6534-7.

208.   Hanes, Sharon M., and Richard C. Hanes. **Great Depression and New Deal: Primary Sources.** Farmington Hills, Mich., U*X*L/Gale, 2003. 260p. illus. index. (U*X*L Great Depression and New Deal Reference Library). $55.00/vol.; $145.00/set. ISBN 0-7876-6535-5.

The Great Depression of the 1930s and President Roosevelt's introduction of the New Deal was a defining moment in American history. These three volumes combine to provide a historical analysis of this time in history. The set is designed for middle school students and is written and arranged to fit their educational needs.

The *Almanac* provides a background for the Great Depression and New Deal. It includes 16 chapters, each of which focuses on a specific topic. The book begins with a timeline, a glossary, and research and activity ideas (e.g., exploring the Internet, political debates, creating political cartoons). The volume then provides 16 chapters, which address such topics as the causes of the Great Depression, farm relief, industry and labor, women and minorities in the Great Depression, and prohibition and crime.

The *Biographies* volume introduces students to key figures of the time, including politicians such as Eleanor and Franklin Roosevelt and J. Edgar Hoover, and activists such as Molly Dewson and Hallie Flanagan. The biographies run several pages in length and include personal and professional information, interesting sidebars, a black-and-white photograph, and resources for further information.

Primary Sources is divided into eight chapters, each of which focuses on a different theme (e.g., "A New Deal for Americans," "Women's Voices") . Each chapter begins with an overview and then provides excerpts from speeches, letters, and essays. The authors help students research by following up with information of what happened next, facts on the document and its author, and posing questions for the reader to ask themselves. Each of the volumes concludes with its own list of books and Websites for further information and an index.

This set will be useful in middle school libraries and children's reference collections in public libraries. The information is straightforward but also includes tips for further research and interesting activities to put them in the time of the Depression and New Deal era.—**Shannon Graff Hysell**

209.   **Westward Expansion: Almanac.** By Tom Pendergast and Sara Pendergast. Christine Slovey, ed. Farmington Hills, Mich., U*X*L/Gale, 2000. 254p. illus. maps. index. (U*X*L Westward Expansion Reference Library). $42.00. ISBN 0-7876-4862-0.

210.   **Westward Expansion: Biographies.** Farmington Hills, Mich., U*X*L/Gale, 2000. 200p. illus. index. (U*X*L Westward Expansion Reference Library). $42.00. ISBN 0-7876-4863-9.

211.   **Westward Expansion: Primary Sources.** Farmington Hills, Mich., U*X*L/Gale, 2000. 200p. (U*X*L Westward Expansion Reference Library). $42.00. ISBN 0-7876-4864-7.
        This three-volume set is designed to bring the American West alive for middle school and high school students. *Westward Expansion: Almanac* offers an overview of the events that took place leading up to the migration west as well as the events that shaped this time period's history. It is arranged into 11 chapters covering such topics as territorial expansion to 1812, driving the Native Americans further west, the gold rush, wars with the Native Americans, religion in the west, and technology of the wild west. This volume also offers a timeline of events, a glossary of terms to know (e.g., *Continental Divide*, *Homestead Act of 1862*), and research and activity ideas. Each chapter contains black-and-white photographs; sidebars on interesting facts, battles, and characters; resources for further information (books and Websites); and a list of sources used in compiling the chapter.
        Westward Expansion: Biographies focuses mainly on the interesting characters of the west. Each 2,000-words essay is presented in alphabetical order and includes such people as Buffalo Bill, George Custer, Wyatt Erp, Annie Oakley, Levi Strauss, Daniel Boone, Lewis and Clark, and John Deere. The *Primary Sources* volume features personal accounts from many of the people who experienced the expansion westward first hand. These include journals, autobiographies, and letters.
        These volumes are best suited for school libraries and larger public libraries. The information will appeal to children and young adults.—**Shannon Graff Hysell**

Almanacs

212.   Engelbert, Phillis. Chenes, Betz Des, ed. **American Civil Rights: Almanac.** Farmington Hills, Mich., U*X*L/Gale, 1999. 4v. illus. index. $127.00/set. ISBN 0-7876-3172-8.
        The *American Civil Rights Reference Library* is composed of four volumes and three titles: *American Civil Rights Almanac* (2 vols.), *Biographies*, and *Primary Sources*. They are designed for use at a fifth-grade and above reading level. The Advisory Board lacks the usual distinguished names; rather, it includes mostly junior faculty (one professor, three assistant professors, and one graduate student), two public school representatives, and one from the American-Arab Anti-Discrimination Committee. The *Primary Sources* volume includes 22 documents with brief profiles of their authors; the *Biographies* volume includes short biographies of 32 individuals. The *Almanac* volumes include major sections covering Africans, Asians, Hispanics, and Native Americans, with much briefer coverage for Irish, Italians, Germans, Jewish, and Arab Americans and for women, gays and lesbians, and persons with disabilities.

The *Almanac* includes much too brief bibliographies at the end of major sections and all volumes are profusely illustrated. Both volumes of the *Almanac* repeat the same chronology, glossary, and "Research and Activity Ideas." The *Primary Sources* and *Biographies* volumes have different versions (though largely the same) of the chronology and glossary. Overall this set serves its purpose well, but it would have been improved by an adequate bibliography and more precise (e.g., location, date) picture captions. Few errors have crept into the text (but there are some, e.g., Highlander Folk School was not founded near New Market, its current location; its founder, Myles Horton, was not African American; and Andrew Young was born in 1932, not 1921). The greatest problem with this set is what has been excluded: groups (e.g., Haitian Americans who are misleadingly classified as "Latinos," Hmong, Appalachians, Greeks, and Polish), individuals (from *Biographies*), and their words (from *Primary Sources*), such as Frederick Douglass, W. E. B. DuBois, and Russell Means.—**Fred J. Hay**

Biography

213.   Hamilton, Neil A. **American Social Leaders and Activists.** New York, Facts on File, 2002. 434p. illus. index. (American Biographies). $65.00. ISBN 0-8160-4535-6.

This useful addition to the publisher's American Biographies series deals with reformers, radicals, and reactionaries from, primarily, the post-revolutionary era to the present, a task complicated by the problem of definition. What is a reformer, a radical, and a reactionary? Essentially, Neil A. Hamilton builds upon an earlier study by Ronald G. Walters, *American Reformers: 1815-1860* (1978), which distinguished the three thusly: whereas a reformer labors to improve the existing system, a radical seeks to replace it with something better; and a reactionary attempts to turn the clock backward to some presumed better time. So the biographies herein run the gamut from William Lloyd Garrison to David Duke, Margaret Sanger to Phyllis Schlafly, Eugene V. Debs to Rush Limbaugh, and Harriet Tubman to Malcolm X.

Hamilton has sought to be representative rather than exhaustive. Thus, the 260 entries offer a sampling of men and women who were prominent "as abolitionists, socialists, communists, temperance crusaders, communards, women's suffragists, peace advocates, civil rights workers, labor organizers, and anti-war protesters" (p. xii). Clearly written and arranged alphabetically, the features average about 300 to 400 words, but a few are considerably longer. The ones on Martin Luther King Jr. and Malcolm X, for instance, run 3,000 words or more. Photographs interspersed throughout enhance the volume's appeal, while a thorough index and a grouping of the entries by area of activity (e.g., "Consumer Rights, Ralph Nader") and year of birth (e.g., "1810-1819, John Humphrey Noyes") add to its utility. This is a work for a general audience, and is a volume that high schools and colleges should consider adding to their reference collections. [R: SLJ, April 03, p. 97]—**John W. Storey**

214.   **Roots of the Republic.** Danbury, Conn., Grolier, 1996. 6v. illus. maps. index. $159.00/set. ISBN 0-7172-7608-2.

This set pulls together, in an attractive, hardbound format, basic information about the founding of and the "movers and shakers" in the U.S. government. The major portion of the material consists of biographical sketches 1.5 to 3 pages in length, with black-and-white photos or pen-and-ink drawings of most persons profiled. This information is usually available only in scattered sources.

Unfortunately, the set lacks a clear sense of audience. The first two volumes especially need to be read with a book on U.S. history at hand. Plenty of adjectives describe the biographees, but there is often a paucity of hard information. Too many references will be puzzling to young readers.

Few are likely to know the meaning of "born to the purple" or "straight-laced" in a day when class and behavior are defined so differently from what they were 200 years ago. Occasionally, someone is described in terms of political outlook without defining phrases; for example, ". . . it was equally difficult to decide whether he was a Federalist or a Democrat." The remainder of the set is stronger, with personalities and achievements of the chief justices of the United States more clearly defined. The sketch of Bill Clinton sounds partisan. All books have useful essays, such as "The Accomplishments of the First Congress" and "The Power of Judicial Review." The set needs a firmer editorial hand.

These volumes could serve as supplementary material for U.S. history classes. The set possesses thorough indexes and scholarly bibliographies. [R: BL, 15 Oct 96, p. 452]—**Edna M. Boardman**

Chronology

215. **The American Scene: Events.** Danbury, Conn., Grolier, 1999. 9v. illus. maps. index. $265.00/set. ISBN 0-7172-9448-X.

This 9-volume set is designed for young readers (grades 4 and up) and highlights many of the important events and people who have helped shape U.S. history. With a total of more than 1,000 pages, an important subject is portrayed on each page. Ranging from the Watson Brake Mounds in Louisiana that were built 3,500 years ago by Native Americans to the Clinton scandal, the books are packed with key information about the United States that will educate students and teachers alike.

The well-designed pages start with a colorful photograph or image of the subject at the top, a location map, and a handy U.S. history timeline along the right margin. Written descriptions vary in length from 200 to 300 words and adequately cover the significance of the event. The page concludes with highly interesting facts in bold typeface under the heading "Did you know . . ."

Including *all* of the important events of U.S. history in a series of this scope is impossible, and selection must be somewhat subjective. For the most part the coverage is thorough, but some glaring omissions are Sitting Bull, Crazy Horse, and the Reconstruction era. Blank space is left at the bottom of each page that would have been a perfect spot for further reading citations or an extra 100 words of text, either of which would have enriched the entries. Occasional oddities also crop up; for example, volume 4, "The Civil War and Its Aftermath," begins in 1863 (the 1861-1862 war years are covered in "Growth and Conflicts"—it would have been more logical to have all the Civil War in one volume). The image for "The Battle of Wounded Knee" actually has nothing to do with the battle—there are far better historical events to choose from that better illustrate this tragedy. These inconsistencies aside, the set serves as an adequate introduction to U.S. history for the young reader. [R: BL, 1 Sept 99, p. 178; BR, Nov/Dec 99, pp. 76-77]—**Mark J. Crawford**

216. **Chronicle of America.** rev. ed. New York, DK Publishing, 1997. 1016p. illus. maps. index. $59.95. ISBN 0-7894-2091-0.

Following nine pages of information on world events that led up to the pivotal 1492 voyage, the *Chronicle of America* chronologically traces the history of this country. Representing the early years, a 2-page spread may cover 5 to 10 years, but by 1764, a spread covers the events of 1 year. Each spread includes a number of colorful illustrations or photographs and a sidebar that pinpoints major events of the time. The work concludes with the events of 1997, which are followed by an illustrated list of facts about the presidents, information on each of the 50 states, a chart on the format of the U.S. government, and an amazingly thorough index.

The index makes clear the value of this attractive work to both student and browser. Among the many entries that identify information on historic persons, places, and events are others that indicate coverage on cultural topics over the years, such as abolition, abortion, actors and actresses, advertising, alcoholic beverages, art, automobile, and aviation. There are four columns of "books, fiction," which are listed in the order of coverage, that enhance access to fiction on a given period.

This sturdy book is appropriate for secondary and public libraries. In academic libraries, undergraduates seeking report topics or an overview of an event or time would find this reasonably priced work of value. A worthwhile companion volume is the 1997 edition of *The Encyclopedia of World Facts and Dates*, by Gorton Carruth.—**Vandelia L. VanMeter**

217.   Rubel, David. **The United States in the 19th Century.** New York, Scholastic, 1996. 192p. illus. maps. index. (Scholastic Timelines). $18.95. ISBN 0-590-72564-5.

Events, photographs, drawings, and maps are brought together here and organized as a timeline to provide an understanding of the history of the United States during the nineteenth century. The book is arranged into chapters, each representing a different era of the 1800s: "Federalism (1800-1814)," "Era of Good Feelings (1815-1828)," "Jacksonian Democracy (1828-1837)," "Industrialization (1837-1845)," "Manifest Destiny (1845-1854)," "A House Divided (1854-1861)," "The Civil War (1861-1865)," "Reconstruction (1865-1877)," "The Gilded Age (1877-1889)," and "The Gay Nineties (1890-1899)." An introduction before each chapter introduces the era and provides some background information. Each chapter is further divided into four categories—science and technology; arts and entertainment; daily life, social movements, fads, and fashions; and politics—that enable the user to better understand the relationships among events that occurred during the same period. Every right-hand page includes an area that features a person (such as Mathew Brady or Horace Mann), an event (such as the Trail of Tears or the Irish Potato Famine), or a trend (such as transcendentalism or urbanization) that further describes the people and conditions that helped shaped the era.

More than 300 photographs and illustrations, a glossary, and a comprehensive index all increase the enjoyment and usefulness of this attractive and easy-to-use reference.—**Dana McDougald**

218.   **ResourceLink: 20th-Century American History.** [CD-ROM]. Santa Barbara, Calif., ABC-CLIO, 1998. Minimum system requirements (Windows version): Pentium-compatible processor at 75MHz or faster. Four-speed CD-ROM drive. Windows 95. 8MB RAM. 10MB hard disk space. SVGA monitor 640x480 (256 colors). 16-bit sound card with Windows drivers. Mouse. Minimum system requirements (Macintosh version): 68040 processor with 25MHz or faster. Double-speed CD-ROM drive. System 7.5.3 or later. 8MB RAM. 10MB hard disk space. SVGA monitor 640x480 (256 colors). $79.00 (stand alone); $199.00 (lab pack); $389.00 (site license). ISBN 1-57607-013-1.

This is essentially an encyclopedia of twentieth-century U.S. history. Approximately 1,500 entries on this subject are presented in the form of video and audio clips, still photographs, maps, definitions, biographical sketches, documents, statistical tables, quotations, and articles of varying length. The term "encyclopedia" is used in this review because of the manner in which users access the contents. Information is in alphabetical lists in which topics may be located either in a single list or via separate lists organized by type (e.g., video clip, audio clip, maps, biographies, organizations).

There is much to be said about this title that is good. Most of the contents will be found useful by both teachers and students. Access to the contents is simple. Users are guided through the various features, search procedures, and methods for carrying out functions in a clearly written and well-organized onscreen manual. A useful feature is the ability to group items for an orderly presentation, to add or edit text to illustrations, and to manipulate and move about text and illustrations in various ways. Topics cover the broad spectrum of the century's history, with emphasis, as one might expect, on the latter half, because this is where the interest of most users probably is. The 27 audio clips are generally excellent, and include such outstanding incidents as Richard Nixon's "Checkers" speech, a "fireside chat by Franklin D. Roosevelt, and Neil Armstrong's moon landing. The same may be said for the 27 video clips, which feature such events as Lyndon Johnson's infamous "Daisy spot" campaign commercial, Woodrow Wilson's 1918 visit to Europe, and scenes from World Wars I and II. The editors also did well in the selection of the 186 biographies and the many still photographs contained in this work.

The content of this CD-ROM is also subject to criticism. With only 1,500 entries, there is not enough information to cover a century as eventful as the twentieth. Related to this criticism is the fact that a significant number of these seem irrelevant. For example, one questions the value of including separate entries for the official seals of 68 government agencies, and illustrations of the flags of all the states and territories. Similarly, few of the 75 state, territorial, and other maps do more than simply list a few of the more populous cities. And, although many of the 178 quotes by famous Americans are interesting, this reviewer does not see their value or need when so many historical events and persons might have been added in their place. A reference work is only as good as its contents, and this one offers less than it could or should have. Despite the above criticisms, this title still has value for teachers and students in secondary schools, and would be a useful addition to their libraries. [R: BR, May/June 99, p. 92]—**Donald E. Collins**

Dictionaries and Encyclopedias

219. **American   History.   http://www.americanhistory.abc-clio.com/.** [Website].   Santa Barbara, Calif., ABC-CLIO. $599.00/year. Minimum system requirements: Internet access with a version 4.0 or later browser. Browser must be cookie and JavaScript enabled. ISSN 1531-1260. Date reviewed: Mar 02.

This electronic resource from ABC-CLIO is designed specifically with teachers and students in mind. Designed much like the other social studies databases from ABC-CLIO, this Website focuses on American history from the early exploration to the American Revolution and the establishment of the 13 original colonies. It covers westward expansion, the Civil War, the Industrial Revolution, and the current threat of terrorism, with much more in between.

The layout of the site is easy to follow. Students can research independently by using the "Reference" section. This page allows the user to search by text (keyword or phrase), topic (a chronological listing of periods throughout U.S. history), or category (e.g., essays, documents, images, maps, quotes). The essays on each topic are thorough and will be easy for middle to high school students to understand and the photographs and maps are clear. A "cybrarian" is available online to answer any questions the user might have using the sight and a Merriam-Webster dictionary is readily available for those having vocabulary problems.

One of the most valuable assets of this reference for the use in schools is that it allows teachers to create a calendar of events and assignments that will specifically meet the needs of their classroom. Under the section titled "Administration" teachers or school media specialists can create research assignments for their students, as well as create subject-specific tests and a class syllabus. Both a student access code and an administrator access code are provided so that students will not have access to the "Administration" page. This also allows students to have access to the Website from school or home and will give parents the opportunity to keep up on their children's assignments.

The *American History* Website is a remarkable tool that will give learning U.S. history new appeal to young adults. Students will enjoy using it and it will give teachers the opportunity to teach U.S. history in a new and exciting format. The cost may keep some schools from purchasing this remarkable tool, but for all of the topics covered and the use it will have in the library, the classroom, and in students' homes this product deserves careful consideration.—**Shannon Graff Hysell**

220. **Encyclopedia of American History.** Gary B. Nash, ed. New York, Facts on File, 2003. 11v. illus. maps. index. $935.00/set. ISBN 0-8160-4371-X.

This 11-volume encyclopedia is designed with high school students in mind. The general editor, Gary B. Nash, was co-director of the National Standards for United States History Project, and has brought his experience with education to this multivolume set. Unlike other encyclopedic volumes it is not organized in the standard A-Z format. Instead, each volume covers a different era of American history and the terms, events, and people relevant to that era are featured in that volume. Each volume provides a list of the entries and an introduction of the time period covered. Entries are typically several pages in length and include biographies of important people and black-and-white photographs and maps. Each volume concludes with a chronology, a list of important documents, a bibliography, and an index to that specific volume. Along with biographies, entries cover topics on events, movements, political developments, the economy, literature, business, art and architecture, and science and technology of the time. Many of the entries provide lists of further reading so students can expand on their research. The use of illustrations and maps is extensive, and they successfully enhance the text. Volume 11 provides a comprehensive index to the set, which serves to pull the 11 volumes together.

This set will be a worthwhile addition to all middle and high school libraries—its intended audience. Unfortunately, at $935 it may be too expensive for some. [R: LJ, 1 Mar 03, p. 78; SLJ, April 03, p. 99]—**Shannon Graff Hysell**

221. **Historic Events for Students: The Great Depression.** Richard C. Hanes and Sharon M. Hanes, eds. Farmington Hills, Mich., Gale, 2002. 3v. illus. index. $225.00/set. ISBN 0-7876-5701-8.

Historic Events for Students: The Great Depression contains 45 entries comprehensively covering such diverse elements of American society as economics, the arts, literature, mass media, labor and industry, international relations, religion, politics, crime, public health, education, and everyday life. It also includes a novel entry, "Effects of the Great Depression—LBJ's Great Society," which highlights the long-term consequences and significance of the Depression in American history. The volume is organized clearly and thoroughly. Every entry begins with a brief introduction, a chronology, and an easy-to-understand, in-depth summary of the topic. A section identified as "Contributing Forces" analyzes the key economic, social, and political forces affecting the particular issue and how these various factors influenced the New Deal's response. Next, under the heading "Perspectives," the reader is provided with differing or competing contemporary opinions, followed by "Impact," which highlights the long-term consequences of the issues and the resulting government action. "Notable People" describes the accomplishments of key individuals in the context of the topic. Every entry contains primary documents, a guide for student research topics, and a thorough up-to-date bibliography (including Internet Web pages) suitable for high school students and undergraduates. The volumes also contain a general chronology of the Great Depression, a consolidated bibliography, a glossary of terms, and a subject index.

Hanes's *Historic Events For Students: The Great Depression* compares well with editor James Ciment's superb *Encyclopedia of the Great Depression and the New Deal* (see ARBA 2002, entry 425). Although there will inevitably be some overlap in two encyclopedic works covering the same period, this feature does not distract from the value of *Historic Events for Students: The Great Depression*. Where there is overlap, such as with Roosevelt's court packing scheme, the Hanes's volumes are far more detailed and specific. Conversely, where the Hanes's volumes are weak—failing to discuss a few issues in detail or at all, such as Aid to Dependent Children, the Silver Shirts, and the Black Legion—Ciment's *Encyclopedia of the Great Depression and the New Deal* provides solid entries. For this reason, the volumes under review complement rather than duplicate Ciment's earlier work. Moreover, the Hanes's volumes stand on their own for their depth of analysis, emphasis on cause and effect in historical events, and creative sidebars. This set is recommended for all libraries.—**E. Wayne Carp**

222. **North America in Colonial Times: An Encyclopedia for Students.** Jacob Ernest Cooke and Milton M. Klein, eds. New York, Scribner's/Simon & Schuster Macmillan, 1998. 4v. illus. index. $375.00/set. ISBN 0-684-80538-3.

This 4-volume set is an adaptation for young adults of the 3-volume *Encyclopedia of the North American Colonies* (see ARBA 95, entry 540), of which Cooke was the editor in chief. Unlike the earlier set, which contained long, scholarly articles arranged topically, this set's articles are arranged alphabetically and have been drastically shortened. For example, the former contains an 83-page section on education with articles on specific topics, whereas the latter's entry for education is only 2½ pages. There are 475 unsigned articles covering a wide range of topics, including people, individual colonies, cities, organizations, events, and social issues (e.g., "Childhood and Adolescence"; "Women, Roles of") . Aside from the British colonies in North America, the authors also cover the French, Dutch, Russian, and Swedish colonies, in addition to the Caribbean and the many Native American groups. The language has also been revised for a younger audience, and the set's layout has been changed to make it more appealing; for example, definitions of unfamiliar words conveniently appear in the left panel, adjacent to the text. The set contains 200 black-and-white illustrations, 16 maps, 16 color plates, and an overall index. Readers are referred to related articles and illustrations by *see* and *see also* references and cross-references. Although each article in the parent set contained a bibliography, this new source contains only an overall list of "Suggested Sources," which does include primary, secondary, and online sources. Materials for young readers are helpfully denoted by asterisks. As with any source of this size, there will be omissions and criticisms that some topics are covered too briefly; one example is that, although the set contains many articles about slavery, the entry on the Declaration of Independence does not mention how Thomas Jefferson's early draft contained a condemnation of the slave trade. This set is recommended for public library young adult reference collections, and for academic libraries that serve young people.—**John A. Drobnicki**

223. **Scholastic Encyclopedia of the Civil War.** By Catherine Clinton. New York, Scholastic, 1999. 112p. illus. maps. index. $18.95. ISBN 0-590-37227-0.

The title, *Scholastic Encyclopedia of the Civil War*, is somewhat misleading if one accepts the traditional definition of an encyclopedia as alphabetically arranged information. Written for juveniles, this slender volume skims the surface, yet contains a great deal of information, much of which is not the kind usually seen in such texts.

The table of contents lists six chapters, which are arranged chronologically. The first, "Before the War," is followed by others for each year, 1861 to 1864. The final chapter, "1865 and After," places much emphasis on the Reconstruction period and the Civil Rights Movement of the 1960s. The volume also includes an alphabetic index. The inside covers provide a clear, color-keyed map showing Union and Confederate capital cities, state capitals, major cities, other locales, places where major battles occurred, and the route of Sherman's March to the Sea.

The text is illustrated with an abundance of period art and photographs, including political cartoons and sketches made by soldiers on the scene. Sidebars with labels like "Eyewitness" (diary excerpts), "Battle-at-a-Glance" (number of troops and casualties on each side and the winner), and "Did You Know" (facts and anecdotes) can be found on nearly every page.

The vocabulary is often above juvenile level, and some might question the author's dwelling on the extended post-war period in a work ostensibly about the war itself. However, the *Scholastic Encyclopedia of the Civil War* provides a lively introduction to a complex subject at a reasonable cost.—**Kay O. Cornelius**

224. **Scholastic Encyclopedia of the Presidents and Their Times.** updated ed. By David Rubel. New York, Scholastic, 1997. 232p. illus. maps. index. $17.95. ISBN 0-590-49366-3.

A revision of the 1994 edition (see ARBA 96, entry 521), this version of the *Scholastic Encyclopedia of the Presidents and Their Times* covers Bill Clinton's reelection; the assassination of Yitzhak Rabin; and the problems, physical and political, of Russia's president Boris Yeltsin. Updated maps and charts are also included.

Attractively arranged and well illustrated, each entry follows the same format. The president's name, term, and picture begin the entry. A mini-fact box containing those items dear to young researchers (e.g., the wife's name and the names of the children) and a personal tidbit —George Bush is cited for his opposition to broccoli and Theodore Roosevelt was the first president to fly in an airplane—follow. Highlights of the administration are given on the outside column of each page, with columns in the interior sections giving cultural events of the period. For example, Gibson Girls, yellow journalism, and breakfast cereals are given as part of the daily life during Grover Cleveland's term. Dates being covered are in blue numbers at the top of each page, making chronology easy to establish.

Added features of this reference book are a history of the White House and a list of presidential election results. A comprehensive index concludes the work. Throughout the essays are words highlighted in red, indicating that the subject is discussed in greater detail elsewhere. The only drawback to this system is that the topic, when found, is not in bold typeface or otherwise noted—one must read the entire page to find the information. This may be discouraging to younger students. A glossary might have been a better approach.

As an overview of the presidents, this is a valuable addition to a reference collection. The format is not overwhelming, concentrated attempts have been made to make the information engaging, and the overall effect of the book is professional and interesting. [R: SLJ, May 97, p. 162]—**Michele Tyrrell**

Handbooks and Yearbooks

225. **American Decades 1900-1909.** Vincent Tompkins, ed. Detroit, Gale, 1996. 589p. illus. index. $78.00. ISBN 0-8103-5722-4.

226. **American Decades 1910-1919.** Vincent Tompkins, ed. Detroit, Gale, 1996. 632p. illus. index. $78.00. ISBN 0-8103-5723-2.

227. **American Decades 1920-1929.** Judith S. Baughman, ed. Detroit, Gale, 1996. 554p. illus. index. $75.00. ISBN 0-8103-5724-0.

These three volumes, covering the first three decades of the twentieth century, are the last to be published in the American Decades series, and, until the volume for the 1990s appears some years hence, complete coverage of this century. As with the others in the series, each, after a helpful encapsulating introduction and a chronological list of world events, treats its decade from 12 different topical perspectives: the arts, business and the economy, education, fashion, government and politics, law and justice, lifestyles and social trends, media, medicine and health, religion, science and technology, and sports.

All sections are similarly organized: a chronology of events; an essay overview; discussions of particular aspects of the topic; brief biographies of "Headline Makers"; biographies, 400 to 1,000 words, of "People in the News"; deaths of notables during the decade; and finally, a list of important publications on the topic that appeared in that decade. (The useful "General References" list toward the end of the volumes contains a selective listing of more recently published items on each of the topical areas.) Black-and-white illustrations are scattered throughout the volume, as well as frequent sidebars on more entertaining, although not necessary, information. Each volume concludes with a list of contributors, an index to the photographs, and a detailed general index.

As with the others in the series, these three volumes can be recommended to a wide audience. The information is accurate and well presented; the bibliographies are brief but helpful; and everything is nicely packaged in sturdy, attractive volumes. While the series is especially aimed at high school and public libraries, it should also prove useful in libraries serving undergraduates. [R: LJ, June 96, p. 56]—**Evan Ira Farber**

228. **American Decades 1980-1989.** Victor Bondi, ed. Detroit, Gale, 1996. 774p. illus. index. $75.00. ISBN 0-8103-8881-2.

Using the same format as the other volumes in the American Decades series (see entries 225-228), this volume chronicles the significant people, events, and issues of the 1980s. It was the decade of the Ronald Reagan administration (and one year of George Bush's) when the federal debt soared to its highest level to date; when the rich were getting richer and their lifestyles were ever present in television shows such as *Dallas* and *Dynasty*; when AIDS deaths multiplied; when gang violence, child abuse, and drug abuse were rampant; and the intergenerational dispute over values was ongoing. The decade, similar to the earlier ones, is surveyed from 13 perspectives (world events, the arts, business and the economy, education, fashion, government and politics, law and justice, lifestyles and social trends, media, medicine and health, religion, science and technology, and sports).

Chapter 1 consists of a chronology of world events, but all other chapters include, in addition to a chronology, an overview, topics in the news, headline makers, people in the news, awards (if applicable), deaths, and publications. The text is interspersed with a variety of photographs (e.g., eruption of Mount St. Helens, Michael Jordan, Prime Minister Margaret Thatcher and Reagan at Camp David) and sidebars and tables ("Vietnam Veterans Memorial"; "Leading Causes of Death in 1981, by Sex and Race") . This work concludes with a general bibliography; a list of contributors; an index of photographs; and a comprehensive subject index of people, books, periodicals, plays, movies, television shows, corporations, government agencies, and the like.

American Decades 1980-1989 is complemented by the chronological/tabular treatment in *Day by Day: The Eighties.* (see ARBA 96, entry 503), a rearrangement of material in *Facts on File Yearbooks.* and to which set readers need to turn for additional information on a person, event, or place cited in *Day by Day. American Decades* is recommended for public, academic, and high school libraries.—**Wiley J. Williams**

229. **The American Dream: The 50s.** Alexandria, Va., Time-Life Books, 1998. 192p. illus. maps. index. (Our American Century). $19.95. ISBN 0-7835-5500-8.

Time-Life Books has produced another attractive volume for general consumption. Not meant to be an in-depth look at the decade of the 1950s, this volume touches on the cultural, political, and historical icons of a complicated 10-year span in U.S. history. For the baby boomer genera-tion, this volume holds many memories. The short narrative format, liberally interrupted with beautiful half-tones and four-color prints, presents the period in an attractive, nostalgic manner. Baby boomers can now see themselves as part of history, along with television and the cultural icons that medium spawned. From black-and-white to living color, from tail fins to sports cars, from James Dean to Marilyn Monroe, the Kennedys to Martin Luther King Jr., this volume has them all. The beautiful book is a welcome addition to any personal, middle school, high school, and public library reference collection.—**Norman L. Kincaide**

230.   **American Immigration.** Danbury, Conn., Grolier, 1999. 10v. illus. index. $325.00/set. ISBN 0-7172-9283-5.
    American Immigration is a 10-volume encyclopedia dealing with the topic of immigration from the earliest Asian settlers of 30,000 years ago to modern-day immigrants such as the Kurds, Haitians, and Bosnians. Volume 1 provides an overview of the subject, discussing immigration in a historical context—immigration laws, patterns, and issues. Volume 2 is dedicated to Ellis Island. The remaining volumes contain topical entries, covering individual ethnic groups, terms associ-ated with immigration, and social issues. Each volume is the same length and each contains a bibliography as an index to the entire work.
    The coverage of the individual groups will prove valuable. The history of the group in its na-tive land is provided as well as the issues prompting the exodus. Problems encountered by the group are discussed, the names of famous members are given, and, in the case of recent immi-grants, some idea of their progress and future is projected. Numerous photographs add interest, and sidebars and inserts giving highlights and little-known facts will get readers' attention.
    No one is given total editorial credit for the work, although names of a project coordinator, writers and editors, and researchers are listed. Also included here are the names of several individ-uals associated with Ellis Island. No credentials are given for any of the participants.
    American Immigration is a fascinating and useful overview of a basic thread in U.S. history. Although not scholarly in nature (data is not footnoted and interviews have been "lightly edited for readability") , the work will prove to be a helpful tool for middle and high school students. [R: BL, 1 Mar 99, p. 1234]—**Michele Tyrrell**

231.   Brownstone, David M., and Irene M. Franck. **The Young Nation: America 1787-1861.** Bethel, Conn., Grolier Educational, 2002. 10v. illus. maps. index. $339.00/set. ISBN 0-7172-5645-6.
    The Young Nation, a 10-volume set, provides an excellent history of the American Colo-nies, their development into a new nation, and the conflict involved in nation-building which led to the Civil War. The set ends in 1861. Organized thematically, the set examines the British, French, and Spanish roots of the United States; the expansion of the new nation; immigration; the conflict over slavery; Native American and women's issues; and many other events and concepts.
    One real benefit of this set is the way in which the authors explain in clear terms the chal-lenges that the forefathers had in conceiving of and creating the new nation. Instead of treating his-torical information as a list of facts, dates and events, the authors show how history happened. Accelerated learners will be able to synthesize and analyze philosophical issues in history. Each volume includes an index to the complete set. Within the text, there are references to related topics, either in the same volume or in another. The final volume includes a glossary, demographic data, and the U.S. Constitution. Each volume also includes references to high-quality, educational Websites and other print publications. The set includes many colorful images and maps, although some images are not placed well contextually. This valuable reference set is recommended for ju-nior and senior high school libraries.—**Tara L. Dirst**

232. **DISCovering U.S. History.** [CD-ROM]. Detroit, Gale, 1997. Minimum system requirements: IBM or compatible 386 (486DX/33MHz or higher highly recommended). CD-ROM drive
(double speed or faster recommended) with MS-DOS CD-ROM Extensions 2.2. DOS 5.0. Windows 3.1. 8MB RAM. 5MB hard disk space. SVGA monitor (256-color display) and graphics
card. Windows-compatible mouse. Printer (optional). $500.00/stand-alone version; $700.00/2-8
users. ISBN 0-7876-0923-4.

This CD-ROM is a comprehensive, interdisciplinary, and cross-linked electronic guide to
the significant events, social movements, and notable and diverse persons of American history
from the prehistoric era through 1996. This interesting and useful reference work contains more
than 2,000 essays covering such topics as government and politics, film and the performing arts,
business and industry, science and technology, and various social movements. These entries are
supplemented by and hypertext linked to more than 1,500 biographies that provide relevant and
personal significance to a variety of historical events. Entries throughout this lively work are concise and factual and should supply users with an awareness of the context under which these events
occurred.

The principal strength of this electronic reference work is the ease by which users can
search, access, and cross-reference materials. Information is sensibly indexed and organized into
five general categories: timelines; names; subjects; places (states, cities, or regions); and primary
documents. The timelines furnish a convenient and effective overview of historical eras and supply descriptive chronologies to an assorted array of nearly 10,000 political, social, and economic
events. The inclusion of 163 primary documents, including such things as speeches, letters, journal
entries, and other personal narratives; contemporaneous newspaper articles; and book excerpts
add an invaluable insight that will be of great and practical benefit to users. Among the other effective and accessible features of this reference work are its linked picture gallery and dictionary. As a
broad-based reference work, the disc effectively introduces a variety of significant events and
persons and will help students to organize and broaden their understanding of U.S. society.—**Timothy
E. Sullivan**

233. Gross, Ernie. **Advances and Innovations in American Daily Life, 1600s-1930s.** Jefferson, N.C., McFarland, 2002. 298p. index. $35.00pa. ISBN 0-7864-1248-8.

This title belies the simplicity of this handy reference volume. Divided into 23 categories,
the book is more of a list of "firsts," such as the first ambulance service or first opera performance
in the United States. Categories run the gamut from agriculture to transportation and include
sports, music, art, religion, education, and finance. Each category is further divided into subtopics.
An example is public service, broken into smaller sections on fire, police, postal, and sewer services. Also typical is the chapter on health, where surgery assumes a major portion of the text, with
references to firsts in cardiac, liver, kidney, and orthopedic surgeries. Despite the easy-to-follow
arrangement, the volume includes an extensive index. Gross is the author of similar titles, including an American historical chronology (see ARBA 2000, entry 407). Although priced a bit high,
reference librarians will find this a useful ready-reference source; school librarians should also
purchase the title.—**Boyd Childress**

234. Kyvig, David E. **Daily Life in the United States, 1920-1939: Decades of Promise and
Pain.** Westport, Conn., Greenwood Press, 2002. 271p. illus. index. (The Greenwood Press "Daily
Life Through History" Series). $49.95. ISBN 0-313-29555-7.

This book is a well-written, encyclopedic guide to the daily life of ordinary Americans in
the 1920s and 1930s based on information in the Fourteenth U.S. Census of 1920, the Fifteenth
U.S. Census of 1930, and numerous secondary sources. Kyvig astutely demonstrates that national
events such as the Eighteenth Amendment and Nineteenth Amendments—prohibition and

women's suffrage, respectively—either had little effect on ordinary Americans or were experienced so diversely, depending on locale, ethnicity, race, or gender, as to make sweeping generalization difficult. Other chapters examine the effect of new technologies, such as electricity and the automobile, and new forms of mass communication, such as the radio and cinema. With these technologies came a growing uniformity in American culture, manifested in the 1930s by increased advertising, mass literacy, and the democratization of music and dance.

Kyvig also skillfully looks at the small and routine features of daily life that appear to change little over generations. He is able to identify significant changes during these decades in everyday activities such as shopping, standards of cleanliness, courtship, marriage, family formation, childbearing, health, leisure, and religion. He also examines the conflicts, crimes, and catastrophes that punctuated American lives. These included the rise of the new Ku Klux Klan and its nativism program, the rise of crime and gangsters in the wake of prohibition, and the natural disasters (e.g., boll weevils, floods, drought) that struck the United States. The final chapters vividly describe the impact of the Depression and the importance of New Deal assistance in the lives of American families. Kyvig is sensitive to regional, ethnic, racial, cultural, and gender differences when making generalizations about the time period; for that reason, this is a valuable work that can be recommended for all libraries. —**E. Wayne Carp**

235.   **U*X*L American Decades.** Tom Pendergast and Sara Pendergast, eds. Farmington Hills, Mich., U*X*L/Gale, 2003. 10v. illus. index. $399.00/set. ISBN 0-7876-6454-5.

*U*X*L American Decades* is a 10-volume set designed to present a broad overview of the major events and people that helped shape American society throughout the twentieth century. Each volume contains a different image in the central panel of the cover reflecting an important icon from that decade. For example, the 1960-1969 volume features a flag bearing the "Peace" symbol. After an overall chronology and a brief essay titled "An Overview," eight chapters comprise each volume: "Arts and Entertainment"; "Business and the Economy"; "Education"; "Government, Politics, and Law"; "Lifestyles and Social Trends"; "Medicine and Health"; "Science and Technology"; and "Sports." Each chapter contains a timeline of significant events within the chapter's field, an overview summary of the events and people detailed in that chapter, short biographical accounts of key people and their achievements during the decade, a series of brief topical essays describing events and people within the chapter's theme, and a "For More Information" section that includes books and Websites. In addition, each volume concludes with a longer "Where to Learn More" listing of books and Websites, as well as an alphabetic subject index for that volume. A paperback cumulative index lists volume and page number for topics covered in all 10 volumes. *U*X*L American Decades* volumes contain many black-and-white photographs and a few scattered sidebars.

Designed for middle school students, this series should not be overlooked for high school use as well. Even reluctant readers could find the sports and pop music statistics fascinating. In fact, researchers of any age who need information about popular culture in a particular decade would probably find this series to be quick and convenient. The language is neither too difficult nor too simple for an average reader. Although *U*X*L American Decades* covers a lot of ground, as with any such series, some of the included material could be open to question as to its political biases or other biases simply because of what is included or excluded. The series is at its best when it quotes important figures and lets the readers draw their own conclusions about what they say. It is perhaps not quite always as successful in choosing the half dozen or so "key people" from each decade. As always, references to Websites will tend to be outdated long before the bibliographic information. For those, however, who can afford the price, *U*X*L American Decades* is an interesting and unique reference.—**Kay O. Cornelius**

236.   Volo, Dorothy Denneen, and James M. Volo. **Daily Life in Civil War America.** Westport, Conn., Greenwood Press, 1998. 321p. illus. index. (The Greenwood Press "Daily Life Through History" Series). $45.00. ISBN 0-313-30516-1.

Based upon journals, newspapers, and diaries, this title provides an account of the daily life of civilians, ordinary soldiers, and slaves, including such information as how they obtained and prepared food and dealt with food shortages, how clothing and fashion were affected by the war, and the role of popular books and magazines, housing, leisure activities, and political ideas. The 1st of the 3 major parts provides the setting by discussing historical and political events and the attitudes of the day in both the North and South. The 2d part concerns all aspects of the lives of soldiers. Part 3 focuses on the lives of civilians. The work begins with a chronology; concludes with a bibliography and an index; and includes some period photographs, illustrations, and original artwork.

Most publications that deal with this time period focus on political and military matters. The introduction to this work makes it clear that it is envisioned as a supplement to other works—to flesh out the bones of statistics and descriptions of battles. Although the intended audience is not clarified in the introduction, this work seems suitable for readers from 8th grade to adulthood. Students will benefit by gaining an understanding of the culture of the day; teachers will find that this information about daily life will enrich the Civil War curriculum.—**Vandelia L. VanMeter**

237.   Volo, James M., and Dorothy Denneen Volo. **Daily Life on the Old Colonial Frontier.** Westport, Conn., Greenwood Press, 2002. 337p. illus. index. (The Greenwood Press "Daily Life Through History" Series). $49.95. ISBN 0-313-31103-X.

This volume in The Greenwood Press "Daily Life Through History" Series covers America between the earliest colonization and the start of the Revolution. The Volos go beyond what is usually considered "daily life" in their book. Along with information about such expected topics as the food, housing, clothing, and education of both colonists and Native Americans, chapters are devoted to the French presence in Canada, intertribal warfare, and the fur trade. Several other chapters cover the military aspects of colonial life, specifically fortifications, weaponry, and the role of the militia. These topics segue into discussions of the early colonial wars and the particularly fascinating stories of colonists captured by the Indians—those that returned to their former lives and those who did not. The book is written in textbook style with numerous paragraph headings calling attention to major and minor topics. The prose is clear and simple with facts following one after another. There are some excerpts from contemporary accounts and occasional illustrations. A selected bibliography and index are also included. This volume is a fine choice for those requiring a basic understanding of daily life in America prior to 1775.—**Deborah Hammer**

ASIAN HISTORY

238.   Benn, Charles. **Daily Life in Traditional China: The Tang Dynasty.** Westport, Conn., Greenwood Press, 2002. 317p. illus. index. (The Greenwood Press "Daily Life Through History" Series). $49.95. ISBN 0-313-30955-8.

Based on a college course taught by the author, this curriculum-oriented book, *Daily Life in Traditional China: The Tang Dynasty*, introduces students of varied disciplines to ancient China during the Tang period, 618-907. Known as the golden age of Chinese culture, Tang China produced the greatest literature, arts, music, dance, law code, and Buddhism during its 300-year history. The book begins with a map of Tang China and its capital Changan and a listing of the tang emperors. There is a wealth of information about historical life that is divided into 12 topics:

history, society, cities and urban life, house and garden, clothes and hygiene, food and feasts, leisure and entertainment, travel and transportation, crime and punishment, sickness and health, life cycle, and death and the afterlife. There are more than 40 illustrations throughout. A list of suggested English- language readings by topics and an index complete the volume.

The text of the book heavily derives from original Tang sources or secondary studies. However, notes of the original sources have been omitted that will undoubtedly diminish the value of the book as a serious scholarly work. However, undergraduates, high school students, and the general public will enjoy the lively account in this excellent introductory work to an ancient time and a faraway place, and gain a better understanding of Tang China. This work is recommended for public, high school, and undergraduate libraries.—**Karen T. Wei**

MIDDLE EASTERN HISTORY

239.   **Ancient Egypt.** David P. Silverman, ed. New York, Oxford University Press, 1997. 256p. illus. maps. index. $35.00. ISBN 0-19-521270-3.

This volume provides a most welcome addition to the many recent books on ancient Egypt. Its editor and contributors rank among the most notable of today's Egyptologists, and each of them describes clearly and succinctly the area about which he or she is writing, including the most recent information on the topic under discussion.

Lavishly illustrated with maps, pictures, and drawings, the book consists of short essays addressing virtually every aspect of the life and times of ancient Egypt under three main topics: the Egyptian world, including a discussion of the dynasties and historical periods, the land, the surrounding world, knowledge in Egypt, and women; belief and ritual, composed of discussions about royalty, mortuary practices, beliefs regarding creation, and ritual actions and beliefs; and finally art, architecture, and language. Under this last heading, the reader learns about pyramids; temples and tombs; Egyptian art; and the signs, symbols, and language of the ancient Egyptians. Each short article includes sidebars or boxes offering brief, detailed discussions of relevant topics, such as the female pharaoh Hatshepsut, the worker's village at Deir el-Medina, and the Egyptian calendar.

A notable and welcome feature is the many in-text page references to the current topic's appearance elsewhere in the volume, permitting the reader to quickly locate other discussions on the subject. The volume's extensive bibliography, arranged by topic, provides another excellent and helpful feature. This book makes a fine addition to any public or school library, and with its bibliography, the library of any undergraduate institution. —**Susan Tower Hollis**

240.   Baines, John, and Jaromir Malek. **Cultural Atlas of Ancient Egypt.** rev. ed. New York, Checkmark Books/Facts on File, 2000. 240p. illus. maps. index. $50.00. ISBN 0-8160-4036-2.

The *Cultural Atlas of Ancient Egypt* comprises a revision of the authors' well-known *Atlas of Ancient Egypt*. The redigitized maps show many details and descriptions that do not appear in the earlier book. Place-names now include modern, classical, and ancient Egyptian, omitting the biblical that was often used previously. Some illustrations are new, others are presented from a different view, and some newer photographs of archaeological activity have been substituted for older images.

The authors have also thoroughly reviewed the text, revising it to include new information and current thinking on many matters. Very significantly, they have revised the dates for the historic periods and for the dynasties and kings prior to dynasty 26, as well as suggesting there are no absolutely firm dates prior to that dynasty. In addition, they have changed the dating terminology from B.C. to B.C.E. and A.D. to C.E. Finally, the bibliography has been considerably revised and updated. The revisions present in this edition suggest that it belongs in any private, public, school, college, and university library that serves people interested in ancient Egypt.—**Susan Tower Hollis**

241.   Brier, Bob, and Hoyt Hobbs. **Daily Life of the Ancient Egyptians.** Westport, Conn., Greenwood Press, 1999. 253p. illus. maps. index. (The Greenwood Press "Daily Life Through History" Series). $45.00. ISBN 0-313-30313-4.

    This book attempts to describe ancient Egyptians—a paradoxical society of startling modern accomplishments with incredibly ancient thought processes, people who looked both forward and back. Ancient Egyptians were stunningly advanced in architecture, food, clothing, and medicine, but their view of the world was closer to that of a prehistoric caveman. Egyptians were among the first people to develop writing, and these writings, along with their accurate tomb paintings, enable archaeologists and historians to study Egyptian life. Egyptians made lists of what they owned, recorded court cases, described battles, preserved recipes, wrote books on medicine and religion, and told stories. Tomb paintings illustrated the clothing, the conduct of professions, and the leisure activities of actual people. Thanks to the recovered objects, inscriptions, paintings, and surviving temples and tombs, today's society knows a great deal about how these ancient people lived and what they thought. The book provides a chronology followed by 10 chapters on various subjects: history, religion, government and society, work and play, food, clothes and other adornments, architecture, arts and crafts, warfare, and medicine and mathematics. An annotated bibliography and an index conclude the work. This is a good introductory reference for archaeology and ancient history students to better understand the Egyptian culture.—**Cari Ringelheim**

242.   David, Rosalie. **Handbook to Life in Ancient Egypt.** New York, Facts on File, 1998. 382p. illus. maps. index. $45.00. ISBN 0-8160-3312-9.

    This handbook presents ancient Egyptian life through an interdisciplinary approach, using the three main sources available to investigators: monuments such as temples and tombs, objects and artifacts from archaeological sites, and written materials available from different times of history. The author, a notable Egyptologist, works with the material through 11 chapters of varying lengths, each with many subsections. She includes discussions of historical background, geography, society and government, religion of the living, funerary beliefs and customs, architecture and building, written evidence, the army and navy, foreign trade and transport, economy and industry, and everyday life. Where appropriate, photographs, line drawings, and maps are included to support the text.

    Each chapter includes references to other readings by topic, thus encouraging the reader to explore further. Unfortunately, a number of revised and recent works do not appear in the bibliography. For example, *The Third Intermediate Period in Egypt (1100-650)* (Aris & Phillips, 1973) published a revised edition in 1996, and *The Origins of Osiris* (Hessling, 1966) published a significantly revised edition as *The Origins of Osiris and His Cult* in 1980 (E. J. Brill). *Ancient Egyptian Kingship*, edited by David O'Connor and David Silverman (E. J. Brill, 1995); *Religion in Ancient Egypt*, edited by Byron Shafer (Cornell University Press, 1993); and A. J. Spencer's *Early Egypt* (Oklahoma University Press, 1993), to note a few, do not appear at all. In addition, some outright errors appear. For example, Tuthmosis III is not the son of Tuthmosis I, King Hor-Aha is now commonly accepted as the first dynastic ruler, and sister marriages are generally seen as rare.

    Despite these concerns, this volume belongs on the shelves of the public and school library. The breadth and thoroughness of its coverage will serve the beginning student well, and there is nothing else known to this reviewer quite like it. [R: BL, 1 Oct 98, pp. 363-364]—**Susan Tower Hollis**

243. Harris, Geraldine, and Delia Pemberton. **Illustrated Encyclopedia of Ancient Egypt.** Lincolnwood, Ill., Peter Bedrick Books/Contemporary Publishing, 1999. 176p. illus. $29.95. ISBN 0-87226-606-0.

This authoritative and entertaining one-volume reference work is an excellent introduction to the world of Ancient Egypt for young students. While its over 200 entries are written for children age 9-12 years of age, older students may also find it useful for ready reference.

The authors, lecturers in Egyptology at Oxford University and the British Museum, effectively communicate their knowledge of the life and times of Ancient Egypt in such a way as to capture the imaginations of their intended audience. The encyclopedia is beautifully illustrated with a predominance of color photographs. A majority of the illustrations depict items that are part of the British Museum collections.

Entries vary in length from one line to two pages, with an average entry approximately a quarter to half a page. The well-researched and well-written entries highlight key terms in bold typeface. Each topic highlighted in this way has its own separate entry in the encyclopedia. Following these cross-references is sometimes difficult. For example, the single-line entry for the Nile highlights the word "Egypt." A reader going to the entry for Egypt will not immediately find the information relating to the Nile in the entry since it does not appear in bold typeface. An index is also available.

A novel means of access is provided through thematic "trails." Selected entries are classified using topics such as "Myth and Magic" or "Egypt and its Neighbors." A listing of the thematic trails and the corresponding entries related to each may be found in the beginning of the book. Every trail is identified by an icon, which appears at the beginning of each entry that is a part of the trail. Using the icon for a particular trail, a reader may browse the encyclopedia looking for entries displaying a particular icon to locate information on a topic.

This encyclopedia is an admirable reference source that provides a wealth of information on Ancient Egypt. School libraries and children's collections will find it a worthwhile purchase. [R: SLJ, Nov 2000, pp. 90-92]—**Elizabeth M. Mezick**

244. Nemet-Nejat, Karen Rhea. **Daily Life in Ancient Mesopotamia.** Westport, Conn., Greenwood Press, 1998. 346p. illus. index. (Greenwood Press "Daily Life Through History" Series). $45.00. ISBN 0-313-29497-6.

Nemet-Nejat's lively account of daily life in ancient Mesopotamia fills an important gap in the literature. The other treatments of this subject, such as the classic work by H. W. F. Saggs, *Everyday Life in Ancient Mesopotamia* (Dorset Press, 1965), are now well out of date. Writing for both students and educated laypeople, Nemet-Nejat begins her book with a useful timeline and then a brief discussion of the rediscovery of ancient Mesopotamia and the decipherment of the ancient texts. This is followed by a description of the geographical setting of Mesopotamia and its peoples and languages in chapter 2 and then a historical overview in chapter 3. Chapters 4 through 11 are arranged topically, treating such subjects as writing, education, city life, private life, science, and religion. She concludes with a brief assessment of the legacy of ancient Mesopotamia. A glossary and selective bibliography provide additional help for the reader. This is a fascinating and authoritative synthesis of an extensive body of material pertaining to life in ancient Mesopotamia, and it will be a frequently consulted reference by those with an interest in this subject. This work is highly recommended.—**Harold O. Forshey**

245. **The Usborne Internet-Linked Encyclopedia of Ancient Egypt.** By Gill Harvey and Struan Reid. Tulsa, Okla., EDC Publishing, 2001. 128p. illus. index. $19.95. ISBN 0-7945-0118-4.

This volume presents lavish illustrations as it describes the major features of ancient Egyptian history and culture beginning in the late pre-Dynastic period and moves forward through the Ptolemaic period. After a brief survey of this history, the text segues into a description of royalty and religion, including discussions of government and its hierarchy, armies and wars, and trading and diplomacy, as well as providing materials on different aspects of religion, including gods, myths, temples, and all aspects of death and the afterlife. Completing the text section is an extensive discussion about everyday life covering houses, women, activities, clothing, education, and more. The volume concludes with a "Factfinder," which includes a timeline of history with contemporaneous events noted for other parts of the world, a list of kings and dynasties, a "who's who" including important non-Egyptian figures, a brief descriptive catalog of deities, a history of Egyptology (the science of the study of ancient Egypt), a list of museums containing major collections, a glossary, and an extensive index.

The unique aspect of this volume is its keyed reference to resources available on the Internet, linking the reader to many different Websites throughout the world where he or she may find pertinent and interesting materials related to the subject at hand. Since the volume seeks to serve children ages 9 to 12, it opens appropriately with caveats about the use of the Internet. Unfortunately, the information provided about needed resources to access the Internet links is out of date, and even the information provided on the Website has changed radically, as one cannot access by page number on Netscape 6.2, but rather one finds a list of site links by type on the home page. Some links that appear in the text seem to be missing from the current Web page (e.g., the Egyptian Museum in Cairo). Changes like these are to be expected when publishing Internet resources, but that they occur foregrounds the complete lack of any print-based references in the volume itself. Since most materials of any significance, even for the ages targeted, appear only in print resources and the targeted age group needs to learn to use print resources as well as the Internet, this omission is very serious. Nevertheless, the collection of sites comprises an excellent resource for anyone, and so the use of the book in public and school libraries is worth the investment.
—**Susan Tower Hollis**

EUROPEAN HISTORY

General Works

Atlases

246.   Kongstam, Angus. **Atlas of Medieval Europe.** New York, Checkmark Books/Facts on File, 2000. 191p. illus. maps. index. $35.00. ISBN 0-8160-4469-4.

In his work, *Atlas of Medieval Europe*, Kongstam has provided readers with a valuable guide to studying the history and culture of Medieval Europe. This book has many valuable points. For instance, its coverage extends beyond Western Europe to the Middle East as well as Eastern and Southeastern Europe. A timeline charts crucial events across the bottom of the pages. The coverage extends to history, art, religion, literature, economics, politics, and other subjects. Kongstam's focus topics call attention to key issues in the study of this era. As with its predecessor (see ARBA 84, entry 330), the maps in this work are colorful and offer the reader a firsthand account of key battles and movements. The introduction's discussion of "The Medieval Myth" will serve readers well. Kongstam's use of excellent contemporary illustrations and the genealogical table in the back are also useful.

However, the book has several flaws that need to be pointed out. First, this work needs a gazetteer and a bibliography. Also, the chronology might have been placed at the front of the book. Finally, it seems as if the Early Middle Ages (400-1100 C.E.) were quickly glossed over to get to the High and Later Middle Ages and the Renaissance. Despite these points, Kongstam has provided scholars with a useful reference tool, especially for the High and Later Middle Ages in addition to the Renaissance. His work is recommended for public, community college, and academic (undergraduate) libraries.—**David J. Duncan**

Dictionaries and Encyclopedias

247. **Ancient Greece and Rome: An Encyclopedia for Students.** Carroll Moulton, ed. New York, Scribner's/Simon & Schuster Macmillan, 1998. 4v. illus. maps. index. $350.00/set. ISBN 0-684-80507-3.

This 4-volume set is designed to provide a single reference source students can go to for information regarding classical Greece and Rome. Some features incorporated into this work include text that is broken down into easy-to-follow subheadings; more than 200 illustrations, maps, diagrams, and drawings; graphic timelines that clarify the chronology of events; sidebars that highlight interesting stories; notations that remind students to refer to the index; difficult words that are marked by an asterisk and defined in the margins; and a complete bibliography that is included for further reading.

Perhaps one of the best designed reference works to come along in a long time, these 4 volumes are beautifully laid out and formatted. Great care and consideration can be seen with the turning of each page, and the extensive coverage of subject matter is remarkable. History, government, culture, the arts, architecture, agriculture, religion, mythology, and famous figures of nonfiction and fiction are all there. The expected subjects are listed as well as some nice surprises. "Euclid" is expected, but "shellfish" is a surprise. The sidebars and margins are so full of fascinating tidbits and pieces of information it is easy to become engrossed in these peripheral data alone. The plethora of maps and illustrations help to break up the text, making research more entertaining, and 4 sections of color plates (1 in each volume) show artifacts of "Daily Life," "Art and Architecture," "People," and "Culture."

The tone of this reference source for middle and high school students is just right. The narrative is easy to follow and understand, although the younger students may find the long (often Latin-based) names of ancient people and places hard to digest, and the older students may find the descriptions blunt and all too brief.

The all-inclusive cross-referencing is to be praised as much as it is to be cursed. By plodding from cross-reference to cross-reference, a fairly decent and complete definition may be obtained on any specific subject. But be forewarned—the majority of descriptions cross-reference an item from volume to volume to volume. If all 4 volumes are not at the student's disposal, he or she might become discouraged and seek out other reference materials. Because of this, the set may be better suited for a small school library over a large public library where books are often off their shelves. However, a public library will probably be in a better position to purchase the set than a small school library because the books are rather pricey.

Often in reviewing reference and research sources such as this, it is the bona fide mission of the reviewer to find that which is missing or not sufficiently detailed. However, this reviewer opted not to spend the many hours and effort to find and therefore criticize the work for the lack thereof, but to thoroughly enjoy all that is there (which is staggering). *Ancient Greece and Rome* is highly recommended to all who can afford it, and it is suggested that the rest save up to get it. This 4-volume set is guaranteed to get a good workout wherever it is. [R: BL, 1 Oct 98, p. 354; SLJ, Nov 98, p. 156; VOYA, Dec 98, pp. 387-388]—**Joan Garner**

248. **Renaissance.** Bethel, Conn., Grolier Educational, 2002. 10v. illus. maps. index. $345.00/set. ISBN 0-7172-5673-1.

Each of the 10 slim volumes in this young adult encyclopedic set that "tells the story of the Renaissance" is a delight to browse and read. Every page has lovely color reproductions of major art and architecture of the period. The narrative is engaging, accurate, and well written. The alphabetic entries in each volume run from 2-5 pages, with text insets drawing attention to key points. The initial paragraph of each entry is an easy-to-understand, bolded summary of the topic. Intriguing sidebars enhance understanding; for example, an illustrated sidebar on Leonardo da Vinci's notebooks explains that they are written back to front and are difficult to read because he was left-handed and wanted to avoid smudging the ink. A *see also* box for each entry makes cross-referencing easy.

Limited to 80 pages, each volume shares the same brief introduction, timeline, glossary, further reading list (with Websites), and set index, plus roughly 20 unique entries. The entries cover broad topics centering on Europe, such as "Artists Workshops, City-States, Inquisition, Fortifications, and Merchants." There are entries for major artists, authors, scholars, politicians, and movements of the period. Appropriately in this global age, there are also entries on Africa, China, India, and the Americas, including the interactions between them.

This set brings history alive for both young and old. While directed to a middle school audience (grades 5-10), it will bring knowledge and pleasure to all readers and is recommended for general libraries as well as school libraries.—**Georgia Briscoe**

Handbooks and Yearbooks

249. **The History of Europe.** John Stevenson, ed. New York, Facts on File, 2002. 512p. illus. maps. index. (Facts on File Library of World History). $75.00. ISBN 0-8160-5152-6.

In one volume, general editor John Stevenson has provided a good, beautifully illustrated history of Europe from the dawn of the Greeks until 2001 and the adoption of the euro as a common currency for most of Europe. The book focuses primarily on the rise of empires, from the Greeks and Romans, the Byzantines, the Carolingians, all the way up until the Soviet empire and its downfall and beyond. The pivotal role of Christianity and the Church to the development of Europe is also emphasized. The resource devotes a substantial amount of space to Europe in the modern era, and does an excellent job of concisely explaining eras such as World War I, World War II, the Cold War, and post-Soviet Europe. It is written at a level appropriate for casual users, many of whom are too young to remember the events of the Cold War and end of the Soviet empire in the late 1980s. One drawback of the book is its focus on major empires; it ignores the less-well-known, but still important, history of pre-Roman European civilization. More information about minority issues and the roles of women in forming the Europe of today would also be appropriate.

As far as organization, the book does very well. There are color-coded tabs for historical eras as well as the different empires and civilizations. The book is beautifully illustrated with a lot of full-color photographs, and there is a timeline provided at the beginning of each section to help the reader put events into chronological perspective. In the appendixes are located lists of important developments in arts and culture, science and technology, and short biographies of key figures. A thorough index is also provided. This survey of European history is recommended for public and school libraries, but its lack of depth probably rules it out for most academic libraries. —**Mark T. Bay**

250.   **Renaissance & Reformation Almanac.** Peggy Saari and Aaron Saari, eds. Farmington Hills, Mich., U*X*L/Gale, 2002. 2v. illus. index. $99.00/2-vol. set; $225.00/5-vol. Set. ISBN 0-7876-5467-1.

251.   **Renaissance & Reformation Biographies.** Peggy Saari and Aaron Saari, eds. Farmington Hills, Mich., U*X*L/Gale, 2002. 2v. illus. index. $99.00/2-vol. set; $225.00/5-vol. set. ISBN 0-7876-5470-1.

252.   **Renaissance & Reformation Primary Sources.** Peggy Saari and Aaron Saari, eds. Farmington Hills, Mich., U*X*L/Gale, 2002. 201p. illus. index. $55.00; $225.00/5-vol. set. ISBN 0-7876-5473-6.

The issue of providing students with a good textbook written at their level challenges teachers as they prepare their lesson plans. Peggy and Aaron Saari have offered one solution to this dilemma. In their *Renaissance & Reformation* set, students have a useful introduction to this period.

The *Almanac* serves students in several ways. It provides coverage of both the Christian and Muslim worlds. All endeavors, viewpoints, and social aspects receive attention here. The timeline grounds the reader in some medieval context for the events and people described in the work. Difficult terms are defined up front. Assignment suggestions and "Further Readings" lists are offered to users. The topical rather than chronological approach will make historical discussions easier for students to understand. There are concerns here, however. Although the forces leading up to the Renaissance and Reformation are discussed in detail here, some of the literary giants (e.g., Dante, Boccaccio, Petrarch) do not get the attention they deserve. The use of Websites in the "Further Readings" section limits the volume's usefulness. Finally, this part of the set would have benefited from further editing as there are some factual errors in the text. For instance, Khayr al-Din was the Ottoman Empire's naval commander not the Ottoman leader; Suleyman the Magnificent held that role.

For the *Biographies* volumes the editors selected people from a wide range of disciplines. Their insight into their accomplishments, lives, and the forces that shaped them is commendable. The editors put certain difficult terms and their definitions in the front of the work. As with the other volumes in the bigger five-volume set, there are "Further Readings" sections available for users. These volumes do have three issues. First, the timeline in the front does not go back far enough. (One does not start discussing the Renaissance in 1377.) Because of this oversight, the user might miss the accounts of those who laid the foundations for these movements. Secondly, the other two works in the larger set mention important non-Western figures, which were omitted here. Finally, the use of Websites in the listing limits the set's shelf life.

The *Primary Sources* volume has several strengths. For example, the focus covers both Christian and Islamic topics. The source materials cover literary, philosophical, religious, and intellectual subjects. Women receive attention here as well. In addition, the editors have annotated the texts well with difficult words and their definitions set off in the margins.

This work has several benefits for the general user if one recognizes the shortcomings cited above. The work is recommended for junior high, high school, and public libraries.—**David J. Duncan**

253.   Singman, Jeffrey L. **Daily Life in Medieval Europe.** Westport, Conn., Greenwood Press, 1999. 268p. illus. index. (The Greenwood Press "Daily Life Through History" Series). $45.00. ISBN 0-313-30273-1.

The subtitle of this work might well read "Northwestern Europe in the High Middle Ages, 1100-1300," for such is its scope. Because the so-called Middle Ages extended over such a long time, Singman concentrates on the period when feudal and manorial systems predominated. He

selects specific examples of medieval institutions, each of which embodies the character of the period: Cuxham, a small English village; Dover Castle in England; the monastery of Cluny in France; and Paris as an exemplar of the town. The result is an intriguing view of life and thought in medieval society and the world of that time. This social history approach delves into practical aspects of everyday life; for example, the structure of medieval society; the life cycle; and material culture with practical discussions on food, sanitation and personal hygiene, and sleeping accommodations, among others. Although Singman's research incorporates important sources, the text of this introductory study is both lively and enlightening and not weighed down with footnotes. This is not a scholarly work, but one that will hold the fascination of the ordinary reader interested in the living history of another time and place. A selected bibliography of English-language materials is appended, along with a brief glossary and appendixes on games, recipes, and music. This book and others in the series are recommended for public, high school, and college libraries.
—**Bernice Bergup**

254. **The Usborne Internet-Linked Encyclopedia of the Roman World.** By Fiona Chandler, Sam Taplin, and Jane Bingham. Tulsa, Okla., EDC Publishing, 2001. 128p. illus. maps. index. $19.95. ISBN 0-7945-0117-6.

This book combines the storytelling of a history textbook and an encyclopedia's quick access to facts. The introduction explains to the young reader the types of sources of data about the Roman world, such as the traditional study of ancient texts and modern pollen analysis. Then readers can begin their journey at the founding of Rome, continue through the fall of the Western Empire in 476 C.E. and the endurance of the Byzantine Empire, as well as learn the many ways in which Roman culture exists today. A glossary; short biographies; a timeline; a table of the emperors; and short articles on the legal and monetary systems, mythology, and other topics complete the final quarter of the book. Every page is richly illustrated by photographs of artifacts or colorful line drawings, such as a cut-away plan of a Roman bath. The publisher's Website offers links to educational Internet sites for every page of text; the links include the highly respected Perseus Digital Library and Kentucky Educational Television's Distance Learning Website. The economical text nevertheless is surprisingly comprehensive, and students can learn about the daily life of citizens and noncitizens, the wealthy and the poor, and women as well as men. The authors are experienced writers of children's reference books; their tone is light, and even the appendixes are fun to read. Libraries needing a textbook for elementary readers may also want to purchase *Find Out About the Roman Empire: What Life Was Like in the Ancient World* by Phillip Steele (Southwater, 2000). This work is recommended for middle school libraries and public libraries' young adult collections.—**Nancy L. Van Atta**

French

255. Butt, John J. **Daily Life in the Age of Charlemagne.** Westport, Conn., Greenwood Press, 2002. 210p. illus. index. (The Greenwood Press "Daily Life Through History" Series). $44.95. ISBN 0-313-31668-6.

Scholars generally agree that the influence of Charlemagne (742-814 C.E.) had as large an impact on history as any other individual of all time, and that his activities preserved the culture of ancient Rome and, perhaps, even the Christian religion. A description of Charlemagne's court, his government, military actions, and his home and social life provides a setting for the book's larger examination of the civilization of his time. Everyday life in the military, the church, and the monasteries is described, as well as that of the common peoples' housing, food, clothing, customs, sports and games, and the ever-present hardships inherent in the times. An introduction gives a brief history of the Franks and places them in relation to contemporary civilizations elsewhere. It also discusses sources of information, primary and secondary, as well as archaeological evidence. The final chapters summarize and evaluate the so-called Carolingian Renaissance and the lasting effects of Charlemagne's legacy. Additional reference value is provided by a chronology of events from 732 to 911 C.E., a Carolingian genealogy chart, maps of the Frankish Kingdom in 800 and the Empire in 814, a glossary of terms relative to the time, a bibliography of print and electronic sources, and an index of names and subjects. Illustrations include facsimiles of manuscript pages showing weapons, tools, and agricultural activities; diagrams of palace and monastic complexes; and photographs of surviving works of architecture. The author is a professor of history at James Madison University and a recognized authority of Carolingian, British, naval, and agricultural history. This work is highly recommended for all subject collections.—**Shirley L. Hopkinson**

Greek

256.   Adkins, Lesley, and Roy A. Adkins. **Handbook to Life in Ancient Greece.** New York, Facts on File, 1997. 472p. illus. maps. index. $45.00. ISBN 0-8160-3111-8.

The authors of this work, both professional classical archaeologists associated with the Museum of London, have written more than 80 pieces on various aspects of ancient civilization, including *Handbook to Life in Ancient Rome* (see ARBA 95, entry 586) and *Dictionary of Roman Religion* (Facts on File, 1996). Their latest offering continues in this tradition of providing readable information about Greco-Roman culture in an accessible format.

The book is organized thematically, with sections on "City-States and Empires," "Rulers and Leaders," "Military Affairs," "Geography," "Economy and Trade," "Towns and Countryside," "Written Evidence," "Mythology and Religion," "Science and Art," and "Everyday Life." The volume features many illustrations, most of which are quite useful; this is a good place to find, for instance, a chart of various pottery shapes. There is also a 32-page, closely printed alphabetic index for easy reference, although users should be careful to take into account spelling variants (e.g., one finds under *khoe* a specific sort of liquid libation, but under *Choes* the name of the holiday on which such libations were made). The bibliography runs to 12 pages, and appears to be fairly up-to-date. The glory of ancient Greece cannot be encapsulated in a single volume by even the best informed and pithiest of scholars, and naturally various details have been omitted. This reviewer was particularly sorry not to find an entry for *kottabos*, the drinking game in which wine dregs were flung at targets from empty cups. All in all, however, the concentration on the daily life of nonelites is useful.

The Adkins's book, nonetheless, has some serious conceptual blindspots; it is shocking that they include only a single page of information about women, and only one-half page about homosexuality, both as subsections under "The Family." We live in the 1990s, not the 1890s, but users would never know it reading the Victorian truisms on gender and sexuality included here. But it is not a trendy book, of course, so perhaps it should not be faulted for being what it is—a solid though not exhaustive guide to ancient Greek life. [R: RBB, Aug 97, p. 1926]—**Christopher Michael McDonough**

257.   Garland, Robert. **Daily Life of the Ancient Greeks.** Westport, Conn., Greenwood Press, 1998. 234p. illus. maps. index. (The Greenwood Press "Daily Life Through History" Series). $45.00. ISBN 0-313-30383-5.

Garland's *Daily Life of the Ancient Greeks* is the newest offering from Greenwood Press's "Daily Life Through History" Series, which also includes titles on Mesopotamia (see entry 244), the Incas, the Mayas, England in various periods (see entry 259), and present-day United States. Of the numerous handbooks to the study of classical Greek civilization now available, this is among the best. It will probably be of most use to middle and high school students. Following a brief historical outline, the book treats these areas: space and time, language (including alphabet and literacy), the people, private life, the public sphere, pleasure and leisure, and the impact of Ancient Greece and modern culture. Garland summarizes usefully what is known about a wide variety of issues in classical antiquity, refraining from the arch tone of older handbooks that only dealt with the lives of the aristocracy. Here one can find out about the daily doings of women, slaves, and children in addition to the generals and politicians. It is also interesting to note in the final discussion dealing with classical impact not only the usual discussion of etymology and democracy but also a half-page summary of the "Black Athena" debate.

Overgeneralization and omission are of course problems in the making of handbooks, and this is no exception; the section on sexual mores, for example, is far too abbreviated. Furthermore, the maps, because they are line-drawn, are not terribly helpful. It is difficult to figure out what is land and what is water. The quality of illustration is otherwise fairly good; the reproduction of a drawing of a monster from the lead curse tablet (p. 129) is striking and informative. But, as with so many handbooks of this variety, the pictures are far too few. Finally, the further reading section includes suggested translations, anthologies, reference works, novels, magazines, videos, and CD-ROMs. It is worth noting that, although several sophisticated scholarly books have been included, there are unfortunately no articles listed in the bibliography. However, with these problems noted, *Daily Life of the Ancient Greeks* is still a well-designed and useful resource. [R: BL, 1 Nov 98, p. 532]—**Christopher Michael McDonough**

258.   **The Penguin Historical Atlas of Ancient Greece.** By Robert Morkot. New York, Penguin Books, 1996. 144p. illus. maps. index. $16.95pa. ISBN 0-14-051335-3.

Before the beginning of the Christian era, Greece was a great intellectual and artistic center. In this book, a timeline from 7000 B.C.E. to 30 B.C.E. displays various elements of ancient Greek civilization, including Greece's interaction with the Near East and North Africa, Europe and the Mediterranean, and its culture and technology. Five parts cover Crete and the Heroic Age, the Dark Ages to Athenian ascendancy, the meteoric rise of Persia on the political scene, the flowering of classical culture and the Peloponnesian War, and Alexander the Great. Each part begins with a brief statement and quotation to set the tone of the material to follow. Overviews of ancient Greek society cover a broad sweep of peoples through an examination of artifacts, architecture, myths and legends, clothing and personal objects, historical events (frequently military campaigns), and political changes. The typeface has delicate serifs and is not an easy read.

The use of minitimelines within articles helps the reader keep a perspective on the changing political climate of the area. Sixty maps, printed in clear, sharp colors with adequate keys, abound. The reproductions of artwork, photographs, and timelines are crisp and well registered with surrounding text. Artwork, photography, and text are smoothly interwoven and allow the reader to move from event to event, gaining a sense of time and place. A current bibliography supplements the text, and an index aids access. Secondary school libraries or small public libraries that need an overview of individuals, events, and other miscellaneous aspects of ancient Greece may consider purchase of this volume.—**Judy Gay Matthews**

United Kingdom

259.   Olsen, Kirstin. **Daily Life in 18th-Century England.** Westport, Conn., Greenwood Press, 1999. 395p. illus. index. (The Greenwood Press "Daily Life Through History" Series). $45.00. ISBN 0-313-29933-1.

This volume is a narrative with 19 chapters on aspects of daily life in eighteenth-century England, including such topics as food, religion, politics, entertainment, and behavior. Each chapter (with the single exception of the food and drink chapter, which contains recipes) ends with a short chronology of important events. The volume also includes more than 40 pages of source notes, a short glossary of terms, a bibliography of more than 75 primary and secondary sources for further reading, an extensive subject index (nearly 40 pages), approximately 50 reproductions of contemporary engravings, and several tables (e.g., cost of living, income by profession). Olsen is the author of several books, including *Chronology of Women's History* (Greenwood, 1994).

Although some excellent specialized studies are available, very few general studies of social life and customs in eighteenth-century England have been published in the past 75 years. None of them have the scope and detail of the present volume, which can be read through with pleasure or (due to its arrangement and extensive index) used for reference purposes. There are a few relatively unimportant errors and infelicities of style, but *Daily Life in 18th-Century England* is recommended for circulating collections of public and academic libraries and for reference collections of libraries that support English or European history curricula.—**Jonathan F. Husband**

WORLD HISTORY

Atlases

260.   Farrington, Karen. **Historical Atlas of Empires.** New York, Checkmark Books/Facts on File, 2002. 192p. illus. maps. index. $35.00. ISBN 0-8160-4788-X.

This atlas is visually appealing. Each empire is described using crisp, clear maps, large color reproductions depicting art or architecture, and a concise timeline. Accompanying text is interspersed with the images to broadly discuss each empire, usually in the span of four pages. The author also provides an introduction and conclusion that nicely defines what she means by the word "empire." The introduction also briefly accounts the author's primary objective, to "chart the structure of empires from a geographical and historical perspective" (p. 9).

Overall, the text is good. Generally, political events and major figures receive primary coverage, although cultural aspects are not neglected. Some entries do a fine job of revealing areas of historic debate, while other issues are glossed over. Unfortunately, no bibliographies are included. The index is adequate.

Finally, in a slim work a major concern revolves around what empires are included. The author's selection is interesting—sometimes a lesser-known empire is discussed, such as the Toltecs in place of the Aztecs. Some major empires are not included, such as the Dutch and the Mughals. Yet some other lesser-known empires are pleasantly included, such as Khazaria, Kalmar, and Axum. The only major fault in selection may be the lack of any major sub-Saharan empire, in particular Great Zimbabwe. This work is recommended for public and school libraries.—**Allen Reichert**

261.   Farrington, Karen. **Historical Atlas of Expeditions.** New York, Checkmark Books/Facts on File, 2000. 189p. illus. maps. index. $35.00. ISBN 0-8160-4432-5.

From antiquity to the present, man has gone exploring for trade, wealth, power, and religious conversion—but above all, out of curiosity. In this reference, biographical essays tell the story of global discovery. It is amply illustrated with photographs, drawings, and timelines but there is limited use of maps. The author begins with early voyages throughout the Ancient world and moves on to explorations before 1600. This account includes interesting individuals, such as Ibn Battuta who traveled all over the medieval Arab world and Willem Barents who was the first European to survive an Arctic winter. The book continues with individual sections for explorations to each continent after 1600. These chapters expand the reader's awareness beyond the usually discussed explorers.

Students are introduced to new names, such as Nain Singh who mapped Tibet for the British in the 1860s while posing as a Buddhist monk; Mary Kingsley who collected zoological specimens during the 1890s in present-day Nigeria, Cameroon, and Gabon; and Fridtjof Nansen who used ice pack drift to travel the Arctic from 1893 to 1895. The narrative also points out changing motivations for exploration. By the end of the twentieth century the world's geography was generally known and explorers turned their attention to wildlife preservation and archaeology. Also interesting is the changing use of technology. Although the men and women profiled are predominately of European origin, the abundance of less well-known figures, from the West as well as the East, is a key strength of this well-written chronology of humans' quest for knowledge about the world and its diversity. [R: LJ, 1 Nov 2000, p. 70]—**Adrienne Antink Bien**

262.   **Hammond Atlas of the 20th Century.** Maplewood, N.J., Hammond, 1996. 239p. illus. maps. index. $39.95. ISBN 0-8437-1148-5.

Hammond, well known for its atlases, has packed a great deal of information into this large-format world atlas dealing with the major events of the twentieth century. The book is divided into five chronological sections: "The End of the Old World Order," "The World Between the Wars," "The World at War," "The Cold War World," and "Towards a New World Order." Not surprisingly, well more than half the book is devoted to wars and the events surrounding them. The sixth section treats world themes, reflecting the globalization of life in the twentieth century, such as migration, epidemics, technology, and the environment.

Each event or theme is allotted a two-page spread that includes a general essay, two to four maps of the regions covered, charts of statistical data, and color and black-and-white illustrations. All illustrations are accompanied by lengthy and informative captions. The more than 250 maps are well drafted and color-coded; map keys and captions add many details to supplement the text.

Richard Overy, the general editor of the atlas, is professor of history at King's College in London. Essays are not signed, but the 12 contributors and their credentials are listed in the front matter. All are British, and British spelling has been used throughout the text. A chronology; a glossary of key people, events, and treaties; a bibliography; and an index add to the book's usefulness. The *Hammond Atlas of the 20th Century* is a browser's delight; its length and scope necessarily limit its use as an in-depth reference source but make it an excellent starting point for further reading and research. Thus it is most suited for home, high school, and public libraries. The atlas' solid construction and heavy paper should stand up to heavy use.—**Lori D. Kranz**

263.   Konstam, Angus. **Historical Atlas of Exploration 1492-1600.** New York, Checkmark Books/Facts on File, 2000. 191p. illus. maps. index. $35.00. ISBN 0-8160-4248-9.

For 20 years, Facts on File has produced cultural and historical atlases combining the best of maps and illustrations with historical accounts. Konstam's *Historical Atlas of Exploration 1492-1600* carries on this tradition in splendid fashion.

This work has many strengths. Konstam's historical account includes every nation of the period, its respective interests, and the issues surrounding its colonizing efforts. The important figures' biographical sketches give perspective to their actions. Important factors such as ocean currents, the ships, the navigational instruments, and techniques enlighten the reader to the environment in which these events occurred. The work's balanced analysis of European, Asian,

African, and Native American cultures is commendable. The timetables at the bottom of each section's first page assist the reader in tracking these events' development throughout the period. The author also blends his maps between contemporary and modern versions. The cultural and archaeological depictions add yet another dimension to the work's account. The index and alphabetical list of explorers are a nice addition.

However, the work has two weaknesses. First, Konstam should have included a gazetteer with his index. Second, a section of further reading materials should be here as well. Despite these issues, the *Historical Atlas of Exploration* should be included with the other Facts on File atlases. Like its counterparts, it provides an apt introduction to its chosen subject field for years to come. This work belongs in public, high school, junior college, college, and university libraries. [R: SLJ, Nov 2000, p. 92]—**David J. Duncan**

264.   Konstam, Angus. **Historical Atlas of the Crusades.** New York, Facts on File, 2002. 192p. illus. maps. index. $175.00. ISBN 0-8160-4919-X.

In the *Historical Atlas of the Crusades*, historian, archaeologist, and museum professional Angus Konstam provides a comprehensive, engaging look at the events and historical impact of the Crusades of Western Europe against the Eastern Mediterranean area during the Middle Ages. While most Americans have at least heard of the Crusades in school, this book gives the reader a far more complete view of their historical significance from both sides of the conflicts. In addition to describing personalities, battles, equipment, and tactics of all sides involved in the Crusades, Konstam examines some of the social and economic motivations for crusading, as well as the religious conflicts between the Roman and Byzantine Christian churches, and between the Islamic centers of Baghdad and Cairo, that influenced the Crusades and their aftermath. Konstam also examines the prejudices and beliefs of both sides of the Crusades and writes about how the Crusades led to the opening of the medieval mind and to the flowering of awareness of the outside world, which led to the Renaissance and had profound effects on our modern world.

The text is well written, in a style that undergraduates, secondary students, and most public library patrons should be able to read and understand. The book is beautifully illustrated with photographs, reproductions of illustrations, and well-rendered maps, which enhance the ability of the text to explain the Crusades. Also included are a glossary of useful terms, a chronology of the Crusades, and family trees of several of the most important dynasties involved. The book is well organized, and the index helps readers locate needed information quickly. The high quality of the *Historical Atlas of the Crusades*, coupled with its relatively low price, make it a useful addition to academic, high school, and public libraries.—**Mark T. Bay**

265.   Konstam, Angus. **Historical Atlas of the Viking World.** New York, Checkmark Books/Facts on File, 2002. 192p. illus. maps. index. $35.00. ISBN 0-8160-5068-6.

Angus Konstam, a museum professional with degrees in history and archaeology, has written a fine, brief introduction to the Viking Age—roughly the three centuries from 800 B.C.E. to 1100 C.E. In 10 concise chapters, Konstam ably surveys Viking exploration, commerce, and settlements as well as Viking families and society, warriors, ships, religion, art, and literature. A one-page appendix lists Viking and Anglo-Saxon kings. Numerous color illustrations and maps enhance a lively, unfootnoted text appropriate for high school students, college undergraduates, and public library patrons.

Like other recent authors on this subject, Konstam incorporates new archaeological evidence into his work in order to revise previous interpretations of Viking activities. Readers intrigued by this volume may wish to examine John Haywood's *Encyclopedia of the Viking Age* (see ARBA 2001, entry 311) and *The Penguin Historical Atlas of the Vikings* (1995). Other important scholarly approaches include the *Oxford Illustrated History of the Vikings* edited by Peter Sawyer

(Oxford University Press, 1999), Colleen E. Batey and James Graham-Campbell's *Cultural Atlas of the Viking World* (see ARBA 95, entry 563), and Else Roesdahl's *The Vikings* (1991). Older but still essential is Gwyn Jones's *A History of the Vikings* (2d ed.; 1984). Eric Christiansen's *The Norsemen in the Viking Age* (Blackwell, 2002) yields in-depth guidance on research methods and sources. Among the many Viking-related Websites, two stand out: *The Vikings* at www.pbs.org/wgbh/nova/vikings/and *Vikings: The North Atlantic Saga*, a Smithsonian Institution exhibit at www.mnh.si.edu/vikings/. [R: SLJ, April 03, p. 98]—**Julienne L. Wood**

Biography

266. Berson, Robin Kadison. **Young Heroes in World History.** Westport, Conn., Greenwood Press, 1999. 269p. illus. index. $45.00. ISBN 0-313-30257-X.

This book of historical narratives chronicles the lives of 17 young heroes, both male and female, whose ages ranged from 12 to 23 at the time of their heroic actions. The heroes profiled were selected from a wide range of cultures and countries and lived during the past 250 years. The biographical entries place the deeds in their historical perspective by giving detailed background information about the times and events leading up to the actions. Each entry includes a bibliography for further reading. Black-and-white photographs of either the hero or an artist's rendition of the hero accompany each section. The appendix categorizes each of the young heroes by gender, century, nationality, and ethnicity within the United States. The book also includes an index. Berson, a former history teacher and the director of the Upper School Library of Riverdale County School in New York City, states that one purpose of these historical narratives is the development of empathy, the root of compassion and compassionate behavior. Although the writing is somewhat uneven, with some entries sounding like a novel and some reading more like a textbook, each person's story is compelling and worthy of being told.—**Janet Hilbun**

Chronology

267. **Children's History of the 20th Century.** New York, DK Publishing, 1999. 344p. illus. index. $29.95. ISBN 0-7894-4722-3.

This compilation of historical twentieth-century information is designed specifically with children and young adults in mind. The short, news-like articles, which are accompanied by brilliant photographs, will appeal to children ages 8 through 14. The book begins with an overview of the century, which features quotes from children with their thoughts on such topics as war, the environment, and the future. Following this introduction, each year in the twentieth century is featured on one page. The book highlights political, technological, and pop cultural hits of that year. The book is arranged in typical DK Publishing style—the layout is not uniform but instead has entries arranged sporadically throughout the text, with different font sizes and both illustrations and photographs. At the bottom of each page is a timeline that highlights news makers from each month. Throughout each decade there are pages discussing important features of the decade, such as the Depression in the 1930s, women at war in the 1940s, the feminist fight of the 1970s, and the end of the Cold War in the 1990s. A section titled "Life in the 21st Century" focuses on the new millennium and how human life will change as a result of new technologies such as Internet shopping, videophones, and high-tech homes. The last section of the work chronologically lists people who are famous in the areas of entertainment, science, sports, politics, and music, as well as famous criminals. An index concludes the work.

Children will enjoy browsing through this book so filled with interesting historical facts. School libraries and public libraries will do well to add this to their collections.—**Shannon Graff Hysell**

268. **Chronicle of the World.** rev. ed. Derrik Mercer and others, eds. New York, DK Publishing, 1996. 1175p. illus. maps. index. $59.95. ISBN 0-7894-0334-X.

The curious idea of telling the story of humankind through newspaper-type reporting is the concept behind a new book published by DK Publishing and touted on its cover as "the ultimate record of world history." An ultimate record it is not, but the book is in its own way intriguing. It opens with a timeline, mapping the milestones of human history from 3.5 million years B.C.E. to 1995 C.E. The chronicle that follows, which covers the same span of time, is a sequence of stories written as though being told by journalists reporting on the event at the time. Consequently, no information (or reference to information) that comes after the date of the event being discussed is contained in the articles.

Each two-page spread begins with a sidebar chronologically listing the highlights (e.g., births, deaths, declarations of war, treaties, inventions) of the period covered on those pages. In the first part of the book, these spreads may cover hundreds of thousands of years, but by the book's end, the average coverage is two years per spread. A number of well-illustrated articles (i.e., line drawings and photographs—many of them in color) follow. This, along with the bold attention-grabbing headlines and clipped journalistic style of writing, makes for lively reading. However, as a reference tool, this work has serious limitations.

A single volume—even of this size and heft—cannot hope to encompass the entire course of world history in any depth. Therefore, coverage is not thorough, nor is it balanced. This is evidenced in the book's index, which includes a page and a half of listings for the United States, more than 20 listings for Armenia, yet not a single entry for Ukraine. The index is itself inadequate for researchers and serious information-seekers. There is no listing for "Holocaust," although some information on this topic can be found under "Jews," "Auschwitz," and the like. Likewise, the term *kristallnacht* is listed only as a sublisting under "Jews" and is not cross-referenced.

Casual readers and history buffs will no doubt enjoy this work with its unique approach and handsome graphics. For reasons cited above, the book is worth considering as an addition to any library collection. It is heartily recommended as a resource for the history section, but only with hesitation for the reference shelf.—**Barbara Ittner**

269. **Chronicle of the Year 1995.** New York, DK Publishing, 1996. 120p. illus. index. $16.95. ISBN 0-7894-0374-9.

This inexpensive, well-illustrated summary of the year's events will remind some readers of the "Year in Review" issues of *Time* or *Newsweek*. The annual review has a chronological arrangement, with each week's stories occupying two facing pages. More significant stories merit photographs with their short narrative, while a sidebar briefly mentions smaller news events. The stories balance a variety of interests: politics, international affairs, science, sports, and entertainment. A few topics, such as the O. J. Simpson trial and the war in Bosnia, receive special treatment. The book has an index and carries *see also* references in the text for continuing stories. It is important to use them both, because stories such as the nomination and eventual defeat of Henry Foster as surgeon general are linked only in the index.

The contemporary report of the annual gives it a sense of immediacy, but there is little here of research value. While an attractive book, it is more likely to be used for browsing than for reference. One clear advantage it holds over other news digests is the presence of high-quality photographs of people and events. The chronicle could be enhanced with a simplified world atlas and a brief analysis of the top stories of the year. The favorable price and breezy presentation should appeal to high school and public libraries seeking to build their chronology collections. [R: RBB, 15 Mar 96, p. 1312; SLJ, May 96, p. 151]—**John P. Schmitt**

270.   **Great Events: 1900-2001.** rev. ed. Hackensack, N.J., Salem Press, 2002. 8v. illus. maps. index. $475.00/set. ISBN 1-58765-053-3.

Great Events combines and updates two earlier reference works from Salem Press: *Twentieth Century: Great Events* (1992) and *Twentieth Century: Great Scientific Achievements* (1994). Nearly all of the entries from these previous works are included, while 283 new entries have been added. More than 200 of these new entries concern events from the mid-1990s up to the September 11th terrorist attack on the United States. All entries share the same format and are at least 1,000 words long. The title is followed by a brief summary, and basic facts are highlighted in a box. After the event is described in detail a concluding section discusses consequences. Most entries are signed, but unfortunately no bibliographies are included. A single black-and-white image or map may be included with an entry. The maps are generally more useful than the pictures. Salem provides five different indexes, arranged by category, timeline, geography, personages, and a general subject index.

This work most strongly covers political and scientific events. Overall, *Great Events* includes a fairly even distribution of global events, although U.S. events slightly predominate. Article quality varies, particularly in the discussion of consequences, but most give a solid account. Indexing quality also varies. The geographical index is very useful, with thorough *see also* references. However, the general subject index could be more robust. For example, while the Salt March and satyagraha are mentioned extensively in the entry concerning Mohandas Gandhi, neither makes the index. Finally, the desire for currency did lead to the inclusion of some events that do not have the magnitude of earlier events, such as the Bridgestone apology or Pets.com. Overall, this set is good and can be recommended for middle school and high school libraries. [R: SLJ, Nov 02, p. 100]—**Allen Reichert**

271.   **Great Misadventures: Bad Ideas That Led to Big Disasters.** By Peggy Saari. Betz Des Chenes, ed. Detroit, U*X*L/Gale, 1998. 4v. illus. maps. index. $99.00/set. ISBN 0-7876-2798-4.

Great Misadventures brings to light examples of human error, greed, incompetence, and poor judgment from ancient to modern times, showing that the qualities that can lead to success can also cause failure and that human beings are inspired by self-interest as often as they are motivated by selflessness. Each entry (generally ranging from five to nine pages in length) offers historical background and a clear description of the event, with a discussion about why the misadventure is significant.

The essays are arranged chronologically within 4 subject volumes: "Exploration and Adventure," "Science and Technology," "Military," and "Society." The table of contents and timeline that open each volume are identical, encouraging an understanding of the relationships among the various events. Cross-references direct users to related entries throughout the set, and sources for further reference at the end of each entry offer direction to more information on each topic. The text is supported by illustrations and photographs, maps, and call-out boxes that highlight related persons or facts to enhance understanding; terms that may be unfamiliar to the target audience are explained within the essays. Each volume closes with a comprehensive index to all four volumes.

Suitable for readers in grades five and up, this unique set will find a wide audience of fascinated readers. No similar publication is known for this audience.—**Vandelia L. VanMeter**

272.   **Junior Chronicle of the 20th Century.** New York, DK Publishing, 1997. 336p. illus. maps. index. $39.95. ISBN 0-7894-2033-3.

Each two-page spread in this colorfully illustrated chronology features events of one year of the century on topics as varied as politics, natural disasters, cultural happenings, war, sports, science, and invention. Each concise account is clearly written for the understanding of the intended audience—intermediate and middle school students. At the bottom of each page is a month-by-month highlight of world events. "Special Feature" spreads cover such topics as the Russian Revolution, the Great Depression, the rock 'n' roll years, and the space race. The work concludes with chronological spreads on Hollywood superstars, scientists and inventors, sports stars, world leaders, music makers, and lawbreakers. A thorough index provides access to people, places, and events.

Complementary works suitable for this age group include David Rubel's *Scholastic Timelines: The United States in the 20th Century* (Scholastic, 1995); *Junior Time Lines on File* by Valerie Tomaselli-Moschovitis (see ARBA 98, entry 499), which covers the range of world history; and the Day by Day series (e.g., *Day by Day: The Eighties* [see ARBA 96, entry 503]) from Facts on File, which thoroughly treats each decade since the 1940s. From the browsing history buff, who will read all the way through, to the student seeking ideas for a report topic, young readers will find this sturdily bound and attractive book a welcome addition to any library.—**Vandelia L. VanMeter**

273.   **Millennium Year by Year.** 2000 ed. New York, DK Publishing, 2000. 896p. illus. maps. index. $29.95. ISBN 0-7894-6539-6.

An entertaining blend of historical fact and editorial journalistic narrative, this volume should help many high school students better understand the cultural highlights and achievements of civilizations around the world—past and present. The basic arrangement is chronological by year (or clusters of years) and the format is that of a basic tabloid newspaper, with approximately 10 major stories per year. Most of the stories average 150 to 200 words, and at least one-half are accompanied by color or black-and-white illustrations. Also included is a sidebar that highlights other major events of the year. Each article has a dateline and location of the story. A full index complements the volume, while a brief five-page chronology chart of the entire millennium prefaces the work. No introduction or criteria for inclusion are to be found anywhere.

For the individual who simply wants an overview of a decade or other extended period, this volume will serve as a good general introduction. However, the interrelationships of historical events and achievements are not to be found between the pages of this work. It is a selected chronology of events, enhanced by a bit of prose and illustration. As such, the armchair historian, trivia buff, and others will find the work of some interest and curiosity. Easily readable, this volume could certainly be used effectively within the contexts of school curricula in the area of world civilization. It is recommended for its readability and illustrations.—**Edmund F. SantaVicca**

274.   Teeple, John B. **Timelines of World History.** New York, DK Publishing, 2002. 666p. illus. maps. $40.00. ISBN 0-7894-8926-0.

This reference shows at a glance what has happened in history across the globe, from 10,000 B.C.E. to September 11, 2001. Users see leaders take the stage, wars start and end, and ideas and technologies emerge and be replaced. Segmented by Asia, Africa, Europe, and the Americas/Australasia, full attention is given to all parts of the world and time periods. Each era is introduced with a narrative essay highlighting the major trends and influences and illustrated with photographs and fold-out maps. The sidebars add depth by featuring interesting individuals who may be politicians, artists, musicians, or cultural insights ranging from the milestones of the Industrial Revolution to the French Wars of religion, the first appearance of the Kabuki theater in seventeenth-century Japan, and the Flatiron Building (the New York City landmark built in 1901 and one of the earliest skyscrapers). In looking at the year 1678, across one page users see that at the same point in time the French explorer and missionary Louis Hennepin discovered Niagara Falls, John Bunyan published Pilgrim's Progress, the French seized Dutch forts in Senegal, and haiku poetry began to appear in Japan. This volume concludes with a concordance that serves as both index and glossary by listing major events and historical figures with page references. These timelines let the reader make connections within the full context of world history to appreciate the richness of its totality. This book is a treat to browse as well as a useful research tool.—**Adrienne Antink Bien**

275.   **20th Century Day by Day.** New York, DK Publishing, 2000. 1558p. illus. index. $50.00. ISBN 0-7894-6856-5.

Probably the first inclination of most readers upon finding this book will be to look up their own birthday to learn what happened in the world on that date in history. About the time of this reader's birth, Britain and France were planning an invasion of the Suez Canal if Nassar pursued his nationalization program; Marilyn Monroe starred in the film *Bus Stop*; Estes Kefauver, rather than John F. Kennedy, was announced as Adlai Stevenson's vice-presidential running mate, while President Eisenhower and Richard Nixon were named the Republican candidates; and West Germany banned the Communist Party.

DK Publishing's reasonably priced tome (it weighs in at 10 pounds) will serve best as a book for browsing, but high school students may find it useful as a point of departure for historical research projects. The layout, as in most DK books, is attractive and well organized. Each month is presented in a half-to four-page spread. A sidebar features the month calendar style, a list of events by day, and births and deaths of famous persons. The rest of the spread consists of short, newspaper-style, dated articles about important events in politics, science and technology, sports, the arts, and other aspects of life from around the world. Numerous captioned, black-and-white and color illustrations, mostly photographic, lend support to the text. The 75-page index is thorough, providing both specific (e.g., Charles Manson, Marshall Plan, FCC) and general (e.g., Labor, Ethiopia, Literature) points of access, indicated by the numerical month and year.—**Lori D. Kranz**

Dictionaries and Encyclopedias

276.   **Ancient History: An On-Line Encyclopedia. http://www.fofweb.com/subscription.** [Website]. New York, Facts on File. Prices start at $299.00 (school libraries) and $450.00 (public libraries). Date reviewed: Feb 2002.

Facts on File's *Ancient History: An On-Line Encyclopedia* is an excellent resource for beginning and intermediate study of ancient cultures. It provides an introduction for beginning scholars and lay readers and a quick reference for more advanced scholars. The database covers the ancient cultures of Africa, Egypt, Greece, Rome, and Mesoamerica. Obviously, much of the material for Egypt can also be found under Africa. The main menu is divided into seven sections: "Introductions," "Subject Entries," "Biographies," "Historical Documents," "Gallery," "Maps and Charts," and "Timelines." The "Introductions" are overview essays of the five ancient cultures, with linked cross-references to various subject entries. More than 6,500 entries for events, places, and cultural developments can be found under "Subject Entries." Users can browse the entries first by the individual civilizations or as a whole and then by additional breakdowns, such as era, topic, civilization, and geographical area. For example, users will find entries on slavery, architecture, deities, athletics and sports, poetry, and building techniques and materials. Users can also search for specific entries by keyword or phrase (exact or relative).

The database contains more than 3,000 biographies for ancient historical figures. Like the subject entries, users can locate the biographies by browsing lists of the entrants or by similar breakdowns used for the subject entries. Biographies for explorers, government officials, religious leaders, and warriors and military leaders are included. Under "Historical Documents" users will find ethnographical and historical materials along with excerpts from poems and novels. The "Gallery" provides access to several paintings, photographs, and coins of the ancient civilizations. Unfortunately, this area is not as extensive as many users would hope. In fact, only coin reproductions are available for the Ancient Rome civilization. Additional illustrations would have been helpful. The majority of the maps contained in the database are political and can by printed via Adobe Acrobat. The charts and tables would be ideal for classroom use, but they are not printable unless users want to try to use a screen print. The timelines are organized by era or topic and they are also not printable. This database is recommended for university and college libraries that support ancient history and mythology curriculums. [R: BR, Mar/April 02, p. 81; LJ, Jan 02, p. 166]—**Cari Ringelheim**

277. **The Concise History Encyclopedia.** New York, Larousse Kingfisher Chambers, 2001. 320p. illus. index. $14.95. ISBN 0-7534-5417-3.

Like the large-format volume on which it was based—the *Kingfisher History Encyclopedia* (see ARBA 2001, entry 492)—this abridged version provides a colorful introduction to world history for upper-elementary and middle school students. The editors have chosen a chronological rather than a thematic approach, with 10 major sections spanning the emergence of the first humans to cautious predictions for the future. An especially nice feature is the "World at a Glance" introduction to each section. Using maps and blocks of text, the editors describe what was happening in North America, South America and Latin America, Europe, Africa, the Middle East, Asia, and Australasia during the time period. Within each section are about fifteen one-to two-page spreads filled with reproductions of artworks, illustrations, and photographs, along with maps, text, key dates, and a timeline that places the entries in historical context. The subjects focus on empires, wars, and civilizations, although topics such as European trade, the Industrial Revolution, and terrorism are included. A subject index completes the text. Although the binding would not stand up to heavy use, this is a beautiful, compact volume that would not only attract young people but anyone who enjoys short, colorful snippets of history. [R: BR, May/June 02, p. 71]—**Hope Yelich**

278. **Encyclopedia of North American History.** John C. Super, ed. Tarrytown, N.Y., Marshall Cavendish, 1999. 11v. illus. maps. index. $459.95/set. ISBN 0-7614-7084-0.

This multivolume encyclopedia will be accessible to at least the well educated among the seventh graders who are its target audience, although many entries are sophisticated enough to be useful to high school students and general readers. The work contains 493 alphabetically arranged entries by a broad array of scholars. Not surprisingly, it is heavily weighted toward U.S. history. Entries range from one to seven pages, all include "causes and effects" sidebars, and the longer ones feature summaries; bibliographies; and six types of sidebars dealing with turning points, daily life, laws and cases, profiles of individuals, temper of the times, and viewpoints. Each volume is indexed, but there is a comprehensive index in volume 11, which also includes biographical, geographical, and various subject indexes; a rather brief bibliography; a glossary; and a timeline. The illustrations are excellent, although it would be nice to have more maps. The selection of topics for entries at times reveals the lack of a sense of proportion (e.g., "Branch Davidian Complex Burns" and "Million Man March" are included, but the presidencies of John Adams and James Madison are not); in fact, a number of U.S. presidents fail to rate individual entries. The choice of battles and treaties is also a bit idiosyncratic. The same is true of religious topics. Although religion is dealt with under several general headings (e.g., Great Awakening, Great Puritan Migration, Separation of Church and State), there are no separate entries on major denominations. All this notwithstanding, there is much useful information in this user-friendly set, and it should help make middle school students more interested in and informed about North American history. [R: BL, 1 Sept 99, p. 179]—**William B. Robison**

279. **Encyclopedia of World History.** New York, Facts on File, 2000. 524p. illus. maps. $85.00. ISBN 0-8160-4249-7.

This reference provides alphabetic entries for key political, social, economic, philosophical, religious, artistic, and cultural events across world history. Notations range from Acropolis, an ancient Mycenaean hilltop fortress, to Emilio Zapata, the Mexican revolutionary. Equal attention is paid to both Western and non-Western nations. Expanded profiles are included for 200 countries and numerous major historical figures.

This volume is amply illustrated with photographs, maps, and drawings. As an appendix, a chronology outlines key historic, scientific, and artistic milestones by continent from 15,000 B.C.E. to the present. This allows the reader to track common themes across the globe. The chronology is followed by listings of emperors, monarchs, prime ministers, and presidents for many countries. Population, religious affiliation, and language preference statistics are also given. This volume is a useful secondary school resource to enable students to understand the facts and interfaces of world history.—**Adrienne Antink Bien**

280. **History of the Ancient & Medieval World.** Tarrytown, N.Y., Marshall Cavendish, 1996. 12v. illus. maps. index. $459.95/set. ISBN 0-7614-0351-5.

This is a beautifully illustrated 12-volume historical encyclopedia, arranged chronologically, beginning with "Origins of Humanity" and continuing through "Asia, Africa, and the Americas." In between are "Egypt and Mesopotamia," "Ancient Cultures," "The Ancient Greeks," "Greece and Rome," "The Roman Empire," "Religions of the World," "Christianity and Islam," "The Middle Ages," and "Medieval Politics and Life." Each volume contains its own index, timeline, glossary, and bibliography of further reading suggestions.

Colorful illustrations make this a rich historical resource; helpful maps, charts, and abundant photographs of locations and artifacts for each period provide fascinating information, greatly enhancing the easy-to-follow text. This reviewer's mid-size public library will put to immediate use the history covered in these volumes; each year, the local middle schools review Egypt and the Middle Ages. This set will be just what is needed for those annual assignments on Egyptian gods; religious and political beliefs; and medieval traditions, wars, and culture.

The index volume provides five valuable sections. "The Chronicles" is a listing of the ancient kingdoms, rulers, and dynasties in order, something frequently asked for in the library. "The Time Line" is an inclusive listing of the periods from all 11 volumes. "A Glossary" covers the entire set. The "Thematic Indexes" are on broad topics, such as arts and culture, religion, wars and battles, and government and politics. Finally, an "Index" to the entire set completes the volume.

History of the Ancient & Medieval World is a versatile, well-organized reference tool. It would be an asset in middle school, high school, and public library reference collections. [R: RBB, 15 Oct 97, p. 428]—**Marcia Blevins**

281. **The Holocaust: A Grolier Student Library.** Geoffrey Wigoder, ed. Danbury, Conn., Grolier, 1997. 4v. illus. maps. index. $169.00/set. ISBN 0-7172-7637-6.

In 4 volumes (511 pages), alphabetically arranged entries cover the causes, events, and results of the Holocaust. The roles of significant persons and groups, related events in many nations, and similar topics are also discussed. The volumes are vastly illustrated and include maps, timelines, sidebars, and other study aids; cross-references connect entries. Non-English-language terms are used sparingly and are fully defined. Each volume is indexed; a cumulative index appears in volume 4. Most helpful is the subject index, which will help the reader locate all of the articles that touch on a particular topic, ranging from anti-Semitism to Zionist activities. The bibliographic essay that describes related titles and indicates the grade level is a helpful collection development tool.

Suitable for students grades 7 and up, this set provides excellent support for junior high school units on World War II, genocide, racism, and related topics. Macmillan Library Reference's 1989 *Encyclopedia of the Holocaust* provides more extensive coverage in a multivolume work suitable for high school and adult readers. [R: RBB, 15 Feb 97, p. 1042]—**Vandelia L. VanMeter**

282.   **Holocaust Series.** William L. Shulman, ed. Woodbridge, Conn., Blackbirch Press, 1998. 8v. illus. maps. index. $18.95/vol. ISBN 1-56711-200-5 (v.1); 1-56711-201-3 (v.2); 1-56711-202-1 (v.3); 1-56711-204-8 (v.4); 1-56711-205-6 (v.5); 1-56711-206-4 (v.6); 1-56711-207-2 (v.7); 1-56711-208-0 (v.8).

The chronology presented in this 8-volume series on the Holocaust begins in ancient times. Volume 1 is an overview of the history of the Jewish people to August 1935 and provides an explanation of this, and other, anti-Semitic movements. The next 5 volumes cover events from 1935 to after World War II. The 7th volume is a collection of primary sources, and the 8th is a resource guide of media for further study.

Each readable 80-page volume is filled with photographs and illustrations. The text blends historical narrative and moving accounts written by survivors as each volume explores the unique aspects and events that shaped the period. Terms unfamiliar to the intended audience are explained in context. Sidebars, insets, maps, and other special features provide further explanation. Each volume has its own index, appendixes, and glossary. The sturdy binding and thoughtful layout add appeal to the series.

This topic is a disturbing one for the intended audience—students grades 4 through 8—but the editorial board made a decision "not to shock or horrify." "Learning about the Holocaust should be disturbing—but there is a delicate line between informative realism and sensationalism. The most brutal accounts and documentation of the Holocaust can be found in many other sources; we believe that in our series, much of this story will be revealed through the powerful and moving images we have selected." This series could have been presented in fewer volumes, but the price for each is reasonable and the 8-volume format does allow access by several students at once. This matter-of-fact account will support curriculum units.

Other coverage of the Holocaust suitable for this same audience is found in a 4-volume alphabetically arranged set entitled *The Holocaust* (see entry 281), and a 1-volume work entitled *The Holocaust: Understanding and Remembering* by Helen Strahinich, from the Issues in Focus series of Enslow Publishers (1996). [R: SLJ, Feb 98, p. 134]—**Vandelia L. VanMeter**

283.   **The Illustrated Encyclopedia of World History.** K. Donker van Heel, ed. Armonk, N.Y., Sharpe Reference/M. E. Sharpe, 1997. 414p. illus. maps. $125.00. ISBN 1-56324-805-0.

In an easy-to-use alphabetic arrangement, this one-volume history of the world offers a broad view of important people, events, wars, treaties, places (but not nations), and cultural trends. Full-color thematic pages that illustrate great historical happenings (e.g., monks and monasteries in the Middle Ages, the Ottoman Turks, Napoleon); illustrations; portraits; and occasional maps provide strong support to the clear, concise text. In the 3-column format, a reader finds 6 lines devoted to Genghis Khan, 30 lines to Adolf Hitler, and 9 lines to Paul Gauguin.

There are *see* references on some thematic pages, as well as occasional *see* references within the text, but there is no indication by bold or italic typeface or other technique that any term within an entry has an entry of its own. This hinders the user in tracing related persons or topics. A scan of the illustrations gives the sense that there is an effort at evenhandedness, but a closer examination leaves many questions—there is a thematic page on China's early dynasties, and another on communist China, but there is no entry or *see* reference for China or any other nation or continent.

This attractive and colorful work is suitable for quick-reference use in school libraries, at the desk, or in the home. Even though the alphabetic arrangement provides access, the necessary sense of context is better provided for students by the timeline/extensive indexing approach used in *The Dorling Kindersley History of the World* (see ARBA 95, entry 587). Libraries serving secondary students and adults who need deeper coverage may prefer to use general encyclopedias, multivolume works, or such one-volume works as *The Hutchinson Dictionary of World History* (see ARBA 95, entry 581), which includes chronologies, lists of leaders, organizations, wars, battles, and disasters.—**Vandelia L. VanMeter**

284. **The Kingfisher History Encyclopedia.** New York, Larousse Kingfisher Chambers, 1999. 491p. illus. maps. index. $39.95. ISBN 0-7534-5194-8.

This large-format reference for elementary and middle school students is designed to be a starting point for further exploration on historical topics. With its profuse and colorful illustrations, both photographic and artist-rendered, it is also an enjoyable book to browse.

Rather than alphabetic, the arrangement is chronological with 10 major sections covering each historical period. Beginning with the ancient world (40,000-500 B.C.E.) and ending at 2000 C.E. with the end of apartheid, the encyclopedia also contains a look toward the world's future. Unlike some historical reference works, a bias toward Euro-American subject matter appears to be absent—the Eastern Hemisphere gets its due in this work. Two pages, occasionally one, are devoted to each major topic. In such space, the main text is necessarily quite general, but annotated maps, captioned illustrations, and sidebars provide related items of interest. A full timeline runs across each spread with a red bar that highlights the period covered. With its global focus, this encyclopedia would have benefited from a two-page map of the world to help place the regions covered in relation to each other.

At the end of the book, a ready-reference section offers tables of dates, historical figures, and facts. The index boasts approximately 3,500 topics and subtopics, making lookup easy. All in all, this encyclopedia should find a place in school and public libraries. [R: BL, 15 Dec 99, p. 799; BR, Jan/Feb 2000, p. 78]—**Lori D. Kranz**

285. McElroy, Lorie Jenkins. **Voices of the Holocaust.** Detroit, U*X*L/Gale, 1998. 2v. illus. index. $49.00/set. ISBN 0-7876-1746-6.

The Holocaust is one of the most horrible events in world history. It is also one of the most difficult to present to young students. With the recurrence of genocide in Bosnia and Rwanda and the increase in hate crimes in the United States, teaching young people about this event is extremely important. *Voices of the Holocaust*, an anthology of excerpts from 34 documents written by people affected by this event, is an excellent tool because it provides primary sources and places them in historical context.

The 2-volume set is divided into 6 chapters that cover broad topics: anti-Semitism, escalation, Holocaust, resisters, liberation, and understanding. Each chapter begins with a historical overview. Each excerpt in the anthology has an introduction to place the document and its author within a historical context and a "Things to Remember" section that provides background information. Difficult words are defined within the text in parentheses. The excerpts themselves appear in their original format, with difficult words in bold typeface. These words are defined in glossaries that appear as sidebars. A "What Happened Next" section follows the text and explains its impact on both the author of the document and the audience. "Did You Know?" provides facts about the document and its author. Each entry has a brief bibliography. Many also have boxed author biographies and related historical information. Black-and-white photographs illustrate the text. Each volume contains a timeline that starts in 1899 and ends with the first disbursement from the Swiss fund for Holocaust survivors in 1997.

The documents excerpted here cover a broad range of subjects that will be of interest to students from middle school through high school: sections of seminal works such as *The Protocols of the Elders of Zion* and *Mein Kampf*; a newspaper account of *Kristallnacht*; sections from memoirs and diaries by Anne Frank, Primo Levi, and Hannah Senesh; Edward R. Murrow's account of the liberation of Buchenwald; and writings by Elie Wiesel and Art Spiegelman. These bring history to life and document both the inhumanity and the courage of those involved. They also demonstrate the importance of remembering the Holocaust and working to prevent a repetition of such atrocities. Two companion sets, *People of the Holocaust* and *Understanding the Holocaust*, provide further background for students and teachers. These sets are excellent resources for school, public, and synagogue libraries. [R: BL, 15 Sept 98, p. 268; VOYA, Dec 98, pp. 388-389]—**Barbara M. Bibel**

286. **The Middle Ages: An Encyclopedia for Students.** William Chester Jordan, ed. New York, Scribner's/Simon & Schuster Macmillan, 1996. 4v. illus. maps. index. $350.00/set. ISBN 0-684-19773-1.

Although designed expressly for students, this reference work will serve the needs of anyone interested in knowing more about the Middle Ages, roughly the period from 500 to 1500 C.E. Based on the authoritative *Dictionary of the Middle Ages* in 13 volumes (see ARBA 90, entry 533), this smaller, less expensive version in 4 volumes has been meticulously compiled by academic experts on subjects ranging from Aachen, the Abbasids, Abelard, and Pierre and Héloïse to Ypres and Zanj. The result is a balanced encyclopedia with focused, compact articles on medieval life. These include half-page profiles (e.g., those on *Beowulf*, the Medici family, and relics), along with more extensive articles on broader subjects (e.g., those on agriculture, feudalism, and Islamic art and architecture).

More than 300 illustrations cover medieval art and architecture; illuminated manuscripts; diagrams depicting the construction of castles; fortifications; medieval clothing; and armor, with numerous maps (showing trade routes, migration patterns, changing political boundaries, and so forth). There are a total of 45 full-color plates, but the vast majority of illustrations are either in black-and-white or limited to, at most, 2 colors. There is a bibliography of suggested readings at the end of volume 4, and a detailed, 28-page index for easy reference.

This encyclopedia of the Middle Ages is an informative and reliable but readable work that will bring the most up-to-date, authoritative understanding of this diverse and complex period within the grasp of younger readers and interested adults alike. It should certainly be included in the reference section of any public library, and would serve well any curious reader with an avid interest in the Middle Ages. [R: SLJ, Nov 96, p. 138; RBB, 1 Sept 96, p. 168]—**Joseph W. Dauben**

287. Moss, Joyce, and George Wilson. **Profiles in World History: Significant Events and the People Who Shaped Them.** Detroit, U*X*L/Gale, 1996. 8v. illus. maps. index. $225.00/set; $29.95/v.. ISBN 0-7876-0464-X/set; 0-7876-0465-8 (v.1); 0-7876-0466-6 (v.2); 0-7876-0467-4 (v.3); 0-7876-0468-2 (v.4); 0-7876-0469-0 (v.5); 0-7876-0470-4 (v.6); 0-7876-0471-2 (v.7); 0-7876-0472-0 (v.8).

This eight-volume set intended for young readers provides a glimpse into the lives of people who had a great impact upon world events. More than 175 individuals who represent many varied viewpoints or groups, or who affected the outcome of a historic event, or exemplify the role of ordinary persons are featured in a chronological presentation from 3100 B.C.E. to the present day. Each biographical profile (approximately 6-10 pages in length) provides a personal background, the role of the individual in the notable event, and the effect of this occurrence upon society and upon the individual's later life. The readable text is enhanced by many portraits, maps, and other illustrations; pronunciation guides; and sidebars that highlight other people of the time or especially interesting cultural practices. A brief bibliography concludes each profile, and a more extensive bibliography is found at the end of each volume.

The individual volumes are indexed, with many cross-references. At the conclusion of volume 8, a cumulative index provides access to the entire set. Unique in reference sets suitable for libraries serving students grades 5 and up, the accessible text and attractive format will find a wide audience. The 12-volume *McGraw-Hill Encyclopedia of World Biography* (see ARBA 74, entry 106); its 4-volume *20th Century Supplement* (see ARBA 93, entry 39; ARBA 89, entries 21-22; and ARBA 88, entry 30); and Salem Press's 5-volume *Great Lives from History: American Series* (see ARBA 88, entry 513) and its 5-volume *Great Lives from History: Renaissance to 1900 Series* (see ARBA 91, entry 549) serve a similar purpose for grades 8 and up. [R: BR, Sept/Oct 96, p. 54; SLJ, Aug 96, p. 182]—**Vandelia L. VanMeter**

288.   **World History. http://www.worldhistory.abc-clio.com/.** [Website]. Santa Barbara, Calif., ABC-CLIO, $599.00/year. Minimum system requirements: Internet access with a version 4.0 or later browser. Browser must be cookie and JavaScript enabled. ISSN 1531-1279. Date reviewed: Mar 02.

Designed with the same format as ABC-CLIO's other education Websites, *World History* provides more than 10,000 reference entries discussing cultures, events, inventions, religious movements, and personalities that have had an impact on history around the globe. The site lists topics chronologically, which will provide students with an overall concept of how history has developed. The site is designed mainly with teachers, school media specialists, and students in mind.

The home page provides a feature story (which changes regularly) and a note on historical things that happened on the day in history the site is being accessed. Students can then use the "Reference" page to research on specific topics of interest. The "Reference" page can be used in three different ways: by entering a keyword or phrase, by clicking on a specific time in history (arranged chronologically), and by category (requesting the information in a specific format, such as essay, image, map, documents, or events, just to name a few). When students find the topic they are researching they will also find related entries located in a sidebar, which will further their research. The site also features access to a Merriam-Webster dictionary and the added feature of contacting a "cybrarian" with specific questions about the site and how to better research a topic.

Teachers and media specialists will find the site useful because it allows them to create assignments, tests, and a syllabus on the "Administration" page. Only teachers and librarians will have access to this page because two user names and passwords are assigned to each school—one for teachers and librarians and one for students. This feature also allows students to access the Website from home and will allow parents to be aware of their children's homework and future assignments.

This database, much like the others from ABC-CLIO, will enhance any school's teaching curriculum. It will bring world history to life for many students and provide a new outlet for learning. The price may be a bit high for many schools, but the amount of material found here may make up for the expense.—**Shannon Graff Hysell**

289.   **World War II Day by Day.** New York, DK Publishing, 2001. 728p. illus. maps. index. $50.00. ISBN 0-7894-7997-4.

World War II Day by Day is an outstanding reference resource for answering questions about World War II. The war is broken down by year and month, with a daily calendar of events for each week that lists the events for each day. For each week, several articles are provided, written in the present tense in the style of newspaper articles. This feature gives the events an immediacy that will help patrons born after the events occurred understand the importance of the events and make them more than just dry factoids in a history book.

The illustrations (in color and black-and-white) add a great deal to the value of the book as a historical reference resource. Examples include wartime recruiting posters, propaganda pieces, and photographs from the front as well as the home front. Materials from the Axis and Allied powers balance the treatment of the war and allow readers to learn about all of the facets of the conflict. Excellent color maps make it easier to follow the action of a particular theater of operations for weeks with a lot of movement. The introduction gives a quick yet useful summary of the major events, themes, and personalities involved in the war, and the book helpfully covers both the buildup to World War II and its aftermath. The comprehensive index makes searching for specific information easy and fast.

World War II Day by Day is an outstanding reference resource. It will be useful in most libraries, from elementary schools to large universities and public libraries. This book is a worthwhile investment for any library reference collection.—**Mark T. Bay**

Handbooks and Yearbooks

290.   **Ancient Civilizations.** Danbury, Conn., Grolier, 2000. 10v. illus. maps. index. $319.00/set. ISBN 0-7172-9471-4.

The staff at Grolier has put together a resource on ancient people and places that is fun and informative. Each of the 80-page volumes in this 10-volume set contains around a dozen articles dealing with ancient civilizations and peoples (Babylonia, Japan, Vikings), archaeological sites and the people who inhabited them (Angkor Wat, Machu Picchu, Ur), and related topics (archaeology, marriage and families, tools and technology). The articles range in length from 2 to 15 pages, with the vast majority between 4 and 6 pages. The volumes are profusely illustrated with photographs, drawings, and maps, all of excellent quality and appropriately placed. In addition to the articles, each volume has a timeline spanning 6500 B.C.E. to 1600 C.E., a glossary specific to the volume, a brief reading list (also volume-specific), and an index to the set.

Though most of the articles are relatively brief, they cover the topics well, if not thoroughly, and are clearly written. At the end of each are one or more cross-references. Thus readers can expand their knowledge of a particular aspect of the ancient world and, at the same time, begin to see the bigger picture. Sprinkled throughout are insets that, although related to the articles in which they are found, are enjoyable to read on their own. Titles include "The Origin of Dice," "How Do We Know What They Ate?," "Plaster People of Pompeii," and "The Use of Zero."

Designed to meet the needs of younger readers, this set will also appeal to some older readers who know little or nothing about ancient civilizations and peoples and want to gain a minimum understanding without being bored. This set is recommended for school and public libraries. [R: BL, 1 Sept 2000, p. 172]—**Craig W. Beard**

291.   **Ancient Civilizations: Almanac.** By Judson Knight. Stacy A. McConnell and Lawrence W. Baker, eds. Farmington Hills, Mich., U*X*L/Gale, 2000. 2v. illus. maps. index. (U*X*L Ancient Civilizations Reference Library Series). $79.00/set. ISBN 0-7876-3982-6.

292. **Ancient Civilizations: Biographies.** By Judson Knight. Stacy A. McConnell and Lawrence W. Baker, eds. Farmington Hills, Mich., U*X*L/Gale, 2000. 254p. illus. index. (U*X*L Ancient Civilizations Reference Library Series). $42.00. ISBN 0-7876-3985-0.

Students, middle school and above, are the target audience of this 3-volume set covering 12 ancient civilizations and biographies of 38 people who influenced those cultures. Beginning with ancient Egypt, the two almanac volumes include Mesopotamia, Israel, Phoenicia, Syria, Arabia, Asia Minor, Persia, India, China, the Americas, Africa, Greece, and Rome. The entry for each country covers its location, history by time period (dynasty, empire, kingdom), political system, religion, and any significant contributions to civilization. There is also an overview of the country's modern history and an explanation of archaeological discoveries. A list of sources to consult for further information follows each chapter and includes books, motion pictures, and Websites.

The biography volume includes well-known historical figures such as Aristotle, Alexander the Great, and Confucius and also lesser-known people like the Indian emperor Asoka and the Celtic woman warrior Boadicia. Biblical personalities such as Jesus, David, Paul, and Moses are included along with philosophers, artists, and rulers. Each of the three volumes has a glossary, a timeline, an index, a pronunciation guide, and suggestions for research topics and activities.

Students using the set to research an ancient culture will find everything they need. Not only can they find information on the details of a specific civilization but also comments on the similarities between cultures, the impact of geography on economics, religious rituals, and political developments over time. Information is well organized and the vocabulary and sentence structure make it easy to access and understand. Words are usually defined within the text of the entry and phonetic pronunciation is given. Sidebars and information boxes highlight other "words to know" and topics of special interest. Upper elementary, middle school, and public libraries will find this set a good value and an outstanding reference source. [R: BR, Sept/Oct 2000, p. 67; SLJ, Nov 2000, p. 92]—**Marlene M. Kuhl**

293. **DK Great Wonders of the World.** By Russell Ash. Illustrated by Richard Bonson. New York, DK Publishing, 2000. 64p. illus. index. $19.95. ISBN 0-7894-6505-1.

This volume focuses on the Seven Wonders of the World and how they came to be known as such. Each of the seven wonders is presented in a two-page spread with color illustrations and sidebars. The author then compares them with other great structures of the time (in order to provide context for the reader) and other similar structures present today. For example, the discussion of the great pyramid at Giza explains in detail the structure of the pyramid, how it was built, and gives examples of other great pyramids (e.g., the Pyramid of the Magician, the Great Temple of Tenochtitlán, Transamerica Pyramid). The book also discusses the statue of Zeus at Olympia, the Mausoleum at Halicarnassus, the Hanging Gardens of Babylon, the Colossus of Rhodes, the Pharos at Alexandria, and the Temples of Artemis at Ephesus in the same format. The final pages list other wonders, such as palaces and castles, "Weird Wonders" (the leaning tower of Pisa), engineering wonders, inventions, and natural wonders (e.g., the Great Barrier Reef, the Northern Lights). The illustrations and photographs, along with the entertaining text, make this resource most suitable for middle school and high school libraries.—**Shannon Graff Hysell**

294. Feldman, George. **Understanding the Holocaust.** Detroit, U*X*L/Gale, 1998. 2v. illus. maps. index. $49.00/set. ISBN 0-7876-1740-7.

Explaining the Holocaust to young students is difficult. The horror of this period is almost beyond comprehension. The U*X*L division of Gale has produced a 6-volume set that brings the events and people of this era to life. The first 4 volumes, *People of the Holocaust* and *Voices of the Holocaust*, cover individuals and primary sources. *Understanding the Holocaust* provides the historical background for the earlier titles.

The 2 volumes, with consecutive paging, are divided into 14 chapters. Each volume contains a complete table of contents and index for the set, a reader's guide, a timeline, a glossary, a bibliography of fiction and nonfiction works, and a list of organizations. They also have an author's note explaining the difficulties involved in determining the exact number of Holocaust victims and their countries of origin.

The chapters cover subjects such as "Germany and the Jewish People Before the Holocaust," "The Rise of the Nazi Party," "The Warsaw Ghetto," "Life and Death in Nazi-Dominated Europe," "Judgments," and "Remembering the Holocaust." Each one explains the historical events clearly and objectively. Illustrations, maps, and charts supplement the text. Sidebars provide explanations of difficult concepts and additional material, such as an account of the Dreyfus Affair, a selection from Yevgeny Yevtushenko's poem *Babi Yar*, and a profile of Hermann Goring. The information is accessible to readers over the age of 10.

Understanding the Holocaust provides an excellent introductory overview of a difficult subject. It is a reasonably priced set that can stand alone. Adding the companion volumes will offer greater depth by bringing firsthand accounts of these events to the students who read them. These books belong in all public and school libraries. [R: BL, 15 Sept 98, p. 268]—**Barbara M. Bibel**

295.   George, Linda S. **The Golden Age of Islam.** Tarrytown, N.Y., Marshall Cavendish, 1998. 80p. illus. maps. index. (Cultures of the Past). $19.95. ISBN 0-7614-0273-X.

296.   Hinds, Kathryn. **The Incas.** Tarrytown, N.Y., Marshall Cavendish, 1998. 80p. illus. maps. index. (Cultures of the Past). $19.95. ISBN 0-7614-0270-5.

297.   Hinds, Kathryn. **The Vikings.** Tarrytown, N.Y., Marshall Cavendish, 1998. 80p. illus. index. (Cultures of the Past). $19.95. ISBN 0-7614-0271-3.

298.   Service, Pamela F. **The Ancient African Kingdom of Kush.** Tarrytown, N.Y., Marshall Cavendish, 1998. 80p. illus. index. (Cultures of the Past). $19.95. ISBN 0-7614-0272-1.

These 4 books of an attractive 14-volume series, designed for older elementary through high school readers, bring key vanished cultures to life as they were at the height of their development. The authors, who are either authorities or persons with a special interest in the culture, use narrative, sidebars, descriptive captions, photographs of places, works of art, and sometimes persons, all currently in existence, to discuss these cultures. The daily lives of the people, including their religions, are brought into focus, as are the culture's legends and political history. The authors note the lives of women and the place of slavery. A chronology, glossary, and two bibliographies—one aimed at the younger student and one for use by the teacher or older student —assist readers in each volume. The titles can be purchased singly as can other titles in the series, including *The Ancient Egyptians*, *The Ancient Greeks*, *The Ancient Maya*, *The Ancient Romans*, *The Aztec Empire*, *The Celts of Northern Europe*, *China's Tang Dynasty*, *India's Gupta Dynasty*, *The Kingdom of Benin in West Africa*, and *The Persian Empire*.—**Edna M. Boardman**

299.   **The Kingfisher Book of the Ancient World: From the Ice Age to the Fall of Rome.** 2d ed. New York, Larousse Kingfisher Chambers, 2001. 160p. illus. maps. index. $22.95. ISBN 0-7534-5397-5.

This book explores civilizations around the world from prehistory to A.D. 600. The authors give interesting glimpses into the daily life of these past cultures to include religion, politics, commerce, food, and amusements. After a brief overview of man's evolution, each chapter focuses on a different region. In addition to the Fertile Crescent, Egypt, Rome, the Greeks and the Celts, ancient civilizations in India, the Far East, the Middle East, Africa, the Americas, Oceania and Europe are also featured. The reader learns such tidbits as that the wheel was originally invented by the Sumerians (5000-2000 B.C.E.) to make pottery and later adapted for carts, the Irish Celts (750 B.C.E.-500 A.D.) had a writing system based on straight lines called Ogam, and the earliest known rock art was done 45,000 years ago by Australian Aborigines. The structuring of the material by continents has logic, but it makes it difficult to understand parallel developments in diverse locations. Readers see a culture in isolation so understanding common themes is a challenge. The authors provide a chronology but it is not as helpful as it could be because it is divided by country and not aligned by the same starting date. A universal timeline would be more helpful but is not included. Appendixes include a glossary as well as an index. This resource will whet the appetite of the elementary school student to learn more about these long-gone but rich civilizations and the impact they have had on today's philosophies, religions, arts, and literature. [R: BR, May/June 02, pp. 71-72]—**Adrienne Antink Bien**

300. **Slavery Throughout History: Almanac.** By Theodore L. Sylvester. Sonia Benson, ed. Farmington Hills, Mich., U*X*L/Gale, 2000. 263p. illus. maps. index. (Slavery Thoughout History Reference Library). $42.00. ISBN 0-7876-3176-0.

301. **Slavery Throughout History: Biographies.** By Theodore L. Sylvester. Peggy Saari, ed. Farmington Hills, Mich., U*X*L/Gale, 2000. 235p. illus. maps. index. (Slavery Throughout History Reference Library). $42.00. ISBN 0-7876-3177-9.

302. **Slavery Throughout History: Primary Sources.** By Judson Knight. Farmington Hills, Mich., U*X*L/Gale, 2000. 168p. illus. index. (U*X*L Slavery Throughout History Reference Library). $42.00. ISBN 0-7876-3178-7.
      Slavery Throughout History: Almanac is the first of three volumes in the Slavery Throughout History Reference Library series. It provides an overview of the institution of slavery from its inception among the "earliest permanent settlers in Mesopotamia (perhaps as early as 3500 B.C.E.) to the present day" (p. xiv). The entries, narrative in form, run approximately 25 pages each. Chapter titles include "Slavery in Ancient Mesopotamia, Egypt, and Israel"; "Colonial Latin America"; "Slave Life in Antebellum America"; and "Slavery in the Twentieth Century." A glossary is provided as well as a timeline of events related to slavery and a general historical timeline. Graphics are provided in each chapter—photographs, illustrations, and maps. This volume also includes an index and a bibliography.
      Many of the 30 men and women in the 2d volume, *Biographies*, are famous figures from the African Diaspora related to slavery. They include Sally Hemmings, Harriet Tubman, and Nat Turner. In addition, a number of well-known white abolitionist leaders are included. True to its billing, however, this volume provides a broad world scope of important historical figures, such as Moses, Aleksandr Solzhenitsyn (slave in Soviet labor camps), Haksun Kim (comfort woman [prostitute] for the Japanese military), and Hammurabi (King of Babylonia). Readers are likely to encounter many people who are new to them as individuals of importance related to slavery.
      Each entry includes a number of graphics: photographs, illustrations, or maps, as well as a sidebar with an interesting fact. The text is straightforward and concise. In addition, a phonetic pronunciation is provided for names that may be difficult to pronounce. At the end of each entry is a further reading section and a bibliography. There are an index and a "Words to Know" section, along with a timeline of events as well as a separate timeline for other historical events.
      The 3d volume, *Primary Resources*, allows students to study 20 full or excerpted speeches, diary entries, newspaper accounts, novels, poems, memoirs, and other materials related to slavery. It includes Hammurabi's code of laws regarding slavery, slave narratives, abolitionist speeches,

legislation, and much more. This series is recommended for public and secondary schools.
—**Leslie R. Homzie**

303. **The Traveler's Guide to . . . Series.** San Diego, Calif., Lucent Books, 2002. 6v. illus. maps. index. $27.45/vol.

This 6-volume series from Lucent Books explores various historical cultures by taking the reader on a tour of the land. Thus far the series covers the historical time periods of ancient Rome, ancient Alexandria, ancient Athens, the California gold rush, Renaissance Florence, and Shakespeare's London. Although written by different authors, all of the books follow the same format, which includes an introduction, a history of the city or time period, the weather and physical setting, transportation and food, markets and shopping, religion, public games, sightseeing, and trips to nearby sites. Each chapter is written in prose that will be easily understood by middle school readers on up and each includes illustrations, simplistic maps, and an index. What makes these works useful for a reference collection are the supplementary materials provided, including notes and lists for further reading, major works consulted, and additional works consulted.

This series creates a unique way for students to learn about other historical cultures. The guidebook format truly makes the reader feel they are experiencing a part of history. Unfortunately, at $27.45 a volume this set will be too expensive for most school libraries. Those needing supplemental information for specific time periods may want to pick and choose which volumes they purchase.—**Shannon Graff Hysell**

304. Volo, Dorothy Denneen, and James M. Volo. **Daily Life in the Age of Sail.** Westport, Conn., Greenwood Press, 2002. 322p. illus. maps. index. (The Greenwood Press "Daily Life Through History" Series). $49.95. ISBN 0-313-31026-2.

The "Daily Life Through History" Series provides a general overview of historical topics, such as Elizabethan England, the Inca Empire, Ancient Romans, as well as 18 other titles. This entry reviews the 400-year period from the late 1400s to the late 1800s from a western European-American perspective. Chapters cover life in port, exploration, navigation advances, make-up of the crew and their daily life, shipboard environment, trading fleets, war at sea, pirates and privateers, the American Revolution, and American sail up to the age of steam. The serviceable writing is descriptive rather than interpretive so that chapters read like long encyclopedia articles. The authors are Connecticut high school teachers and wrote one other work in the series as well as two other titles published by Greenwood Press. Chapters are documented by a few dozen footnotes, each from a five-page bibliography of respected secondary sources. The 11-page index misses lots of words or concepts and many terms are undefined. For example, the Bight of Benin is mentioned but only by context does one know it is a place and it never tells where it is located. A glossary would help and the work could use more maps and illustrations. Overall, it is an acceptable survey with a lot of information, but it may be a tough read for junior high students. Suitable for senior high schools, lower division college libraries, and public library circulating collections that have found other titles in the series that circulate well.—**Patrick J. Brunet**

8 Law

GENERAL WORKS

Biography

305.   Harer, John B., and Jeanne Harrell. **People For and Against Restricted or Unrestricted Expression.** Westport, Conn., Greenwood Press, 2002. 224p. illus. index. (The Greenwood Press "People Making a Difference" Series). $50.00. ISBN 0-313-31758-5.

This work looks at the lives and influences of 50 people who have been at the forefront of the freedom of speech law in this country. It is designed for use by students who are researching freedom of speech or preparing for a debate on the subject. The 50 people profiled became involved in the debate for different reasons. Some had careers that are affected by freedom of speech, including author Judy Blume and intellectual freedom advocate for the American Library Association Judith Fingeret Krug. Others became involved due to religious beliefs, such as the founder of the Christian organization Focus on the Family James C. Dobson and Martin Mawyer of the Christian Action Network. Many of the people listed here are concerned with pornography as it relates to children and the Internet. And others, such as Danny Goldberg and Frank Zappa, are fighting to keep music from censorship. Each biography is two to three pages in length and provides the education and career information for the individual, a history of their influence in the debate, and a list of suggested reading. Many of the individuals have black-and-white photographs. The work provides many supplementary materials for further research, including a reprint of the first amendment to the U.S. Constitution, historical documents related to the first amendment, a glossary of terms, a bibliography for further reading, a list of resources, and an index. This work will be useful in middle and high school libraries.—**Shannon Graff Hysell**

Dictionaries and Encyclopedias

306.   **Courtroom Drama: 120 of the World's Most Notable Trials.** Elizabeth Frost-Knappman, Edward W. Knappman, and Lisa Paddock, eds. Detroit, U*X*L/Gale, 1998. 3v. illus. index. $79.95/set. ISBN 0-7876-1735-0.

Courtroom Drama: 120 of the World's Most Notable Trials presents 25 centuries of intriguing and influential trials that have helped shape the course of world history. Falling into 13 categories, the cases cover assassinations, murders, war crimes, courts-martial, religious crimes, espionage, treason, negligence, political corruption, freedom of speech, family law, human rights, and constitutional cases.

The earliest courtroom drama dates from 399 B.C.E.; for refusing to worship the gods of the city of Athens, the philosopher Socrates was sentenced. The Timothy McVeigh trial, which deals with the worst act of terrorism in U.S. history—the bombing of the Oklahoma City Federal Building in 1995—is among the most recent trials. Others are the *Jones v. Clinton and Ferguson* lawsuit brought by Paula Jones against President Bill Clinton for sexual harassment that allegedly occurred when he was governor of Arkansas. *Vacco v. Quill* and *Washington v. Glucksberg* together make up the right to die cases heard by the Supreme Court.

Volume 1 contains cases on the Constitution, family law and reproductive rights, freedom of speech, human rights, and negligence. Volume 2 contains cases on assassinations, espionage, murder, and political corruption. Volume 3 features cases on military trials and courts-martial, religion and heresy, treason, and war crimes. Each volume begins with an alphabetic listing and a chronological listing. Each entry covers who was involved in the trial, where it took place, when it occurred, what the outcome was, and what the significance is. Most of the cases in this book resulted in true trials, meaning that a court—usually a judge or a panel of judges—followed established rules and procedures and impartially examined disputes between parties over fact or law. Others are jury trials in which lawyers presented evidence to a jury that delivered a verdict. Others are not real trials at all. The Salem witchcraft persecutions, for example, were not true trials because no attorney was present to represent the accused. Still, they were among the great social upheavals in colonial New England. Communist dictator Joseph Stalin's "show trials" made a mockery of justice because their verdicts were foregone conclusions.

The trials are arranged chronologically by category. There is an alphabetic listing as well. For easy reference, a "Words to Know" section at the beginning of each volume defines key terms. More than 120 sidebars provide related information, whereas 172 photographs add to the text. A cumulative index concludes each volume.

Each trial begins with a bold box in which the principals of the trial are listed. The claims of either the plaintiff or defendant are listed. The lawyers' names are included as well as the place and date of the trial. The verdict is listed and, most important, the significance of the trial. Following is a profile of the trial in a two-to five-page entry. An in-depth essay follows, describing the events leading up to the trial, key moments of the trial, and the aftermath of the decision. This 3-volume set will be a welcome addition to a middle school, high school, or public library. Once again, Gale has produced a book of high quality. [R: SLJ, Aug 98, pp. 188-190; BR, Sept/Oct 98, p. 68]
—**Barbara B. Goldstein**

Handbooks and Yearbooks

307. Carleton, David. **Student's Guide to Landmark Congressional Laws on Education.** Westport, Conn., Greenwood Press, 2002. 227p. index. $49.95. ISBN 0-313-31335-0.

Perhaps it is the exasperation the law brings that manages to tease the best ripostes out of people when it comes to attorneys. It remains, nevertheless, that regardless of how we feel about law or lawyers, we still have to understand the courts, even when they speak out of both sides of their mouths.

The current volume attempts to distill one aspect of legalese: education. The coverage is not exhaustive. The cases considered have more to do with why we have education than with the legal means to secure it for given individuals. Hence, decisions that deal with the federal government's expanding role in education, or, to look at it more historically, the triumph of the federalists over the anti-federalists are covered here. Individual chapters treat the Land Ordinance of 1785, the Northwest Ordinance, the Morrill Acts, Smith-Hughes, The National Defense Education Act, the Elementary and Secondary Education Act, the disastrous Bilingual Education Act, and more.

In all, there are 18 bills discussed and thoroughly dissected. Students, especially those in education, will find this book especially helpful. Each chapter provides either a full reprint of the bill or key portions of it, a discussion of its background, and a few paragraphs or pages on the bill's impact. An index and a chronology help to place the acts in their proper historical landscape. [R: SLJ, Nov 02, p. 95]—**Mark Y. Herring**

308. Livingston, Steven G. **Student's Guide to Landmark Congressional Laws on Social Security and Welfare.** Westport, Conn., Greenwood Press, 2002. 258p. index. (Student's Guide to Landmark Congressional Laws). $49.95. ISBN 0-313-31343-1.

This volume in the Student's Guide to Landmark Congressional Laws series examines the history and the impact of 21 social insurance laws, from the Homestead Act of 1862, which aided the unemployed by selling public land on easy terms, to the Senior Citizen's Freedom to Work Act of 2000, which eliminated the benefit reduction for retirees earning income above an often changed and debated limit. In each historical overview, the author explains the basic controversies behind each law, such as the food stamp program's dispute over whether the stamps should be given to the poor or sold, as they were in the orange and blue stamp programs of the 1930s. In this way, high school students can understand how conflicting interests lead to sometimes complex and not wholly satisfying laws.

Each 8-to 14-page entry ends with an edited version of the text of the law. The volume's 10-page introductory essay can be useful for debate on how far government assistance should extend, although its first sentence, "America is a welfare state," may bias younger readers before they have read the mixed bag of examples of benefits traditionally granted and benefits traditionally denied by the federal government. Other study tools include a glossary, timeline, index, and bibliography. The author, a professor of political science at Middle Tennessee State University, teaches courses about public and foreign policy and the U.S. Congress. This volume is recommended for high school and public libraries. Undergraduates looking for more in-depth background on the development of U.S. welfare policy may prefer Walter Trattner's *From Poor Law to Welfare State: A History of Social Welfare in America* (Free Press, 1999.)—**Nancy L. Van Atta**

309. Pohlmann, Marcus D., and Linda Vallar Whisenhunt. **Student's Guide to Landmark Congressional Laws on Civil Rights.** Westport, Conn., Greenwood Press, 2002. 284p. index. (Student's Guide to Landmark Congressional Laws). $49.95. ISBN 0-313-31385-7.

This work, designed for high school and college undergraduate students, looks at the civil rights movement in the African American community by studying 36 individual laws. The authors have chosen to look at African American civil rights specifically because of their unique position in American history and because of the vast improvements made in the past three centuries. Each law is written in an edited form that will make it easier for students to understand. After an introduction from the author and a nine-page timeline of significant events in the movement, the work is broken down into three parts. Part 1 provides an in-depth analysis of 12 laws passed during the period of slavery (1776-1863), including the Fugitive Slave Law (1793), the Missouri Compromise (1820), and the Emancipation Proclamation (1863). Part 2, "Postwar Reconstruction," discusses the laws passed from 1865-1875, including the Reconstruction Act (1867) and the Klan Act (1871). Part 3 discusses the Civil Rights era from 1941-1968, with in-depth discussion of the Civil Rights Acts of 1957 and 1960 and the Voting Rights Act (1965). Each law discussed provides notes at the bottom for further research. A bibliography and an index conclude the volume. —**Shannon Graff Hysell**

310. Willis, Clyde E. **Student's Guide to Landmark Congressional Laws on the First Amendment.** Westport, Conn., Greenwood Press, 2002. 232p. index. (Student's Guide to Landmark Congressional Laws). $49.95. ISBN 0-313-31416-0.

The massive amount of literature on the First Amendment can be overwhelming to anyone, especially those wanting some direction in beginning research on First Amendment issues as found in congressional statutes. The book opens with a "Timeline of Events" that directly or indirectly contributed to congressional statutes relevant to the First Amendment. The author's introduction offers a brief and clear overview of the First Amendment. Eight chapters focus on different congressional legislative acts that directly affected the First Amendment. Each chapter begins with a general introduction followed by a more specific introduction to each of the statutes included. Typical examples of statutes, and, in parentheses, the chapter title, are the Espionage Act of 1917 (Internal Security), the Draft Card and Mutilation Act of 1965 (Symbolic Speech), the Federal Election Campaign Act of 1971 as Amended (Election Campaign Activities), the Child Online Protection Act of 1998 (Obscenity), the Copyright Act of 1976 (Intellectual Property), the National Labor Relations Act of 1935 (Labor-Management Relations), the National Foundation of the Arts and Humanities Act of 1990 (Federally Funded Programs), and the Religious Freedom Restoration Act of 1993 (Freedom of Religion). The book concludes with two extremely helpful appendixes (a "List of Cited Statutes" and a "List of Cited Cases") and an excellent index. This reference work definitely belongs in high school and college libraries. [R: SLJ, Nov 02, p. 95]—**Michael A. Foley**

CRIMINOLOGY AND CRIMINAL JUSTICE

Biography

311. Bijlefeld, Marjolijn. **People for and Against Gun Control: A Biographical Reference.** Westport, Conn., Greenwood Press, 1999. 324p. illus. index. (The Greenwood Press "People Making a Difference" Series). $49.95. ISBN 0-313-30690-7.

As both accidental and deliberate shootings occur more frequently in upscale neighborhoods and young people are increasingly the targets, gun control becomes a more intense controversy. It is often a topic for student papers and debates. This volume, part of a series titled "People Making a Difference," is intended to help high school and college students involved in such projects to explore the complex issue of gun control through the lives of 50 people who are very much involved in the debate. They include doctors, elected officials, lobbyists for various organizations, and victims. The one trait they all have in common is their dedication to making a safer society.

Preceding the biographies is an excellent introduction by the author that covers the main elements of the gun control debate; the roles of law enforcement, gun manufacturers, health professionals, and others; statistics; and public opinion. The profiles contain such information as where and when the person was born, family background, education, and present position. More important, however, is the story of how each of these persons became involved in the gun control debate, the contributions they have made to the movement, and the obstacles they have faced from the opposition. Readings by or about the person are appended to each profile and photos frequently accompany the text. Material appended to the main section is helpful in itself, but also to a certain extent in evaluating the evenhandedness of the author. Included are summaries of state and federal gun control laws and state constitutional clauses relating to the right to bear arms; lists of the biographies by pro- and anti-gun control legislation, by profession, and by states represented; a general bibliography; and an index.

All of the profiles were written by the author, a freelance writer and former director of the Educational Fund to End Gun Violence. She also worked with the Coalition to End Gun Violence —activities that obviously put her in the pro-gun control category and would most likely raise questions about her objectivity in presenting both sides of the issue fairly. The text itself, however, gives no indication of bias. Neither is any bias shown in the selection of those profiled—25 for gun control and 25 against it—nor was any detected in the types of persons or geographical locations, as both showed a wide variation. The value of this work is that it presents gun control issues from a different perspective than what students usually find available. The profiles are well written and compelling; they enable the student to consider a reasoned presentation of an opposing viewpoint. It would be particularly helpful for students taking a pro or con side in the gun control debate. Although recommended for school and college libraries, it would also be useful for public libraries where interest in the subject is high.—**Lucille Whalen**

312. Helmer, William, and Rick Mattix. **Public Enemies: America's Criminal Past, 1919-1940.** New York, Facts on File, 1998. 368p. illus. index. $35.00; $17.95pa. ISBN 0-8160-3160-6; 0-8160-3161-4pa.

The period between 1919 and 1940 has been described as a "golden age" of U.S. crime. Many colorful criminals—including Al Capone, Clyde Barrow, John Dillinger, Baby Face Nelson, and Pretty Boy Floyd—were active during this time (coinciding with Prohibition and the Depression). Much has been published during the years on these criminals and their era. The principal author of the present volume has made some noteworthy contributions to this literature. This volume provides readers with an engagingly written, systematically organized guide to the "public enemies" and their associates who dominated the crime scene during the two decades in question. Many of the stories recounted, and much of the information, will be quite familiar to dedicated students of this era; however, the authors make a reasonably credible case that they present a more reliable account than can be found in the many competing publications of Jay Robert Nash (e.g., *Bloodletters and Badmen*, 1973).

More specifically, this volume includes brief biographical sketches of all the better-known, and many of the lesser-known, public enemies of the Jazz Age and Desperate Years eras. Accounts of the major events (e.g., the Noble Experiment, the St. Valentine's Day Massacre) are also provided. Readers are also given descriptive accounts of principal gangs or mobs, such as the Black Hand; investigative enterprises, such as the Wickersham Commission; and crime-fighting technological breakthroughs, such as bulletproofing cars. A detailed chronology may prove especially useful to serious students of crime and crime control during these years. The more casual reader will surely find the many featured boxes on a variety of topics—for example, the man responsible for giving Scarface Al Capone his scars—entertaining and informative. The volume concludes with an extensive, annotated bibliography. Altogether, this volume is an attractive and well-informed work that will both entertain and enlighten those who wish to know more about a colorful and noteworthy era in the history of U.S. crime and its control.—**David O. Friedrichs**

313. Phillips, Charles, Alan Axelrod, and Kurt Kemper. **Cops, Crooks, and Criminologists: An International Biographical Dictionary of Law Enforcement.** updated ed. New York, Checkmark Books/Facts on File, 2000. 322p. illus. index. $18.95pa. ISBN 0-8160-4076-1.

The 1st edition of this work appeared in 1996 (see ARBA 97, entry 504) and received generally good reviews. Concise biographical sketches were offered on more than 600 current and past criminologists, police personnel, attorneys, pathologists, penologists, criminals, and others who had significantly shaped the history of law enforcement (particularly in the United States and

England). This "updated" trade paperback edition is nearly a virtual reprinting of the earlier edition. It even contains the same page count. Updated entries (a brief perusal yielded less than 10) consist of minimal revisions. One sentence mentioning the Branch Davidian debacle in Waco, Texas, is appended to Attorney General Janet Reno's entry. FBI Director Louis J. Freeh fares somewhat better. The authors add a paragraph to his entry. An updated edition usually implies significant revision and additional entries. In the years between editions the authors managed to find only six individuals worthy of inclusion in an international biographical dictionary of law enforcement. These include acquitted murder suspect O. J. Simpson, Oklahoma City bomber Timothy McVeigh, Unabomber Theodore Kaczynski, and Megan Kanka ("Megan's Law") . To accommodate these new entries, 8 entries from the 1st edition are dropped. These include Josef Stalin, Ed Masterson (brother of Bat), Stephen Kennedy, and W. Freeland Kendrick. The sole criteria for dropping these individuals appears to be that they are unfortunate enough to fall within the alphabetic range of a new entry. This is a common, and lazy, practice that some publishers adopt to present new material without having to dramatically change the format of the original edition. This "updated" edition at $18.95 is obviously targeted at individuals. No library that paid $45 for the 1st edition would or should purchase this new edition. [R: BR, Nov/Dec 2000, p. 80]—**David K. Frasier**

314.   **Villains and Outlaws.** Judy Culligan, ed. New York, Macmillan Library Reference/Simon & Schuster Macmillan, 1998. 361p. illus. index. (Macmillan Profiles, v.4). $75.00. ISBN 0-02-865058-1.

As part of the Macmillan Profiles series, this volume draws from other works in the series to present an introduction to the lives and times of world and American figures who are perceived to be villains and outlaws. Because this would be a lengthy list, the editors have based their criteria for selection on three factors: importance in history, relevance to standard curricula, and representation of a broad cultural range. Within these criteria biographees are selected from seven groups, including gangsters, assassins, old west outlaws, and corrupt political leaders. Although most of the material is taken from other Macmillan reference works, the biographies have been rewritten by scholars to appeal to a younger audience, and approximately 30 have been written specifically for this volume. Within the 113 biographical articles, a few are for more than one person—for example, the infamous Bonnie and Clyde and the Rosenbergs, a husband and wife spy couple.

The table of contents indicates the pages for each biographee although access is quick by going straight to the alphabetic list. Additional material includes a list of sources—the specific Macmillan works used and the authors of the original articles, along with the authors of the new articles; suggested readings for each person included; and a glossary and an index. Several features accompanying the biographical texts make the volume especially useful, such as photographs and illustrations, timelines and relevant quotations, frequent "pull quotes" highlighting essential facts from the text, and definitions of some uncommon terms. Occasionally, there are half-page insets of explanatory material as, for example, information on the Salem witch hunt accompanies the article on Lizzie Borden. The use of this added material is enhanced by the excellent typography and page layout. A slightly larger text print with bold black headings, wide margins, the use of shaded violet coloring for the timelines and insets, and violet ink for the other margin material not only enhance the attractiveness of the volume but make it easier to find pertinent information quickly.

As a reference tool, this work provides convenient access to well-written biographical material that is not always easily available elsewhere. It should be in all school and public libraries and would be useful in community colleges and undergraduate libraries also. For pleasurable reading, especially for students, this should have a wide audience.—**Lucille Whalen**

Dictionaries and Encyclopedias

315. Newton, Michael. **The Encyclopedia of Serial Killers.** New York, Checkmark Books/Facts on File, 2000. 391p. illus. index. $75.00. ISBN 0-8160-3978-X.

An overview of the famous infamous, both well known and relatively obscure, *The Encyclopedia of Serial Killers* provides information on serial killers, FBI profiling techniques, the psychology of serial killers, and other related topics. The photographs in the work are mainly of the criminals themselves; very few are grisly in nature. The work follows the standard Facts on File format—entries are arranged alphabetically, an index and bibliography are provided, and there are three appendixes. The writing is somewhat pedestrian (e.g., "shot him dead in his tracks") .

Although the information provided in this volume is exhaustive and comprehensive, the appendixes ("Solo Killers," "Team Killers," and "Unresolved Cases") are less so. Appendix C, "Unresolved Cases," is merely a list of unsolved crimes that may or may not be serial murders.

The publication meets a need for this type of information and attempts to do it in a nonsensationalistic manner. It will be useful for students' projects and will appeal to the casual browser. [R: LJ, 15 Feb 2000, p. 152; Choice, Sept 2000, p. 88]—**Michele Tyrrell**

316. **Outlaws, Mobsters, & Crooks: From the Old West to the Internet.** By Marie J. MacNee. Jane Hoehner, ed. Detroit, U*X*L/Gale, 1998. 3v. illus. index. $84.00/set. ISBN 0-7876-2803-4.

Outlaws, Mobsters, & Crooks is a collection of short biographies (on average 8-10 pages in length) of a wide range of North American outlaws. Written for a middle/high school audience, the 3 volumes present familiar figures such as Jesse James or Al Capone as well as the more obscure (Roger Touhy or JoAnne Chesimard). The 75 outlaws (the editor's introduction, called the "Readers Guide," indicates 73 but counts pairs as one) are grouped into 10 categories. Volume 1 includes mobsters, racketeers and gamblers, and robbers; volume 2 includes computer criminals, spies, swindlers, and terrorists. Volume 3 covers bandits and gunslingers, bootleggers, and pirates. The set contains such contemporary figures as Timothy McVeigh and Aldrich Ames. Each article contains basic biographical information as well as interesting sidebars—for example, the Bonnie and Clyde article contains a poem written about them; the Carlo Gambino section contains a family tree.

Each volume is organized in the same fashion. There is an overall table of contents that lists the contents of all three volumes, followed by the reader's guide, a list of the outlaws alphabetically, and a timeline. In addition, all volumes are indexed. There should be no reason not to find an individual, even if the reader is unsure of the figure's category. Numerous black-and-white photographs, charts, and small graphics add to the appeal of the information. Chapter headings look as if done on an old, manual typewriter, the typeface found in newspaper offices.

This work will be appealing both for research needs and for browsing. Students looking for blood and gore, however, may be disappointed—the editor has chosen not to include serial killers and mass murderers. [R: BL, 1 Nov 98, p. 540]—**Michele Tyrrell**

317. **Outlaws, Mobsters & Crooks: From the Old West to the Internet. Volumes 4 and 5.** Marie J. Hermsen MacNee, Sarah and Allison McNeill, eds. Farmington Hills, Mich., U*X*L/Gale, 2003. 2v. illus. index. $95.00/set. ISBN 0-7876-6482-0 (v.4); 0-7876-6483-9 (v.5). ISSN 1540-739X.

The crimes committed by the outlaws whose stories this series compiles range from murder, pirating, and robbery to swindling, computer hacking, and spying. Volumes 4 and 5 each contain 23 essays relating not only the criminals' biographies and crimes, but also the cultural background that influenced them. Along the way, the author dispels myths, such as the legendary butcheries by

Blackbeard the pirate, who, recent evidence shows, likely killed none of his robbery victims and whose most feared crime, for the class-based British, might have been the democratic principles of his criminal organization. The essays also examine the crime busters, who showed their own failings. In Baby Face Nelson's biography, an insert notes that the FBI spent so much of their resources on targeting "Public Enemies" that they had little time to stem the growth of the now formidably powerful organized crime syndicates. The combination of fact and analysis written in a style suitable for young adult readers makes this series an excellent addition to school and public libraries. Study aids include a timeline, in-text definitions, illustrations, a series and volume index, and a crimes index. Although a number of biographies of individual criminals exist, encyclopedic books are unusual. Younger readers may also enjoy Donald Sobol's *Encyclopedia Brown's Book of Strange but True Crimes* (Scholastic, 1991) or Richard Platt's *Villains: Traitors, Tyrants, and Thieves* (DK Publishing, 2002.)—**Nancy L. Van Atta**

Handbooks and Yearbooks

318.   Outman, James L., and Elisabeth M. Outman. **Terrorism: Almanac.** Farmington Hills, Mich., U*X*L/Gale, 2003. 235p. illus. index. (U*X*L Terrorism Reference Library). $55.00/vol.; $145.00/set. ISBN 0-7876-6566-5.

319.   Outman, James L., and Elisabeth M. Outman. **Terrorism: Biographies.** Farmington Hills, Mich., U*X*L/Gale, 2003. 235p. illus. index. (U*X*L Terrorism Reference Library). $55.00/vol.; $145.00/set. ISBN 0-7876-6567-3.

320.   Outman, James L., and Elisabeth M. Outman. **Terrorism: Primary Sources.** Farmington Hills, Mich., U*X*L/Gale, 2003. 192p. illus. index. (U*X*L Terrorism Reference Library). $55.00/vol.; $145.00/set. ISBN 0-7876-6568-1.
   Since the terrorist attacks on the United States on September 11, 2001, there has been a need for more information and history surrounding terrorism both at home and abroad. This need for information extends to children and young adults who are often the most confused and frightened by these acts of violence. This set provides just the type of information that middle school and high school age young adults will be looking for concerning terrorism and its roots.
   The set begins with an *Almanac*, which provides nine chapters covering the history and role of terrorism throughout the world. The chapters discuss the legal definition of terrorism, the tactics used, the training of terrorists, political and economic warfare, and state-sponsored terrorism. Sprinkled throughout the text are black-and-white photographs and sidebars with interesting facts and stories concerning terrorism. Each volume in the set provides a timeline of terrorism history beginning with 1793 as well as a glossary for that volume. The *Almanac* volume concludes with an appendix listing and describing some of the terrorist groups operating today, including Colombia's National Liberation Army, Ireland's Irish Republican Army (IRA), and Al Qaeda.
   Biographies alphabetically lists 26 notorious terrorist leaders, political figures, and freedom fighters associated with terrorism. Those profiled include Osama bin Laden, Timothy McVeigh, George J. Mitchell, and freedom fighters John Brown and Michael Collins. Each biography includes a black-and-white photograph. The final volume, *Primary Sources*, provides excerpts from speeches and documents concerning terrorism. These are separated into five chapters, including "Philosophy of Terror," which provides excerpts from Charlotte Brontë's *Shirley: A Tale* (1849); "Terrorism and Race in the United States," which includes an article from Claire Safran about a member of the Ku Klux Klan; and "Conflict in the Middle East," which provides an excerpt from

Osama bin Laden's "Jihad Against Jews and Crusaders" (1998). Each volume concludes with an index to the entire set.

This resource will be valuable to middle and high school libraries as well as the children's reference departments of public libraries. The information is timely and written at a level that young adult students will be easily able to comprehend.—**Shannon Graff Hysell**

9 Military Studies

GENERAL WORKS

Biography

321. **Generals in Muddy Boots: A Concise Encyclopedia of Combat Commanders.** By Dan Cragg. Walter J. Boyne, ed. New York, Berkley, 1996. 196p. illus. $29.95. ISBN 0-425-15136-0.

Concise is an appropriate adjective for this work on combat field commanders. Not intended to be all encompassing, this volume identifies some of the more noteworthy commanders in the history of warfare from ancient times to the Vietnam era. Entries provide a brief biography, describe military education, and discuss combat career. The alphabetic presentation eliminated the need for an index, making this a quick-reference guide. Cragg has written a more popular and anecdotal rather than a strictly scholarly work. Notable omissions from an otherwise star-studded assembly of commanders are Wilhelm Balck, Kurt Student, James Gavin, and Hasso von Manteuffel. Oversights and a lack of a more scholarly treatment aside, this is a solid, competent survey of combat commanders, and is recommended for middle school, high school, public library, and private reference collections. [R: LJ, Feb 96, p. 142; RBB, 1 May 96, p. 1519;]—**Norman L. Kincaide**

Dictionaries and Encyclopedias

322. Adams, Simon. **World War II.** New York, DK Publishing, 2000. 63p. illus. index. (Dorling Kindersley Eyewitness Books). $15.95. ISBN 0-7894-6298-2.

This volume in the Dorling Kindersley Eyewitness Books series focuses on the Second World War. Designed with middle school and high school students in mind, this volume uses photographs, short bits of information, and paragraph overviews of specific topics to tell the story of the war. The book is in chronological order, beginning with events that led up to the war and ending with the victory of the Allied countries and the aftermath of the war. Other topics included in this volume are the German army, the Battle of Britain, America in the war, women's role in the war, Japan at war, the Holocaust, D-Day invasion, and the atomic bomb. Young adults will find this book interesting because of its many photographs and sidebars. It is a very brief overview and can only be used as a supplement to more substantial works on the subject.—**Shannon Graff Hysell**

323.   **The Grolier Library of World War I.** Danbury, Conn., Grolier, 1997. 8v. illus. maps. index. $249.00/set. ISBN 0-7172-9065-4.

Written for students in grades 7 and higher, *The Grolier Library of World War I* has as its purpose the explication of the conflict that "affected the modern geopolitical landscape of our planet" more than any other. The set is divided into 8 chronologically arranged, 128-page volumes: "The Causes of Conflict, 1914"; "The Race for the Sea, 1915"; "The Lines Are Drawn, 1916"; "The Year of Attrition, 1917"; "The U.S. Enters the War, 1915-17"; "The Eastern Front, 1918"; "A Flawed Victory"; and "1919-39, the Aftermath of War." Each volume contains indexes (subject and biographical) to the entire set, the same 32-word glossary, and the bibliography for the encyclopedia. The format of each volume is identical. Each begins with a comprehensive table of contents listing the subjects covered in the book as well as additional features, such as biographies. This is followed by an introduction explaining the arrangement of the book and a map that focuses on the location of the action in the individual volume. This similarity in format allows each volume to stand alone and makes the information highly accessible.

The editors of *The Grolier Library of World War I* have provided the student researcher with an engaging and information-rich resource. While providing good coverage of the military and political aspects of the war, they have also contributed insights into social history, literature, and medical and technological advances. The use of numerous sidebars giving short biographies of political leaders and military commanders, quotations from letters and diaries, and cross-references to related topics give insights into homefronts as well as battlefronts. The many maps and black-and-white photographs contribute to visual interest.

With its exploration of the causes of the war, ranging back to 1879, and its discussion of the effects of the war, projecting to 1939, this encyclopedia becomes a valuable research tool for issues beyond those indicated in its title. This publication, because of its readability and accessibility, will be a valuable addition to any library or media center.—**Michele Tyrrell**

324.   **Modern Campaigns.** Danbury, Conn., Grolier, 1997. 15v. illus. maps. index. $319.00/set. ISBN 0-7172-7678-3.

Modern Campaigns is a series of 15 volumes, each covering an important military conflict of modern times. The conflicts treated cover Civil War campaigns (First Battle of Bull Run, 1861; Antietam, 1862; Chickamauga, 1863; and Vicksburg, 1863); World War I campaigns (Gallipoli, 1915, and Kaiserschlact, 1918); World War II campaigns (France, 1940; Midway, 1942; Guadalcanal, 1942; Kursk, 1943; Normandy, 1944; Operation Bagration, 1944; Arnhem, 1944; and Ardennes, 1944); and a Vietnam campaign (Tet offensive, 1968). Designed for junior high and high school students, each volume describes the events that precipitated the specific conflict; the events of the campaign; and details on the participants, armaments, geographic influences, and other factors that helped determine the outcome of the engagement.

Each volume has 112 pages with numerous captioned photographs (both color and black-and-white), maps, drawings, and timelines, making the set appealing to young adults as well as adults. A table of contents and a master series index in each volume simplifies their use for both researchers and browsers. Also contained in each volume are a chronology of the important dates and events, a guide to further reading, and recommendations for "wargaming" the specific campaign. This series will be a welcome addition to school and public libraries and is within the price range of most libraries.—**Vik Brown**

325.   Purcell, L. Edward, and Sarah J. Purcell. **Encyclopedia of Battles in North America: 1517 to 1916.** New York, Facts on File, 2000. 383p. maps. index. $60.00. ISBN 0-8160-3350-1.

This encyclopedia covers nearly 400 alphabetically arranged battles in Mexico, Canada, and the United States—from Francisco Hernández de Córdoba's battle against the Maya at

Champoton, Mexico in 1517 to Major Frank Tompkin's fight against the forces of Pancho Villa in Parral, Mexico, almost 200 years later. Small encounters are excluded, as well as those that little information is available for (e.g., pre-European, Native American conflicts). But, the definition of "battle" is flexible enough to include encounters not found in other standard works, such as Mark M. Boatner's *The Encyclopedia of the American Revolution* (David McKay, 1966) and *The Civil War Dictionary* (rev. ed.; David McKay, 1988).

Each entry is headed with the name of the battle; any alternate names; and the place, date, and name of the larger conflict (e.g., American Revolution). The text describes the battle; its context, outcome, and significance; and the military figures, units, geographic locale, and casualties. Entries also feature brief bibliographies for further reading. Supplementary features include a glossary of military terms, dozens of maps (up to a full page in size), several appendixes (battles listed alphabetically, chronologically, and by war, and a directory of battlefield sites), an extensive bibliography, and a subject index. This is an accessible, reasonably priced, and comprehensive military history reference work that is appropriate for all school, public, and academic libraries' history collections. [R: LJ, July 2000, p. 79]—**Kenneth W. Berger**

Handbooks and Yearbooks

326. **World War II: Almanac.** By George Feldman. Farmington Hills, Mich., U*X*L/Gale, 2000. 2v. illus. maps. index. (U*X*L World War II Reference Library Series). $79.00/set. ISBN 0-7876-3830-7.

327. **World War II: Biographies.** By Kelly King Howes. Christine Slovey, ed. Farmington Hills, Mich., U*X*L/Gale, 1999. 288p. illus. index. (U*X*L World War II Reference Library). $42.00. ISBN 0-7876-3895-1.

328. **World War II: Primary Sources.** By Barbara C. Bigelow. Christine Slovey, ed. Farmington Hills, Mich., U*X*L/Gale, 2000. 229p. illus. maps. index. (U*X*L World War II Reference Library Series). $42.00. ISBN 0-7876-3896-X.

These three titles complete the Gale/U*X*L World War II Reference Library Series. The *Almanac* volumes provide in-depth information and current commentary on World War II. The 2 volumes provide 17 chapters covering subjects such as the war's background (beginnings in Europe), its expansion, American's entry into the war, the U.S. home front, and occupied Europe. These chapters also discuss the Holocaust, impact of the war, the Allied and Axis sides, the war's turning points, D-Day, defeat of Germany, war against Japan and its defeat, spies and scientists, the arts and propaganda, and the post-war world.

Each volume includes a reader's guide, timeline, words to know, research and activity ideas, where to learn more, and an index. The "Words to Know" section is a useful glossary for World War II units. The "Research and Activity" section is a boost for teachers and students looking for project ideas. Over 150 black-and-white photographs and maps enhance the text, as do the numerous sidebars that highlight individuals and facts. Despite a few proofing errors, this is an excellent title to add to World War II reference collections.

The *Biographies* volume focuses on 31 people who played key roles in World War II. These include such well-known figures as Winston Churchill, Charles de Gaulle, Dwight D. Eisenhower, Adolf Hitler, Douglas MacArthur, George S. Patton, and Joseph Stalin. The biographies are generally 8 to 10 pages in length and feature photographs, interesting sidebars, and resources to consult for further research (e.g., books, periodicals, Websites).

The *Primary Sources* volume provides 16 full or excerpted documents, such as speeches and memoirs from soldiers, nurses, and Holocaust survivors. Documents from Winston Churchill, Franklin D. Roosevelt, Adolf Hitler, Ruth Minsky Sender, Ernie Pyle, and Stephen E. Ambrose, and many more are included. Over 70 black-and-white photographs illustrate the text and maps help explain the logistics of the war.

This volume also includes a reader's guide, a timeline, a list of words to know, and an index. Each chapter begins with an introduction to set the stage for the reproduced document and concludes with a list of where to find more information. Sidebars and boxed information further help clarify the text. Bold typefaced words in documents are defined in the margin. As always with such a limited collection of documents, readers can quibble over what was selected. But this work does provide secondary students with some key primary resources for their research needs. All in all, these three titles, like others in the Gale/U*X*L Reference Library Series, deserve a place in reference and circulating collections for grades 6 through 12. [R: SLJ, Aug 2000, p. 128]—**Esther R. Sinofsky**

10 Occultism and Parapsychology

OCCULTISM

329. **The Greenhaven Encyclopedia of Witchcraft.** By Patricia D. Netzley. San Diego, Calif., Greenhaven Press/Gale, 2002. 288p. illus. index. (Greenhaven Encyclopedias). $74.95. ISBN 0-7377-0437-3.

The Greenhaven Encyclopedia of Witchcraft is a collection of articles that explore all aspects of witchcraft, including magical tools, rituals, concepts, traditions, witchcraft-related deities, historical events, and important figures in the field of witchcraft. It covers from the medieval witch trials to the modern-day, Neo-pagan witchcraft religious movement. The book includes a table of contents, the articles, a short list of books for further reading, a more extensive list of works consulted, and an index. Most of the illustrations are of articles relating to medieval witchcraft; oddly enough there are few if any pictures of modern-day Pagan leaders.

The articles are brief and unsigned. As there is no list of contributors it can be assumed all of the articles are written by Netzley. She is aware of current scholarship and mentions it, also explaining where it and the beliefs of modern witches are the same or where they differ. For example, her article on Margaret Murray explains that Murray was a scholar whose books postulated the existence of a witch cult from the Stone Age through the medieval witch trials and into the present, arguing that although the witch trials gained their information through torture, the features of witchcraft brought out in the trials were too similar for coincidence. Netzley also explains that modern scholars discount Murray's theories, while some witches accept them and some do not.

The Greenhaven Encyclopedia of Witchcraft begs to be compared to *The Encyclopedia of Witches and Witchcraft* by Rosemary Ellen Guiley (2d ed.; see ARBA 330). They cover much of the same material from a similar viewpoint. Each has articles the other does not. Guiley's articles tend to be longer with more illustrations, and tend to have suggestions for further reading. Comprehensive collections on alternative religions or the occult will want both. Those who must choose will probably prefer Guiley's *The Encyclopedia of Witches and Witchcraft.*—**Mary A. Axford**

330. Guiley, Rosemary Ellen. **The Encyclopedia of Witches and Witchcraft.** 2d ed. New York, Checkmark Books/Facts on File, 1999. 417p. illus. index. $50.00; $24.95pa. ISBN 0-8160-3849-X.

Guiley knows her witches. In the book's acknowledgements she thanks a "Who's Who" list of today's major leaders of Neo-Paganism (of which Witchcraft, or Wicca, is a denomination). Guiley is the author of more than 20 books, most dealing with aspects of Eastern and Western metaphysics. Her books are shining examples of professionalism in fields plagued by books that are poorly researched and written.

The book focuses on the magic and witchcraft in Western culture, covering classical to modern witchcraft. Classical witchcraft is a term often applied to the medieval conception of witches who worshipped Satan and performed vile deeds. The encyclopedia applies modern research to the concepts and cases of medieval witchcraft. Modern Neo-Pagan Wicca is a nature religion centering on the worship of a mother Goddess, her consort God, and the practice of self-empowering and transformative white magic. Another category of articles are on folk magic and include topics such as village wise women and Pennsylvania Dutch hex witches. Guiley also covers related religions such as Santeria and Vodoun (or Voodoo), which are usually treated by the media as inaccurately as it treats witchcraft.

The articles are arranged in alphabetic order. There are many *see also* references, although many more could be added. Most of the articles include a further reading list, and the book has an extensive bibliography. The index looks rather sparse, but is adequate to an encyclopedia that is already organized alphabetically.

The 2d edition adds new articles and updates many of those from the original 1989 edition (see ARBA 90, entry 755). New articles primarily deal with the modern religions and their developments since the earlier edition, although Guiley also reviewed new publications on classical witchcraft. Any encyclopedia deals with the problem of being out-of-date as soon as it is in print. For example, the wonderful Doreen Valiente, author of some of the most widely cherished Wiccan rituals, died in 1999 after the book went to press. Guiley might also want to consider if she publishes another edition adding an article about the dynamic Neo-Pagan Internet presence in newsgroups, mailing lists, and Web pages. *The Encyclopedia of Witches and Witchcraft* is highly recommended. It is a comprehensive source of accurate information concerning topics too often misunderstood. [R: LJ, 1 Oct 99, p. 80]—**Mary A. Axford**

PARAPSYCHOLOGY

331.   Ogden, Tom. **Wizards and Sorcerers: From Abracadabra to Zoroaster.** New York, Facts on File, 1997. 246p. illus. index. $40.00. ISBN 0-8160-3151-7.

This one-volume reference provides a historical overview of enchantment, magic, and the occult based on both fact and fiction. The author has been a professional magician who has toured around the world during the past 20 years and who has been interested in the occult all of his life. In the foreword, Ogden states that terms such as *wizard*, *shaman*, *witch doctor*, *warlock*, and *necromancer* are often used interchangeably because people do not make the distinction between practitioners of beneficent magic and their malicious counterparts—a distinction necessary to respectively divide practitioners of so-called white versus black magic. Ogden is also quick to add that these names do not always offer a gender choice (*wizard*, for example). The inclusion of popular supernatural characters with magical powers from films—the Blue Fairy from *Pinocchio*, for example—and of the thumbnail sketches of nearly 200 films makes this reference especially innovative.

The entries range in length from less than a quarter-page to several pages in a generous two-column layout. Topics include magicians and events from world history. Black-and-white illustrations and drawings enhance the work. Most of the dozen or so black-and-white photographs were taken by the author on his travels around the world; in fact, the one criticism of this work is the lack of any color plates or photographs that greatly enhance other encyclopedias of magic. The work includes an index and an extensive bibliography of more than 150 books, as well as 41 articles, 35 sound recordings, and 14 videos. This reference is a real value and is recommended for all libraries.—**Edward Erazo**

11 Political Science

GENERAL WORKS

332. **Opposing Viewpoints Resource Center. http://www.gale.com.** [Website]. Farmington Hills, Mich., Gale. Price negotiated by site. Date reviewed: Aug 02.

Opposing Viewpoints is designed specifically with students and researchers of contemporary issues in mind. It will be an ideal source for those researching debate topics, writing a paper on a controversial topic, or those simply looking to find out every side of an issue. Designed around Greenhaven Press's Opposing Viewpoints series, this site also includes information from Gale and Macmillan Reference USA, including *Bioethics for Students* (see entry 441), the *Encyclopedia of Sociology* (see ARBA 2001, entry 835), and *Great American Court Cases* (see ARBA 2000, entry 523). Articles from more than 30 newspapers are provided as well, including *U.S. News and World Report*, *Newsweek*, and *The New York Times*—all trustworthy sources of news.

The homepage of *Opposing Viewpoints* displays more than 50 of the most popular topics of debate, including birth control, capital punishment, genetic engineering, pollution, and gun control. The easiest way to search is to simply click on one of these topics. Users can also search by keyword, subject, of full text, or conduct a more selective advanced search. Search results provide brief citations to reference articles (displayed according to title) and journal articles (displayed chronologically with most current articles first). At this point the relevant entry or article is just a click away. Users can either e-mail or print all search results. Additional features include tips on how to search effectively, a dictionary, and a research guide. Researchers can also check out more information on Gale's selected topic of the week by looking at "Spotlight On" or can vote on "This Week's Poll," which features a question about a current topic of interest.

This is an ideal resource for high school and undergraduate college libraries. The only worry with a source such as this is that users will stop researching with this tool and not consult other, equally valuable tools. [R: BR, Sept/Oct 02, p. 83]—**Shannon Graff Hysell**

333. **Pro/Con.** Danbury, Conn., Grolier, 2002. 6v. index. $309.00/set. ISBN 0-7172-5638-3.

This attractive six-volume set could be a boon to librarians and teachers assisting young researchers with such perennial term paper and debate topics as gun control, bilingual education, global warming, abortion, and euthanasia. The six volumes represent major subject areas: "Individuals and Society," "Government," "Economics," "Environment," "Science," and "Media." Each volume within the set is divided into major sections containing 16 topical questions. For example, topic number 14 in the "Media" volume asks: "Does Napster Encourage Copyright Infringement?" Topics begin with a brief introduction and are centered around a yes (pro) and no (con) essay. Marginalia supplement the essays with added information and quotations by historical figures such as Winston Churchill and Henry David Thoreau. Citations for print and Web resources for further research and a summary of that issue's pros and cons follow each topic. Finally, a "key map" provides a schema of the issue's central points. One-page sidebars on topics such as Watergate, the history of cloning, and civil rights are interspersed throughout the set to contribute further insights and historical context. A full index to all six volumes and a glossary conclude each volume. Pro and con essays have been chosen from a variety of authors, including those from previous centuries such as Rousseau, Montesquieu, Machiavelli, and Joseph Goebbels. Most, however, are contemporary writers who run the gamut from economist Milton Friedman to feminist teacher, writer, and provocateur bell hooks.

Public, high school, and community college librarians will want to consider purchase of this excellent reference tool. It brings together disparate aspects of topics, yet it is not so conveniently packaged as to preclude critical thinking or to push for a particular point of view. *Pro/Con* could occupy shelves near favorite debate reference tools such as *CQ Researcher* and *Editorials on File*. There are also excellent Websites for pro/con analysis such as the Multnomah County (Oregon) Library Social Issues Homework Center at http://www. multcolib.org/homework/sochc.html.

A shortcoming of this otherwise valuable set is a failure of the publisher to provide more complete credentials for the writers. Some are undoubtedly from the popular press and some from academe, although it is impossible to verify without consulting other biographical or reference sources. Since librarians and teachers justifiably emphasize that researchers closely scrutinize authors' credentials, such an oversight is significant and may be a deal breaker for some purchasers. [R: VOYA, Oct 02, p. 318; SLJ, Nov 02, p. 105]—**Linda D. Tietjen**

POLITICS AND GOVERNMENT

United States

Biography

334.   Wilson, Richard L. **American Political Leaders.** New York, Facts on File, 2002. 444p. illus. index. (American Biographies). $65.00. ISBN 0-8160-4536-4.

This collection of more than 250 biographies of American political leaders covers men and women who were elected or appointed to office or have, in some other way, exerted considerable influence in American history. Those chosen for inclusion in this book are frequently mentioned in high school or college textbooks or appear prominently in the news. Biographies range in length from two-thirds of a page to four pages and each entry is accompanied by a short bibliography. Entries are arranged alphabetically. Listings by offices held or sought and by date of birth are included. The index has references to offices, places, political parties, historical events, and cross-references among the entries. The book has a bibliography of other collective biographies and about 60 well-selected photographs.

The aim of the book, to include biographies of prominent individuals in American politics, is achieved. The entries are more substantial than those found in other one-volume collections. The scope differs from most similar collections, which limit their selections by race, gender, or holders of particular offices. The writing style is accessible to the intended audience and the content of the entries would meet the needs of readers seeking more information on the accomplishments and importance of the subject in American politics. As a one-volume collection of biographies, this book is an excellent addition to collections serving general readers, high schools, and undergraduates. [R: SLJ, April 03, p. 97]—**Jeanne D. Galvin**

Dictionaries and Encyclopedias

335. **Encyclopedia of American Government.** Joseph M. Bessette and R. Kent Rasmussen, eds. Englewood Cliffs, N.J., Salem Press, 1998. 4v. illus. maps. index. $210.00/set. ISBN 0-89356-117-7.

The *Encyclopedia of American Government* (EAG) is a reference work developed around current curricular design for students in middle and secondary school social studies and civics units of study. The 200 alphabetically arranged articles are supposed to be written in a jargon free language, stressing essentials and defining terms as they are introduced; however, the definition of *conservatism* is regarded as modern and *liberalism* is defined as welfare liberalism. The definitions are not jargon free; the bibliographies include contemporary works, but most listings are university press volumes and do not appear to be suitable for middle school and ninth-grade level civics units.

The format is awkward; it has continuous paging for the four volumes, yet lacks a complete four-volume table of contents in each volume. It also places the U.S. Constitution in the back of a volume as an appendix instead of making it an article on its own with an essay analyzing it, which would be more appropriate. The primary resource should be in the text, not an appendix to a reference source on U.S. government. From this set, students would not know that freedom of speech, press, assembly, and petition are in the Bill of Rights. An essay should be included on each of these basic U.S. freedoms. There is an essay on religion that deals with the basic facts from the First Amendment. The EAG is adequate and can be recommended for middle school libraries with some hesitation.—**Gerald D. Moran**

336. **The Presidents.** Fred L. Israel, ed. Danbury, Conn., Grolier, 1997. 8v. illus. maps. index. $259.00/set. ISBN 0-7172-7642-2.

The Presidents is an eight-volume set that details the presidencies from George Washington through the 1996 election of Bill Clinton. Coverage includes a chronology; an extensive biography; excerpts from inaugural addresses and other noteworthy speeches or documents; information about family, cabinet, and vice president; and key places associated with various presidents. The set is lavishly illustrated with both color and black-and-white photographs and drawings. A stunning full-page color portrait begins the section on each president. Entries are 20-plus pages, giving a complete overview of each administration. Although the set is easily accessible for middle school students, it will appeal to high school students and adults as well. Volume 8 includes returns for each election with color-coded maps and state-by-state voting statistics, allowing the reader to visually see the country grow. An adequate index is also provided.

The information here is more extensive than the one-volume *Facts About the Presidents* (6th ed.; see ARBA 94, entry 499) or *The Presidents, First Ladies, and Vice Presidents* (see ARBA 2002, entry 715). The set under review is more readable than *The Presidents: A Reference History* (2d ed.; see ARBA 97, entry 589), which does not include the 1996 election. Because of its currency, its visual appeal, and its content, this set is a must-buy for all schools and public libraries.
—**Lynda Welborn**

337. **Scholastic Encyclopedia of the Presidents and Their Times.** updated ed. By David Rubel. New York, Scholastic, 2001. 232p. illus. maps. index. $18.95. ISBN 0-590-49366-3.

Rubel's *Scholastic Encyclopedia of the Presidents and Their Times* is truly an inexpensive resource for elementary school students. It provides concise information in an easy-to-read format where young readers will enjoy learning about the accomplishments and disappointments of each president, from George Washington to George W. Bush.

Little-known facts are what make this *Encyclopedia* different and interesting. Such as the fact that Herbert Hoover was the first president to have an asteroid named for him, or that Calvin Coolidge had an electric horse installed in his White House bedroom.

Each entry in the *Encyclopedia* includes the president's birth date and place, date of death, party, vice president, family member names, and nickname. Throughout the book certain words are highlighted in red, indicating that the subject is discussed in greater detail in another section of the book. Using the subject index at the end of the book, the reader can then find the page for the most detailed explanations of an entry. Black-and-white photographs of events and people, political cartoons, and artifacts reflecting the period in history as well as maps detailing the growth of the country can be found throughout the book. Rubel's *Encyclopedia* is recommended for the children's section of public libraries and elementary school media centers.—**Vang Vang**

Handbooks and Yearbooks

338.   **American Inaugurals: The Speeches, the Presidents, and Their Times.** Woodbridge, Conn., Blackbirch Press/Gale Group, 2002. 312p. illus. index. $64.95. ISBN 1-56711-584-5.

American Inaugurals is a collection of the inaugural speeches of the American presidents, from George Washington through George W. Bush. Published by Blackbirch Press, Gale Group's educational imprint, it is aimed at elementary and middle school students. It thus contains very little political or historical analysis.

A six-page introduction discusses the significance of the inaugural ceremony in American history and political life. This is followed by a chronological listing of presidents. Each entry consists of a brief overview of the president and his times, followed by the complete text of the inaugural address. Both speeches (or, in the case of Franklin D. Roosevelt, all three) are included for multiterm presidents. The book includes brief chapters on the two presidents who did not give inaugural speeches (John Tyler and Andrew Johnson). Each entry also contains various sidebars describing facts about the president, historical events that occurred during his time in office, and notable quotations from the speech.

The book is heavily illustrated. It includes many excellent color photographs and reproductions of the presidents, the inaugural events, as well as contemporary figures. It contains an index and a bibliography (called "For Further Research") of useful books and electronic sources. While the listed sources are current, it includes some Websites of questionable quality. *American Inaugurals* is a lively, well-organized, and attractive book that is highly recommended for any school or public library.—**Scott Johnston**

339.   **The American Presidency.** [CD-ROM]. Danbury, Conn., Grolier, 1996. Minimum system requirements: IBM or compatible 486DX/33MHz. Double-speed CD-ROM drive. MS-DOS 5.0. Windows 3.1. SVGA 256-color monitor. Microsoft or compatible mouse. Wave table sound card. Speakers or headphones. Printer (optional). Optional online requirements: Modem. Access to the World Wide Web using an Internet service provider. $19.99. ISBN 0-7172-3367-7.

A wag once said that the opposite of progress is Congress. That may well be, but citizens of the United States have long hallowed their presidency. Even after scores of scandals like the XYZ Affair, Teapot Dome, and more have rocked the Oval Office, people of the United States still rally around the office of the president, even after they have abandoned those who sit in the honored seat. The current CD-ROM is a testament to the deification of that office. Grolier has culled from its three basic encyclopedias—*New Book of Knowledge* (see entry 26), *Academic American Encyclopedia*, and the *Encyclopedia Americana* (see entry 22)—all materials relating to the U.S. presidency and loaded them on disc. The result is a fascinating piece of work that is as informative as it is fun to use.

When users first load *The American Presidency*, they will get QuickTime, AT&T's World Net Service, and Netscape Navigator Software. The World Net Service is AT&T's own browser that relies on Netscape for safe launching. Installation is easy and quick, but users should be advised, for space allocations alone, that the install feature automatically loads these programs. The "Presidential Assistant" takes users on a tour of the disc, but one is hardly needed. Depending on the depth of the information sought, clicking on the appropriate encyclopedia will guide users there. The screens are beautifully arranged and easy to read. Hardly ever is there an occasion for misunderstanding what one needs to click on next. Clicking is just what users will do. More than 800 biographies, general interest articles, facts, figures, and more are here. The "Quick Facts Browser" provides patrons with a brief résumé of any one of the 42 presidents. General articles discuss topics as wide-ranging as suffrage, the ballot box, and the electoral college to documents, speeches, the Constitution, and more. The presidential summaries range in length according to the historical importance of the president. Thus, Chester Arthur's sketch is brief compared to Abraham Lincoln's lengthy article.

The CD-ROM does not miss much chance for fun, either. By clicking on the first line of the opening screen, users will hear "Hail to the Chief" vigorously played. The multimedia section of minidocumentaries contains movie clips of everyone from Franklin Delano Roosevelt to Bill Clinton. Teachers will be particularly delighted to see quizzes for students from grade 3 through adult. The disc is not, however, without it faults. Even as information-rich as this resource is, much of it is of sound-bite quality. The section on scandals is selective, and bias is evident throughout. For example, Ronald Reagan "jammed" through his tax bill relief, "claimed" to have forced Mikhail Gorbachev and the Soviet Union to its knees, while combining "inspiration over management" with "simplistic" leadership. Compare this to the hagiography that passes for biography under Lyndon Johnson, John F. Kennedy, and even the current White House occupant.

The CD-ROM mimics some parts of *Vital Statistics on the Presidency* (Congressional Quarterly, 1996), but the book has fewer articles and more statistics. The disc is also somewhat like National Geographic Society's CD-ROM, *The Presidents: A Picture History of Our Nation* (Educational Media Division, 1996). Yet the current disc has fewer picture and clips, but three times as many articles and biographies. Not all academic librarians will find this CD-ROM useful unless they serve large undergraduate constituencies. Special, public, and school libraries, not to mention many homes, will see this multimedia disc as the godsend it is. [R: RBB, 15 Feb 97, p. 1040]—**Mark Y. Herring**

340.   Vile, John R. **The United States Constitution: Questions and Answers.** Westport, Conn., Greenwood Press, 1998. 316p. illus. index. $39.95. ISBN 0-313-30643-5.

Intended to help high school students understand the constitutional dimensions of U.S. government, this guide uses a question-and-answer format to present detailed information about the U.S. Constitution (i.e., can a president be sued for actions he took before assuming the office of the presidency?). Each chapter covers a specific issue or set of amendments. The final chapter focuses on key dates and events in U.S. constitutional history. The answers given vary in length from a simple sentence to a short paragraph. Following the question-and-answer chapters are eight appendixes that contain the text of the U.S. Constitution, the Declaration of Independence, and the Articles of Confederation; "100 Questions and Answers Used By the Immigration and Naturalization Service"; and lists of the speakers of the House, the U.S. presidents, the U.S. Supreme Court justices, and the 50 states with their dates of admission to the union and the number of representatives based on the 1990 census. The work concludes with a comprehensive subject/name index.

Given its intended audience, this is a somewhat useful supplement to general encyclopedias and specialized guides and handbooks. However, the guide is of little value to anyone other than secondary school students because the questions and answers are not placed in any historical, political, or social context; the bibliographies concluding each chapter cite only general survey texts; and the legal cases accompanying the bibliographies are not referenced back to the question or answer in which they were mentioned.—**Robert V. Labaree**

IDEOLOGIES

341. **Political Theories for Students.** Matthew Miskelly and Jaime Noce, eds. Farmington Hills, Mich., Gale, 2002. 429p. illus. index. $85.00. ISBN 0-7876-5645-3.

There are 19 major political theories and systems (e.g., anarchism, capitalism, communism, pacifism, populism, utopianism) discussed in *Political Theories for Students*, a volume written by academics and journalists and targeted at high school students, undergraduate college students, and general researchers. A 2-page spread of comparison tables of the 19 theories is introduced to readers, which precedes the detailed and thorough chapter entries for each political theory or system. The comparison tables include categories such as who controls government, who controls production of goods, and historical examples. Each chapter entry includes an overview of the political system, the history of the system, who controls government, how the government is put into power, what roles the people have, who controls production of goods, who controls distribution of goods, major figures, and historical examples. Additionally, significant writings and potential study questions are included in each entry as well as biographical entries (for instance, Aristotle is featured within republicanism). Relevant and current examples of the systems are outlined in the "Theories in Action" section. Other sections included in each entry are analysis and critical response, further readings (for the most part current citations), and an informational sidebar of facts. The work also includes a glossary, a master index, a chronology, and images.—**Leslie R. Homzie**

12   Recreation and Sports

GENERAL WORKS

Biography

342.   Edelson, Paula. **A to Z of American Women in Sports.** New York, Facts on File, 2002. 278p. illus. index. (Facts on File Library of American History). $44.00. ISBN 0-8160-4565-8.

The latest in the Facts on File Library of American History series, this book documents the contributions of women to sports in American society, primarily during the twentieth century. The author clearly defines her criteria for inclusion in her opening note, and follows this with an excellent introductory essay. The alphabetically arranged entries are focused on the sports and competitive aspect of each woman's biography, with only brief notes on personal matters. Each entry ends with a "Further Reading" list, which contains references to more in-depth articles, books, and Web pages on each individual. Entries are presented from a wide selection of sports, some rarely associated with women, such as boxing, wrestling, shooting, automobile racing, and bowling. A list of recommended sources on American women in sports, a standard index, and two uniquely helpful indexes in which entries are organized by sport and by year of birth close the book. This work is highly recommended for public libraries, high school libraries, and community college and undergraduate libraries. [R: LJ, 1 Oct 02, p. 81]—**Lynn M. McMain**

343.   Paré, Michael A. Carnagie, Julie L., ed. **Sports Stars, Series 5.** Farmington Hills, Mich., U*X*L/Gale, 1999. 348p. illus. index. $39.00. ISBN 0-7876-3683-5.

The fifth volume in this series continues the format that has been generally praised in reviews appearing in *Book Report*, *School Library Journal*, and *Booklist*. In this volume, 22 athletes have been profiled, and 12 others have had their entries in earlier volumes brought up-to-date (late 1999). The comprehension level is pitched at young people. The biographies, though called "full-length" in the introductory matter, run only 8 to 10 pages of text and pictorial matter; they are written in an undemanding style. While many of the subjects here may be thought of as role models for the young, the author has not left out examples of past indiscretions, such as law-breaking and drug use. Entries include the athlete's address and a list of sources for the essays (most often newspapers and magazines, including *Sports Illustrated*, *USA Today*, *Newsweek*, *People*, *Ebony*, and the occasional book.

The *Sports Stars* series does, in general, most of what it sets out to do. The essays are sometimes too praising. To be sure, athletes who have "overcome physical obstacles or social constraints" are most likely to be chosen for inclusion, along with stars who are merely currently active or at the top of their games. Minor sports, such as those that do not get much press and media attention, are also included: track and field, yachting, swimming (with its teenage heroes), and skiing. Girls and women are given an equal place. Even some of the "bad boys" of sports, such as the media-wary Albert Belle of baseball, are recognized. Except for some minor and rare editing miscues (e.g., Nyland Stadium for Neyland Stadium and Washington State "Huskies" instead of "Cougars") , *Sports Stars, Series 5*, along with its predecessors, deserves consideration for school libraries and young adult areas in public libraries.—**Randall Rafferty**

344.	Woolum, Janet. **Outstanding Women Athletes: Who They Are and How They Influenced Sports in America.** 2d ed. Phoenix, Ariz., Oryx Press, 1998. 412p. illus. index. $49.95. ISBN 1-57356-120-7.

In this 2d edition, Woolum has revised and expanded several sections, including the chapter that provides an overview of the history and development of women's sports. Unfortunately, there is no discussion of issues concerning minorities other than African American and disabled athletes in this section. The largest section of the book is the biographical section. More than 20 additional entries, including a boxer and a bullfighter, have been included in this edition. There are bibliographies for some of the individuals, but all titles listed are books. A new chapter concentrates on selected teams in selected sports that have received national recognition. Each entry has information on the history of the team, a list of achievements, and a brief biography of members of the team. It is puzzling why other teams were excluded that deserve mentioning, such as the 1984 women's volleyball team and the 1998 women's ice hockey team. There is no discussion on issues in women's team sports, including the changes in the training venues for the national teams or the advent of professional teams. The selected bibliography contains book titles and is sport-specific.

One problem that could have been discussed is the issue of locating information on women athletes and women's sports and additional resources that could be checked because identifying information on outstanding athletes is not always an easy task. The national organizations only include addresses; many have Websites that could have been included. At a time when several reference sources on women athletes and their sports are prevalent, *Outstanding Women Athletes* updates the previous edition and complements *Encyclopedia of Women and Sports* (see ARBA 97, entry 644) and *Encyclopedia of Women and Sports in America* (Oryx Press, 1998). The title at hand is recommended for libraries with the earlier edition and public, school, and academic libraries. [R: SLJ, Nov 98, p. 159]—**Mila C. Su**

Handbooks and Yearbooks

345.	Craig, Steve. **Sports and Games of the Ancients.** Westport, Conn., Greenwood Press, 2002. 271p. illus. index. (Sports and Games Through History). $49.95. ISBN 0-313-31600-7.

This is the first volume in Greenwood Press's Sports and Games Through History series. It has two primary goals: to provide a comprehensive, worldwide view of sports, play, and games of the ancients and to make suggestions for modern play. The author, the winner of the New Hampshire Sports Writer of the Year award, identifies sports and games that were popular at least 1,500 years ago. He defines "sports" as activities that are rule governed, determine a victor, have social or religious meaning, and are used as preparation for some greater concern to the community. "Play" includes activities that did not require an audience and were not associated with important cultural events. "Games" are either board games or dice games. Some activities, such as the gladiatorial contests of the Roman Empire and several animal-related sports, were purposefully omitted.

The entries are divided into seven regions of the world, and each section starts with an introduction, followed by the subcategories "Sports," "Play," and "Games." Each entry describes the history, purpose, equipment, rules, and suggestions for modern play. In addition to the source list under each entry, there is a separate comprehensive bibliography and index.

This book is valuable in that it covers lesser-known sports and suggests applications for modern play. Some sports are addressed in multiple sections, and the differences that are reflective of their culture and similarities are described thoroughly. Photographs and diagrams illustrate how the games and sports were played, and geographical coverage is well balanced. Libraries that emphasize sports or physical education may want to offer this publication. [R: LJ, 1 Nov 02, p. 78; SLJ, April 03, pp. 95-96]—**Mihoko Hosoi**

346. Fortin, François. **Sports: The Complete Visual Reference.** Willowdale, Ont., Firefly Books, 2000. 372p. illus. index. $39.95. ISBN 1-55209-540-1.

Sports have long been a national obsession in the United States. Whether one is an active participant or an avid spectator of athletics, *Sports: The Complete Visual Reference* will answer many questions about many different kinds of sports for readers consulting this reference. The book is divided into 20 categories, including such topics as track and field, aquatic sports, snow sports, ball sports (both large and small), and combat sports. Each section is further divided into smaller sections; for example, under "Aquatic Sports" the topics of swimming, synchronized swimming, water polo, apnea free diving, and diving are discussed. Each entry is generally discussed in two to three pages, and color photographs, illustrations, charts, and fact boxes are provided. Famous athletes are showcased throughout the work, with brief explanations of their contributions to their sport. A three-page introduction discusses the history of sports, from their transformation from local competitions to the cultural phenomena they are today. The book concludes with an index.

With its easy-to-understand text and colorful illustrations, *Sports: The Complete Visual Reference* will get a lot of use in junior high, high school, and public library collections. Researchers will likely find new sports they were unaware of as well as new information about their current favorite sports. [R: LJ, July 2000, p. 80; BL, 1 Dec 2000, p. 758; SLJ, Nov 2000, p. 96]—**Shannon Graff Hysell**

347. Hastings, Penny. **Sports for Her: A Reference Guide for Teenage Girls.** Westport, Conn., Greenwood Press, 1999. 254p. illus. index. $45.00. ISBN 0-313-30551-X.

As this book notes, one in three high school girls are involved in a sport and this number is growing each year. The number of athletics offered to young women is growing as well. The author of this work wrote this book in an attempt to get information about sports and their benefits out to young women. Besides the obvious benefit of promoting good health, sports also provide young women with self-confidence, socialization skills, leadership skills, and time management skills.

The top eight most popular sports among teenage girls are given their own chapters. These include basketball, field hockey, soccer, softball, swimming and diving, tennis, track and field, and volleyball. Another chapter titled "Other Sports to Try" includes less familiar sports, such as badminton and crew, and male-dominated sports, such as football and baseball. Each of these chapters provides practical advice on trying out for the team, equipment used, and most common injuries of the sport, among others. One of the most interesting chapters discusses the special issues that can arise from participating in athletics, such as eating disorders, over-involved parents, and problems with coaches. The book concludes with a list of resources and an index. This book will be a valuable addition to any middle or high school library.—**Shannon Graff Hysell**

348. Wilkins, Sally. **Sports and Games of Medieval Cultures.** Westport, Conn., Greenwood Press, 2002. 325p. illus. index. (Sports and Games Though History). $49.95. ISBN 0-313-31711-9.

Recreational activities are important in every society. In *Sports and Games of Medieval Cultures*, Wilkins discusses the recreational activities of people from all areas of the globe between the fall of Rome and the rise of printing. She answers such questions as: Where did sports and games come from? How did societies share ideas and contribute toward forming the games that we play today?

This work has many strengths. The work's individual consideration of each continent merits praise. In addition, each section is subdivided by game and play (sports). The activities' descriptions vary in length, but have detailed summaries. Where possible, Wilkins includes how to adapt methods of playing modern games to their medieval equivalents. The path that a game took in being introduced to various cultures also receives attention here, especially when the modern descendant(s) came from a common ancestor. Where she needs to make a geographical distinction, the author does so, especially where specific societal groups are concerned.

There are a few areas in which the book is lacking. First, what were Wilkins' sources? She might have included a list of further reading for the user's benefit. Also, the work suffers from the author's imposition of the Western medieval dates upon the rest of the world. Not every society's medieval period can be dated between 476 and 1476. Given the rest of her organization and planning throughout the book, this oversight is unfortunate.

Despite these issues, this work will provide a useful reference for medieval social activities. This work is recommended for public, school, and academic libraries.—**David J. Duncan**

Indexes

349.   Meserole, Mike. **The Ultimate Book of Sports Lists 1998.** New York, DK Publishing, 1997. 224p. illus. index. $17.95pa. ISBN 0-7894-2134-8.

Meserole, creator and editor of the *Information Please Sports Almanac* (see ARBA 94, entry 818, and ARBA 91, entry 800), has compiled more than 1,000 lists in the sports of baseball, football, basketball, hockey, golf, tennis, track and field, swimming, soccer, Olympics, horse racing, auto racing, and a miscellaneous category that includes movies. The majority of the lists are documented, so the reader understands the time span or context of the list. For example, in the section on college basketball, under the category of streaks, there is a list of longest winning streaks for the full season with an explanation that this includes post-season and tournaments. The lists mainly highlight single game and single tournament results.

The material is arranged in an easy-to-use format with a good index; however, this resource is far from being the ultimate authority in either sport or list coverage. The author does not address why he chose the information he did other than as entertainment value. This title may be of more interest for personal collections than a library's collection. *Guinness Sports Record Book* (see ARBA 94 entry 825, and ARBA 91, entry 811) covers many more sports even though the focus is on world records. Aside from trivia and statistical use, this volume does not satisfy the reader's curiosity. Andrew Postman's *The Ultimate Book of Sports Lists* (see ARBA 98, entry 727) has more entertaining lists than this volume.—**Mila C. Su**

FOOTBALL

350.   Buckley, James, Jr. **Super Bowl.** New York, DK Publishing, 2000. 64p. illus. index. (Dorling Kindersley Eyewitness). $15.95. ISBN 0-7894-6300-8.

Part of the Dorling Kindersley Eyewitness series, this slim volume covers many interesting facts about "the world's most popular single-day sporting event." As with all DK Publishing books, this volume is filled with color photographs and sidebars containing little-known bits of information. The book begins with chapters on how the Super Bowl was created and then goes on to feature highlights of Super Bowls I-XXXIII. The text and photograph captions provide information on star coaches and players, as well as interesting facts about commemorative patches and trophies and events of the half-time shows. The chronological layout demonstrates the high points and low points the NFL teams.

The second half of the work offers pictures and information on topics unique to the Super Bowl, such as the trophies, Super Bowl rings, records made during the games, and the pregame and halftime shows, among others. The final chapter is an overview of the latest Super Bowl between the St. Louis Rams and the Tennessee Titans. An index concludes the volume.

Probably best suited for children and young adults, this work as well as others in the series will work well in school libraries and the children's sections of public libraries. Adult fans are better off with *The Sports Encyclopedia: Pro Football* (see ARBA 98, entry 745) or *Total Football: The Official Encyclopedia of the National Football League* (see ARBA 98, entry 746).—**Shannon Graff Hysell**

OLYMPICS

351. **Chronicle of the Olympics, 1896-2000.** New York, DK Publishing, 1998. 330p. illus. index. $29.95. ISBN 0-7894-2312-X.

This volume updates the previous edition (see ARBA 97, entry 660) with complete results for the Olympic Games in Atlanta, Georgia. The chronology provides an overview for each of the Olympic Games, with highlights of the opening ceremony and various events. This section is the major focus of this title, along with a variety of photographs that capture different moments of competition. The snippets of drama, tension, and competition that highlight each of the Olympic Games and attempt to capture the spirit experienced at that time is the main difference between this and other titles on the Olympics. A total of 26 new entries have been added. An overview of expectations and the new events at the 1998 Winter Games and the 2000 Summer Games in Sydney, Australia, is presented. The next section contains statistics on all of the Olympic Games by each game, the total number of participants (further broken down by gender and country), and the medallists for each event. Other tables and charts include the top five medal-earning countries and the top five "outstanding athletes." *Chronicle of the Olympics, 1896-2000* is recommended for public and school libraries. Individuals and academic libraries may want to consider its purchase as a supplemental resource. [R: SLJ, July 98, p. 114]—**Mila C. Su**

SOCCER

352. Woog, Dan. **The Ultimate Soccer Encyclopedia.** Los Angeles, Calif., Lowell House, 1999. 144p. illus. maps. $9.95pa. ISBN 0-7373-0399-9.

Intended for young readers, this encyclopedia provides interesting tidbits of information about the game of soccer. It is not a comprehensive or in-depth examination of the game, but is more of a fun and entertaining introduction for young fans and players. Alphabetic entries of only a few sentences cover various players such as Mia Hamm, Thomas Dooley and, Tony Meola; rules and regulations; famous teams; and soccer terminology. Black-and-white photographs and educational maps enhance the work. Sidebars provide interesting facts and trivia, such as how Cobi Jones made a guest appearance on *Beverly Hills 90210* in 1994 and how much distance does an average soccer player cover during an average 90-minute game? (7 miles). Woog was the 1990 National Youth Coach of the Year and has written several other books about the sport, including *The Parent's Guide to Soccer* (Roxbury Park, 1999) and *The Ultimate Soccer Almanac* (Lowell House, 1998). This volume is recommended for juvenile reference and circulating collections.—**Cari Ringelheim**

TAE KWON DO

353.   Park, Yeon Hee, Yeon Hawn Park, and Jon Gerrard. **Tae Kwon Do: The Ultimate Reference Guide to the World's Most Popular Martial Art.** updated ed. New York, Facts on File, 1999. 218p. illus. index. $26.95; $14.95pa. ISBN 0-8160-3838-1; 0-8160-3839-2pa.

A literal translation of Tae Kwon Do (TKD) is "the way of punching and kicking." The term was developed in the late 1950s in an attempt to unify Korean martial arts. It was not until 1973, with the formation of the World Tae Kwon Do Federation (WTF), that a single organization was recognized by the Korean government as an international regulatory body. However, various systems of TKD continue to be practiced worldwide under the auspices of numerous organizations not endorsed by the WTF.

This book then reflects the TKD as endorsed by the WTF. The volume's principal contribution is a graphic depiction of sequential movements, known as forms, that have been officially sanctioned by the WTF. Practitioners of a particular martial arts style are required to execute forms for advancement through various levels of their art. The rest of the book contains little not included in other books about TKD or martial arts of other countries. Warm-up exercises, sparring, breaking, and self-defense are neither unique nor well covered. Of some value are the various sections on Korean martial arts terminology, officially sanctioned WTF associations worldwide, and rules of competition used for the Olympics. A grossly sexist section on etiquette tells readers how to chew their food and attend to their superiors.

Library collections do not usually carry martial arts books because they are likely to be vandalized. Despite the current emphasis on martial arts in the media, this book will not likely enjoy that notoriety. Unless readers need to be informed on the doings of the WTF, they are better off with books that provide better coverage on self-defense and a balanced view of oriental martial arts.
—**Andrew G. Torok**

13 Sociology

SUBSTANCE ABUSE

354. **Drug Information for Teens: Health Tips About the Physical and Mental Effects of Substance Abuse.** Karen Bellenir, ed. Detroit, Omnigraphics, 2002. 452p. index. (Teen Health Series). $58.00. ISBN 0-7808-0444-9.

Although teen substance or drug abuse fluctuates over time and with different drugs, the overall pattern of abuse is alarming. The physical, mental, emotional, and behavioral effects of hallucinogens, inhalants, tobacco, ecstasy, cocaine, steroids, and others can be substantial. This handbook, written for a teenage audience, provides information on the causes, effects, and preventive measures related to drug and substance abuse among teens. Overall, there are 57 chapters grouped into 8 sections or parts: understanding substance abuse; alcohol; tobacco; other abused drugs; other drug-related health concerns; treatment; drug statistics and policy controversies; and resources for help and additional information.

The chapters in section 1 explain many of the common physiological effects of various drugs, patterns of addiction, effects on the brain, and the influence of peer pressure. There is even a self-diagnostic quiz on one's knowledge of drugs. Sections 2 through 4 address alcohol, tobacco, and a range of other common drugs and substances that are abused. The section on related health concerns deals with such topics as teen suicide, AIDS, rape, youth violence, and other problems that are drug-influenced. There are an additional number of chapters dealing with treatment, statistics, and policy controversies. All chapters are excerpted or adapted from other sources, which are cited. Chapters also include definitions of "weird words" (i.e., technical terms), things to remember, quick tips, and important facts. A final section of the book provides directory information on state and national organizations that provide additional information or assistance. There are also suggestions for further reading, as well as a combined subject/name/title index.

Except for the chapter on the physiology of the brain, the chapters are quick to make a connection to their teenage reading audience. The prose is straightforward and the book lends itself to spot reading. It should be useful both for practical information and for research, and it is suitable for public and school libraries.—**Stephen H. Aby**

355. **Drugs and Controlled Substances: Information for Students.** Stacey L. Blachford and Kristine Krapp, eds. Farmington Hills, Mich., Gale, 2003. 495p. illus. index. $99.00. ISBN 0-7876-6264-X.

Learning about drugs and controlled substances is useful for maintaining health. It is also a common assignment for middle school and high school students. Finding accessible, current, objective material can be a challenge. *Drugs and Controlled Substances: Information for Students* is a good place to start. The contributors are physicians and medical or science writers. The entries cover legal addictive drugs, illegal drugs, other controlled substances, and commonly abused prescription and over-the-counter drugs. The 50 signed alphabetic entries contain the official and street names of the drugs; the pharmacological class; the chemical composition; ingestion method; therapeutic use; usage trends; mental and physiological effects; interactions with other substances; treatment and rehabilitation information; and the personal, social, and legal consequences of use. All entries begin with an overview and end with a resource list of books, articles, and Websites. Definitions of key terms appear in boxes. Sidebars offer additional information such as myths, current news, and historical data. Black-and-white photographs and charts illustrate the text. A chronology from 5000 B.C.E. to 2002 provides a brief history of substance use and abuse in various cultures. A photograph gallery of commonly used and abused prescription drugs, a glossary, an appendix with the text of the Controlled Substances Act, and variant name and general indexes complete the work.

Drugs and Controlled Substances: Information for Students is very useful because it covers a wide range of substances, including diuretics, herbs, diet pills, and steroids, in addition to the usual narcotics and psychedelics. The information is current, objective, and accessible to young adults and adults reading at the high-school level. Students doing reports will get a great deal of information here, but they may want to consult other resources such as *Uppers, Downers, All Arounders* (CNS Publications, 2000) for more background. Patrons who need basic information about drugs will be satisfied with this source. It is an excellent addition to school, public, and consumer health library collections.—**Barbara M. Bibel**

YOUTH AND CHILD DEVELOPMENT

356. **Being Human.** Danbury, Conn., Grolier, 2000. 8v. illus. maps. index. $229.00/set. ISBN 0-7172-9419-6.

With the help of artists and three editorial consultants, the editors of this work have produced a set, intended for schools and libraries, that endeavors to encompass the full range of what it is to be a young human. Attractive two-page spreads include boxes, color illustrations, and action figures of young people. Boldfaced subheads and short sentences break up the sometimes complex information. The editors clarify the scope and purpose of the set and individual volumes with introductory material, and each book has suggested activities and a glossary. Volume titles are "Human Body," "Brain and Senses," "Health and Illness," "Keeping Safe," "Personality and Behavior," "Communication," "Relationships," and "Human Race." The first volume is a fine introduction to human anatomy, and each spread throughout is well done, but the set as a whole ranges too widely to offer focused, usable information. Students will enjoy browsing the excellent individual blocks of material during free time, but the grab bag collection of often tenuously integrated material makes the set of limited usefulness to educational curriculum. [R: BL, July 2000, p. 2055; SLJ, Aug 2000, p. 132; BR, Sept/Oct 2000, p. 76]—**Edna M. Boardman**

357. Fenwick, Elizabeth, and Tony Smith. **Adolescence: The Survival Guide for Parents and Teenagers.** New York, DK Publishing, 1996. 286p. illus. index. $14.95pa. ISBN 0-7894-0635-7.

Attempting to write a "survival guide" designed for use by both parents and teenagers is an ambitious goal, yet this work has potential for helping many parents and adolescents find their way through the teen years. Several features help set this book apart from others with a similar goal. The authors obtained input from adolescents; the results of a questionnaire sent to 100 high school students helped determine the content of this book. As a result, the volume deals with such concerns as "The Milestones of Adolescence" (including physical development); "Learning to Live

Together" (talking to teenagers, rebellion, the quest for freedom); "The Adolescent and the Outside World" (friends, social life, sexuality, sexual abuse, school, money matters, facing up to adulthood); and "The Adolescent in Trouble" (drugs, running away, emotional problems). Another advantage is that within each chapter is a section designed for parents as well as a separate section for adolescents, very obvious because it is printed in blue. Real-life case studies are presented that give both the parent's and the youth's viewpoint. Through these case studies, the authors help the reader to see a situation from the other person's perspective.

Both adult and teen readers may browse through this book at the library or even check it out. Although it may not necessarily serve as a focal point for discussion among members of the same family, its strength may be that it helps teen readers to see common situations through their parents' eyes (even if the parent has not read the book), and thus helps the teen communicate with parents. It also gives teens—especially those who are uncomfortable with discussing certain situations—practical suggestions as to where they can get information, help, or advice beyond the family. In other families, it may be only the adult who receives insight and guidance. Ideally, several members of the family will read the guide and use it as a jumping-off point to solve problems jointly. This book may be especially useful in larger group discussions where both parents and teens are willing to open up communication avenues.

This book has reference value because of the index and because the independent—yet integrated—nature of the chapters allows readers to consult just those pages that would be most useful at a given time. A cautionary note for librarians: Not all parents will want their adolescents to have access to the frank discussions of some issues, especially those dealing with sexuality. On the whole, this is a well-intentioned and well-designed reference that most libraries serving adolescents and their families will want to have in their collection.—**Jan Bakker**

14 Women's Studies

ALMANACS

358. **Women's Almanac.** Linda Schmittroth and Mary Reilly McCall, eds. Detroit, U*X*L/Gale, 1997. 3v. illus. index. $85.00/set. ISBN 0-7876-0656-1.

Women's Almanac is a 3-volume collection of assorted information about women that is designed primarily for youthful readers. The set is an independent component of U*X*L's projected 13-volume "Women's Reference Library." Although the 3 volumes are subtitled, respectively, *History*, *Society*, and *Culture*, the focus of each volume is not as narrow as the subtitles imply. Each volume contains a wide assortment of material about women of the past and present, about gender roles in various cultural settings, and about critical issues that have had significant impact upon women of different times and places. The volumes cover a wide range of topics, including essays on women in politics, education, sports, science, medicine, the military, music, the arts, religion, and the family. The almanac also includes more than 200 black-and-white photographs and illustrations of people and events, scores of excerpts from important historical documents, dozens of charts of pertinent statistics depicting the place of women in society, a glossary of words readers need to know, and a comprehensive index.

Academic historians will quiver at the frequent oversimplifications and erroneous historical facts scattered throughout the volumes. These imperfections notwithstanding, *Women's Almanac* is an appealing and readable introduction to a large number of pertinent topics relating to women worldwide. The set is recommended for high school libraries.—**Terry D. Bilhartz**

BIOGRAPHY

359. **The Grolier Library of Women's Biographies.** Danbury, Conn., Grolier, 1998. 10v. illus. index. $319.00/set. ISBN 0-7172-9124-3.

The Grolier Library of Women's Biographies surpasses the usual list of notable women to find the unusual contributors to medicine, the arts, teaching, activism, and government. A well-conceived, beautifully executed series, this work entices young researchers as well as teachers, librarians, and parents from cover to index. Each volume opens with a table of contents that lists the entry, a brief description, and page number. In bold typeface are the titles of 20 essay articles, such as "Women's Employment Issues," "Suffrage," and "Women and Islam." A delightfully readable preface discusses the issues of patriarchy and marginalization without rancor through thoughtful commentary and passages from the Bible, Koran, Aeschylus's *Eumenides*, and Elizabeth Cady Stanton's *History of Woman Suffrage*. Equally forthright are 1,750 succinct, informative entries, 1,300 of which are accompanied by photographs or drawings. Concluding each volume is a master index. General headings list entries under groupings such as law, Swiss women, espionage, and performing arts. A puzzling omission is the absence of subheadings for African American women. The final volume appends a 36-page list of works cited and their authors.

The overall plan and coverage of the Grolier biography set is remarkably balanced and useful. Diction and composition set a good example of clear, objective writing and wise selection of data. A worthy adjunct to the work's success is the selection of appealing typefaces, layout, and pagination. A dismaying fault is the near absence of Native American women. The obligatory Pocahontas and Sacagawea receive mention, but editors have omitted them from the subheading "Heroism." Passed over are the best known Native American leaders and role models—Wilma Mankiller, Milly Hayo Francis, Datsolali, Sarah Winnemucca, Martha Brae, Molly Brant, Kateri Tekakwitha, Nancy Ward, Maria Tallchief, Marjorie Tallchief, Gayle Ross, Maconagua, Maria Chona, Buffy Sainte Marie, and Suzette La Flesche Picotte (Bright Eyes). The glaring slight of American Indian women is a serious drawback to a set that otherwise demonstrates sensitivity and appreciation for women's struggles to excel. [R: SLJ, Nov 98, p. 152]—**Mary Ellen Snodgrass**

360.   Jackson, Guida M. **Women Rulers Throughout the Ages.** Santa Barbara, Calif., ABC-CLIO, 1999. 471p. illus. index. $75.00. ISBN 1-57607-091-3.

According to the author of the volume, *Women Rulers Throughout the Ages* includes a biographical listing of "every known ruling queen, empress, prime minister, president, regent ruler, de facto ruler, constitutional monarch, and verifiable ruler who was female, from the oral tradition and written history of the world's kingdoms, islands, empires, nations, and tribes down to present time" (p. xxxi). Each of the 508 alphabetically arranged entries contains a 50-to 350-word overview of the life and career of the woman ruler, and a brief reference section that includes a bibliography of 1 to 6 sources. About one in five entries also contains an illustration. The volume also contains a 12-page introduction that discusses the role of women in political history; a 15-page geographical chronology of entries, which lists the subjects by country and century; a 16-page bibliography that lists the references cited in the text; and a 17-page general index.

Although the entries include some interesting information and are generally well written, much of the material in the volume is drawn from world history textbooks, dated monographs, encyclopedias, almanacs, and newspapers. The brevity of the entries also limits their usefulness. The work is more a reference text for nonspecialists than a guide for scholars in the field of women's history. This work is recommended for high school libraries. [R: BL, 15 Dec 99, pp. 804-05]—**Terry D. Bilhartz**

361.   Kort, Carol, and Liz Sonneborn. **A to Z of American Women in the Visual Arts.** New York, Facts on File, 2002. 258p. illus. index. (Facts on File Library of American History). $44.00. ISBN 0-8160-4397-3.

Comprised of clearly written, concise essays on more than 130 American women artists, *A to Z of American Women in the Visual Arts* offers a starting point for research on a rich topic. Essays are approximately one to two pages in length, and each ends with a short bibliography (a longer list of suggested reading appears at the end of the book). Biographical details and a summation of the artist's career are given. A black-and-white photograph of the artist accompanies many, but not all, of the essays. No other images are included. In addition to the standard index, three others are present and list artists by medium, artistic style, and year of birth. Artists from the eighteenth century to the present are covered and represent a variety of ethnic backgrounds. Painters, sculptors, photographers, printmakers, architects, and a few decorative artists are mentioned. Artists working solely in nontraditional media, such as performance and installation art, are overlooked, leaving out groundbreaking artists such as Laurie Anderson and Yoko Ono.

The addition of a glossary would have been useful; within essays, some terms (*abstract expressionism*) are defined while others (*minimalism*) are not. The authors indicate that only artists about whom a significant amount of material has been written are included. So researchers of lesser-known American women artists will have to look elsewhere for assistance. If added alongside other works on women artists, the *A to Z of American Women in the Visual Arts* will make a useful addition to reference collections in secondary school, public, and academic libraries. [R: LJ, 1 May 02, pp. 90-92; BR, May/June 02, p. 75; VOYA, Oct 02, p. 318]—**Terrie L. Wilson**

362.   Langston, Donna. **A to Z of American Women Leaders and Activists.** New York, Facts on File, 2002. 288p. illus. index. (Facts on File Library of American History). $44.00. ISBN 0-8160-4468-6.

If you are seeking information on American women activists, past or present, this is the reference tool to consult. The work contains biographical information on approximately 150 women who represent a variety of ethnic and regional backgrounds. Entries are alphabetically arranged by name, range from one to two pages in length, and include facts on the family background. Education and public activities of the biographees as well as some more personal information is often included. Each entry is accompanied by a list of further reading. There is a bibliography of recommended sources on American women activists, and indexes by the type of activity, by year of birth, and a general index of personal names and organizations referred to. This work is easy to consult, but the writing style is somewhat choppy and dry. Overall, one cannot argue about persons included here, although this reviewer would have added a prominent figure like Jane Fonda based on her activities opposing the Vietnam War. Also, one might wonder about the necessity of including information on personal relationships—as in the case of Eleanor Roosevelt—in a reference work.—**Leena Siegelbaum**

CHRONOLOGY

363.   Franck, Irene M., and David M. Brownstone. **Illustrated History of Women.** Danbury, Conn., Grolier, 1999. 10v. illus. index. $295.00/set. ISBN 0-7172-7497-7.

The *Illustrated History of Women* is a comprehensive, well-written history of women from ancient times through the twentieth century. The text is enriched with illustrations, photographs, charts, sidebars, and many timelines and boxes. There is a set index in each of the 10 volumes. The reading level is appropriate for middle school and high school students.

The topics discussed in "HerStory" are religious battles, childbirth and midwives, education, women of power, women of medicine, scientists and inventors, slaves, art patrons, writers, and heroines and villains. Each of the volumes presents an overview of the period and a timeline for that period. A short bibliography and cross-references are provided and a cumulative index is provided in each of the volumes. This set is recommended for middle and high school libraries due to the reading levels and the limited bibliographies. [R: BR, Nov/Dec 99, pp. 88-89]—**Kay M. Stebbins**

364.   **Women's Chronology: A History of Women's Achievements.** Peggy Saari, Tim Gall, and Susan Gall, eds. Detroit, U*X*L/Gale, 1997. 2v. illus. index. $55.00/set. ISBN 0-7876-0660-X.

This two-volume chronology of women's history includes prehistory to 1996 in a series of short (one-to two-paragraph) entries. Volume 1 covers approximately 4000 B.C.E. to 1849, and volume 2 covers 1850 to the present. Other than the first few entries, which deal with Sumerian,

Greek, and Chinese gods, the book covers individual women who are notable for their accomplishments and achievements. The entries are brief, simple, aimed at middle and high school-level readers, and provide minimal information about the people, events, and historic or social context. The 10-page introduction gives a sketchy overview of women's history since the Bronze Age.

Like any chronology, this book is selective and misses many interesting people. For example, a random check showed no entries for Josephine Baker, Rachel Carson, or Lucretia Borgia. However, it does provide more international coverage than many women's chronologies, especially of Asian and Middle Eastern women. It is also well illustrated and includes a useful glossary. Words not normally within a middle school vocabulary are defined parenthetically within the entries.

The major weakness of this set is the inaccessibility of the information. The entries are in chronological order, and the index is limited to proper names and titles. It is impossible for a user to look up women by country, profession, contribution, achievement, or any other general category of interest, which turns an otherwise useful reference source into a source of great potential frustration. In addition, it lacks a bibliography.

Women's Chronology is clearly aimed at general use by middle school and high school students or public library patrons looking for introductory information. It is not suitable for academic or research libraries or for anything beyond simple reference use.—**Susan Davis Herring**

365. **Women's Firsts.** Caroline Zilboorg, ed. Detroit, Gale, 1997. 564p. illus. index. $44.95. ISBN 0-7876-0151-9.

Christine Todd Whitman, first female governor of the state of New Jersey, proclaims in the foreword to this volume, "*Women's Firsts* offers a tribute to women of achievement whose stories can inspire, enlighten, and motivate." After careful review of the text, most would probably agree.

This reference source covers many fields of endeavor and is arranged by subjects that include activism, the arts, business, education, literature, religion, science, and sports, to name only a few. It is further arranged by date, with special emphasis on the nineteenth and twentieth centuries. Each entry identifies the achievement, describes it, summarizes its content, and is immediately documented by its source. The more than 150 illustrations of clear photographs and reprints are impressive. Other features include a timeline of events in women's history; an index by day of the month; an index by year; a keyword index listing women, important events, issues, and locations; and a bibliography.

With the growing interest in women's history, this volume should prove useful to scholars, historians, students, and all who seek information on women's concerns. This addition would be great for academic, public, and school libraries. [R: RBB, 15 Mar 97, p. 1261]—**Mary L. Bowman**

DICTIONARIES AND ENCYCLOPEDIAS

366. Kuhlman, Erika. **A to Z of Women in World History.** New York, Facts on File, 2002. 452p. illus. index. (A to Z of Women). $49.50. ISBN 0-8160-4334-5.

In this one-volume encyclopedia of women's history, Kuhlman presents snapshots of various women throughout the ages. Crossing many centuries and many countries, stories of courageous women are brought forth. Many are well known, but many more are not. Yet all of the women demonstrate uniqueness in their lives and are important to a new understanding of history. With 260 biographies, Kuhlman provides details of each woman's life and her contributions as well as additional references to other works about the individual in each entry. As she states in her introduction, "*A to Z of Women in World History* is an attempt to reveal not only the distinction of the women it covers but also the ingenious ways in which women skirted the numerous barriers society placed in their paths" (p. viii). This she does in a lively and engaging manner.

Arranged alphabetically within fields of accomplishment (journalists, performers, scholars, and so on), Kuhlman also provides appendixes that list each woman by country of birth and year of birth, as well as an extensive index that provides subject searching. More than 30 photographs of various women are included. This volume is very well organized and easy to navigate. *A to Z of Women in World History* will be an excellent introductory volume for high schools, community colleges, and public libraries.—**Deborah L. Nicholl**

367.   **Scholastic Encyclopedia of Women in the United States.** By Sheila Keenan. New York, Scholastic, 1996. 206p. illus. index. $17.95. ISBN 0-590-22792-0.

Scholastic Encyclopedia of Women in the United States is a valuable illustrated profile of women who have made a difference in U.S. history, from Pocahontas to Hillary Rodham Clinton. The biographies are brief and represent a broad range of women's lives. Women treated are from every walk of life and from every ethnic group. A significant number are included because they filled nontraditional roles.

Entries are divided into six broad categories covering a period from the 1500s through the 1990s. Most entries are biographical, but a significant number of cameos are included that highlight women whose broader lives are not detailed. A section called "Women's Words" presents quotations by and about women. A section entitled "Women's Sphere" is a sidebar that provides information on what women's lives were really like during a certain period.

This source contains both a topical and an alphabetic index. It is recommended for both public and school libraries.—**Mary L. Bowman**

368.   **Women's Firsts: Milestones in Women's History.** Peggy Saari, Tim Gall, and Susan Gall, eds. Detroit, U*X*L/Gale, 1998. 2v. illus. index. $55.00. ISBN 0-7876-0653-7.

Why would one want one's children to read *Women's Firsts*? It is one of those curious books about which praise is due because it is fun and full. Its scope is enthusiastic, covering women who were the first in the fields of activism, the arts, business, education, government, media, the professions (e.g., architecture, law, medicine, and the military), religion, science, and sports. Women from ancient to modern times and from all over this planet are listed first by domain, then by the year(s) of their most notable accomplishment. The women's birth and death dates, formal education, special awards, photographs, and anecdotes are published, and sources are credited.

Why would one not want one's children to read this book? Because "children" is spelled "childran." Because "Renaissance" and "consumption" and "naval" and "Colombian" are misspelled, and "principle" is used as an adjective. Mother Teresa is said to have joined the Sisters of Loretto (American-founded) when she actually joined the Sisters of Loreto (Italian-founded). Katharine Graham manages to be both Katharine and Katherine in the same paragraph. Whether it is sloppy cut-and-paste or simple disregard of the facts, the accuracy of this book suffers.

The book mentions many obscure, although consequential, women and is a wonderful place to start if you have the Internet or an encyclopedia next to you. Nonetheless, a reader deserves and expects a book that has been proofread. [R: VOYA, Oct 98, pp. 308-309]—**Mary Pat Boian**

HANDBOOKS AND YEARBOOKS

369.   **Women in History on File.** New York, Facts on File, 2002. 1v. (various paging). illus. maps. index. $185.00 looseleaf w/binder. ISBN 0-8160-4646-8.

A new publication in the On File series, *Women in History on File* features reproducible materials on women from prehistoric times through the twentieth century. These materials are organized into seven sections: "The Prehistoric World," "The Ancient World," "The Medieval World," "The First Global Age," "The Eighteenth Century," "The Nineteenth Century," and "The Twentieth Century." Information is geographically sorted under the sections.

More than 250 timelines, chronologies, and other resources that can be used for classroom handouts are included in this looseleaf binder. For example, there are timelines on the lives of Nefertiti, Cleopatra, Queen Elizabeth I, Pocahontas, Betsy Ross, Florence Nightingale, Louisa May Alcott, Harriet Tubman, and Indira Gandhi. Several chronologies of events in various time periods and civilizations are also included along with various articles about women in society and other topics that have affected women throughout time (e.g., the right to vote, equality, feminism). A table of legal marrying ages in the United States and around the world, a list of Internet resources, a chronology of twentieth-century leaders and female enfranchisement, and an index conclude the volume. This resource is recommended for middle and high school libraries.—**Cari Ringelheim**

370. **Women's Voices: A Documentary History of Women in America.** Lorie Jenkins McElroy, ed. Detroit, U*X*L/Gale, 1997. 2v. illus. index. $55.00/set. ISBN 0-7876-0663-4.

Women's Voices, geared toward the secondary-school library market, provides students with an opportunity to read firsthand the words of many of the women who have helped shape social issues during the past two centuries. The set's 32 documents are organized by topic: education, abolition, suffrage, property and labor, civic and social equality, and reproductive rights. Coverage includes many classics, such as Virginia Woolf's "A Room of One's Own," Sojourner Truth's "Ain't I a Woman?," and excerpts from Simone de Beauvoir's *Second Sex*, as well as more contemporary writings by Gloria Steinem and Betty Friedan. Emphasis is on the expansion of women's rights and the speeches, writings, and documents (such as the Supreme Court's *Roe v. Wade* decision) that have supported this trend.

Each excerpt includes biographical information about the speaker or writer plus historical overviews that place the issue in a broader context. Words students may not understand are explained in sidebars throughout the 32 sections. Other teaching points include "What Happened Next" and "Did You Know" sections that highlight interesting information. More than 100 photographs and portraits, a glossary, an index, and a timeline supplement the text.

The speeches, diary entries, newspaper articles, poems, and reminiscences recounted in these two volumes provide a fascinating overview of women's halting but irresistible progress toward a society that embraces equal rights for both sexes. It should be in every secondary school library.—**G. Kim Dority**

15 Fine Arts

GENERAL WORKS

Biography

371.   Cummings, Robert. **Great Artists: The Lives of 50 Painters Explored Through Their Work.** New York, DK Publishing, 1998. 112p. illus. index. (DK Annotated Guides). $24.95. ISBN 0-7894-2391-X.

This oversized book gives two facing pages to each artist. One painting is selected to represent the artist's body of work. A few are fortunate enough to have another piece printed, but the focus is on the one painting, where captions and enlargements of particular portions of the piece explore the where and why of color, texture, composition, symbolism, purpose, and so forth. Other captions give insight into the artist's life, chronicle important events during the artist's most productive period, and list other notable works of the painter. Two primary paragraphs begin each section, reviewing the artist and giving an overview of the painting highlighted.

The key to this book is that it is part of the series DK Annotated Guides. Curiously, there is no foreword or introduction. In looking to the subtitle, "The Lives of 50 Painters Explored Through Their Work," a hint of purpose is presumed. If the purpose of this book is to encourage the reader to seek out more in-depth sources on the artist, then it succeeds well. The brevity of the text and visuals will certainly compel most to find out more about each of these 50 artists.

When a specific number is drawn from an established group, personal preference (and admitted bias) always makes one question why this one was chosen but the other not. Of course, Leonardo da Vinci, Michelangelo, and Titian are included, but why not El Greco? Peter Paul Rubens, Rembrandt, and Jean-Honoré Fragonard are there, but not Thomas Gainsborough. The first artists in this compilation are the Limbourg brothers (mid-1440s), and the last mentioned is Jackson Pollock (1912-1956). Are readers to believe the contributors felt there were not any great artists before 1400 or after 1950? Of the 50 artists selected, only 2 are women, and only 3 are from the United States. No Latin American artists are represented. In fact, 45 of the 50 artists here are European. This complaint is not meant to dismiss the artists that are here. Each is a master deserving recognition. However, a more international selection would have been nice to see.

Another curiosity is the formatting of the book. As stated, each artist is given two facing pages. Some of the facing pages read horizontally, and some read vertically. Because the two formats are intermixed, turning the page often requires flipping the book up on its end. At its vertical format, the book is awkward to hold, text is difficult to read, and visuals are arduous to view.

On the plus side, the reproductions are of high resolution and vibrant color, and the captions placed around the paintings are of essential and important information. Also, the book is reasonably priced. This book is marginally recommended to scholastic libraries because students may be able to complete a sketchy one-page essay on an artist from the data supplied here. Otherwise, *Great Artists* is purely a quick coffee-table browsing book. [R: SLJ, July 98, p. 115]—**Joan Garner**

Handbooks and Yearbooks

372.   **Art: A World History.** New York, DK Publishing, 1997. 720p. illus. index. $59.95. ISBN 0-7894-2382-0.

As quoted on the book's jacket, "Encyclopedic in Scope—Conceived as a journey through a huge museum, *Art: A World History* looks at the development of art from its earliest beginnings to the contemporary innovations of the late 20th century. From the art of the great preclassical civilizations to the treasures of five continents, all the major movements in the history of world art are chronicled. Developments in art, architecture, and design are set in their social and historical context." This resource combines text, pictures, and special "aside" boxes to highlight relevant historical events and cultures that contributed to the art of that time. It reflects the setting and mood of world societies from the beginning of human expression to the present, showing what happened to shape the art of the time, and it goes on to speculate what art will be in the future. Selected pieces of art are examined, defining what makes them masterpieces (i.e., composition, light and shadow, mastery of drawing technique, symbolism, and the like).

There is an incredible amount of information here. Readers can see the careful thought process put into each page layout and the formatting of data, and the text is concise and intelligent. For example, in defining Egyptian art, one line of the narrative nails it: "Objects are presented as they are conceived, not as they are seen." A simple sentence that explains an entire culture. This exceptional text is worth the acquisition of the book alone, and the numerous masterpiece dissections are invaluable to anyone wishing to gain a better understanding of art. Overall, this art book is a remarkable endeavor.

But the book is not without a few problems. As in this reviewer's look at another DK art book, *Great Artists* (see entry 371), this art source—although greatly improved over the above—still concentrates too heavily on European art. Credibly, Asian and South American art is explored, but not much beyond antiquity. The art of North America is more often than not given an "honorable mention" treatment, and the review of the latter part of the twentieth century is rushed through and too sketchy. For example, the Hudson River School movement of nineteenth-century America gets a 2-by-4-inch box footnote. The more well-known artists of this movement do not have a single painting displayed in this book. And the expansion of the art through the wide variety of new medias developed and improved upon in the last 60 years, such as photography, film, and computer art, only receive one-quarter to one-half page.

Art: A World History may be used as a textbook for upper high school and collegiate settings as long as one recognizes that certain areas and eras will need to be augmented independently. And if looked upon this way, it can be recommended to schools and public libraries. [R: LJ, 15 Nov 98, p. 63]—**Joan Garner**

373.   Janson, H. W., and Anthony F. Janson. **History of Art for Young People.** 5th ed. Bergenfield, N.J., Harry N. Abrams, 1997. 632p. illus. index. $49.50. ISBN 0-8109-4150-3.

Three decades of university students have learned about art history using an imposing textbook called *History of Art*, written originally by Horst Janson in 1962 and now continued by his son Anthony. Just as the university textbook has undergone periodic review, so has a shorter version for high school and junior college audiences called variously the *History of Art for Young People* or *Basic History of Art*. This new edition includes revisions to the treatment of art before the Renaissance as well as an extended look at the art of the twentieth century, including postmodernism.

Every public or school library needs a basic survey of art history in its reference collection. This one continues to be a popular choice because of the clarity of the prose, useful tables and maps, and the ever-increasing number of spectacular color illustrations. Several editorial changes have increased its value as a library reference book. An attractive redesign has simplified the process of identifying key artists and their works in the text. The reformatting also allows for extensive explanatory marginalia defining terms (*silkscreen* or *Augustine of Hippo*, for example) and line drawings illustrating key concepts. In addition, new boxed sections relate art historical movements to contemporary developments in music and theater. The changes continue to improve a good thing and update a valued intellectual guidebook for a new generation.—**Stephanie C. Sigala**

16 Language and Linguistics

ENGLISH-LANGUAGE DICTIONARIES

Grammar

374. **English Matters.** Danbury, Conn., Grolier, 2000. 10v. illus. index. $299.00/set. ISBN 0-7172-9437-4.

This small, 10-volume set provides easy-to-understand explanations about writing and speaking style, grammar, usage, and punctuation. Some of the alphabetically arranged entries answer questions about commonly confused words, parts of speech, thinking skills, literary terms, and research. Entries provide definitions, simple explanations and examples, or a cross-reference to an alternative keyword. Some pages are highlighted by blue side borders to emphasize important entries that are essential to proper English skills. For example, one such entry demonstrates the proper usage of commas—when it is absolutely necessary and when it is optional.

Entries go beyond just the rules of English to include explanations of concepts and examples of a business letter, a pie chart, and a Venn diagram. Dialog boxes also provide helpful hints, checklists, Internet sources, vocabulary word checks, and memory joggers. Indexes to the complete set are included in each volume for further ease of reference. This is a very useful resource for not only middle and high school students, but for adults as well. It is a quick and easy reference to the often-confusing English language. [R: VOYA, Oct 2000, p. 298; BR, Nov/Dec 2000, p. 76; SLJ, Nov 2000, p. 90]—**Cari Ringelheim**

Juvenile

375. **English Dictionary for Students.** Middlesex, Great Britain, Peter Collin; distr., Chicago, Independent Publishers Group, 1999. 907p. $15.95pa. ISBN 1-901659-06-2.

Designed for students whose age or grade level is not defined, this dictionary presents short definitions with a sentence or phrase demonstrating the term's use, the pronunciation (using international phonetic symbols that are explained only once at the beginning of the book), and the part of speech. The pages have narrow margins, but with the entry words in larger dark type, phrases or sentences in bold italics, and pronunciations in brackets, the book is readable.

According to the unpaged preface, some 300 terms include "encyclopaedic" comments. British definitions are preferred as are British spellings, usually with a U.S. spelling given second. Relatively recent terms such as "mad cow disease" are included, as are names of body parts and functions frequently excluded from student dictionaries. Some slang or vulgar language is included, but apparently not for sexual activities. Tables at the back give examples of how to "say" numbers, give metric equivalents for weights and measures, and list irregular verbs.

The front cover states that over 25,000 terms are included compared to over 3 times that many claimed by *Merriam-Webster's School Dictionary* (see entry 381). This dictionary would be helpful for middle school or high school students, especially to give an international flavor, but when used in the United States it needs to be supplemented by an American dictionary.—**Betty Jo Buckingham**

376. **The Kingfisher Illustrated Junior Dictionary.** Heather Crossley, ed. New York, Larousse Kingfisher Chambers, 1997. 192p. illus. $18.95. ISBN 0-7534-5096-8.

Designed for children age seven and up, the *Kingfisher Illustrated Junior Dictionary* lives up to its name—illustrated. There are 2-5 colored illustrations per page, with a number of half-page and nearly 20 full-page illustrations in the 192-page dictionary. The illustrations are appealing and useful, although sometimes items are not carefully tied to definitions on that page; for example, a nilgar and an eland are pictured near a definition of antelope with no connection other than proximity.

There is a guide at the beginning of the dictionary that explains three shapes used for homophones, pronunciation and rhyming words, and opposites. It does not seem likely that the average user will remember what the symbols mean, although the context may be clear enough. However, the fact that pronunciation is provided for less than 13 percent of the words, according to the reviewer's sample, indicates that this dictionary will not provide the kind of support needed by children just learning to read and pronounce words.

Some of the appendixes are helpful, especially those about states and countries. The alphabet on the pages could also be useful, but it tends to make the page too busy.

This is a colorful dictionary that may supplement but will not replace the need for more traditional dictionaries for children, such as *The American Heritage Children's Dictionary* (Houghton Mifflin, 2003).—**Betty Jo Buckingham**

377. **The McGraw-Hill Children's Dictionary.** Columbus, Ohio, McGraw-Hill Children's Publishing, 2003. 830p. illus. maps. index. $24.95. ISBN 1-57768-298-X.

378. **The McGraw-Hill Children's Thesaurus.** By the Wordsmyth Collaboratory. Columbus, Ohio, McGraw-Hill Children's Publishing, 2003. 294p. illus. $19.95. ISBN 1-57768-296-3.

The colorful cover of *The McGraw-Hill Children's Dictionary* claims it is "The Only Dictionary Your Child Will Ever Need!" With 830 entry pages and 97 more "reference" pages, this volume may seem at times to contain almost too much information. Many of the illustrations are in full color and useful. Others, like that of a girl standing with her hand to her head beside the entry for the word "misunderstanding," are less useful. Double-page spreads on subjects such as "Musical Instruments" and "The Solar System" are impressive, as are the word histories and a color-coded system to relate a word to 10 areas, ranging from the human body and communication to economy and government and law. Younger children may be overwhelmed by *The McGraw-Hill Children's Dictionary*, but this volume would be a great addition for those from the fourth grade up.

A companion volume, *The McGraw-Hill Children's Thesaurus*, claims to be "the only thesaurus your child will ever need." Its aim is "to help the young reader build a vocabulary that is expressive, versatile, and precise." Many entry words have been keyed to the same topics used in the companion dictionary. This volume contains fewer illustrations, but most are well chosen. Full-page spreads on words like "dogs," "insects," and "trees" encourage the user to employ specific, rather than generic, terms. With or without its *Dictionary*, *The McGraw-Hill Children's Thesaurus* will be a valuable addition to the upper elementary classroom, library, or any place where children write or do homework.—**Kay O. Cornelius**

379.   **The Merriam-Webster and Garfield Dictionary.** Springfield, Mass., Merriam-Webster, 1999. 800p. illus. $12.95pa. ISBN 0-87779-626-2.

The Merriam-Webster and Garfield Dictionary is the most child-friendly dictionary to be published. This innovative dictionary actually encourages use by utilizing a cartoon character that appeals to children of all ages.

This dictionary features the cartoon cat Garfield, in collaboration with its creator Jim Davis, to highlight featured words in the dictionary. At the bottom of the pages that use the highlighted featured word is a comic strip illustrating that particular word's usage.

This dictionary, inspired by Jim Davis, is designed just like every other dictionary and includes a list of common English given names; a list of foreign words and phrases; a section on biographical, biblical, and mythological names; a section on geographical names; signs and symbols; a handbook of style section; and a section on documentation of sources. There is even a special list of wacky definitions that only Garfield could dream up. In the front is a section of explanatory notes, abbreviations used in the work, and a page devoted to pronunciation symbols. It is an extraordinary combination of both dictionary and comic book and is highly recommended. —**Pamela J. Getchell**

380.   **Merriam-Webster's Intermediate Dictionary.** Springfield, Mass., Merriam-Webster, 1998. 943p. illus. $15.95. ISBN 0-87779-479-0.

This dictionary, of about 40,000 word entries, is intended for middle and junior high students. It is preceded by *Merriam-Webster's Elementary Dictionary* (Merriam-Webster, 1994) and followed by *Merriam-Webster's School Dictionary* (see entry 381). All three volumes are highly respected and widely used. For each entry in the main body of this work, syllabification is given, followed by variant spellings, phonetic pronunciation (the pronunciation key is found on each double-page spread), usage indication (e.g., slang, substandard), grammatical classification, and irregular plurals or tense formations when necessary. The definitions follow. They are clear, concise, and suited to the intended audience. As in other Webster dictionaries they are in chronological order. Separate entries are given for homographic words. A few basic words have synonym entries with definitions and usage pointers for each synonym. Some words with interesting origins are given a separate short paragraph called "Word History." There are about 300 "Word Histories" and an equal number of synonym entries. Brief etymologies or usage indicators are sometimes given, but there are no antonyms. The word coverage seems up-to-date. *Dork*, *Internet*, and *World Wide Web* are included, but not *search engine*. Many words considered obscene are absent; for example, *fornicate* is here but not its more frequently used synonyms. Running heads at the top of each page give both the first and last word on the page. Small black-and-white drawings are used to illustrate objects or animals. Special features include several mini-dictionaries at the back; a list of abbreviations, which includes chemical symbols; a biographical directory of more than 1,000 names with one-line identifications; a gazetteer of nearly 3,000 place-names with their pronunciations; and a short section of signs and symbols. The format is attractive, type size is suitable, and the binding is sturdy. This dictionary is highly recommended for students in grades six through nine.—**John T. Gillespie**

381.   **Merriam-Webster's School Dictionary.** Springfield, Mass., Merriam-Webster, 1999. 1158p. illus. $15.95. ISBN 0-87779-380-8.

Designed for high school students, this dictionary indicates the expertise of the staff of one of the preeminent dictionary makers in the United States. It compares well with the *Merriam-Webster's Collegiate Dictionary* (11th ed.; Merriam-Webster, 2003), including about 75 percent of the same words. The definitions, while frequently shorter with few subsections, reflect a strong influence from that volume. The etymologies are also very similar, but with fewer abbreviations, making them easier to understand. The introductory material includes topics such as guidewords, pronunciation, function, form and meaning of words, cross-references, usage, synonyms, abbreviations, and pronunciation symbols. The pronunciation guide also appears on each two-page spread. General abbreviations; a biographical dictionary with historical, biblical, and mythological names; a geographical dictionary; and a brief article on style complete the book.

The back cover of the dictionary claims that it contains 85,000 entries and 91,000 definitions. Terms omitted from this volume that are present in the *Collegiate* volume would probably not be of pressing interest to the average high school student. There are no terms appearing in the *School Dictionary* that are not in the *Collegiate*. Terms such as *CD*, *RAM*, *ROM*, and *grass* as marijuana, are included, as are body parts relating to sexual functions, but not the slang words defined in the *Collegiate* volume.

Nearly every two-page spread includes at least one helpful drawing or chart. The pages have enough white space to be appealing and easy to read. This will be a good dictionary for senior high school students, libraries, and for some middle school students. Libraries and some high school students may also wish to consult the *Collegiate* in book or CD-ROM (see ARBA 98, entry 998) format.—**Betty Jo Buckingham**

382. **Scholastic Children's Dictionary.** rev. ed. By the Editors of Scholastic, Inc. New York, Scholastic, 1996. 648p. illus. maps. index. $16.95. ISBN 0-590-25271-2.

Perhaps if every variant of a word, defined or undefined, was counted, the 30,000 words claimed for this dictionary by some reviewers might be reached. Defined terms are closer to half that number; main entries are still fewer. This dictionary, designed for children in grades 3 through 6, and based on an English dictionary, provides its own pronunciation, which is given only once. The pronunciation helps are rather standard sounds such as "a" for the sound in "mad" and "ah" for the sound in "father" and should be fairly simple to follow.

Most entries provide pronunciation, part of speech, and definition. Many include more than one definition and related words, and some include sample sentences. Homophones are given when appropriate, introduced by the phrase "sounds like." Very little information is provided on the history of words—only 5 in the 1st 25 pages. Those provided are designed to catch the interest of the readers. For example, the word history of *girl* points out that *girl* used to refer to a child of either sex and *gun* came from a huge crossbow from the fourteenth century named a "Lady Gunilda." Many colorful drawings and photographs illustrate further some complex terms, such as *ice-skating movements*, and suffix and synonym notes expand some definitions.

Supplements include the Braille alphabet, sign language symbols, world and U.S. maps, flags, facts about the states and presidents, and an index of picture labels. These last appear to be words that are not otherwise defined in the dictionary, although this is not always true and all labels are not included.

The editors have made an effort to address newer terms. *Kwanzaa* is defined, as are *Islam*, *Christianity*, and *Catholic*. Although *Protestant* is included, individual denominations are not. More body parts are defined than has been typical of children's dictionaries, but there are functions that are not included. For example, *manure* is defined, but *human waste* is not. More notice is taken of inclusive terminology, but *mankind* is defined and *humankind* is not.

This is a physically appealing dictionary, probably best used as one of several children's dictionaries, such as *The American Heritage Children's Dictionary* (Houghton Mifflin, 2003) or the *Macmillan Dictionary for Children* (see ARBA 2002, entry 1022), in school and public libraries. —**Betty Jo Buckingham**

383.   **Thorndike-Barnhart Junior Dictionary.** By E. L. Thorndike and Clarence L. Barnhart. New York, HarperCollins, 1997. 1024p. illus. maps. $19.00. ISBN 0-06-270161-4.

The *Thorndike-Barnhart Junior Dictionary* defines approximately 68,000 words, including a number of geographic terms and biographical entries; some basic scientific terms are also defined. Syllabication, part of speech, and pronunciation (including variants) are given; pluralizations of nouns and the participles and past tenses of verbs are frequently given. In addition, there are 1,200 photographs and illustrations; 34,000 illustrative examples; 900 usage notes and synonym studies; and a concluding section that contains world maps, a table of elements, and pictures and information about the U.S. presidents.

One does not expect a dictionary intended for middle school students to include obscenities, and this one does not. At the same time, one hopes for a dictionary to present information accurately, clearly, and concisely, and the *Junior Dictionary* again does not; its flaws are disturbing and manifest. There are persistent problems with names: Pseudonyms and birth names are rarely revealed, leading putative users to suppose that such figures as George Orwell, Houdini, and Boris Karloff had no other names. Full names of people are inconsistently given, and the first names of T. S. Eliot and F. Scott Fitzgerald remain mysterious. Also, the editorial decision to lump together all entries for people sharing a similar last name leads to some thoroughly misleading juxtapositions. One has the Franklins (Aretha and Benjamin), the O'Connors (Flannery and Sandra Day), and the Adams (Abigail, Ansel, John, John Quincy, and Samuel), to name but three examples.

Cross-referencing between entries is similarly weak: The entry for Buckminster Fuller mentions his role in creating the geodesic dome, but the entry for geodesic dome does not mention Fuller. Similarly, Karloff's entry mentions his role in *Frankenstein* (without providing the year of the motion picture), but the definition for *Frankenstein* provides an unidentified picture of Karloff, the caption stating only that it is the monster "as played by an actor." (Nor does the definition of *Frankenstein* provide the scientist's first name.) Finally, the quality of the definitions is poor. For example, to define *tzarina* only as *czarina* is of no help (and there is no cross-reference to the fuller definition given under *czarina*). This dictionary was also published as the *Scott Foresman Intermediate Dictionary*.—**Richard Bleiler**

384.   **The World Book Dictionary.** millennium ed. Chicago, World Book, 2000. 2v. illus. $87.00/set. ISBN 0-7166-0297-0.

This is a new printing of a two-volume dictionary that first appeared in 1963 and last appeared in 1996. Although major updating has occurred since the 1st edition, there is no evidence of any, or at least any significant, updating since 1996. Indeed, this "millennium edition" fails to define Y2K.

The dictionary defines 225,000 words, terms, or abbreviations, arranged in a single alphabetical list. Since it is intended for use with the *World Book Encyclopedia*, it has no entries for biographical names or geographic entities. With nice clear print, the dictionary is easy to read. It includes well-done line drawings, an average of more than one per page.

This dictionary is intended for use by students from junior high school level through college undergraduate level, although some material is aimed as low as third grade. The introductory material, running to 124 pages, includes information on correct English usage, vocabulary, punctuation, spelling, grammar, English language history, and word construction in English. These sections are intended as instruction to students and help make the dictionary very useful.

This is a good solid dictionary of American English and pronunciation. The binding is apparently sturdy and should hold up to student use in a school library. It would also be good for home use. There is, however, no compelling reason to replace recent editions of the work.—**Florence W. Jones**

385.   **The World Book Student Dictionary.** 2002 ed. Chicago, World Book, 2002. 900p. illus. $31.00. ISBN 0-7166-1550-9.

The 2002 edition of *The World Book Student Dictionary* is colorful, attractive, and very heavy. In addition to providing the usual information about main entries, its stated aim is to foster vocabulary and development and encourage an interest in words for students in grades three through six. Exercises and graded word lists suitable for each grade level are provided.

Introductory material covers how to use the main entries as well as detailed information about parts of speech, spelling helps, and plurals of nouns. Idioms, identified by a red dot in the main listings, should be helpful to the increasing number of children for whom English is a second language. Brief, nontechnical word histories are scattered throughout the main entries. For example, the main entry on *cloud* defines it as a noun and verb, followed by the idiom "on cloud nine," and states: "Cloud comes from an Old English word meaning 'rock.' It is also related to an Old English word meaning 'lump.' Many clouds look like large floating lumps of rock."

A reference section following the main entries contains student exercises and lists of presidents of the United States and Canada, the 50 states and their capitals, independent countries of the world and their capitals, and major languages of the world. An eclectic collection of facts about oceans and seas, longest rivers, metric conversion tables, and gods and goddesses is followed by a series featuring word games. Also included is a section on the meaning of selected first names and how last names evolved.

While *The World Book Student Dictionary* is obviously designed for classroom use with teacher guidance, it should also be useful in a general elementary library setting.—**Kay Cornelius**

Spelling

386.   **The Scholastic Dictionary of Spelling.** By Marvin Terban. New York, Scholastic, 1998. 223p. illus. $15.95. ISBN 0-590-30697-9.

This very simplistic approach to spelling offers the beginner many ways to search the spelling of words, and also different tricks to help the reader memorize these spellings. In the section entitled "How to Look Up a Word," some useful tricks of the spelling trade are offered, such as guide words, syllables, words that have confusing sounds, blends, silent letters, and compounds. Follow this with the section titled, "A Dozen and One Spelling Rules," and the reader will have all the information needed to begin using the remainder of the book, which is packed with more than 600,000 commonly used words in the English language. "The Dictionary of Spelling" section is set up in alphabetic order, and parts of the word that help the search by means offered in the earlier sections are set in bold typeface. The words are broken up into syllables, and many also have "sounds like" hints to assist the reader in finding the right word.

The back of the book offers a few hundred common misspellings for words, such as those which begin with "ph" in place of an "f," or use the letter "g" instead of "j." This section may help to ease the frustration that can occur when one is searching for words simply by sounding them out. In all, this reviewer found this guide to be a complete introductory tool for children learning to spell and a worthwhile addition to school libraries. [R: BR, Sept/Oct 98, p. 72]—**Michael Florman**

Synonyms and Antonyms

387. **The American Heritage Children's Thesaurus.** By Paul Hellweg, with the editors of the American Heritage Dictionaries. New York, Houghton Mifflin, 1997. 279p. illus. $17.00. ISBN 0-395-84977-2.

In a kid-friendly format and size, Hellweg introduces young students to the concept and use of a thesaurus. An opening how-to chapter will be useful to the students and teachers designing first lessons in word-use reference books beyond the dictionary. Most two-page spreads have color pictures that relate in some way to a word on the page, and many have a color-border box that contains antonyms. (Antonyms are not mixed with the synonyms.) The author uses color, space, bold typeface, four-point stars, italics, and numbers to set apart groups of definitions and parts of speech. This reviewer prefers Roget's traditional thesaurus over dictionary formats such as this, but this is the best way for a young person to start. The grade-level recommendation is better at the high than at the low end of the grade spectrum. Schools will appreciate Houghton Mifflin's effort to keep down the price.—**Edna M. Boardman**

Visual

388. **Scholastic Visual Dictionary.** New York, Scholastic, 2000. 224p. illus. index. $21.95. ISBN 0-439-05940-2.

This visual dictionary for children from Scholastic is just that—visual. There are no definitions of terms, only illustrations of the topic and a one-word explanation of what it is. The table of contents and the detailed index are essential in finding what users are looking for in this volume. The dictionary provides illustrations on such topics as the animal kingdom, the plant kingdom, the human body, architecture, clothing, communications, transportation, music, sports, energy, machinery, and symbols, among others. The illustrations are detailed, but without any explanation it will be difficult to find out much information about the subjects.

This book's main use will be for children to understand the names of components of particular items. For example, for the picture of a portable CD AM/FM cassette recorder the antenna, speaker, tuning control, and compact disc player are pointed out. This dictionary will have limited use in the children's reference department because of its lack of definition. School libraries might be able to use it, but only as a supplement to more substantial children's reference materials. [R: SLJ, Nov 2000, p. 88]—**Shannon Graff Hysell**

389. **Ultimate Visual Dictionary 2001.** New York, DK Publishing, 2000. 640p. illus. maps. index. $40.00. ISBN 0-7894-6111-0.

Although selective in its coverage as any book of this kind would have to be, there are visual answers in this book to many of the common questions that present themselves to readers every day. This is a new edition of the picture dictionary that was first published in hardback in 1994 as the *Dorling Kindersley Ultimate Visual Dictionary* (see ARBA 95, entry 52) and as a paperback in 1998. The content of the 2001 edition is identical to the 1994 edition with the exception of a 64-page addendum of new advances, processes, and devices that have emerged since 1994.

The original part of the book is arranged into 14 chapters covering such vast topics as the universe, the human body, sea and air, architecture, music, and everyday things. Illustrative of the information included is the section on baseball in the sports chapter. A brief description of the game is followed by color photographs of baseball equipment (the batter's helmet, the catcher's mask, a shoe, a bat, and a glove), a diagram of the baseball field, and the pitching sequence (windup, release, and follow-through). With such broad topic arrangement, a detailed index is the key to finding precise information. The new section in the 2001 edition contains topics such as the Hubble space telescope, genetic advances, body healing, the 2000 Olympics, digital photography, and the World Wide Web.

The *Ultimate Visual Dictionary* is ideal for school, public, and home libraries. Libraries owning the 1994 or 1998 editions may decide not to purchase the 2001 edition because the content is identical except for the 64-page addendum.—**Elaine F. Jurries**

17 Literature

GENERAL WORKS

Bio-bibliography

390. **Cyclopedia of World Authors.** 3d ed. Frank N. Magill, McCrea Adams, and Juliane Brand, eds. Pasadena, Calif., Salem Press, 1997. 5v. index. $350.00/set. ISBN 0-89356-434-6.

This 5-volume encyclopedia of more than 2,000 authors from Aesop (3d century B.C.E.) to Sherman Alexie (born 1966) has dual purposes: to combine, revise, and expand the 2 previous sets, *Cyclopedia of World Authors* (1974) and *Cyclopedia of World Authors II* (see ARBA 91, entry 1105); and to complement *Masterplots* (2d ed.; see ARBA 97, entry 906). The revisions are substantial: 25 percent of the entries are new to this edition. Although the greatest number of entries still come from the anglophone world, this edition includes new essays in major ethnic areas—African American, Latino, Asian American, Native American—and women's literature. The sketches consistently average a page in length, regardless of the writer's reputation, stressing biography over literary criticism.

Unlike other sources of this type, the *Cyclopedia* includes two unique aspects: writers whose primary claim to fame is not literary (Thorstein Veblen and Elizabeth Cady Stanton, for example), information about whom this source may not be the most obvious or intuitive choice, and one-hit wonders, such as Shelby Steele, Harriet Wilson, and Darryl Pinckney. The searcher is furthermore rewarded with ready access to contemporary writers (approximately 25 percent of the authors are still living). The 1997 copyright date, furthermore, reflects current biographical data, such as the recent death of Jose Donoso. In addition, most of the authors' works lists and bibliographies have been updated, if not expanded. As previously, the works lists are sorted by the genre in which the writer is best known; the bibliographic sources were selected on the basis of availability, timeliness, and usefulness, with a heavy slant toward English-language materials. The lack of page references for periodical citations, however, inhibits the effectiveness of the tool somewhat.

New to this edition are two indexes, one by a birth date timeline and one by where the writer flourished or was born. The geographic index inspires some caveats; for example, the cases of Albert Camus and Jacques Derrida, who are listed under both Algeria and France, are symptomatic of several duplications. Galicia, Silesia, and Numidia are designated as separate geographic entities. The master list of authors in volume 5 merely replicates the table of contents from each of the individual volumes; there is no additional index to names embedded within entries. All entries are signed, but an unusually high proportion of the contributors to this edition (nearly 15 percent) are designated as "independent scholar" under affiliation.

Although the set is almost beyond comparison in terms of sheer numbers of entries, its coverage is more superficial than that of Scribner's European, Ancient, British, American, and Latin American Writers sets (see ARBA 97, entry 961). *Cyclopedia*'s approach is more biographical and less interpretive than *Contemporary World Writers* (2d ed.; see ARBA 94, entry 1144). Its style is less colorful, but scholarship is more current than all but the most recent Wilson Authors series (see ARBA 97, entry 887). All in all, the set is a useful stepping-stone for works by and about the most influential and studied writers in today's curriculum.—**Lawrence Olszewski**

391.   Galens, David, ed. **Literary Movements for Students: Presenting Analysis, Context, and Criticism on Literary Movements.** Farmington Hills, Mich., Gale, 2002. 398p. illus. index. $125.00/set. ISBN 0-7876-6517-7.

Gale's series of books "for students," whose ever-expanding volumes already cover the standard genres, adds yet another set. The 28 lengthy entries—14 in each volume—treat movements such as humanism, Renaissance literature, magic realism, or existentialism in a consistent scheme, which consists of a brief description or history of the subject, representative authors and works, typical themes, and styles. Other features include a movement's variations, its historical context, and an overview of criticism, plus one or more critical essays, the latter occasionally overly academic for the intended audience. Bibliographic sources are listed, as are suggestions for further reading. Meant to appeal to a younger audience are sidebars, which include "What Do I Study Next?," "Topics for Further Study," and "Media Adaptations," as well as a liberal sprinkling of attractive illustrations.

Volume 1 treats pre-twentieth-century movements, while the twentieth century and beyond are found in volume 2. Rather than listing the movements in typical chronological order, the movements are listed alphabetically. Contributors of the signed entries are identified in a separate list as various writers, students, and scholars. Each volume ends with a glossary of literary terms, an author/title index, a national/ethnicity index, and a subject/theme index. Unfortunately, the indexes are by no means comprehensive. Numerous themes listed in the main section are not found in the subject/theme index, even though the introduction assures us they will be there in boldface (for example, Dreams and Visions is not listed for the Romanticism entry). Also, many authors and works mentioned in the larger entries do not appear in author/title index.

High school teachers and students and college undergraduates will find these volumes useful. They offer a one-stop introduction to literary history and themes. The steep price, however, may make its purchase debatable. —**Willa Schmidt**

392.   **Literary Lifelines.** Danbury, Conn., Grolier, 1998. 10v. illus. index. $319.00/set. ISBN 0-7172-9211-8.

Literary Lifelines is a disappointing set that gives cursory information about 1,000 alphabetically arranged authors of the past and present (100 per volume). The writers range from the well known (Charles Dickens, Honoré de Balzac) to the relatively obscure (Marina Tsvetaeva, Andrei Bely, Earl Birney) and cover all fields of literature.

Each author is given a double-page spread. On the first page a small, muddy, 2-by-2-inch portrait appears, followed by 4 or 5 brief paragraphs that cover basic biographical information and supply a few critical comments. A small reproduction of a dust jacket, again poorly reproduced, is provided, as is a list of important works by the author (with a maximum of 10). No secondary of critical sources are listed. On the opposite page, there is a list of more than a dozen authors related to the main one either by nationality, period, or genre. Lastly, a timeline is given that lists, by decade, approximately 15 important world events that occurred while the author was alive. Each decade has a small, unattractive drawing illustrating one of the events. For authors with approximately the same birth and death dates, these timelines are virtually the same, including the drawings. No attempt is made to correlate the world events with incidents or influences in the author's life.

Each volume ends with the same glossary of literary terms and an index to the entire set. Author and title entries are listed alphabetically; writers are arranged by century, nationality, and genre. The index is confusing, and a random check showed many omissions, particularly of titles.

It is difficult to suggest an audience for this set; it is too superficial and lacking in substantial information for adults, and many of the entries would be of no value to middle school students. Only a handful of contemporary children's and young adult writers are included, and the information given on appropriate authors is so slight that youngsters would be better served by using a general encyclopedia or a biographical dictionary of children's authors. [R: BL, 15 Sept 98, pp. 264-266; BR, Nov/Dec 98, pp. 76-77; SLJ, Nov 98, p. 154]—**John T. Gillespie**

393. **Literature Resource Center. http://www.gale.com/LitRC.** [Website]. Farmington Hills, Mich., Gale. Price negotiated by site. Date reviewed: Aug 02.

The *Literature Resource Center* from the Gale Group is an easy-to-use resource full of biographical and critical information on literary figures from the Classic period to today. The information found within comes from the literature resource standards from Gale (e.g., *Contemporary Authors, Contemporary Literary Criticism, Dictionary of Literary Biography*), the full text of Merriam-Webster's *Encyclopedia of Literature*, more than 5,000 author-related Websites, and full-text articles form 130 literary journals. In all, user's will have access to biographical information on 2,500 of the most-studied authors, synopses of the 4,000 most-studied titles, and access to information on an additional 3,000 to 4,000 authors that will be added annually.

The site is both attractive and intuitive to the needs of the user. The easiest, and most likely the most popular, searches are by keyword, title, and author. Users are also able to conduct a search selecting "Authors by Type" or by going to the "Literary-Historical Timeline." For those conducting a more complicated search, an advanced search option is available with the use of Boolean operators. Additional features include a "Spotlight On" section, which links to a featured author that changes with each session; a link titled "Authors on the Highway," which provides a schedule of upcoming events for selected authors; and access to the *Modern Language Association International Bibliography*, which provides additional links to 1.4 million bibliographic citations.

When conducting a search users are provided with biographical information as well as a bibliographic information. If new information has been added recently, it will be found under a section titled "Recent Update on This Author." Searches can be "infomarked" for later use, sent to an e-mail address, or printed, making the site very useful for students researching at the library and writing the research paper at home.—**Shannon Graff Hysell**

Biography

394. **Biography Today: Author Series. Volume 12.** Cherie D. Abbey, ed. Detroit, Omnigraphics, 2002. 222p. illus. index. $39.00. ISBN 0-7808-0610-7.

This volume in the *Biography Today: Author Series* is the 12th volume in the series, which now covers 130 authors of interest to young adults. Unlike many biography series that are presented in multiple volumes as well as annual cumulations, the biographies found here are not duplicated in the annual *Biography Today* volume.

This work brings together 10 authors that are currently of interest or currently studied by middle school and high school students. The authors listed here include: Meg Cabot, author of *The Princess Diaries*; Linda Sue Park, winner of the 2002 Newbery Medal for *A Single Shard*; and Virginia Hamilton, award winner for her stories about the African American experience. For each author a black-and-white photograph is provided, along with information on their childhood, education, career highlights, family, and interests. Each biography concludes with a list for further reading (periodicals and Websites). The index includes all individuals profiled in *Biography Today*. It includes a place of birth index as well as a birthday index.—**Shannon Graff Hysell**

395.   **DISCovering Authors: Biographies & Criticism on 400 Most-Studied Canadian & World Authors.** Canadian ed. [CD-ROM]. Toronto, Gale Canada, 1996. Minimum system requirements: IBM or compatible 286 (386 or faster recommended). ISO 9660-compatible CD-ROM drive with cables, interface card, and MS-DOS CD-ROM Extensions 2.1 (double speed or faster recommended). MS-DOS 3.3. 640K RAM. 10MB hard disk space. VGA monitor and graphics card. Mouse (optional). Printer (optional). $750.00. ISBN 0-8103-9955-5.

DISCovering Authors provides fast access to biographical, bibliographic, and critical information on the most well-known authors from ancient times to the present. More than 400 writers from all over the world have been included in the database. This version of *DISCovering Authors* includes biographies and criticism of more than 70 Canadian authors. In addition, 250-plus portraits are included.

Each entry in the biography section provides an introduction to the author; a portrait (if available); a full-text biography (usually approximately 1,000 words); personal background data including family, education, awards received, and so forth; a bibliography of the author's work; any media adaptations of the author's works (i.e., movies, television programs, books on tape); and any additional sources of information. In addition, there is a criticism section that consists of selected critical essays on the author's best-known works. These criticism entries supply subject headings that make it possible to search them and the bibliographic citation indicating the source. Additional features of the CD-ROM include a copy of the 10th edition of *Merriam-Webster's Collegiate Dictionary*, a glossary of literary terms, research paper topics, a timeline of literary and world events, and something called a "notepad editor" that allows the user to personalize the search to some extent. Much of the information included on this CD-ROM has been obtained from the Gale literary and biography series entitled Contemporary Authors, Contemporary Literary Criticism, Twentieth-Century Literary Criticism, the Dictionary of Literary Biography, Black Literature and Criticism, and others. The publisher contends that this information has been updated and corrected when necessary, but it appears that much of the material has been entered as it was in the original Gale publications.

The database is easily set up and used. It is possible to use it on local area networks with multiple users or as a stand-alone system. Search times are quick, and the printing setup is adequate. (The number of pages printed in one search session can be limited when the program is set up.) This disc is recommended for larger public and academic libraries (especially ones in Canada), and for libraries that do not already own many of the Gale biographical publications that provide the basic information. It is not recommended for smaller public and academic libraries because of the cost.—**Robert L. Wick**

Dictionaries and Encyclopedias

396.   **Cyclopedia of Literary Characters.** rev. ed. A. J. Sobczak and Janet Alice Long, eds. Pasadena, Calif., Salem Press, 1998. 5v. index. $350.00/set. ISBN 0-89356-438-0.

This comprehensive set contains all the titles from the original *Cyclopedia of Literary Characters* (1963) and the *Cyclopedia of Literary Characters II* (see ARBA 91, entry 1104), as well as titles included in *Masterplots* (2d ed.; see ARBA 97, entry 906) and the *Masterplots II* set (see ARBA 96, entry 949). However, only the *Masterplots II* volumes that survey novel-length fiction and drama are covered. This revision analyzes 3,300 titles, an increase of 574 titles. As with the previous editions, the volumes can be used alone or as a companion to *Masterplots*.

Entries are arranged alphabetically by the title of the work. Additional information includes the original foreign title (if appropriate), the author's name, birth and death dates, date of first publication or production (for drama), genre, locale, time of action, and plot type. Within each entry, characters are arranged in order of importance, with main characters receiving more detailed descriptions. Three indexes complete the set and enhance its usefulness. The 1st is a complete list of titles covered, including cross-references. The 2d provides access to the titles grouped by author. The final index is a comprehensive alphabetic list of the more than 20,000 characters described.

There is no other treatment of the subject that equals this set in scope and detail. It is helpful both for quick reference and more in-depth research and criticism. With all of the new and updated material included, even those libraries owning the previous editions should consider its purchase. This set is recommended for public, academic, and high school reference collections. [R: Choice, Sept 98, p. 86]—**Barbara E. Kemp**

Handbooks and Yearbooks

397.   **Epics for Students: Presenting Analysis, Context, and Criticism on Commonly Studied Epics.** Marie Lazzari, ed. Detroit, Gale, 1997. 440p. illus. maps. index. $65.00. ISBN 0-7876-1685-0.

Gale has performed a service for librarians, literature teachers, and students, who will benefit from this elegant and useful compendium. Designed with Gale's usual attention to detail, it covers the most popular world epics: *The Aeneid, Beowulf, El Cid, Song of Roland, The Divine Comedy, Gilgamesh, The Iliad, Kalevala, Mahabharata, Niebelungenlied, The Odyssey, Omeros, Paradise Lost,* and *Sundiata,* the epic of Mali. The work opens with a superb essay by Helen Conrad-O'Briain of University College, Dublin, in which she celebrates the action, tension, passion, and thought of the epic. An introduction to the text enumerates each entry's focus, including introduction, author biography, book-by-book plot summary, characters, themes, style, historical and cultural context, critical overview, criticism, sources for further study, media adaptations, comparisons and contrasts, list of complementary readings, and study questions. A literary chronology precedes the body of entries. A glossary covers 161 literary terms, most without models. Indexing covers author/title, nationality/ethnicity, and subject/theme.

Every turn of the page of this monumental reference work is a treat. The cover, layout, icons, and illustrations are appealing. Phrasing is informative, direct, and neither overly literary nor dumbed-down. Useful information includes chronological lists of media adaptations, uncomplicated definitions of literary terms, and brief discussions of historical context; for example, the Bronze Age, the Dark Age, and the Iron Age in the entry on *The Iliad.* The book would have profited from a comprehensive list of world epics, but, overall, the coverage, tone, and appreciation for student difficulties in reading world epics make this work a must-have for public and school libraries.
—**Mary Ellen Snodgrass**

398.   **Twayne's World Authors.** [CD-ROM]. New York, G. K. Hall/Simon & Schuster Macmillan, 1997. Minimum system requirements: IBM or compatible 486. CD-ROM drive. 16MB RAM. 16MB hard disk space. SVGA monitor. $1,243.75. ISBN 0-7838-1718-5.

Twayne's World Authors, using the Macmillan Library Reference interface, shares many of the same assets as *Scribner's Writer's Series on CD-ROM* (see ARBA 99, entry 978), with real production value without sacrificing load time (though one might expect a bit more lag using Windows 3.1), contextual help a click away, and a variety of ways to search by taking advantage of hyperlinks to related chapters and books. Like *Scribner's*, it gives the option of accessing chapters and entire entries from an alphabetical author list or of doing an in-depth search by genre, sex, time period, or other options. This product, however, contains 200 articles, some nearly book length, which provide thorough introductory criticism and overviews of the lives and writings of writers from ancient Greece to the present. One may also search or browse the authors or search a short list of research ideas, the strength of which is in showing connections between authors. The researcher will likely make the most use of the options under "In Depth Search," where searches using drop-down menus in sex, genre, and other fields can be combined with an implied "and," or do a full-text keyword search. Keywords can be combined with Boolean terms in the keyword text box. Each author entry has a hyperlinked table of contents, timeline, and bibliography, including a link to how the entry can be cited in a research paper, which is a valuable feature. Keyword searches scan full text, and the results are displayed in full chapters, as opposed to pulling out individual paragraphs that include the keyword(s); *Twayne's* gives a bit of context and continuity. Also, if searching the keyword "African American" pulls up a given chapter of the monograph on Lorraine Hansberry, the searcher is given the option of seeing the chapters that precede and follow the chapter displayed.

The CD-ROM's box indicates that readers would feel compelled to read the original monographs from which the entries were derived, to bring to the reading a basic knowledge. That is precisely what the reader will gain from this collection. This product will be useful for upper-level high school students as well as liberal arts students needing cogent and well-presented introductory insights. [R: BL, 1 Sept 98, p. 165]—**Jennie Ver Steeg**

CHILDREN'S AND YOUNG ADULT LITERATURE

General Works

399.   Helbig, Alethea K., and Agnes Regan Perkins. **Myths and Hero Tales: A Cross-Cultural Guide to Literature for Children and Young Adults.** Westport, Conn., Greenwood Press, 1997. 288p. index. $49.95. ISBN 0-313-29935-8.

Compiled for use by both teachers and students, this work annotates 189 volumes, representing 1,455 retellings of myths and hero tales, published from 1985 through 1996. A majority of the entries are from Native American or African sources, although tales from most cultures are included. Short, critical reviews cover both single-tale books and multistory collections ranging from children's picture books to scholarly publications suitable for the high school reader. The guide has seven indexes that organize the works by writer (meaning the reteller or editor); story type; culture; characters, places, and other significant items; grade level; and illustrator. All entries are keyed to the review section.

A general index lists all works by individual authors who are annotated in the guide, the titles for each story within any collected works, and the cultural source for most individual tales. Preface matter defines and differentiates between myths and hero tales, and the "stories by type index" organizes the reviewed works in this manner. The authors provide a list of standard and classical books of myths and hero tales still available. The annotated entries summarize individual stories and either summarize or categorize all stories included in anthologies. These annotations evaluate the bibliographic and source information as well as the overall effect of the work, including illustrations. Particularly useful is the comparison of works when more than one book on the same subject is reviewed.

This bibliography should prove itself a valuable tool for teachers and librarians as well as for the serious student. Its extensive and complete coverage of works for children and young adults from kindergarten through high school provides concise and easily accessed information.—**Janet Hilbun**

400. **Masterplots II: Juvenile and Young Adult Literature Series Supplement.** Frank N. Magill, ed. Pasadena, Calif., Salem Press, 1997. 3v. index. $275.00/set. ISBN 0-89356-916-X.

With well-written articles on 377 titles, the *Masterplots II: Juvenile and Young Adult Literature Series Supplement* is a welcome addition to an excellent series focusing on literature for children and young adults between the ages of 10 and 18. The supplement follows *Masterplots II: Juvenile and Young Adult Fiction Series* (see ARBA 92, entry 1128) and the *Masterplots II: Juvenile & Young Adult Biography Series* (see ARBA 95, entry 1150).

Titles included in this supplement represent a broad range of genres, periods, cultures, and countries of origin. For the first time, poetry collections (23 titles), plays (25 titles), short story collections (41 titles) and nonfiction books on the arts (4 titles), history (30 titles), sociology (4 titles), and science (22 titles) are included in addition to fiction. This work extends the Biography series by including 21 additional titles of autobiography and biography. Also represented are 53 Newbery Medal and Newbery Honor Books. Titles in the supplement are arranged alphabetically for easy access. Each article begins with informative ready-reference information about the title, followed by three subsections on "Form and Content," "Analysis," and "Critical Context." Four cumulative indexes in volume 3 allow the user to quickly locate articles in the series by title, author, subject, or name of an individual profiled in an autobiography or biography. A helpful annotated bibliography of general works about children's literature, selection aids, and further sources for finding information about some of the important children and young adult authors precedes the indexes. This work is highly recommended. [R: RBB, 15 Oct 97, pp. 428-29]—**Elizabeth B. Miller**

Children's Literature

Bibliography

401. Wright, Cora M. **Hot Links: Literature Links for the Middle School Curriculum.** Englewood, Colo., Libraries Unlimited, 1998. 173p. illus. index. $30.00pa. ISBN 1-56308-587-9.

This book contains some 280 children's literature titles, which represents a small, selective mix of recent and older titles that the author indicates would be of use for integrating literature into a middle school curriculum. Titles are suggested for use within several content areas and genres, and for recreational reading. The book is intended primarily for the classroom teacher, but is of use to librarians and parents as an introductory source for identifying and discussing children's literature in the middle-level curriculum. Books were included based on "their quality of writing, how well the illustrations accompany the text, the interest to students, availability, and a strong curriculum connection" (p. ix). Entries are listed within the book for several content areas: English classics; books that contain English usage; poetry; fine arts; mathematics; multicultural aspects; science; social studies (U.S. and ancient cultures); and sports and games. Certain genres are also included: biographies; recently published titles; high interest-low reading level books; myths, folktales, and legends; read aloud books; and books with a "unique presentation." Entries are annotated and contain basic citation information, including the ISBN and price. *See* references are also provided to other subject areas.

There is a chart at the end of the book that lists the titles alphabetically and has indicators to show the content and genre areas covered by each title. There is an indicator that shows under which content area the annotation can be found. An alphabetically arranged author/title index provides page numbers for the titles and authors listed. The book is useful for those interested in literature for students at the middle grades. This book would be more useful in a school or public library setting.—**Jan Squire Whitfield**

Biography

402.   **Eighth Book of Junior Authors and Illustrators.** 8th ed. Connie C. Rockman, ed. Bronx, N.Y., H. W. Wilson, 2000. 592p. illus. index. $75.00. ISBN 0-8242-0968-0.

Now in its 8th edition, and well over 70 years old, *Junior Authors and Illustrators* continues to be an essential reference tool for biographical information on the individuals who create literature for children and teenagers. Updated from the 1996 edition (see ARBA 97, entry 937), this volume contains 202 entries that cover fiction, picture books, poetry, and nonfiction. Each entry includes a personal essay, biographical information, a list of selected works, and often a list of suggested readings. The entries are enlivened with a photograph of the author or illustrator, jacket covers, and the signature of the subject. The personal essays make for very interesting reading and are sure to inspire potential writers.

The usefulness of the biographical information is about the same as the Contemporary Authors series from Gale in that it answers basic questions but is not sufficient for in-depth research. A listing of awards and honors granted to children's literature is included as well. Perhaps most useful of all in this edition is the cumulative index to the previous seven editions. Beneficial for the inside glimpse of an author's or illustrator's view on their work, inspiration, and life, this 8th edition will be of use in school and public libraries and in academic libraries that support education or library science curricula. [R: SLJ, Oct 2000, p. 199]—**Neal Wyatt**

403.   McElmeel, Sharron L. **100 Most Popular Children's Authors: Biographical Sketches and Bibliographies.** Englewood, Colo., Libraries Unlimited, 1999. 495p. illus. index. (Popular Authors Series). $48.00. ISBN 1-56308-646-8.

The compilation of this volume is based upon more than 3,000 teacher and student responses to a 1997 survey that attempted to identify the top 100 of the most important authors and illustrators of children's literature. Teachers, librarians, and students will find this easy-to-read volume useful in identifying and reading about popular authors' backgrounds and their works. Most of the books listed here are intended for an elementary or middle school audience. Please note that the author has also published a volume entitled *The 100 Most Popular Young Adult Authors: Biographical Sketches and Bibliographies* (see entry 414).

Entries are alphabetically arranged by the author's last name, and in some cases include a photograph. Each entry includes a birth and death date, an indication of the broad genre the author's work falls into, any books they have written in a series, and a biographical essay. Under the books and notes section of the entry is a bibliography (sometimes annotated) of the author's books on a certain subject, books in a series, and sources to consult for further information on the author. An appendix is included for photography credits and there are two indexes.

The genre index is alphabetically arranged and includes genres such as adventure fiction, biographies, contemporary realistic fiction, fantasy, historical fiction, humorous stories, mystery, nonfiction, poetry, and sports fiction. Underneath each genre the author is listed in alphabetic order by last name. Page numbers are not included. The general index is an alphabetic list that includes the author's name and titles of works mentioned in the author's biography. Page numbers are provided and the ones that reflect the main entry for an author are in bold typeface. Books listed in the bibliographies of each section and genres are not included in this index. [R: BL, 1 Sept 99, p. 182]—**Jan Squire Whitfield**

404.   McElmeel, Sharron L. **100 Most Popular Picture Book Authors and Illustrators: Biographical Sketches and Bibliographies.** Englewood, Colo., Libraries Unlimited, 2000. 579p. illus. index. (Popular Authors Series). $49.00. ISBN 1-56308-647-6.

Teachers, librarians, and students will find this volume easy to read and very useful in identifying picture book titles and reading about their authors and illustrators. Over 100 persons are included due to the listings of husband-and-wife teams. Most of the books listed here are intended for the very youngest of readers, but they hold much utility for the older reader as well. The compilation of this volume is based upon a 1997 survey that attempted to identify the top 100 authors and illustrators of children's literature. There were more than 3,000 teacher and student responses. Top authors and illustrators included were identified by 90 percent to no less than 15 percent of survey respondents. The author has also written other useful volumes on popular children's authors, young adult authors, and nonfiction authors for children.

Entries are alphabetically arranged by the author's last name, and in some cases include a photograph. Each entry includes a birthplace, birth and death dates, an indication of the broad genre the author's work falls into, and books of note. There is also a section about the authors or illustrators that contains biographical information and background information on the books written or illustrated. Under the section on books of note is an introduction that provides additional information on the works created. A bibliography of works follows that usually groups the books under several categories like picture books, wordless books, early readers, journey books, books in a series, genre books, books written by the person, books illustrated by the person, and joint collaborations. Under a section of more information are references to other articles, books, and Websites that might be consulted for further information.

There is an appendix of photography credits, a genre or theme index, and a general index. The genre index is alphabetically arranged, with the author or illustrator listed alphabetically by the last name. Genres included are African American culture, community, family relationships, folklore, historical fiction, humor, poetry, and wordplay. The general index is an alphabetic list that includes all titles mentioned in the book and the authors' names. Page numbers are provided, and the ones that reflect the main entry for an author are in bold typeface. Books listed in the bibliographies of each section and genres are not included in this index. This work is highly recommended for school, public, and academic libraries, especially those with an early childhood education or children's literature program. [R: SLJ, Nov 2000, p. 94]—**Jan Squire Whitfield**

405.   **Something About the Author Series.** Farmington Hills, Mich., Gale Group. 143v. illus. $128.00/vol. ISSN 0276-816X.

In 1971, the 1st volume of this biographical dictionary on authors and illustrators of children's books was published as an aid to librarians besieged by students who were required by their teachers to include in their book reports "something about the author." Now, more than 100 volumes and 10,000 biographical sketches later, this set has become the most extensive (and expensive) source of material on past and present writers and illustrators of children's books published in English in this country. Each volume contains approximately 70 to 80 entries that are of 2 kinds. The 1st gives a brief (about 2-page) introduction to the subject of his or her work, whereas the 2d provides an in-depth profile extending over several pages illustrated with photographs, jacket art, and examples of the subject's illustrations (when appropriate). In addition to career and personal data, these entries include excerpts from diaries, letters, and interviews; detailed chronologies; and lists of both the writer's works and sources of further information. Beginning with volume 57, a cumulative index to the set appears in odd-numbered volumes. Each volume usually contains a few updated, expanded profiles of important authors covered in previous editions. The volumes also have a policy of featuring 3 or more specially commissioned autobiographical essays per volume, each about 10,000 words in length and heavily illustrated with photographs. Although this set is a handsome, useful addition to any children's literature collection, its price and the fact that five or six volumes are added per year make it a luxury for school and small public libraries. However, for school district libraries, larger public libraries, and universities that support children's literature collections, it continues to be a quality mainstay in the reference collection.—**John T. Gillespie**

Dictionaries and Encyclopedias

406.   **The Dictionary of Characters in Children's Literature.** Beverly Ann Chin, ed. Danbury, Conn., Grolier/Children's Press/Franklin Watts, 2002. 128p. illus. index. $34.00. ISBN 0-531-11984-X.

407.   **The Dictionary of Folklore.** David Adams Leeming, ed. Danbury, Conn., Grolier/Children's Press/Franklin Watts, 2002. 128p. illus. index. $34.00. ISBN 0-531-11985-8.

These two children's dictionaries from Franklin Watts follow a similar layout. Both contain a table of contents; sections entitled "Note to Reader," "How to Use This Book," and "Note to Educator"; alphabetic entries; a selected bibliography; and an index. *The Dictionary of Characters in Children's Literature* also includes a master list of major characters with the title of the work they appear in. Sidebars throughout both volumes provide complementary material, such as information on similar works or works by the same author, data on the authors, excepts from stories, and quotes from critics.

The Dictionary of Characters in Children's Literature briefly discusses the major characters from some of the more popular juvenile novels that are often taught in elementary and middle school curriculums. For example, classics such as *Black Beauty*, *The Wonderful Wizard of Oz*, and *The Secret Garden* are covered, along with contemporary favorites like *Harry Potter and the Sorcerer's Stone*, *Wayside School is Falling Down*, and *The Giver*. The entries are alphabetic by title and, following a brief plot synopsis, the editor has designed the character entries to reinforce critical thinking. In other words, educators can use this resource to encourage classroom discussion about how a character changed throughout the book, whether the character is multidimensional or narrow, and how the character is similar or different from other characters.

The Dictionary of Folklore covers myths, superstitions, nursery rhymes, folk songs, legends, fairy tales, tall tales, fables, game rhymes, and riddles. Works from writers such as Mark Twain and Charlotte Brontë are featured as well. This work emphasizes American folklore that has developed from American Indian, European American, African American, Asian American, and other North American group traditions. The editor hopes that this dictionary will help young readers further explore American folklore and encourage their interest in other countries and regions. All in all, the material in these dictionaries may to be too superficial for any substantial classroom use, but they may help inspire teachers in developing their curriculum plans. [R: BR, Sept/Oct 02, p. 71]—**Cari Ringelheim**

Young Adult Literature

Bibliography

408. **Best Books for Young Adult Readers.** Stephen J. Calvert, ed. New Providence, N.J., R. R. Bowker/Reed Reference Publishing, 1997. 744p. index. $59.95. ISBN 0-8352-3832-6.

Bowker's The Best Book series was established to assist librarians and teachers in meeting both the curriculum-related and recreational reading needs of their students. The present volume covers recommended titles for readers in grades 7 through 12 and supplements the previously published titles *Best Books for Children* (5th ed.; see ARBA 95, entry 1130) and *Best Books for Junior High Readers* (see ARBA 92, entry 1116). The main part of the book is arranged by subject with three indexes—author, title, and subject/grade level. Annotations are brief and provide citations to published reviews in several standard sources. All in all, this well-balanced and professionally prepared volume should be in the hands of all juvenile libraries and most public libraries.—**Bohdan S. Wynar**

409. **Books for You: An Annotated Booklist for Senior High.** 13th ed. Lois T. Stover and Stephanie F. Zenker, eds., with the Committee on the Senior High School Booklist of the National Council of Teachers of English. Urbana, Ill., National Council of Teachers of English, 1997. 451p. index. (NCTE Bibliography Series). $16.95pa. ISBN 0-8141-0368-5. ISSN 1051-4740.

A standard tool on school library and departmental reference shelves, this overview of the published works during the period 1994 to 1996 suited for secondary readers maintains the National Council of Teachers of English's criteria for print matter. Pleasantly laid out and easy to use, the book opens with a table of contents that divides the text into 40 categories of selections, totaling nearly 1,400 works of fiction and nonfiction, reference, self-help, and collections. Following a prefatory note by senior editor Michael Greer, the usual acknowledgments, and a foreword by Chris Crutcher, editors Stover and Zenker speak directly to young readers, suggesting how to locate works by favorite authors and how to apply the codes ER, WL, and MC, which stand for easy reading, world literature, and multicultural. Each chapter contains numbered entries followed by additional titles incorporated under other listings. Appendix A names award-winners in 14 listings of the Coretta Scott King Award and IRA Children's Book. The 2d appendix presents 12 pages of multicultural titles; the 3d follows the same procedure for 3 pages of titles from world literature. Appendix D names eight of the most common dealers: Econo-Clad, Houghton Mifflin, Penguin Books, Perma-Bound, Random House, Scholastic, Sundance, and William Morrow. The final 44 pages are the most helpful—indexes by author, subject, and title.

Weaknesses in this reference work are few. The editors could have included Internet addresses and advice on accessing online distributors and reviewers of young adult literature. The list of 57 committee members who made the choices for this work names 45 from Maryland. The fact that there is one lone southwesterner from Colorado and a sprinkling from Ohio leaves in doubt the fairness of the final call on titles to be included, especially works that address concerns and interests of readers along the Pacific Coast and in Hawaii. A final question that hovers over the work is the absence of explicit commentary on Random House's 1996 edition of Mark Twain's *The Adventures of Huckleberry Finn*, one of the most significant alterations in the high school canon in recent years.—**Mary Ellen Snodgrass**

410. **Outstanding Books for the College Bound: Choices for a Generation.** Marjorie Lewis, ed. Chicago, American Library Association/Young Adult Library Services Association, 1996. 217p. index. $25.00pa.; $22.50pa. (ALA members). ISBN 0-8389-3456-0.

Lewis's catalog of must-read books for young readers reflects a shift in education from standardized lists to increasing vitality and creativity in education. According to her preface, as a result of the Young Adult Library Services Association's role in the change, librarians, teachers, students, and parents have a fuller choice of titles and a greater range of learning. A precise introduction establishes the parameters of book selection by defining outstanding works and anthologies, college-bound readers, and genre listing. The section concludes with a chart of books that have been on the list from 6 to 10 times.

The text opens on a 110-page listing by genre. Beautifully spaced in readable typeface and a single-column arrangement, the entries vary from two to five lines in length. Each entry names title, author, publication date, and dates the title appeared on the list. Part 2 presents the unannotated lists by year, beginning with 1959 and continuing to 1994. A two-page appendix states the guidelines for book selection. A 27-page double index lists authors and titles.

The American Library Association provides a valuable service in performing this tedious task of collating lists of books suited for bright young readers. The usual questions surface from a hasty perusal, such as, Why is Elie Wiesel's *Night* not named? It would also aid the first-time user to have a model entry explaining the series of dates that follow the publication date. Quibbles aside, the cataloging of reading lists offers librarians, teachers, students, and parents a worthy place to start.—**Mary Ellen Snodgrass**

Biography

411. **Authors & Artists for Young Adults, Volume 20.** Thomas McMahon, ed. Detroit, Gale, 1997. 261p. illus. index. $79.00. ISBN 0-7876-1136-0.

412. **Authors & Artists for Young Adults, Volume 21.** Thomas McMahon, ed. Detroit, Gale, 1997. 239p. illus. index. $79.00. ISBN 0-7876-1137-9.

This set of books is arranged in the same format as the Something About the Author (see entry 405) and Contemporary Authors series. The 20 to 25 authors in each volume are listed alphabetically, and entries include personal information, addresses, career data, awards and honors, writings, adaptations, and sidelights. Pictures of the authors and their work add interest to the entries. The information is written for young adults and is intended to entertain and inform them. The unique part of this series is the variety of artists, such as cartoonists, photographers, music composers, and playwrights, that are included. The people in these volumes range from children's authors, such as Louisa May Alcott, to young adult authors, such as Janet Bode, to adult authors, such as Dick Francis. However, it does not stop with just authors. Artists such as Kenneth Branagh, Mike Judge (creator of *Beavis and Butt-Head*), and Georgia O'Keeffe are also included.

The index in this set is similar to that in Something About the Author. However, it does not include references to the other Gale author series. In comparing 29 authors in *Authors & Artists for Young Adults* to the authors included in Something About the Author, only 9 were not included in the latter. Those 9 were actors, artists, and adult authors.

Authors & Artists for Young Adults offers the same great information found in other Gale publications. For those who serve young adults and do not own many biography sources, this set would be an excellent purchase. However, if the budget is tight and the library already owns Something About the Author and Contemporary Authors, *Authors & Artists* would be a nice purchase, but not a necessity.—**Suzanne Julian**

413. **Authors4Teens.com. http://www.authors4teens.com.** [Website]. Westport, Conn., GEMonline/Greenwood Press. Price negotiated by site. Date reviewed: Oct 02.

Authors4Teens.com was created to provide a place for teenagers, teachers, librarians, and researchers to locate thorough information on contemporary authors who write primarily for the young adult audience. The Web format was chosen because it provides a means of increasing the number of entries, a means of updating and expanding the existing material, and the ability to add links to other sites of related information.

Through the "Frequently Asked Questions" section the criteria for inclusion is provided. The primary factor is authors who focus on writing for teenagers; other factors include notability, quality, recent award winners, and those considered at the top of the field. These authors are mainly writers of fiction. Don Gallo, who is noted in the field of education, conducts all of the interviews. Inclusion is influenced by whether or not he has met the author, his familiarity with an author's works, and the type of material he prefers to read. Another determining factor is whether or not authors agree to participate and whether or not they are online since all interviews are conducted via e-mail. The number of writers of color is low, and this is attributed to the proportionally low number who write for teens.

After Gallo completes the interview process and initial editing, an editor at Greenwood Press also reads and edits the interviews. Interviews are lengthy and include information on the author's teenage years, the sources of their material, and their writing process. Pictures often include the author in their childhood, their office, and with family members. Interviews are interspersed with many links to sound files, pictures, video, e-books, and related Websites. Teens will enjoy the interviews and the snapshots. In the left frame of each interview is a list of links for bibliography and awards, reviews, images, and upcoming appearances. Bibliographies include fiction by age categories, nonfiction titles, essays, novelizations of movies, and general awards. The site has a conference/message board feature, which allows the user to post questions for a particular author. Postings and replies can be read by other users. This feature shows little activity and postings were basically trivial. There is no guarantee that an author will respond.

Navigation of the site is easy. The linked list of authors is given on the home page of the site along with buttons for the conference board, search, and a list of recommended links to author's Web pages and sites related to young adult literature. A pull-down menu is provided on the interview pages that allows the user to easily change to another author. The search function is a keyword search with Boolean search features. Updates are made regularly to the interviews and the site promises to continue adding new authors. Information is provided on how to purchase access, contact the publisher, and contact tech support.

This is a subscription site, and the cost is relatively low. However, the subscriber will need to have an active teen audience who is interested in interview-type material in order to justify a site with information on only 40 authors. The limitations noted above in the selection process will influence the ability of the site to expand. —**Elaine Ezell**

414.   Drew, Bernard A. **The 100 Most Popular Young Adult Authors: Biographical Sketches and Bibliographies.** rev. ed. Englewood, Colo., Libraries Unlimited, 1997. 531p. index. $55.00. ISBN 1-56308-615-8.

This collection covers 100 popular contemporary and classic young adult authors. Novelists are predominately American, with several British and other nationalities represented. It includes a few upper middle school authors, such as Judy Blume, Betsy Byars, and Phyllis Reynolds Naylor and several adult authors read by young adults—V. C. Andrews and Stephen King. The genres covered range from science fiction and historical fiction to recent horror authors like Christopher Pike and R. L. Stine.

The entries are listed alphabetically by surname of the writer. Each author's entry is listed with a genre type, birth date, date of death, birthplace, and most recognized works of fiction. The text includes a brief biography of the author; critical comments on his or her works from magazines, interviews, and other reference sources; a list of titles written; series information; and bibliographic information suggesting further reading about the author.

The entries represent an adequate list of authors read by the designated age group, but as a reference tool it is lacking in consistency and organization. The biographical information is too brief and lacking in substance. The writing careers of the individuals portrayed through interviews and critical sources are not organized chronologically and are difficult to follow. Criticism of specific works by the novelists is not mentioned uniformly or skillfully. The title contains some useful, concise information about the authors, but a more complete source such as the Something About the Author Autobiography series (see ARBA 99, entry 988) would be a more helpful tool.—**Marlene M. Kuhl**

415.   **Lives and Works: Young Adult Authors.** Danbury, Conn., Grolier, 1999. 8v. illus. index. $255.00/set. ISBN 0-7172-9227-4.

Lives and Works: Young Adult Authors is an eight-volume set of brief author biographies designed especially for the middle school student. The more than 250 authors profiled include both modern and classical writers ranging from William Shakespeare to Anne Frank to Francesca Lia Block. Each three-to four-page biography includes a picture; a quote from a major work; a brief overview of the author's life; a description and brief, critical analysis of the author's major works; a list of selected works by and about the author; and when available, a Web address. All eight volumes include a table of contents for the individual volume and a master index for all volumes. The master index has references to authors, titles, and subjects, which makes it useful for finding multiple books about a topic. Although the set is designed for the middle school reader to learn about individual authors, the design of the index should also prove useful for teachers and librarians looking for additional works on specific subjects.

The format of the volumes makes for easy, interesting reading but does not allow for any in-depth student research. The strength of the set lies in its up-to-date coverage of both modern and historical authors who are frequently read as part of the curriculum or for pleasure reading. [R: BL, 1 May 99, p. 1632; BR, Sept/Oct 99, p. 74]—**Janet Hilbun**

Handbooks and Yearbooks

416.   Gillespie, John T., and Corinne J. Naden. **Characters in Young Adult Literature.** Detroit, Gale, 1997. 535p. illus. index. $60.00. ISBN 0-7876-0401-1.

This compendium of more than 2,000 characters from 232 works by 148 authors is a must for reviewers, school and public libraries, teachers, and college and university education departments. The text is illustrated with cover and movie art from 70 titles, for example, Gregory Peck in the role of Atticus Finch arguing his case before the jury in the entry for *To Kill a Mockingbird*. The layout is neatly marked with icons indicating plot and characters and includes birth and death dates of authors, genre and publication date of each work, and an extensive list of critical commentaries for additional data. Guide words and pagination are clearly marked. The preface explains the plan of each entry and of sequels, series, and trilogies. The text precedes a 57-page character and title index.

The appeal of this reference work begins with its manageable size and a colorful, intriguing cover, which duplicates the illustration on page 145, an action shot of Alexandre Dumas *pere*'s Three Musketeers dueling their challengers. The writing style of plot summaries and character studies is also upbeat and accessible to young researchers. Coverage is perhaps the major strength of this volume, which features standard works by J. R. R. Tolkien, Arthur Conan Doyle, Louisa

May Alcott, and Hermann Hesse as well as significant young adult favorites by Cynthia Rylant, Gary Paulsen, Lois Lowry, Anne Rice, Avi, and Scott O'Dell. Science fiction buffs will find Jules Verne, Ursula K. Le Guin, H. G. Wells, Madeleine L'Engle, and Isaac Asimov. Nonwhite authors include Amy Tan, Walter Dean Myers, Alice Walker, Alice Childress, Toni Morrison, and Ernest Gaines. All in all, this volume deserves attention from the book world.—**Mary Ellen Snodgrass**

417.   **Writers for Young Adults.** Ted Hipple, ed. New York, Scribner's/Simon & Schuster Macmillan, 1997. 3v. illus. index. $235.00/set. ISBN 0-684-80474-3.

This 3-volume set is a great addition to secondary school libraries and the young adult section of public libraries, especially those that cannot afford Gale's *Authors & Artists for Young Adults* (see entries 411 and 412). Robert Cormier's foreword should be read. Signed articles cover 129 classical and contemporary authors, with the emphasis on the latter category. Teachers and students looking for background information will vie to use this set. It is also a browser's delight.

Each article includes the author's picture or illustrations, biographical information, critiques or interpretations of the author's important books, a selected bibliography of the author's works, works about the author, and how to contact the author. Many articles include a note indicating quotations are from current correspondence with the writer. Even though the articles provide typical information about the authors, each article is slightly different. This gives each entry a unique feel and lets the author discussed shine. The articles are written with young adults in mind.

The easy-to-read page layout includes outside margins used for definitions, brief explanations, suggestions for other authors to read who write in a similar vein, and so on. The list of contributors gives affiliations and articles written. The category index lists titles alphabetically by genre and theme; it certainly aids in reading list preparations. The general index lists authors and titles. In typical Scribner's fashion, the authors' names are listed on the spine of the book. There is a similar list on the back cover. These user-friendly additions ensure no fumbling with a table of contents, although the one for this set is well laid out. This set will definitely be requested at report-writing time. [R: RBB, 15 Oct 97, p. 430]—**Esther R. Sinofsky**

DRAMA

418.   **Drama for Students Series.** Farmington Hills, Mich., Gale Group. 19v. illus. index. $83.00. ISSN 1094-9232.

In *Drama for Students* conveniently arranged guides for the appreciation of commonly studied dramatic works are found. Designed chiefly for high school and undergraduate college students, each volume covers 12 to 20 plays. The works are selected mainly on the basis of their popularity as study texts in literature courses; thus, the selection is extremely eclectic, ranging from classics such as *Antigone* and *A Doll's House* to such contemporary works as *The Odd Couple* and *Twilight: Los Angeles, 1992*. Each entry consists of an author biography, plot summary, description of the main characters, overview of the themes and style, and a critical essay commissioned by the editors. The analyses are straightforward and conventional, not unlike those found in *Cliff's Notes*. The distinguishing feature here is the rather cloying attempt to be politically correct, both in the selection of titles and in the relentless effort to show each play's relevance to contemporary concerns. For example, most entries include a "Compare and Contrast" section in which parallels are drawn between the cultural milieu of the time the play was written and that of today. In *Rosencrantz and Guildenstern Are Dead*, the editors are reduced to comparing the prevalence of credit cards between 1966 and today. Unfortunately, this kind of "reaching" is not uncommon in an otherwise useful and engaging work.—**Jeffrey R. Luttrell**

FICTION

419. **Novels for Students Series.** Farmington Hills, Mich., Gale Group. 19v. illus. index. $83.00. ISSN 1094-3552

Intended for high school students, undergraduates, and teachers, this work can also be used by anyone seeking further information on selected novels. Various sources on teaching literature and analyses of course curricula were used to obtain the titles, which include a mixture of classics and contemporary works. Each 20-page entry includes an introduction, an author biography, a plot summary, character descriptions, themes, style, historical context of the work, a critical overview, and three critical essays. Rounding out the entries are mentions of media adaptations, topics for further study, "Compare and Contrast" and "What Do I Read Next?" sections, and a list of books for further study. Other useful features include a literary chronology, a subject/theme index, and cumulative indexes covering authors, titles, nationalities, and ethnicities.

The biographical information is more detailed than that found in *Something About the Author* (see entry 405) and *Contemporary Authors* (Gale Group). Although *Twentieth Century Literary Criticism* (see ARBA 97, entries 919, 920, 921, and 922) is more sophisticated, it groups criticism of the major works of an author together, thus offering less coverage on each book. The advantage of this reference work is that by concentrating on one book per entry, it can provide a comprehensive overview of each work, its author, and its place in literature in an inviting format that encourages further research. A minor quibble concerns the distracting typeface used for the headings. At $83 these works will be a nice addition to public and academic reference collections. —**January Adams**

420. **Short Stories for Students Series.** Tim Akers, ed. Farmington Hills, Mich., Gale Group. 19v. illus. index. $83.00. ISSN 1092-7735.

High school teachers of literature will want this series on their school's standing order. They will be especially pleased with it if they are looking to expand their teaching repertoire beyond a textbook or traditional author group but are concerned about usefulness and literary status. With input from practicing teachers, the editor provides author biographies, plot summaries, characters, themes, styles, and bibliographies. In addition, the information given for each of 17 stories includes a critical overview, sources, media adaptations, complementary works, study questions, and comparison and contrast with the time of the author or the story context and the present. The mix of classic and contemporary titles treated in this volume have been published across more than a century, with the oldest being published in 1877 and the newest in 1989. This work is also for student research projects where teachers see themselves as "guides on the side," not direct purveyors of information. Good students who struggle with scholars' critical treatments will find this readable. This source will feed the interest in expanding the canon of literature "to include international, women, and multicultural authors." A glossary, suggestions for citing stories and critical comments, text of stories not included, and nationality and ethnicity indexes are included.—**Edna M. Boardman**

NATIONAL LITERATURE

American Literature

421.   **Great American Writers: Twentieth Century.** R. Baird Shuman, ed. Tarrytown, N.Y., Marshall Cavendish, 2002. 13v. illus. index. $459.95/set. ISBN 0-7614-7240-1.

This 13-volume set from Marshall Cavendish introduces students to notable U.S. and Canadian writers. While some of the writers included were born in the nineteenth century, all of the writers included in this set published their works during the twentieth century. Overall, this set covers trendsetters that broke away from the genteel writing of the nineteenth century—such as Jack London, Upton Sinclair, and Gertrude Stein—along with groundbreaking authors throughout the twentieth century, including F. Scott Fitzgerald, John Steinbeck, Toni Morrison, and Margaret Atwood. Playwrights, such as Eugene O'Neill, Arthur Miller, and Tennessee Williams are also covered.

The alphabetic entries begin with a summary of the vital facts about the author (i.e., birth and death dates and writing genres) and a paragraph about the writer's significance in American literature followed by four main sections. "The Writer's Life" discusses important events in the writer's life and "The Writer's Work" focuses on the writer's literary contributions, including issues they addressed, recurrent themes, and character development. The "Reader's Guide to Major Works" section provides essays on a selection of the writer's most notable and representative works. This section also includes lists of sources for further study. The last section, "Other Works," briefly summarizes the writer's other works not covered in the previous section. The entries then conclude with an additional list of resources, including books, Websites, and videos.

Color photographs and illustrations are present throughout the volumes. Each volume contains a volume-specific index and volume 13 contains a comprehensive index for the entire set. This volume also includes a glossary; a list of Noble Prize winners in literature; a list of Pulitzer Prize winners; a further reading list; a guide to the writers by genre; and additional indexes by literary works, visual arts, visual artists, films, literary characters, and geographical locations. At nearly $460, this set is recommended for larger middle school, high school, and college libraries and smaller libraries that can afford it. It is a good introductory resource to many of the writers that are commonly studied in today's curriculum. [R: SLJ, Nov 02, p. 106]—**Cari Ringelheim**

422.   **Twayne's United States Authors on CD-ROM.** [CD-ROM]. new ed. New York, G. K. Hall/Simon & Schuster Macmillan, 1997. Minimum system requirements: IBM or compatible 486. CD-ROM drive. 16 MB RAM. 16 MB hard disk space. SVGA monitor. $1,243.75. ISBN 0-7838-1715-0.

A revision of the DiscLit series, this new compilation of literary criticism and interpretation includes 59 additional authors or topics, bringing the total to 201 authors. New among these are topical treatments of Native American poetry, Jewish American fiction, late-nineteenth-century American diary literature, and Native American literature. The range of additional authors includes Nikki Giovanni, Rita Mae Brown, Dr. Seuss, Chaim Potok, Thomas Pynchon, Toni Morrison, Margaret Titchell, and Edgar Rice Burroughs, to name a few.

Users will appreciate the new browser interface, similar to Netscape. Of equal value is the ability to move among chapters, search for bibliographies or chronologies, ask for on-screen help, or choose from a variety of menu commands. An initial menu provides a choice of "In Depth Search," "Research Ideas," or "Authors A-Z," as well as options for searching tips and printing tips. Color-coded screens remind the user of the context of any given search.

Search capabilities are more powerful in this revision, allowing for wild cards, truncation, and Boolean operators. References can be retrieved across all works on the disk, and additional keywords are suggested to assist the user. Printing options are expanded to allow single page, chapter, or highlighted sections. Citation information is provided in pop-up windows and is printed automatically for each section.

Price aside, most libraries should strongly consider acquiring this disk for its ease of use, compact storage, and the scope and nature of the criticism included. [R: BL, 1 Sept 98, p. 165; BR, Sept/Oct 98, p. 90]—**Edmund F. SantaVicca**

British Literature

General Works

423.   **Twayne's English Authors on CD-ROM.** [CD-ROM]. New York, G. K. Hall/Simon & Schuster Macmillan, 1997. Minimum system requirements: IBM or compatible 486. CD-ROM drive. 16 MB RAM. 16 MB hard disk space. SVGA monitor.$995.00. ISBN 0-7838-1717-7.

Nearly 200 books on British authors from the popular Twayne's Author Series have been reproduced on this CD-ROM and made searchable with Netscape software. Advanced searching allows one to search by period, genre, or keyword as well as by author's name. A search for tragic heroes (keyword) and Renaissance (period) yielded more than 50 chapters. One of the Shakespeare chapters had many hits, but it is not clear how to find them beyond reading the complete chapter. The most efficient way of finding them was to use "CTRL F" to bring up a "find" box and type in the phrase. However, in another chapter discussing the works of Robert Greene, the phrase "tragic hero" brought no results, yet searching each word separately leads one to information on tragedy or heroes. Common Windows conventions such as drop-down menus allow the user to see which periods and genres are available. Online help is available for those who want more explanations and examples for citing CD-ROM versions of the books.

Other offerings on the main menu include "Research Ideas" and "Authors, A-Z." The first is a selection of well-known authors arranged by literary period and by gender. More specific topics for research (for example, "the tragic hero in Shakespearean drama") are not offered. The second is a dictionary listing of the British authors included.

At the top of each search screen and at the beginning of each document is a navigational bar that takes the user to any of the main menu options and to the help menu. Only when one is deep into a book is there no program-specific navigation assistance. This, however, is when the Netscape software is useful. The "back" option on the top bar quickly takes you out of the text and back to the "table of contents" of the book. High school and college students for whom this is designed will have no trouble with the search software.

Loading the CD-ROM is easy following the instructions in the technical reference pamphlet that accompanies the product. However, due to some organization-specific network software on this reviewer's personal computer, the program would not work. Using the technical support telephone number, I was able to talk to a helpful technician who walked me through several procedures, and finally sent me some additional software to ensure that the program worked.

Users may not want to read long chapters directly from the computer screen, so printing is likely to be excessive. To help avoid this, at the top of each chapter are simple instructions for printing out sections of text. However, for popular authors whose criticism is frequently checked out of the library, this reference source will be much appreciated by librarians and users. [R: BL, 1 Sept 98, p. 165]—**Juleigh Muirhead Clark**

Individual Authors

William Shakespeare

424. O'Dell, Leslie. **Shakespearean Characterization: A Guide for Actors and Students.** Westport, Conn., Greenwood Press, 2002. 294p. index. $76.00. ISBN 0-313-31144-7.

425. O'Dell, Leslie. **Shakespearean Language: A Guide for Actors and Students.** Westport, Conn., Greenwood Press, 2002. 269p. index. $76.00. ISBN 0-313-31145-5.

426. O'Dell, Leslie. **Shakespearean Scholarship: A Guide for Actors and Students.** Westport, Conn., Greenwood Press, 2002. 413p. index. $91.00. ISBN 0-313-31146-3.
     Each of these volumes are written to highlight critical areas for the performance of Shakespeare—to enhance actors' and students' understanding of how Elizabethans interpreted the plays of their day and thus to bring the spirit and truths of those plays to the twenty-first century. Focused on performance, O'Dell discusses passages to help the student understand the meaning of the text, and how that meaning can be conveyed to the audience through inflection, body movements, and psychological identification. In the volume on scholarship, O'Dell recommends worthwhile books that will be valuable to collection management librarians as they evaluate their burgeoning collections of Shakespearean criticism. The arrangement is topical rather than by dramatic work, thus the indexes are necessary for the actor interested specifically in the interpretation of a major role. The general index is followed by an index of plays and characters at the end of each volume.
     Each book is a separate work, but as all the parts contribute to the understanding of the plays, libraries will want to purchase all three. A worthy addition to the huge body of advice, illumination, and directions for producing Shakespearean plays, O'Dell's works will be a welcome addition to libraries that support drama departments or community theater. Leslie O'Dell is an associate professor of English and theater at Wilfrid Laurier University and text consultant for the Stratford (Ontario) Shakespeare Festival.—**Juleigh Muirhead Clark**

POETRY

427. **Poetry for Students Series.** Farmington Hills, Mich., Gale Group. 20v. illus. index. $83.00. ISSN 1094-7019.
     Much value can be seen in this type of teaching tool, poetry being the most difficult genre for literature novices. The series provides a useful method for close reading and a thorough look at poems by its small selection (this volume highlights 18 poems). Each poem is accompanied by a biographical sketch of the author, a historical context, a line-by-line summary, a description of its themes, two critical articles, suggested topics for discussion and composition, and a bibliography of other critical works on the author. In that respect, the instructor has at hand a good choice of approaches and materials to examine individual works in a larger context. The abundance of material can be useful but can also be detrimental. The summaries and the articles provide overpowering a priori interpretations of the poems that can excuse—or even impede—students from a process of discovery. The discussion themes are very broad and seldom reflect back to the poems, which are dwarfed by the huge critical work around them. This is underscored by the fact that they appear in a font much smaller than the rest of the text. However, the

biggest omission in this series, and especially in this particular volume, is in the selection that, judging by the cumulative index, does justice only to African Americans among all American ethnic groups, and relies too much on the canon. One can only hope for better representation of non-canonical groups and people of color in future volumes.—**Stella T. Clark**

18 Music

GENERAL WORKS

428. Earls, Irene. **Young Musicians in World History.** Westport, Conn., Greenwood Press, 2002. 139p. index. $44.95. ISBN 0-313-31442-X.

Author Irene Earls selected 13 musicians who mastered their instruments while they were very young to feature in this volume. The child prodigies include Louis Armstrong, J. S. Bach, Beethoven, Pablo Casais, Sarah Chang, Ray Charles, Charlotte Church, Bob Dylan, John Lennon, Midori, Mozart, Paganini, and Isaac Stern. The author states: "The goal was to provide role models who came from different types of backgrounds and different periods in history. Many were selected because they had to rise above adversity in order to achieve. All became publicly successful before the age of twenty-five." The volume should be of interest to young musicians and teachers. One hopes that the book will make apparent to the young student the difficulties of obtaining success at an early age and the great determination involved in mastering an instrument. The volume includes bibliographies, illustrations, a glossary, and a general index. *Young Musicians in World History* is especially recommended for the juvenile section of general libraries and for music department libraries.—**Robert Palmieri**

429. Kuhn, Laura, comp. **Baker's Student Encyclopedia of Music.** New York, Schirmer Books/Macmillan Library Reference, 1999. 3v. illus. index. $295.00/set. ISBN 0-02-865315-7.

An up-to-date, comprehensive encyclopedia, these three volumes are extensively researched and provide information on a wide range of musical subjects and personalities. Entry lengths range from brief, dictionary-type definitions to longer, more complete explanations and biographies. Adding to the completeness and comprehensibility are margin notes that give the pronunciation of difficult words, identify which entries pertain to musical instruments and people, and provide anecdotal explanations of more esoteric entries such as those for collective compositions, color hearing, and dodecaphonic music. Photos and timelines of important events enhance composer biographies. Each volume includes a full-color insert highlighting special topics such as music and musicians as portrayed in art, music around the world, and popular performers. For easier use, a complete index concludes each volume.

Written in an easy-to-read manner for students from middle school through college, the volumes are impressive in their scope and depth. The encyclopedia contains more than 5,500 entries on all aspects of music: composers, performers, songwriters, conductors, critics, scholars, organizations and societies, instruments, musical styles, major compositions, and terminology. The appealing style of writing combined with the completeness of the entries makes this a worthy volume for school, academic, and public library purchase. [R: SLJ, May 2000, p. 88; RUSQ, Sept 2000, pp. 401-402]—**Janet Hilbun**

MUSICAL FORMS

Popular

430. **DK Encyclopedia of Rock Stars.** By Dafydd Rees and Luke Crampton. New York, DK Publishing, 1996. 951p. illus. $29.95pa. ISBN 0-7894-1263-2.

This hefty compilation and rewrite of text from news clippings and press releases could more appropriately be titled *Chronologies of Pop Music Artists*. It lacks the analytic tone of an encyclopedia, is not limited in scope to the famed, and covers folk, pop, and world music artists as well as those in rock. In articles that vary in length to reflect career longevity, yearly summations for solo artists and groups list events such as album and single releases, selected concert appearances, drug arrests, musician and management changes, and all manner of personal data bordering on (and venturing into) gossip. A warhorse outfit such as Jefferson Airplane and its permutations is granted nearly 3 pages of coverage for a 30-year career, while relative newcomers such as Candlebox earn a single column.

Entries are sectioned by year and month, with dates of specific events given in brackets. Information is current through early 1996. The book is neither indexed nor illustrated throughout, an anomaly and disappointment for a publisher so respected for its visual presentation of information. The evaluation of artistic output in a medium this popular and pervasive tends to sound either conformist or capricious as readers of these books come to them with strong opinions. The authors, veterans of music industry writing and research, avoid the issue by doing no overt judging or even categorizing of the musical acts included in their book. Factual mistakes are impressively rare, although the common misspelling of the R.E.M. *Lifes Rich Pageant* album as *Life's Rich Pageant* is made.

The listed criteria for inclusion of artists are rather generic, but in execution display a preference for British over American acts, and the 1960s versus other decades, although very current personalities are featured. It is the odder inclusions that are most valued, as they are entities not represented in other rock reference sources. The British jazz-rock group Caravan is here, for example, but not the stylistically similar and better-documented Soft Machine. There is value, too, in the atypical depth of detail to the chronologies—one reader's minutia being another's revelatory fact. Students and music collectors will have their browsing rewarded. Popular music collections should have this title, priced reasonably given its girth.—**Ed Volz**

431. Knight, Judson. McNeill, Allison, ed. **Parents Aren't Supposed to Like It: Rock & Other Pop Musicians of Today, Volumes 4-6.** Farmington Hills, Mich., U*X*L/Gale, 2002. 3v. illus. index. $115.00/set. ISBN 0-7876-5387-X.

Volumes 4, 5, and 6 of *Parents Aren't Supposed to Like It* have changed format from the first three volumes (U*X*L/Gale, 1998). While the title of the work has remained the same, the entries are now alphabetically arranged instead of being organized by musical genre. But the entries are still categorized by genre in the table of contents in the front of each volume. The premise of the work is that most popular music sounded like "noise" to parents in the early days, but that the genres (e.g., rock, rap) often provide an insight to our culture. Each volume begins with an in-depth overview of the particular genre that provides a basic explanation of what that particular music is trying to communicate. The first three volumes covered popular musicians performing and recording in the 1990s. More than 150 biographical entries were included. The present set of volumes continues this process by covering bands and artists relevant to the later 1990s and early 2000s. Previously covered musicians and bands are updated with new entries, and many more have been added. Each volume begins with a "Musical Genre Overview" that provides a background to the particular style being covered.

The entries generally cover several pages and include a history of the performer or group, photographs (which are usually provocative in some manner), lists of awards and hit songs, and a selected discography. In the case of well-known groups or individuals, the entry includes a bibliography listing items for further reading. The histories are amazingly candid. Some list arrests of individuals and other trouble with the police. The discussions of lyrics can be used by parents, or other listeners, to determine the appropriateness of the music for younger listeners. The entry for Bone Thugs-n-Harmony points out that "the five youths supported themselves by selling crack cocaine [and that later one of the members] had been arrested for assault four years . . . before he was a star" (v.4, pp. 45-46)]. This type of information is generally not available in other sources where the intent is simply to sell recordings. The series is recommended for both young adults and parents. It is not recommended for younger children. The work should be considered for junior high, high school, and public libraries.—**Robert L. Wick**

19 Mythology, Folklore, and Popular Culture

FOLKLORE

432. **The Folklore of American Holidays.** 3d ed. Hennig Cohen and Tristram Potter Coffin, eds. Farmington Hills, Mich., Gale, 1999. 573p. index. $105.00. ISBN 0-8103-8864-2.

Arranged by the calendar year, this compendium contains 140 religious, political, seasonal, and regional holidays celebrated in the United States and includes more than 630 items. The editors state that the "traditional lore surrounding a given holiday, regardless of its origin, comprises the heart of the book." This certainly seems to be the case. Each entry is unique in that the information presented depends entirely on the type of folklore that could be obtained. For example, the section on St. Valentine's Day consists of eight pages, with entries as diverse as "Valentine's Day in the Classified Ads," "Valentine's and Lupercalia," "Signing an 'X' for a Kiss," recipes, and "Valentine's Massacre and Its Ghosts." The entry for August 16, the anniversary of Elvis Presley's death, is four pages long and is comprised more of excerpts from articles tackling such topics such as "Taking Care of Elvis," "Did Elvis Fake His Death," and "Elvis and an NFL Exhibition Game."

The preface explains the rationale and format of this volume and the introduction covers the development of formal calendars; agricultural communities and the seasonal cycle; the pagan influence on Christian holidays; and the three types of folk festivals, genuine (May Day), revived (Ground Hog Day), and fabricated (Mother's Day). There are five indexes to round out the journey through the year: the subject index; the ethnic and geographic index; the collectors, informants, and translators index; a song titles and first significant lines index with specific indicators to musical scores included in the text; and a motif and tale index. There is no indexing of the holiday entries that include recipes.

This is a volume that is not only informative but also fun to browse. Although some of the holidays are universal and celebrated elsewhere, there are many that are place specific, and for that reason this reference can be recommended for public libraries and school libraries in the United States and for collections in other places that have a strong Americana section.—**Gail de Vos**

MYTHOLOGY

433. **The Kingfisher Book of Mythology: Gods, Goddesses, and Heroes from Around the World.** 2d ed. New York, Kingfisher, 2001. 159p. illus. index. $22.95. ISBN 0-7534-5317-7.

The Kingfisher Book of Mythology: Gods, Goddesses, and Heroes from Around the World contains information about myths and legends in general, divided into various areas of the world. In all, more than 500 characters from mythology are listed, along with their functions and capsule summaries of some of the major stories associated with them. The introductory essays are simple enough to be understood by middle school age and up. Timelines and other helpful additions are provided for each section, and the many full-color illustrations are superb. A glossary defines some terms, such as *avatar*, which are also explained in the text. An alphabetic index lists the page numbers on which each entry can be found. However, material in the individual mythologies section is hard to follow. For example, the North American section lists the Iroquois creator gods, Hahgqwehdiyu and Hahgwehdaetgah, but gives no clue as to how their names might be pronounced. Another drawback is that the alphabetic listings are a mixture of so many different ethnic groups that it is hard to follow. Natos, the Blackfoot Sun god, is followed by Nayehezgani and Tobadziztzini, Navajo war god brothers. It is almost impossible to get an idea of the myths of any one Native American group (such as the Zuni, Hopi, or Cheyenne), and many prominent Native American groups (such as the Cherokee and Shawnee) are not included at all.

The Kingfisher Book of Mythology has a strange juxtaposition of mythologies, in which Celtic is paired with Slavic, with Norse in a separate category. Also included are myths and characters from Africa; the Mediterranean lands (the Near East, Egypt, Greece, and Rome); Eastern Asia (India, China, Japan, and Southeast Asia); Central and South America (Mesoamerica, the Amazon, and South America); and the South Pacific lands. The scholarly nature of this work might confuse more than inform younger users, while its lack of organization could put off even the most serious scholars. [R: BR, May/June 02, pp. 71-72]—**Kay O. Cornelius**

434.   Wilkinson, Philip. **Illustrated Dictionary of Mythology: Heroes, Heroines, Gods, and Goddesses from Around the World.** New York, DK Publishing, 1998. 128p. illus. index. $24.95. ISBN 0-7894-3413-X.

This richly illustrated volume attempts to present the major and some of the minor deities and related myths from around the world. More than one-half of the material relates to the ancient Near East, including ancient Egypt and the classical world, with the rest providing information about India, China, Japan, the Native peoples of the Americas, Africa, Australasia, and Oceania. The volume seeks to present its material through major themes common to different peoples, including narratives and deities related to the creation of the universe, battles of the gods, destruction of the cosmos (especially through floods), trickster gods, and moving to the demi-gods/super humans.

This dictionary presents little more than the basics for any topic. Although it is supposed to appeal to readers of all ages, the print is rather small for younger readers and the content is rather shallow for the young adult. Given its specific content, the volume would have benefited greatly from a basic bibliography, something to which the interested reader could turn to for further reading. Unfortunately, not everything presented is accurate (e.g., an illustration on the opening page is the Egyptian god Thoth (later so identified) but titled here Seshat). In addition, the promise of the book jacket to reveal why Kronos ate his children is never answered in the text. The volume is thus not for every library, but it can be recommended for its lavish illustrations, many not commonly seen.—**Susan Tower Hollis**

POPULAR CULTURE

435.   Ash, Russell. **Factastic Book of 1001 Lists.** New York, DK Publishing, 1999. 208p. illus. index. $19.95; $14.95pa. ISBN 0-7894-3769-4; 0-7894-3412-1pa.

The world's most famous criminals, countries with the most workers, oldest underground railroad systems, largest flightless birds—these are just 4 of the 1,001 superlative-type lists included in the *Factastic Book of 1001 Lists*. It is divided into 11 general sections such as "The Arts,"

"World Sports," " and "Science," and further into 2-page spreads such as "Travel and Tourism," "Insects and Spiders," and "Murder and Punishment." The lists are presented in box format and accompanied by colorful illustrations. A general index is provided. Ash, also author of *The Top Ten of Everything* (see entry 33), has derived his data from many sources—print, online, and "experts"—but for the most part does not provide specific sources. This makes the volume less a reliable reference than a fun book for the browser and the trivia buff. [R: BR, Sept/Oct 99, p. 77]—**Lori D. Kranz**

436.   Griffin, Robert H., and Ann H. Shurgin. **Junior Worldmark Encyclopedia of World Holidays.** Farmington Hills, Mich., U*X*L/Gale, 2000. 4v. illus. index. $149.00/set. ISBN 0-7876-3927-3.
    Brazil has Carnival, Germany celebrates Fasching and the United States has Mardi Gras. How each country celebrates its pre-Lenten festival is described in this encyclopedia of world holidays. The four volumes are arranged by topic and cover secular, religious, and national holidays of 30 countries. Holidays of Europe, Asia, South America, Africa, the Middle East, and the United States are represented.
    Each chapter begins with an overview of the featured holiday followed by information on its celebration in specific countries. Coverage of the selected days is extensive and includes history, customs, food, and music. Examples of folklore, legends, and stories associated with the days are included along with recipes for holiday foods. Fact boxes and sidebars provide a synopsis of the holiday or supplemental and comparative information. For example, the entry for Thanksgiving in the United States includes a fact box about Canada's Thanksgiving. Also, the Ramadan article has a box giving information about mosques. Furthermore, entries do not focus only on traditions but also discuss modern trends, such as the commercialization of Christmas and the adaptation of Christian holidays by non-Christian countries.
    The arrangement of the book allows for the comparing and contrasting of holidays in several countries. For example, a student (fifth grade and up) can easily find out that rice dishes and sweets are served on New Year's Day in Iran while in Scotland Hogmanay black buns are favorites. Each volume has a history of calendars, a glossary, a calendar of world holidays, and a subject index. Suggested titles and Websites to use for additional information follow each chapter along with a list of print and Web sources. Sources include standard titles such as the *Illustrated Encyclopedia of World Religions* (see ARBA 98, entry 1356), *Celebrations Around the World* (Fulcrum, 1996) and *The Worldmark Encyclopedia of Cultures and Daily Life* (see entry 129).
    The strength of this set is the ability to compare holidays across cultures, but it is not a comprehensive source. The number of holidays for each country runs from one to six, with several countries having only one holiday included. Elementary and school librarians will find the encyclopedia useful as a supplement to standard titles and to the Festivals of the World series. [R: BR, Jan/Feb 01, p. 74]—**Marlene M. Kuhl**

437.   Kronzek, Allan Zola, and Elizabeth Kronzek. **The Sorcerer's Companion: A Guide to the Magical World of Harry Potter.** New York, Broadway Books, 2002. 286p. illus. $15.00pa. ISBN 0-7679-0847-3.
    J. K. Rowling's Harry Potter novels have become a worldwide phenomenon appealing to audiences of all ages, genders, and ethnicities. With this adoration, readers have also become intrigued by the magic, mythology, and folklore behind the stories. The Kronzeks, a father and daughter team, have developed this resource to introduce readers to the history behind many of the aspects found within the first four volumes of the Harry Potter saga. Since most of the magical practices taught at Hogwarts and the imaginary creatures found in Harry's wizardry world are from the Western tradition (i.e., the Middle East, Greece, and Rome), the authors do not cover the

magic and mythology found in other countries and cultures, such as China, Africa, India, Japan, Australia, and South America.

Beginning with "Amulet" and ending with "Zombie," alphabetic entries cover topics such as broomsticks, divination, hippogriffs, owls, transfiguration, and werewolves. Within the entries, topics that have their own entries are in bold print. References to an item's first appearance in the Harry Potter volumes are provided at the end of each entry. These references include an abreviation for *Harry Potter and the Sorcerer's Stone* ("SS") , *Harry Potter and the Chamber of Secrets* ("CS") , *Harry Potter and the Prisoner of Azkaban* ("PA") , or *Harry Potter and the Goblet of Fire* ("GF") along with chapter and page numbers. The authors note in their introduction that the references are for the American editions.

Unfortunately, an index is not included so the table of contents is the reader's only clue as to what topics are covered. Furthermore, the table of contents only provides guidance to the main entries. Thus, if readers want to look up all of the references to dragons, besides the main entry, they are out of luck. Nevertheless, the entries provide a good introduction to topics covered and a bibliography lists resources that can be used for further research, including online sources. Numerous black-and-white illustrations are also scattered throughout the work.

Overall, *The Sorcerer's Companion* is fun and entertaining. The entries are appropriate for older Harry Potter fans, most likely upper middle school and above. Obviously, the work will need to be revised as future Harry Potter volumes are released and the addition of an index is advised. This edition is recommended for middle and high school libraries as well as public libraries. At $15, larger libraries should consider acquiring multiple copies for both reference and circulating collections. [R: BR, Mar/April 02, p. 68]—**Cari Ringelheim**

438.   Wilsdon, Christina. **Everyday Things: An A-Z Guide.** Danbury, Conn., Franklin Watts, 2001. 138p. illus. index. (Watts Reference). $32.00. ISBN 0-531-11792-8.

A scaled-down encyclopedia of common objects, *Everyday Things: An A-Z Guide* describes for elementary-aged readers where these things have come from, what they do, and how they work. Contemporary technology is well represented alongside prosaic entries such as paper, frozen food, and the jump shot. Every entry is accompanied by a photograph or other illustration and includes a *see also* cross-reference to related entries. The index includes not just the entry names but also subjects, nations of origin, and individuals to aid readers in tracing relationships between objects. The design is clean, the reproductions and typography crisp, the bibliography helpful, and the language inclusive. The content of *Everyday Things* seems relevant to contemporary children with a healthy dose of "where do things come from?" The 126 topics cover a broad range but this book is best seen as a jumping-off point for younger readers. [R: BR, Mar/April 02, p. 73]—**R. K. Dickson**

20   Performing Arts

GENERAL WORKS

439.   **Creative and Performing Artists for Teens.** Thomas McMahon, ed. Farmington Hills, Mich., Gale, 2000. 4v. illus. index. $350.00/set. ISBN 0-7876-3975-3.

The authors of these volumes have made a decided effort to cover a vast range of talented people, in all areas of the creative and performing arts. The choices may be questioned, but it is an eclectic collection with Mary Cassatt sharing a volume with Puffy Combs and Salinger with Seinfeld. The short articles are well written and include biographical data, an essay of commentary and criticism along with a listing of major works, and a further reading list. The black-and-white photographs, frequently movie stills or book jackets, are an additional attraction. Each volume includes an index to the entire set, and the first has an index by field. The work is attractively produced and the columnar design replicates many of the more popular contemporary magazines. With limited budgets, this may be a questionable purchase for junior and high school libraries. Most young fans probably know most of the information about their favorites and much is available in other resource material. It might prove to be useful in setting an example of how to write an interesting, informative, brief summary of the life and accomplishments of a public figure. [R: SLJ, May 2000, p. 88; BR, May/June 2000, p. 65; VOYA, Aug 2000, pp. 210-211; RUSQ, Winter 2000, pp. 183-185]—**Paula Frosch**

440.   Sonneborn, Liz. **A to Z of American Women in the Performing Arts.** New York, Facts on File, 2002. 264p. illus. index. (Facts on File Library of American History). $44.00. ISBN 0-8160-4398-1.

This reference work provides short biographical and bibliographic information on 150 American women whose talent has entertained audiences worldwide. The author defines "women in the performing arts" fairly narrowly, focusing on performers rather than talents working behind the scenes. The term "American" is used much more loosely, including foreign-born women such as Claudette Colbert, Ingrid Bergman, and Elizabeth Taylor, given their influence on American culture (although Sofia Loren was not included). Younger women performers were also not included, although the author seems to have made the decision to include Jodie Foster and Julia Roberts.

Overall, the author states her reasons for inclusion and exclusion of important American women in the performing arts in her introduction. The book is alphabetically arranged. An index of entries by area of activity and an index by year of birth accompany a general index. A short bibliography of recommended sources on American women in the performing arts is included as well. This book is a quick and selective guide to information on this subject area, with entries determined by the author's personal and professional judgment. [R: LJ, 1 Mar 02, pp. 88-90; Choice, May 02, p. 1554]—**Bradford Lee Eden**

21 Philosophy and Religion

PHILOSOPHY

Dictionaries and Encyclopedias

441. **Bioethics for Students: How Do We Know What's Right?** Stephen G. Post, ed. New York, Macmillan General Reference/Simon & Schuster Macmillan, 1999. 4v. illus. index. $295.00/set. ISBN 0-02-864940-0.

Today's young people want to be knowledgeable about medical technology in order to help them to make personal choices in the future. *Bioethics for Students* examines issues in medical ethics, animal rights, and the environment at a level that will be understood by young people. Easily comprehensible language is used to explain difficult medical terms, procedures, and concepts.

This work is heavily illustrated, with close to 500 photographs. It contains about 200 individual articles. Each volume contains some 50 articles. Feature articles cover topics such as death and dying, fertility and reproduction, one's duties to animals and the environment, genetics, health care, mental health, population control, research on humans, and artificial organs and transplantation. Broad summaries are given for each of the key topics. In the section on transplantation, six key articles are provided. Discussions range from the historical, legal, and social issues involved in organ and tissue transplants to the medical, ethical, and philosophical ones. A full range of topics related to organ transplants include donor death, artificial hearts, and various types of organ transplants, cryonics, kidney dialysis, and the marketing of organs.

This multivolume set examines issues such as euthanasia, along with the associated public debates and court cases. After extensive research, the best of the case studies (e.g., the Karen Ann Quinlan case) were selected to illustrate the complexity of the decisions concerning euthanasia and sustaining life facing the patient's family and physicians. Significant legislation is also noted. The Uniform Determination of Death Act (UDDA), adopted by more than one-half of the states and the District of Columbia, establishes brain death as the standard for determining the time of death.

This reference work is based on the revised edition of the *Encyclopedia of Bioethics* (see ARBA 96, entry 1429). Continuing the tradition, *Bioethics for Students* brings this topical subject to young people because of its easy-to-read style. This work is written at an appropriate reading level for students beginning middle school.

The two-color format (blue and white with black typeface) is clear and concise. Numerous page features include sidebar definitions, quotations, *see also* references, and bold section heads. Overall, the presentation is appealing to the eye. Bibliographical references and an index are included. Volume 4 contains 3 appendixes. The glossary is comprehensive.

A strength of this work is that both sides of controversial issues are presented with equal coverage. A good addition for public libraries in both the young adult and adult reference collection. [R: BL, 1 May 99, p. 1606; BR, Sept/Oct 99, p. 78; SLJ, Aug 99, p. 187]—**Marilynn Green Hopman**

442.   **Ethics and Values.** Danbury, Conn., Grolier, 1999. 8v. illus. index. $265.00/set. ISBN 0-7172-9274-6.

This work is aimed at providing clear, unbiased information about ethical issues and concerns. It is oriented to students of all ages, but is particularly relevant for intermediate and high school levels. It contains more than 200 entries that reflect a broad range of issues related to ethics, morals, and values. A sample of the topics included is abortion, addition, animal rights, anti-Semitism, capital punishment, censorship, cults, discrimination, euthanasia, child abuse, corruption, Nazism, pornography, gun control, genocide, the Holocaust, racism, and sexism.

The entries are arranged alphabetically. Most are only two pages long, with one black-and-white photograph as illustration. The photographs are well chosen and interesting. The articles are subdivided into shorter sections, which makes for easier reading. The type is large and presented in two-column format. Each volume has an index to the entire set; however, individual entries do not include bibliographic information. There is a one-page listing of references ("further reading" in the last volume that focuses on ethics in general rather than on specific topics included.

Individual articles are not signed. There is a list of contributors hidden on the back of the title page of each volume, with no indication of their qualifications or positions. The authority of the work appears to rest on the reputation of the publisher. However, the information included does clarify and present a balanced, objective, easy-to-understand introduction to complex moral and ethical issues. The set is a useful starting point for discussion and work with students on many important, critical issues that impact today's society. It is recommended for children's and young adult collections in public libraries, as well as for intermediate and high school library collections. [R: BL, 15 Nov 98, p. 612]—**Susan J. Freiband**

Handbooks and Yearbooks

443.   Magee, Bryan. **The Story of Philosophy.** New York, DK Publishing, 1998. 240p. illus. index. $29.95. ISBN 0-7894-3511-X.

Purists, such as this reviewer, are inclined to see such a book and turn up their noses. Coffee-table claptrap, they might say. But this purist breaks ranks, seeing a book like this and heaving a sigh of relief. In a discipline of arch-feminist studies, where people say things like "linguistify [my] positionality," and "Queer Studies," wherein places like Duke University are seriously considering serious study of transsexuals, philosophy needs all the help it can get. When that help comes in the form of a luscious and enticing book filled with ruminations both great and small, this reviewer exults.

This book, exorbitantly filled with pictures, drawings, etchings, and more, covers nearly all of western thought. From the Greeks and their world to the rationalists to the empiricists past Henri-Louis Bergson and Karl Popper to Jostein Gaarder's 1991 novelization of this subject in *Sophie's World*, Magee's book is water to a dry and thirsty land. Even the glossary is valuable. Yes, there are pitfalls in such an undertaking: Greek philosophy (all 500-plus years of it) is covered in less than 50 pages, pages covered with as many illustrations as text. The inscrutable medievals, wherein we get nearly all modern philosophy in some rechauffed form, is covered in eight pages, and so it goes.

But adversity's sweet milk, philosophy, finds its finest hour. Since sound bites have taken over the world, one cannot hope to hold the attention of modern minds much longer than 15 seconds. In an age so ripe for introspection beyond the "e" of me, this book comes as a must, not only for all libraries, but surely for all homes as well.—**Mark Y. Herring**

444.   **A Young Person's Guide to Philosophy: "I Think, Therefore I Am."** Jeremy Weate, ed. New York, DK Publishing, 1998. 64p. illus. index. $16.95. ISBN 0-7894-3074-6.

A Young Persons Guide to Philosophy: "I Think, Therefore I Am" is a fascinating way of introducing the great philosophers to young readers. Why am I here? Am I dreaming? Is there a God? These are all questions that have perplexed young minds throughout the ages. The editor of this book presents to the reader philosophers who have grappled with these questions for centuries.

The 1st section of the book is a chronological journey through the history of Western philosophy, looking at the lives and the times of some of philosophy's greatest thinkers. The pronunciation guide after each philosopher's name is helpful. The 2d section looks at the philosophers in the context of their ideas and groups them into different schools of thought: early Greeks, cynics, stoics, idealists, materialists, scholastics, rationalists, empiricists, pragmatists, phenomenologists, existentialists, post-modernists, and a separate list of feminist philosophers. Socrates, the father of Western philosophy, receives special attention. An index, a glossary, and beautiful illustrations add to the usefulness of this book, which is recommended for public, elementary, and high school libraries.—**Mary L. Bowman**

RELIGION

General Works

Dictionaries and Encyclopedias

445.   **DK Illustrated Dictionary of Religions: Rituals, Beliefs, and Practices from Around the World.** By Philip Wilkinson. New York, DK Publishing, 1999. 128p. illus. index. $24.95. ISBN 0-7894-4711-8.

This is a richly illustrated, informative, easy-to-read and -understand survey of rituals, beliefs, and practices of world religions from a publisher well known for its pictorial guides. Fifteen key world religions, from ancient civilizations such as Egypt and Greece, to present-day living religions, are treated chronologically and topically in 10 major sections of definitions and illustrations.

The work is organized on the basis of two-page spreads. The general introduction analyzes the nature of religion, the function of myth and doctrine, and the idea of ritual and sacred places. Next, an introduction to each section is presented in a box on the right side of a full-color, illustrated spread. Treatment of two to six topics (or themes) follows; for example, origins and texts, teachings, worship, and festivals. The treatment of each theme opens with an introductory paragraph and is then followed by definitions for an average of 18 terms per spread, some of which appear in subtheme boxes, along with 10 to 12 colored illustrations. A *see also* box of 4 to 14 related entries appears in the bottom right corner of every spread. At the back of the work are a glossary of 89 general terms, a 6-page index to all the key terms found in the text, and a short list of suggested readings (mostly from the 1990s). Although this dictionary was written for readers of all ages and is exceptionally well produced, it will be especially appropriate for school media centers.—**Glenn R. Wittig**

446.   **The Usborne Internet-Linked Encyclopedia of World Religions.** By Susan Meredith and Clare Hickman. Tulsa, Okla., EDC Publishing, 2001. 127p. illus. index. $19.95. ISBN 0-7945-0182-6.

   The Usborne Internet-Linked Encyclopedia of World Religions explains the major world religions as well as several ancient Western belief systems. It is intended for late elementary to middle school-aged children but even adults will find it useful. Several pages are devoted to each religion, with lots of beautiful photographs and illustrations to support the text. The entries are written with the juvenile audience in mind, but adults and college students could use the resource for quick overviews of the history and beliefs of each religion covered. The coverage of the work seems balanced, with no preference of place or language given to particular types of religions. The work begins with some ground rules of Internet safety for children, and moves on to an overview explaining for younger readers what religion is and is not before examining specific religions.

   While this encyclopedia stands alone as a great resource, as an added bonus the publisher has a Website where links for more in-depth information on each topic are listed and kept up-to-date. Each section of the encyclopedia points users to appropriate sections of the publisher's Website. The book is well indexed, and contains a map and timeline of world religions in an appendix. This is a great reference resource for public library children's collections, school libraries, and academic libraries with collections of juvenile materials.—**Mark T. Bay**

Handbooks and Yearbooks

447.   Bowker, John. **World Religions.** New York, DK Publishing, 1997. 200p. illus. maps. index. $34.95. ISBN 0-7894-1439-2.

   DK Publishing has produced another eye-catching, informative volume in *World Religions.* The author won the HarperCollins Religious Book Award in 1993 for his work, *The Meanings of Death* (Cambridge University Press). Bowker served as dean of Trinity College, Cambridge, and is currently Gresham Professor of Divinity at Gresham College, London. In the United States, Bowker is an adjunct professor of religious studies at the University of Pennsylvania. At the end of the book, the publisher acknowledges experts consulted in each area.

   World Religions looks at the beliefs and practices of many different religions, from the ancient Egyptians through Zoroastrianism and the major faiths practiced today—Christianity, Judaism, Hinduism, Buddhism, Jainism, Sikhism, and Islam. Each of the major faiths is examined through its sacred texts, imagery, key beliefs, and religious artifacts. The author's preface "What Is Religion?" successfully makes the transition to the subsequent chapters, each page generously illustrated with detailed annotations of superb reproductions of the symbolism and meaning of religious imagery and iconography. Of special interest is the section examining the Golden Rule as it exists in each of the religions. The appendixes contain useful religious timelines and maps. The work concludes with a bibliography on each religion's history, beliefs and practices, and art and architecture.

   While the illustrations are stunning, the scope is somewhat limited. Macmillan's 16-volume *Encyclopedia of Religion* (see ARBA 88, entry 1392) is preferred for more in-depth discussion. DK's *World Religions,* however, is highly recommended for a colorful and informative overview of the topic and should be purchased both as a reference and as a circulating item for middle and secondary schools and all public libraries.—**Sharon Thomerson**

448.   Breuilly, Elizabeth, Joanne O'Brien, and Martin Palmer. **Festivals of the World: The Illustrated Guide to Celebrations, Customs, Events and Holidays.** New York, Checkmark Books/Facts on File, 2002. 160p. illus. index. $29.95. ISBN 0-8160-4481-3.

This companion volume to *Religions of the World* (see ARBA 98, entry 1348) uses liturgical calendars of the world's religions to introduce students to the major (and some minor) religious festivals. The yearly cycle of feasts and festivals is used to illustrate how these events celebrate the historical events of each faith.

Festivals of the World's major religions covered—Judaism, Christianity, Muslim, Hinduism, and Buddhism—are presented in extensive entries. Other traditions covered include festivals of the Sikhs, Taoists, Zoroastrians, and Shintos. Baha'i, Jain, and Rastafarian celebrations are covered to a lesser degree.

Entries for each religion begin with a summary of its origin, history, religious practices, sacred texts, and customs. Major festivals and their significance to the faith are explained in depth. The background of each event is told through stories and legends from sacred texts that put the festival in context of the religion's history and beliefs. The liturgical calendar for each is a major feature of each entry. The calendars are depicted cyclically and each festival is briefly described on the same page, making the calendar page a useful quick reference guide. Color photographs, illustrations, and sidebars catch the eye of the reader and serve to supplement the clearly written text. For example, the Passover entry contains a full-page color spread of the elements of the Seder plate; the Hajj rites are outlined in detail, as are some Christian symbols. There are also recipes for traditional dishes such as latkes and kiribat. A glossary, bibliography (print and Websites), and an index complete the book.

Some of the information presented here is covered in less depth in *Religions of the World*. Certainly, books on specific religions will offer similar information but this is a bright, attractive book that offers visual appeal and just the right amount of information for students researching religious festivals. [R: SLJ, April 2003, p. 95]—**Marlene M. Kuhl**

449.   **Faith in America Series.** J. Gordon Melton, ed. New York, Facts on File, 2003. 5v. illus. index. $30.00/vol.

As one of the most religiously diverse nations in the world, the United States' population represents nearly all practicing religions in the world today. This series, edited by J. Gordon Melton, the director of the Institute for the Study of American Religion, looks at how each of the religions profiled has affected society politically, culturally, and spiritually. The five religions profiled by the series thus far are Catholic, Jewish, African American, Islam, and Hindu and Sikh.

Although each volume is written by a different author, each hits on the same primary points of interest. Each discusses the religions basic belief system, how it became established in the United States, discusses key events of the religion's history in the United States, discusses how the followers represent themselves in U.S. culture, the religion's impact on society, their role in U.S. politics, key figures in U.S. society, and the future of the religion in the United States. Each volume ends with a glossary, timeline, a list of resources for further study, and an index. The black-and-white photographs are well placed to illustrate various religious dress, practices, and forms of worship from each religion.

This series will be a useful resource for middle and high school libraries and many public libraries. Those religions that are often misunderstood by American citizens (e.g., Islam, Hindu) may be the most useful; however, the entire set is well done and provides valuable information.
—**Shannon Graff Hysell**

450.   Hartz, Paula R. **Zoroastrianism.** New York, Facts on File, 1999. 128p. illus. maps. (World Religions). $26.95. ISBN 0-8160-3877-5.

451.   Lugira, Aloysius M. **African Religion.** New York, Facts on File, 1999. 128p. illus. maps. index. (World Religions). $26.95. ISBN 0-8160-3876-7.

Each of these two small volumes, the most recent in Facts on File's World's Religion series, provides an excellent resource on its topic. *Zoroastrianism* opens with a brief overview of this religion with very few members. In the following chapters, the reader learns about its founder, Zarathushtra, essentially a reformer; the religion's history, including information about its Persian homeland and later Iran; and then Zoroastrianism in India, where its members are termed Parsis, the religion's largest group in the world. The following three chapters expand on the Avesta, the Zoroastrian scripture; its religious ethics and philosophy; and its rites and rituals. Finally, the author explores the future of this non-proselytizing religion, which has stringent rules against inter-marriage and converts and whose members are so dispersed throughout the world that many are separated from any significant group of like-minded individuals.

African Religion discusses the indigenous religions present in the 35 reporting nations, while noting as well the presence of Christianity and Islam. Thus its title is something of a misnomer. After opening with a general overview of Africa, the author notes the topics of significance for African religion—oral tradition and creation myths, the Supreme Being, the spirit world, rites and rituals, sacred spaces and places, and mystical forces—addressing each in greater depth in the subsequent chapters. The final chapter reviews African religion in today's world, noting the increased respect accorded the different indigenous beliefs in contrast to the earlier days when these religions were not considered true religion. Currently, missionaries generally recognize that any conversion represents a graft onto the basic "Africanness" of the individual.

In sum, both of these volumes provide excellent introductions to their respective subjects, with useful glossaries, chapter notes, suggestions for further reading, and comprehensive indexes. Thus these two books deserve a place on the shelves of public, high school, and church libraries, if not even those of colleges, due to both their readability and their clarity.—**Susan Tower Hollis**

452.   **The Kingfisher Book of Religions: Festivals, Ceremonies, and Beliefs from Around the World.** By Trevor Barnes. New York, Larousse Kingfisher Chambers, 1999. 160p. illus. index. $22.95. ISBN 0-7534-5199-9.

This book serves as a general introduction to world religions. It is very attractively packaged and filled with lots of color pictures and illustrations. There is a special focus throughout on the roles that children play within each religion to give readers a real insight into a host of different beliefs. Chapters cover ancient religions, traditional beliefs, Hinduism, Jainism, Sikhism, Buddhism, Shinto, Chinese religions, Judaism, Christianity, Islam, and modern-day beliefs. The text varies from being general in nature to specific on selected facts within each chapter's sections. Sections vary within the chapters covered.

Coverage appears to be more substantial on the Eastern religions. The Hindu religion has more substantial sections introducing the religion, the origins of the religion, Hindu gods and goddesses, the sacred writings, the Hindu trinity, Hindu worship, and Hindu beliefs. Children are reflected in three captioned photographs, but not in the text. The chapter on Chinese religions provides focused sections on Confucianism, Taoism, and folk religion, but not on Buddhism, which is covered in an earlier chapter. Under the chapter on Christianity there is a section devoted to divisions in Christianity, but it might have been helpful to have separate chapters on Roman Catholicism and Protestantism.

There is some unevenness in what aspects were described or highlighted for each religion mentioned. Worship and festivals may have a whole section within a religion or a highlighted box describing different festival days. The glossary is very good and so is the index. Despite its unevenness, school libraries may find it useful for some of the chapters, and especially for its photographs that reflect children in many different religious groups.—**Jan Squire Whitfield**

Bible Studies

453. Waller, Lynn. **International Children's Bible Dictionary.** Dallas, Tex., Word Publishing, 1997. 128p. illus. maps. $12.99pa. ISBN 0-8499-4013-3.

This 128-page book contains more than 1,200 simple definitions of biblical words, phrases, people, and events. The definitions are arranged in alphabetic order to make the entries easy to locate. Entries include references to where the term can be found in the Bible as well as cross-references to other entries in the dictionary. Many words also have a pronunciation guide to help children pronounce unfamiliar words. In addition, the author has included approximately 100 realistic-looking illustrations and maps to help readers understand the terms defined and how they were used in biblical times. The two-page introduction suggests that this dictionary has been prepared for elementary school-age children; although the definitions are clear and straightforward, the typeface size would suggest that this book is not directed to younger elementary students. Parents and teachers who work with elementary or middle school children, however, will find this a useful resource that seems to address many terms and phrases that would be encountered in teaching the Bible to younger children.—**Kay Mariea**

Judaism

454. Morrison, Martha A., and Stephen F. Brown. **Judaism.** rev. ed. New York, Facts on File, 2002. 144p. illus. index. (World Religions). $30.00. ISBN 0-8160-4766-9.

This revision of the 1991 edition is part of the World Religions series aimed at grades 7 through 10. The eight chapters discuss the modern Jewish world, early history of Jews and Judaism, Jewish history from the Restoration to the present, the Hebrew Bible, the branches of Judaism and their basic beliefs, rites of passage, the impact of Judaism, and the future of the religion. The books identified for further reading have copyright dates ranging from 1938 through 2002, with some more adult-oriented titles, but no Websites are mentioned for further reference. A glossary, index, and black-and-white photographs and illustrations are included. The lucid narrative is complemented by a clean layout and uncrowded pages with plenty of space for boxed sidebars with additional facts. This is an excellent title, but will be more appropriate for circulating rather than reference collections.—**Esther R. Sinofsky**

BIOGRAPHY

455.   **Biographical Encyclopedia of Scientists.** Richard Olson, ed. Tarrytown, N.Y., Marshall Cavendish, 1998. 5v. illus. index. $299.95/set. ISBN 0-7614-7064-6.

This 5-volume set profiles some 472 figures in the history of science that have been gathered from across disciplines and throughout history, with the focus being on the hard sciences at the exclusion of the social sciences. Included is a mixture of scientists from the famous to the little known, from ancient Greeks to today's working scientists.

Each volume includes an index and pronunciation key. Entries are arranged alphabetically, ranging in length from 750 to 1,250 words, although some longer essays are included that cover individuals who made significant contributions to the field of science. Each entry begins with the scientist's name along with their area of achievement and contribution to the sciences, followed by a biography. Photographs, drawings, and diagrams are included along with separate boxed-off areas within the articles that further explain theories and research related to the scientist's work. Bibliographies are also listed along with the author of each biography. The 5th volume of this work also includes a glossary, country list, achievement list, and timeline. Of these, the most useful is the country list—a listing of each scientist under the primary country or countries where he or she lived and conducted scientific work. Also useful is the separate listing for members of minority groups and women (and the achievement list) and a listing of scientists under categories such as astronomy, biology, chemistry, and others.

This work compares favorably to other biographical encyclopedias already available. High school and undergraduate college students will find the biographies accompanied by their illustrations informative. The separate listing for locating biographies on minority groups and women is also useful. This biographical set is recommended for purchase. [R: SLJ, Aug 98, p. 194; BL, 1 Dec 98, p. 694; BL, 15 May 98, p. 1651]—**Julia Perez**

456.   **Biography Today: Scientists & Inventors Series. Volume 7.** Cherie D. Abbey, ed. Detroit, Omnigraphics, 2002. 205p. illus. index. $39.00. ISBN 0-7808-0636-0.

This is the latest volume in the *Biography Today: Scientists & Inventors* set from Omnigraphics. With the 7th volume, more than 80 scientists have been profiled in the set so far. Omnigraphics also offers biographical works on artists, authors, sports figures, and world leaders, as well as their annual *Biography Today* volume that includes influential people from all types of professions.

This volume provides biographies for 10 famous scientists. Written in a style and format that will appeal to young adults age 9 and above, the work features such well-known scientists as Steve Irwin (the "Crocodile Hunter"), Jerri Nielsen (the doctor who dealt with breast cancer at the

South Pole), and John Forbes Nash (the mathematician whom *A Beautiful Mind* was written about). Each biography provides a black-and-white picture of the scientist as well as information about their childhood, education, career highlights, and family. Each biography concludes with a list of the scientist's writings, honors and awards, and a list of further reading (including books, periodicals, and Websites).—**Shannon Graff Hysell**

457. **Scientists: Their Lives and Works, Volume 5.** Marie C. Ellavich, ed. Detroit, U*X*L/Gale, 1998. 224p. illus. index. $39.00. ISBN 0-7876-2797-6.

458. **Scientists: Their Lives and Works, Volume 6.** Marie C. Ellavich, ed. Farmington Hills, Mich., U*X*L/Gale, 1999. 193p. illus. index. $39.00. ISBN 0-7876-3682-7. ISSN 1522-8630.
    Scientists: Their Lives and Works provides information about 34 scientists from around the world and from the Industrial Revolution to the present are covered in such diverse fields as animal ecology, astronomy, biology, climatology, ecology, forestry, mathematics, medicine, oceanography, physics, zoology, and more.
    The volume begins with a cumulative list of the scientists by their field of specialization. More than 80 fields are categorized and each scientist is mentioned by name followed by the volume number and page number where the information can be located. A timeline of major scientific breakthroughs follows, with brief descriptions of these events. Parallel to the timeline is another timeline that includes major world historic events. A glossary of "words to know" follows that includes definitions of scientific terms. The explanations are clear, brief, and easy to understand.
    The biographies comprise the majority of the text and are in alphabetic order. Each entry begins with the scientist's name, birth date, death date (if deceased), and a photograph. The content focuses on the scientist's early life, formative experiences, and inspirations. When the article refers to the scientist's educational years, it is done candidly and contains details about any difficulties they may have had, which should have great appeal to students. All entries are easy to read and clearly and concisely written.
    Impact boxes are located in each article, which contain important information and summaries of why each scientist's work is revolutionary. Other highlighted areas in each article, biographical boxes, have information about other individuals who were influential in the work of the featured scientist or who conducted the same type of research. Finally, each article concludes with an excellent list of sources for further reading so students know where to seek other information.
    A wonderful cumulative index to all six volumes completes the book. It is annotated with italic type that indicates volume numbers, boldface type that indicates entries and their page numbers, and "(ill.)," which indicates illustrations.
    This series is an excellent source for all public and school libraries. Marie Ellavich has written an outstanding tool for research work or for personal knowledge seekers that is appropriate for all ages.—**Mary L. Trenerry**

459. **The Grolier Library of Science Biographies.** Danbury, Conn., Grolier, 1997. 10v. illus. index. $299.00/set. ISBN 0-7172-7626-0.
    This 10-volume set of science biographies by Grolier contains 2,000 entries of basic biographical data on the world's most influential and well-known scientists. Intended for students from grade 7 to adults, each biography includes a portrait of the scientist, the period in which he or she worked, and the scientific field to which the person made a contribution. In addition, there are an index for the entire set, a glossary for the entire set, and a useful "Chronology" or timeline that places the scientists and their discoveries in order.
    After comparing other well-known scientific biographies such as Scribner's *Dictionary of Scientific Biography* (see ARBA 91, entries 1461 and 1462), this set by Grolier is not as complete.

Some famous scientists have been left out, such as Gottfried Leibniz, and eighteenth century physicist, and the entries are not as detailed and informative. Although there is a section called "Sources and Further Reading" in each volume, it would be more convenient to have this information at the end of each biography for faster and easier reference by students, especially because some entries are not very detailed. *The Grolier Library of Science Biographies* is useful for middle school, high school, and public library collections; however, it is not as scholarly as other available biography collections.—**Natalie Brower-Kirton**

460.   Haven, Kendall, and Donna Clark. **100 Most Popular Scientists for Young Adults: Biographical Sketches and Professional Paths.** Englewood, Colo., Libraries Unlimited, 1999. 526p. illus. index. (Profiles and Pathways Series). $56.00. ISBN 1-56308-674-3.

This 1-volume resource focuses on uncovering the "early intentions and plans and the early life events that shaped" the lives of the scientists discussed. Each 5-page entry contains 6 sections: Career Highlights, Important Contributions, Career Path, Key Dates, Advice, and References. The advice section explains in the scientist's own words, "how to start a successful career in that field of science" (p. xv). Some entries include a black-and-white photograph of the scientist. The appendix provides Internet references and a list of scientists by field of specialization. The 100 scientists include some of the ones most frequently researched by students in grades 5 through 10 (e.g., Isaac Asimov, Robert Bakkar, Robert Ballard, Luther Burbank, Rachel Carson, Albert Einstein, Enrico Fermi, Dian Fossey, Edwin Hubble, Bill Nye, Sally Ride, and Carl Sagan). The entries are arranged alphabetically by last name, but the table of contents and page guide words, instead of listing last name first to make scanning for a name easier, the names are listed first name then last name, making the reader work a little harder to scan the last names. The emphasis on the scientist's career makes this a useful research tool. —**Esther R. Sinofsky**

461.   **Notable Black American Scientists.** Kristine Krapp, ed. Farmington Hills, Mich., Gale, 1999. 349p. illus. index. $75.00. ISBN 0-7876-2789-5.

This biographical resource records the accomplishments of 254 African American scientists and physicians from colonial times to the present. The selection criteria for inclusion in this book included several areas, such as scientists who have worked or work in the natural, physical, social, and applied sciences; scientists with notable first achievements; those with an overall contribution to scientific progress; and those familiar to the general public. Some well-known scientists as well as lesser-known individuals have been selected for inclusion. The majority of the biographies are of men, although 59 women are featured here.

The book is divided into several sections—an entry list (an alphabetical list of names with page numbers included to locate the individual biographies); a timeline, which includes scientific milestones of the book's entrants; the biographies; and indexes. The biographies are arranged alphabetically with each list beginning with, if available, a photograph or drawing of the individual, then the scientist's name, birth and death dates, and field of specialty. The biographical essays range in length from 400 to 2,000 words and cover the salient points of the person's early life, accomplishments, and current status if still living. Enough information about the person is contained in the essay in order to get a good introductory background about the person's life and achievements. Other items included in the essay are a list of publications written by and about the entrant. Other useful items in the book are the separate indexes used to locate the biographies by gender, specialization, or subject.

The subject content alone will make it a desirable purchase because not many resources gathered in one place are available about the endeavors of African Americans in the sciences. This book is recommended for any library that has use for biographical information, particularly public, school, or academic libraries. [R: BL, 15 Feb 99, p. 1085; Choice, Sept 99, pp. 114-115; RUSQ, Spring 99, p. 311]—**Julia Perez**

462. **Scientists, Mathematicians, and Inventors: Lives and Legacies, an Encyclopedia of People Who Changed the World.** Doris Simonis, ed. Phoenix, Ariz., Oryx Press, 1999. 244p. illus. index. (Lives and Legacies). $69.95. ISBN 1-57356-151-7.

Biographical reference sources in the sciences continue to be published at a fast pace, at least in part serving the popularity of biographical assignments among children. This volume follows the lead of many other recent titles by striving to include those who have been traditionally ignored in science biographies, especially women and minorities. The work's unique slant is the choice of those scientists whose lives and work had a significant impact on either their own disciplines after their lives or else on society as a whole. Thus, those scientists and inventors who demonstrated influential and creative thinking were included in favor of those who merely made discoveries that followed from accepted knowledge. Most of the 200 subjects lived during the past two centuries, and the scope is broad enough to include key figures in medicine and physiology.

Each subject receives a 1-page treatment, which includes an outline of his or her life and work, an interpretation of that person's legacy, a timeline, and a brief bibliography. The several appendixes include further chronologies, a fuller bibliography, and a solid index. The splitting of life and work from legacy often seems artificial; whereas some essays (such as that on Werner Karl Heisenberg) include a thoughtful analytical treatment of the subject's impact, many of the other essays (such as that on Nikolaus Otto) continue the same type of historical discussion in the legacy section that appeared in the life section. The writing is usually clear, although not especially lively, and the coverage is fairly brief and thus would be most appropriate for high school or later junior high age on up. The sources in the bibliographies generally indicate an intended audience beyond elementary school as well. Overall, this source is competently executed, but it may have little new information to add to collections that have purchased other recent works. [R: BR, Sept/Oct 99, pp. 66-67]—**Christopher W. Nolan**

463. **Scientists: The Lives and Works of 150 Scientists.** Peggy Saari and Stephen Allison, eds. Detroit, U*X*L/Gale, 1996. 3v. illus. index. $99.95/set. ISBN 0-7876-0959-5.

This 1,000-page, 3-volume guide to the lives and works of 150 scientists is a highly selective, even arbitrary catalog of some well-known and a greater number of lesser-known scientific figures. The profiles range in time from Johannes Kepler to living scientists, many of them Nobel prize-winners. The tone is set by the "Reader's Guide," which notes that "budding scientists and those entering the fascinating world of science for fun or study will find inspiration in these volumes."

The preface states that the biographies range from Louis Pasteur to Bill Gates. Individual articles are meant to recount each scientist's upbringing, formative experiences, and major inspirations, details meant to "keep students reading." A timeline of scientific breakthroughs is provided, which begins with the industrial revolution (which many may argue does not reflect science but rather technology, and that a significant distinction ought to be drawn between the two) and ends with Mark Plotkin's ethnobotanical studies of the Amazon rain forest. Because most of the biographies of living scientists provide no sources concerning their lives, it is not clear how the research for this book was actually conducted. Nor is there any indication of what criteria were used in selecting the individuals presented here. Although all have made commendable contributions, not all are equally distinguished, and the biggest surprises are the omissions.

What should be emphasized is that the editors have gone out of their way to include women and minorities to a larger extent than is the case with most comparable reference works. Among women, for example, the biographies include women whose names are probably not so well-known outside their own circles, such as Angeles Alvariño, Elizabeth Blackburn, Helen Caldicott, Sylvia Earle, Dorothy Horstmann, Ruth Patrick, Berta Scharrer, and Florence Seibert. Why, if these relative unknowns are listed, were not such better-known women as Maria Gaetana

Agnesi, Mary Cartwright, Sofia Kolaveskaya, Sophie Germain, Christine Ladd Franklin, Julia Robinson, Olga Taussky, Dorothy Wrinch, or Grace Chisholm Young?

As for bibliographies to "stimulate further reading," these seem inadequate in many cases. For example, the list for Albert Einstein does not recommend any of the major, authoritative biographies, including those by Jeremy Bernstein and Abraham Pais. Similarly, for the prominent mathematician Carl Friedrich Gauss, only one article from *Scientific American* is given. Despite the arbitrary selection of the scientists included in these three volumes and the unfortunate lack of substantial bibliographic references, this collection of biographies may still be a useful resource for high school students or for anyone in need of brief information about the scientific figures included here, especially lesser-known women, blacks, and other minorities.—**Joseph W. Dauben**

CHRONOLOGY

464.   Bridgman, Roger. **1,000 Inventions & Discoveries.** New York, DK Publishing, 2002. 256p. illus. index. $24.99. ISBN 0-7894-8826-4.

This visually rich reference covers three million years of creativity and curiosity that have produced tens of thousands of inventions and discoveries that have played an important part in shaping our world. The first section, "Learning the Basics," starts with stone tools, the oldest being crude stone tools found in Africa, which date back to c3,000,000 B.C.E. Covering this first discovery through 500 B.C.E., this section includes a wide diversity of discoveries including, cave paintings, houses, the usefulness of dogs and sheep, making fire, pottery, boats, tools for farming, silver, alcoholic drinks, the wheel, the calendar, cosmetics, writing, bathrooms, the corset, shoes, money, stores, and so on. Other sections are "The Age of Authority, c499 BC-1400"; "New Worlds, New Ideas, 1401-1750"; "Revolutionary Changes, 1751-1850"; "Science Takes Control, 1851-1900"; "Inventions for Everyone, 1901-1950"; and "Information & Uncertainty, 1951-2001."

Each entry includes a clearly written explanation and description of the invention or discovery as well as the approximate date that it first appeared. There are 1,000 inventions and discoveries compiled from a panel of scientific experts, with hundreds of full-color pictures and illustrations from the Smithsonian Institution. Special features include a running timeline at the bottom of each page and insets of special topics interspersed throughout the text, as well as essays that discuss ground-breaking discoveries such as the Pythagoras theory, Archimedes' discovery of how things float, Gutenberg and the printing press, and Bell and the telephone. There are indexes of inventions and discoveries and inventors and discoverers.

This is a book that will serve elementary students through adults as a history of civilization through man's ingenuity. It is a visual delight for browsing and will serve as a ready reference for students doing research on inventors and inventions.—**Dana McDougald**

DICTIONARIES AND ENCYCLOPEDIAS

465.   **The American Heritage Student Science Dictionary.** New York, Houghton Mifflin, 2002. 376p. illus. $18.00. ISBN 0-618-18919-X.

The 376 pages of alphabetic entries featured in this volume include information about pronunciation, irregular plurals, closely related words, and cross-references and chemical formulas. Entries are complemented by 425 color photographs and drawings. Supporting tables and charts include a timeline of computing, geologic time, measurement, organic compounds, a periodic table, rocks, the solar system, and taxonomy. There are 21 biography sidebars that support 300 biographical entries of major men and women in science. Front matter includes a table of contents; a list of special entries; a preface; an excellent, diagrammatic explanation of the elements found within the dictionary; and a pronunciation guide. End matter consists of a listing of picture credits.

There are several features that make this volume user-friendly and increase the utility of this dictionary beyond that of most simple-definition dictionaries. The 12 "A Closer Look" text boxes (side bars) explain broader concepts, such as the greenhouse effect or photosynthesis. There are 105 "Did You Know" text boxes provided to expand information about concepts and processes, such as acid rain, the big bang, or transcription. The 31 "Usage" text boxes explain how similar words are incorporated into language, such as bacteria and bacterium or the differences between fruits and vegetables. There are 19 "World History" text boxes that expand upon the definition to include its interaction with people, cultures, and events. More than 300 entries address the men and women of science. In addition, there are 21 "Biography" text boxes providing greater detail about the lives and efforts of those individuals generally recognized as the scientific "greats." In some instances, significant additional information is provided to expand upon the basic definition, such as the supporting data for "organic compounds."

This is a comprehensive, affordable reference volume that would be useful to students in upper-elementary grades and above or as a general household, nontechnical science dictionary. It does not affect its usage, but the separation of expanded entries into variously named text boxes may be confusing to some readers. It may be difficult to understand why photosynthesis is listed as "A Closer Look" while plate tectonics is "Did You Know." [R: SLJ, Feb 03, p. 85]—**Craig A. Munsart**

466.   Bruno, Leonard C. **Science and Technology Breakthroughs: From the Wheel to the World Wide Web.** Detroit, U*X*L/Gale, 1998. 2v. illus. $55.00/set. ISBN 0-7876-1927-2.

The 1,300 entries in this work cover major scientific and technological achievements and vary in length from two sentences to eight or nine. The paragraphs provide the date or approximate period in which the milestone occurred, location, person responsible, and the individual's nationality.

Each volume comprises six subject areas, which are arranged chronologically, allowing the reader to follow the development of a discovery or invention through its stages and understand the progression and influences. Cross-references to related entries in that section are provided. The indexes found in each volume are comprehensive for the set and provide quick access to specific topics with illustrations noted. Each volume is prefaced with a 362-word glossary, a table of contents to the set, and a bibliography with suggested titles for each of the 12 categories. The earliest milestone was the introduction of the bow and arrow in 50,000 B.C.E.; the most recent entry was the birth of Dolly, a genetically engineered lamb on June 25, 1997.

The boldfaced headings and the visually pleasing page format make it easy for the student to focus on the date and the milestone. Approximately 150 black-and-white photographs and drawings illustrate the set. Twenty-one sidelines provide further interesting and fascinating facts on topics, such as measuring earthquakes. Three of the sidelines are biographical, providing information on George Washington Carver, Charles Darwin, and Rosalind Franklin. Grades four through eight will find this set useful, especially for following the influences of early milestones on later discoveries.—**Elaine Ezell**

467.   **The Concise Science Encyclopedia.** New York, Larousse Kingfisher Chambers, 2001. 320p. illus. maps. index. $14.95. ISBN 0-7534-5418-1.

This is a quick reference source for science topics. The broad field of science is divided into nine chapters: "Planet Earth," "Living Things," "Human Biology," "Chemistry and the Elements," "Materials and Technology," "Light and Energy," "Forces and Movement," "Electricity and Electronics," and "Space and Time." There are 15-25 subtopics in each chapter with each topic receiving 1 to 2 pages of coverage. In relation to the amount of information, concise is the correct term. The information is valid; however, it is basic. Each chapter opens with an introduction and concludes with a "Facts and Figures" page related to the topic. The information on the "Facts and Figures" pages range from key dates to branches of the scientific discipline, laws, and definitions. The "Ready Reference" section in the back of the book includes numbers and units of measurement, geometric shapes, famous scientists, inventions and discoveries, a glossary, and an index. There are 21 scientists and 22 inventions included; these are all well known and the information is given in a few sentences.

Cross-references are provided throughout the book and are consistently placed in the lower right hand corner of the pages. These references make the book more useful to students. The volume is attractive and well illustrated throughout with color photographs, drawings, and diagrams. But the binding is not very durable—the stitching holding the sections together is very visible. It will not endure heavy use and the text is too close to the edges for rebinding. This book will be most useful in school and public libraries looking for quick reference sources and not in-depth coverage. [R: BR, May/June 02, p. 71]—**Elaine Ezell**

468.   **The DK Science Encyclopedia.** rev. ed. New York, DK Publishing, 1998. 448p. illus. index. $39.95. ISBN 0-7894-2190-9.

The DK Science Encyclopedia is an outstanding, comprehensive reference work. That so much can be packed into one volume and still maintain clarity, organization, and scope is a tribute to the efforts of the exceptional team of science writers and specialists. The encyclopedia is divided into 12 topical sections covering matter, reactions, materials, forces and energy, electricity and magnetism, sound and light, Earth, weather, space, living things, how living things work, and ecology. Within the topical sections are more than 280 main entries describing such topics as the chemistry of foods, elements, friction, robots, lasers, fossils, forecasting, Mars, viruses, blood, conservation, and more. More than 1,900 subentries include biographies of great scientists and inventors, time charts, and fact boxes on information highlighting specific aspects of a main entry. In addition to the concise table of contents, a detailed index assists the user. The illustrations are colorful, clear, and accurate.

Even though the encyclopedia was planned to support elementary and middle school science curricula, it is so well written that even the most nonscientific person would benefit and understand the concepts presented. DK Publishing has provided an excellent resource for all. [R: BL, 1 Dec 98, p. 690]—**Mary L. Trenerry**

469.   **DK Ultimate Visual Dictionary of Science.** New York, DK Publishing, 1998. 448p. illus. index. $29.95. ISBN 0-7894-3512-8.

DK Publishing has established a tradition of excellent visual works of reference; this work continues that tradition. Following the precept of "a picture is worth a thousand words," the publishers have produced a volume that seems to be worthy of its title.

The book is user friendly. Contents are divided among nine chapters: physics, chemistry, life sciences and ecology, human anatomy, medical science, earth sciences, astronomy and astrophysics, electronics and computer science and mathematics. Each chapter begins with a guide to the topics within that chapter, a historical overview of the subject matter, and a timeline of discoveries. Important names within the historical overview are shown in bold typeface and are detailed in the biography section at the back of the book. Each topic is shown on a facing, two-page spread and contains a short introductory text supported by many illustrations and explanatory notes. Words in bold typeface are defined in the glossary. Color photographs are supplemented by detailed artwork in color.

The "Useful Data" appendix contains such reference material as conversions; formulas; geometric figures; star charts; and a diverse group of facts, among which are the energy requirements of animal species, lengths of cave systems, and binary codes of various numbers. In addition to appendixes containing biographies and a glossary, the back matter also includes an excellent index that also references the appendixes. If there is a shortcoming to this work, it is a minor one. Some pages in the volume were reproduced from the Visual Dictionary Series, published earlier by DK Publishing.

This is a well-designed and well-executed dictionary that would be an excellent addition to any library, classroom, or home. At a time when some books seem to offer little for the price, it is an excellent value and quite affordable. [R: SLJ, Nov 98, p. 151; BL, 1 Dec 98, p. 690]—**Craig A. Munsart**

470.   **Eyewitness Encyclopedia of Science.** [CD-ROM]. New York, DK Multimedia, 1996. Minimum system requirements (Windows version): IBM or compatible 486DX/33MHz. Double-speed CD-ROM drive. Windows 3.1. 8MB RAM. 22MB hard disk space. 640 x 480 pixels, 256-color monitor (16-bit colors preferred). Mouse. 8-bit sound card. Loudspeakers or headphones. Minimum system requirements (Macintosh version): 68LC040 25MHz. Double-speed CD-ROM drive. System 7.0. 12MB RAM. 25MB hard disk space. 640 x 480 pixels, 256-color monitor (thousands of colors preferred). Mouse. 8-bit sound card. Loudspeakers or headphones. $39.95. ISBN 0-7894-1230-6.

This CD-ROM product is a visually intriguing and entertaining attempt to deliver information about the sciences in a multimedia, encyclopedic format. Its major coverage includes mathematics, physics, chemistry, and the life sciences, with further subject breakdown for each area. Chemistry, for example, further refines into such topics as physical states and changes, reactions, chemical elements, organic chemistry, and so forth. Clicking on any of these categories offers the user another set of even more specific subcategories. Once at this level, a short hypertext article (with highlighted keywords to click on for further information) appears on the screen and is narrated. A "see also" box and a "find out more" list are also offered.

Complementing the core subject areas are other features. Biographical information about scientists, arranged alphabetically, is included in a "Who's Who" area. A "Virtual Molecule" program displays moving, 3-D images of a dozen different molecules, along with a short description and an opportunity to click on related articles. A "Matter Explorer" offers a chance to select and increasingly magnify a variety of objects—view an aphid with the naked eye, then at 10 times its size, for example. Forty different short, narrated videos on various topics are also available for viewing. "Earth and the Universe" offers information on astronomy. (One may wonder why astronomy was not included as a topic in its own right.) A "Quiz Master" feature gives users a chance to test their knowledge in the areas of scientific facts, principles, and people. Finally, indexes to videos, animations, and articles are offered, along with a search engine allowing keyword Boolean and other refined searches of the encyclopedia's contents.

There are some significant weaknesses to this multimedia tool, however. The most striking is that, although the graphics are attractive and the sound is of professional quality, there are no clear clues for navigation. The graphics are fun, but they are not terribly intuitive. From the initial screen the major options seem somewhat obvious at first, but closer inspection reveals much more going on in the background: a tiny "A-Z" icon for the index and an almost invisible question mark where one may click to find help information, for example. It is simply not clear which are clickable image areas versus simple illustrations, and what will happen when one does click. Beyond the main screen, it is not clear how to exit an area, return to an earlier screen, or close a text box. These problems detract considerably from ease of use.

It is a bit of a stretch to label this product an encyclopedia. For all its bells and whistles, the CD-ROM's scope and depth of topic coverage do not begin to approach that of a print encyclopedia—articles are brief and the content and language simplistic. Instead, it may be wiser to market this tool as simply an entertaining introduction to science. Finally, selectors would find it helpful if academic credentials had been included with the credits for the science information included on the disc.—**Judith A. Matthews**

471. Graham, Ian, and Paul Sterry. **Questions & Answers Book of Science Facts.** New York, Facts on File, 1997. 80p. illus. maps. index. $19.95. ISBN 0-8160-3655-1.

Large typeface, nice color illustrations, and interesting information make this a great browsing book for a middle school-age student. It contains broad categories of information on space, the world, nature, and science and technology. "Space" deals with four topics related to stars and space exploration. "Our World" has five subjects that range from the Earth to habitats. "Nature" is a large section with 15 categories that start at evolution and work through pets into plant life. The "Science & Technology" category contains 14 subjects moving from physics to machines and structures. Each subject has six or seven questions and their answers. For example, in the category of science and technology, one of the subjects is "materials." Such questions as "What are materials?" and "How is paper made?" contain brief, general information. A color illustration accompanies each question and answer.

Some entries are simple, such as "What is gravity?" but can become complex, such as "What is an Archimedes' Screw used for?" Each question has a clear, understandable answer to a child with good reading skills and basic science background. It is not clear how questions were chosen for inclusion in the book. Surprisingly, computers are not included in the "machine" subject of "Science & Technology." The book contains an excellent index but does not include any other supplementary materials, such as a glossary or a bibliography.

The strength of this book is in the intriguing questions with a brief but clear answer that will encourage a student to explore a science topic in greater detail. Although the volume could not be used as a source for a science report, it can give students ideas for their reports.—**Suzanne Julian**

472. **The Grolier Student Encyclopedia of Science, Technology, and the Environment.** Danbury, Conn., Grolier, 1996. 11v. illus. maps. index. $219.00/set. ISBN 0-7172-7517-5.

This 11-volume set provides an introduction to many aspects of science and technology for children at a 3d-or 4th-grade reading level. The books are colorful, lightweight, and accessible. The entries are in alphabetic order, and an index in the last volume directs the reader to topics that are not necessarily the titles of specific entries. Each entry is short and clear, and explanations are simple and understandable. Inevitably, the entries are superficial, but the reader is referred to other sections that have more information on a particular aspect. The entries stimulate curiosity and interest without being overwhelming.

The entries cover a broad variety of subjects. Science, in general, is defined in an operational way rather than as a collection of facts; the aspect of answering questions and explaining things is emphasized. The many branches of biology are described, chemistry and mathematics are covered, and technology is considered broadly. Generous photography, much from public domain sources, illustrates the entries. Diagrams are clear and uncluttered, and the writing is crisp and engaging.

Despite the fact of being published in Danbury, Connecticut, an Australian influence is felt. Many photographs originate in Australia, such as the Southern Cross in the entry on constellations and the Australian opera in the entry on voice. This is not a negative influence, however. One error was found: The diagram in the entry on Genetics is mislabeled; brown hair and blond hair are reversed. Nonetheless, these volumes are captivating and should grab the interest of any child. [R: RBB, 1 April 96, p. 1388; SLJ, Aug 96, p. 181]—**Margretta Reed Seashore**

473.   **Illustrated Science Encyclopedia.** Austin, Tex., Raintree/Steck-Vaughn, 1997. 24v. illus. maps. index. $499.50/set. ISBN 0-8172-3943-X.

This encyclopedia is intended to be a student-friendly, comprehensive science reference work for middle school students. Most articles are illustrated with color photographs or drawings. Many article titles have phonetic pronunciation shown, with a pronunciation key at the beginning of each volume. Some articles include an "Activity Box" containing a simple project students can complete to enhance understanding of the subject. Articles often go beyond the clinical exposition of their title. "Agriculture" and "Plastic," for example, also include a subsection about the environment, important information for students. The encyclopedia contains a useful student bibliography annotated with the grade level appropriateness of the citations. It is arranged by subject and includes CD-ROMs. Many bibliographic citations are of other Raintree/Steck-Vaughn publications. The final volume contains 75 science projects, easily completed by students, that are tied to and reinforce articles in the main text. The index lists article titles as well as other locations of the keyword.

Overall, the encyclopedia is done well, but there are some areas that could have been improved. An occasional article contains misleading information. Under "Airplane," the *Concorde* is indicated as a French airplane; the information is corrected under "Aviation," where it is correctly described as being developed by the British and the French. Under "Astronautics," the caption of the space shuttle drawing describes the shuttle as being launched into orbit by two recoverable, solid rocket boosters; the description omits the large, nonrecoverable, external tank containing the liquid fuel for the *Orbiter*'s own engines. The "Engine" article omits the two-stroke type, a common, small engine students may know. Some articles without an illustration could benefit from one, such as "Plimsoll Line" and "Halibut." At other times, an illustration supports the article poorly, such as the photograph of a wild almond tree in bloom for "Almond," when students may be more interested in the edible nut of the plant and its products. The price of the set would preclude it from most classrooms, but, despite some editorial shortcomings, this set could be a useful addition to the middle school library.—**Craig A. Munsart**

474.   **Interactive Science Encyclopedia.** [CD-ROM]. Austin, Tex., Raintree/Steck-Vaughn, 1997. Minimum system requirements (Windows version): IBM or compatible 486DX/33MHz. Double-speed CD-ROM drive. Windows 95. 8MB RAM. 10MB hard disk space. 256-color monitor. SVGA video card. Mouse. Sound card. Speakers or headphones. Printer (optional). Minimum system requirements (Macintosh version): 68040 microprocessor. Double-speed CD-ROM drive. OS system 7.1. 8MB RAM (16MB with PowerMac). 10MB hard disk space. 13-inch, 256-color monitor. Mouse. Speakers or headphones. Printer (optional). $99.95. ISBN 0-8712-3914-6 (Windows version); 0-8172-3913-8 (Macintosh version).

This electronic encyclopedia is a collection of nearly 3,000 articles covering numerous aspects of science, with more than 3,000 graphics, 50 video clips, 50 animations, 75 sound effects, and 8 narrated slide shows. In addition, it contains more than 150 experiments called "ProActivities" in 3 levels of difficulty. Twenty of these activities can be performed onscreen, whereas the rest are offline activities. Learners can also study the history of science through eight timeline capsules that show key historical events and important scientists in context. Overall, entries are current and appear to be well written.

The disk was easy to load. The contents are easily navigated either by searching the topical subcategories or by clicking on an alphabetic index. Hypertext entries link various topics. Keyword searching is also available, with advanced features such as proximity searching. The sound bites did not work even though two different personal computers were tried. This may have been the fault of the review disk. Animations worked well, and the speed could be regulated. Overall, the technical characteristics are generally user-friendly and reliable, and the quality of graphics is excellent.

The level of interactivity is generally better than with many other similar encyclopedias that act principally as reference sources. Instructional characteristics include the ability to make notes about the projects or entries. One could easily envision collaborative team projects or group viewing for demonstration. The multimedia support for text makes the product more appealing for visual learners; children in the earlier grades will especially benefit. [R: LJ, Jan 98, pp. 157-158]—**Andrew G. Torok**

475.   **The Kingfisher First Science Encyclopedia.** By Anita Ganeri and Chris Oxlade. New York, Larousse Kingfisher Chambers, 1997. 112p. illus. index. $14.95. ISBN 0-7534-5089-5.

This colorful science encyclopedia is a great introduction to science for young children as they begin to do simple research. Each entry includes a definition, step-by-step instructions for experiments, fact boxes that contain extra information, facts and figures, pictures to illustrate the word(s), and a section that helps the students find out more about each topic. Some pictures show the different parts of an object and label each part for clarification.

An alphabetic table of contents provides a fast way to find information on the main topics in the book. The alphabetic index gives a more detailed listing of topics and helps the student to find additional subjects not found in the table of contents. Main entries are in bold typeface in the index. A glossary is included, which lists words and their definitions that the science students may encounter for the first time. The illustrations and pictures are appropriate for a young child. Most children would find this encyclopedia interesting and entertaining as they learn basic science facts. The experiments can be easily performed with common household products, making the book a fun resource to learn about scientific experiments. The "find-out-more" feature of the encyclopedia allows further research into related topics. The design of the book and the illustrations add to the book's appeal for young children. This book is highly recommended. Every elementary school should own several copies of this creatively designed science encyclopedia.—**Betty J. Morris**

476.   **The New Book of Popular Science 2000.** Danbury, Conn., Grolier, 2000. 6v. illus. maps. index. $269.00/set. ISBN 0-7172-1222-X.

This set is designed to present modern science to a general audience. It is largely successful in combining significant scientific detail with numerous examples of topical relevance and clear prose to make the books interesting and useful. There are 13 sections divided throughout the 6 volumes in this collection. They include astronomy and space science, mathematics, Earth science, energy, environmental science, chemistry, physics, general biology, botany, zoology, "human sciences" (essentially human anatomy and health), and technology. Most articles are well illustrated with color photographs and diagrams and plenty of charts that are useful for junior high science reports. Each volume repeats the thorough index in its final pages, which is convenient because of the overlap of many issues through the sections.

The work of more than 200 authors is represented in this set, so there are some inconsistencies in coverage and accuracy. Many of the authors are science writers rather than scientists. This means that the writing is almost always accessible to readers of about age 12 and above, but some articles are seriously dated and have annoying errors. For example, the article on evolution looks 40 years old with its black-and-white illustrations, obsolete terminology, and paucity of modern genetics. Paleomagnetism is included as a "subdiscipline" of paleontology, apparently because the words start the same way. The discussion of space probes ends in 1997, leaving out some significant advances (and bitter failures). In contrast, there is a fine history and explanation of computers and the Internet, and the human health and mathematics sections are especially good.

It will be difficult to sell this set of volumes to households in this age of easy World Wide Web access and comprehensive CD-ROM and DVD products. Families who can afford the steep purchase price have no doubt already invested in the competing computer technology. Libraries will still find it useful for casual shelf reference. [R: BL, Aug 2000, pp. 2197-2198]—**Mark A. Wilson**

477.   Sachs, Jessica Snyder. **The Encyclopedia of Inventions.** Danbury, Conn., Franklin Watts, 2001. 192p. illus. index. $29.95. ISBN 0-531-11711-1.

This single volume includes alphabetic entries to more than 200 inventions, many illustrated with photographs or drawings to show what they do. Within the entries, words written in small capitals refer the reader to other articles addressing the same topic. Pages follow a two-column format and entries vary in length from a few sentences to multiple pages. Contained in the volume are 12 articles of broad subject interest such as "Agriculture" and "Power Generation." Profiles are provided for six inventors and are placed in the book near their respective subjects. Throughout the book, inventions are placed within a temporal framework. Eleven one-page articles (sidebars) provide an overview of events and inventions in a given year, from 250,000 B.C.E. to 1995. A three-page chronology at the back of the book shows the date of an invention with corresponding events in world history. The index lists inventions, inventors, articles, and illustrations.

The strength of this book is its presentation of many inventions as an evolution of ideas and process in a single, useful volume. Many of the inventions listed can be credited to a single individual. Others (like soap or concrete) have merely evolved though common usage. Still others are wrongly credited to an individual who improved or refined a preexisting device. Their contribution was significant nonetheless, but it is erroneous to credit James Watt with the invention of the steam engine when his important contribution was to dramatically improve the efficiency and power of the existing steam engine developed by Thomas Newcomen. Other inventions involved a continuum of refinements, developments, and combinations of other newly invented engineering components.

There are many publications showing how inventions work, containing detailed biographies of dozens of inventors, or merely listing who invented what and when. The attempt of this work is not to create the world's most comprehensive publication of inventors and inventions. Instead, this work is a useful, user-friendly single volume about inventions that would be useful in both the home and school library, serving virtually all grade levels and adults. [R: BR, Nov/Dec 01, p. 82]—**Craig A. Munsart**

478.   **Scholastic Science Dictionary.** By Melvin Berger. Illustrated by Hannah Bonner. New York, Scholastic, 2000. 224p. illus. index. $19.95. ISBN 0-590-31321-5.

School children today are bombarded with a myriad of technical and scientific terms that extend beyond their vocabularies. Recognizing this, the author states that he has compiled this dictionary in order to provide a quick, easy way for young children to familiarize themselves with the vocabulary, ideas, objects, and people of science. In order to contain the immensity of "science" into one manageable dictionary, the author focused the scope of the dictionary to those areas that he felt would have most relevance to a school child's daily exposure. Entries were culled from basic elementary school science curricula, current scientific journals, magazines, newspapers, and the author's own 40 years of experience writing children's science books.

There are more than 2,400 entries covering the major branches of science. In addition to scientific terminology, there are entries for many diseases, drugs, treatments, and medical specializations. More than 140 biographies of important scientists representing a diversity of backgrounds are also included. All of these entries are intermingled in alphabetic order. True to its intention to be an elementary school level tool, the definitions are written in very basic language, and most are kept to a couple sentences in length. All entries include pronunciations —etymologies are given sparingly. The work is carefully formatted, utilizing cross-references, guide words, and bold text within definitions to indicate words defined elsewhere in the dictionary.

A very valuable feature is the "How to Use This Dictionary" guide. These two pages provide a thorough diagram of all that a dictionary offers, a valuable lesson in itself. The dictionary is generously illustrated with engaging renderings that avoid looking like cartoons, and that incorporate a variety of ethnic and gender representations. An "Index of Picture Labels" covers words that are not entry words. The dictionary concludes with a two-page guide of resources that lists museums, science competitions, and Websites, but it is too superficial to be of much use. Yet, this is a minor flaw in an otherwise useful and appealing work. It is highly recommended for school and public libraries.—**Diane Donham**

479.   **U*X*L's Science Fact Finder.** Phillis Engelbert, ed. Detroit, U*X*L/Gale, 1997. 3v. illus. index. $79.95/set. ISBN 0-7876-1727-X.

The volumes are organized around the natural world, the physical world, and the technological world. Within each volume, information is further separated into chapters and smaller subject listings. For instance, volume 1 (The Natural World) contains a chapter entitled "The Human Body," with subject headings of "Characteristics and Functions," "Parts of the Body," and "Senses and Sleep." Although touted as a middle-school reference containing answers to 750 commonly asked student questions, those about Batesian mimicry, the Great Boston Molasses Disaster, or Ralph Nader and the Corvair may be obscure for many students.

Each book in the 3-volume set contains an 18-page listing of recommendations for further reading, online sources, and CD-ROMs. Although helpful, they might have been more student-friendly if arranged by subject. Each volume also contains a comprehensive index of entries in all 3 volumes; cross-referencing of entries could have helped students find additional information about subjects more easily.

Answers to many specific questions provide a springboard to a more in-depth discussion of a general subject. ("Are there any mammals that fly?" evolves into a detailed discussion of bats.) Certain questions of general interest are highlighted throughout the text. Each entry provides a reference citation for additional information, which is a useful feature. Although well-illustrated with black-and-white photographs and diagrams, some entries on such subjects as the recycling symbol, universal product code, or types of bridges might be more helpful to students with an illustration.

Although organized within the framework of specific questions, this three-volume set functions like an informal encyclopedia of science and, as such, could be useful to middle-school libraries or a home setting. [R: BL, 1 June 98, pp. 1818-1820]—**Craig A. Munsart**

480.   **The World Book Encyclopedia of Science.** Chicago, World Book, 2000. 8v. illus. maps. index. $259.00/set. ISBN 0-7166-3396-5.

This eight-volume scientific reference set, last published by World Book in 1997 (see ARBA 98, entry 1409), includes volumes on astronomy, physics, chemistry, the planet Earth, the plant world, the animal world, and the human body. The final volume, entitled "Men and Women of Science," contains a cumulative index to the entire set as well as information about the most important scientists from the time of Aristotle to the present day. Written in a straightforward and concise manner, this set will be easily accessible to adults and children alike.

The content of the new 2000 edition includes a number of important updates and improvements. Almost 200 pages have been revised to include important updated information in all scientific fields. The volume on astronomy features the most additions, including new discoveries and updated theories in the field, as well as recent data and photographs captured by Hubble and other current space probes.

Each volume, with the exception of *Men and Women of Science*, begins with a description of careers in the scientific field that it covers. Each volume also includes a well-organized table of contents, glossary, and index. Some volumes include useful and informative appendixes, such as a table of astronomical data or a table summarizing the taxonomic classification of the animal kingdom. Colorful and eye-catching illustrations, photographs, diagrams, and charts are used profusely throughout all volumes in this set. Such vibrant visual aids will certainly stimulate the imagination and sense of curiosity in all readers.

The last volume in the set includes biographical information on 111 men and women of science and a cumulative index. Arranged chronologically, this volume features a colored timeline at the bottom of every page, which highlights the most significant scientific accomplishments of that era. Numerous drawings, illustrations, and photographs make the volume appealing and interesting. A full cumulative index to the entire set appears as the second part of this volume. This set will certainly make a useful and interesting addition to many library collections, particularly school and public libraries. [R: BR, Sept/Oct 2000, p. 78; RUSQ, Summer 01, p. 393]—**Bronwyn Stewart**

481.   **World Book's Young Scientist.** Chicago, World Book, 1997. 10v. illus. maps. index. $140.00/set. ISBN 0-7166-2796-5.

This series of reference books is designed to be a student-friendly science source for upper-intermediate and middle school students. Unlike encyclopedias, which have articles in alphabetic order, each of the 10 volumes addresses specific subjects, such as space technology and computers (volume 1) or the human body and communication (volume 7). The format makes the work well suited to student needs, such as researching basics of a particular subject for a report. Each of the volumes contains a detailed table of contents, a glossary, and an index. Keywords within articles are indicated in bold typeface and are included as the index entries. Articles are well illustrated with combinations of drawings and photographs, all in color. Students of multiracial backgrounds are included in many of the illustrations. Easily completed student activities are incorporated within the text, allowing students the opportunity to explore various concepts; when necessary, these include a logo that indicates the need for adult supervision. Cross-references within a volume indicate pages that provide additional information.

The final volume includes a comprehensive index to the entire series and a minimal glossary that includes words already defined in the individual volumes. Some questions are posed within the text, and the answers to these are given in volume 10. The remainder of the final volume is more of an introduction and might be more likely used by students if they were directed to it in volume 1 or if the information was in volume 1. General information about science and scientists, a guide for researching and using the set, methods and units of measurement, and helpful ideas about completing the activities in the book are included here.

Some opportunities were missed to make the books even more student-centered. Possible damage to hearing by listening to loud music is absent in both the discussions of the human ear (volume 7) and the discussion of sound energy (volume 8). In an effort to simplify text, some information provided is misleading. In volume 8, only wind and gasoline are indicated as energy sources for boats, omitting diesel fuel, other petroleum products, and nuclear energy. Minor editorial errors also exist. Materials listed for an activity on water level (volume 4) and the supporting illustrations indicate a can should be used; the description of the activity cites a glass jar.

Such minor errors detract only a little from the overall quality of these books. The price, format, and content make this set an excellent addition to either an elementary school, middle school, or home library.—**Craig A. Munsart**

HANDBOOKS AND YEARBOOKS

482.   **Arty Facts Series.** New York, Crabtree, 2002. 6v. illus. index. (Linking Art to the World Around Us). $17.95/vol. (reinforced library binding); $8.06pa./vol. ISBN 0-7787-1108-0 (v.1); 0-7787-1109-9 (v.2); 0-7787-1110-2 (v.3); 0-7787-1111-0 (v.4); 0-7787-1112-9 (v.5); 0-7787-1113-7 (v.6).

Arty Facts is a six-volume series from Crabtree Publishing that introduces young readers to various topics in science and nature through easy-to-follow text and accompanying arts and crafts projects. The series is designed to appeal to a child's natural curiosity while reinforcing information about science and nature. The six volumes cover animals, insects and bugs, the Earth, plants, space, and structures and materials. Each volume covers 21 topics with complementary art activities. For example, the volume on insects and bugs contains an entry on caterpillars with a project for making a caterpillar out of yarn pompoms and the volume on space contains an entry on how stars are formed with a project to make a stargazer.

The projects range in level of difficulty and most will need adult assistance and supervision. Many of the projects can also be used for science fairs. All of the volumes contain a glossary, an index, and a materials guide. This series is recommended for elementary school libraries and juvenile collections in public libraries. They provide a good introduction to several topics in science and nature and they are a good resource for science-oriented arts and crafts projects.—**Cari Ringelheim**

483.   Burgan, Michael. **Science in Everyday Life in America.** Westport, Conn., Greenwood Press, 2002. 5v. illus. index. $160.00/set. ISBN 0-313-32235-X.

This five-volume set is a chronologically arranged encyclopedia of scientific discoveries and inventions that either occurred in the United States or significantly impacted American life. Volume 1 starts with the period of Native Americans to European settlement (1799); the remaining volumes each cover 50-year spans. This arrangement provides the user with an awareness of other inventions and discoveries made during the same time period. Each volume consists of 124 pages covering 20 to 25 main articles. The standard format for each volume includes an introduction, a section on "Inventions and Technologies," a bibliography, and an index. Each volume is independent from the set in that it covers a separate time period; has its own introduction; is alphabetized independently; has its own pagination; and has its own bibliography, list of Websites, and index. The one-to three-page introductions give an overview of the scientific advances made during that time period. The articles are not in-depth but do give background on the discovery or invention and expand to related and future developments and improvements. Issues, such as the controversy over who invented the sewing machine and the negative side effects like DDT, are mentioned within the articles. Brief biographical information is included on the individuals associated with the discoveries or inventions. The topics range from early agricultural methods, factories, money, and medical hygiene to skyscrapers, plate tectonics, personal computers, and DNA structure. The set is lacking a comprehensive index with cross-referencing to related inventions. For example, nylon in volume 4 mentions the previous discoveries of celluloid and rayon but does not cross-reference to these articles in the other volumes. This set is written at a fifth-grade reading level and is best suited for the middle school level. The information is not in-depth; however, it is another useful resource for libraries looking for information on inventions and discoveries. —**Elaine Ezell**

484.   Clark, John O. E. **Under the Microscope: Science Tools.** Bethel, Conn., Grolier Educational, 2003. 9v. illus. maps. index. $239.00/set. ISBN 0-7172-5628-6.

Unlike must reference sets for children that focus on broad aspects of a topic and provide simplistic information, this set takes a specific area of scientific study and breaks it down into explanations that children can understand. This set focuses solely on the instruments and methods that scientists use to measure and record observations. Each volume provides a specific aspect of scientific research, which then builds on the other research methods in the subsequent volumes. The volumes are titled: "Length and Distance," "Measuring Time," "Force and Pressure," "Electrical Measurement," "Using Visible Light," "Using Invisible Light," "Using Sound," "Scientific Analysis," and "Scientific Classification." Illustrated with color photographs and diagrams, the work explains to students how scientific tools are used and what they have helped scientists discover. The text also features biographies throughout of scientists who developed or discovered the principles that the tools employ. Each volume provides a glossary of terms used throughout that volume and the index to the set. There are cross-references throughout the volumes that refer users to other volumes with related material. Although not a necessary purchase, this set will be useful as a supplementary reference material in middle school libraries. —**Shannon Graff Hysell**

485.   Engelbert, Phillis. **Technology in Action: Science Applied to Everyday Life.** Jane Hoehner, ed. Farmington Hills, Mich., U*X*L/Gale, 1999. 3v. illus. index. $79.95/set. ISBN 0-7876-2809-3.

This is a valuable and informative 3-volume compendium of most of the major inventions that have transformed modern civilization in dramatic ways and have had significant impacts on the lives of countless people all over the world. It does not forget the roots or the ancestors, both ancient and of the recent past, of the technological world. The volumes are introduced with a timeline that starts from 8000 B.C.E. when the first canoes were used and ends with 2002 when the International Space Station is scheduled to be completed, and lists in between more than 500 items. There is also a glossary of technical terms right at the outset to which the reader may refer to as the need arises. The topics are presented as short essays and arranged under eight broad themes. The essays not only succinctly discuss the principles and functioning of the inventions, but they give brief histories that refer to the countless originators, some of whom who may have amassed much wealth through their patents but would be forgotten otherwise. The writing is clear and crisp and simple enough to be within reach of the average educated person. This book belongs in all public libraries and in homes where there is an interest in learning about the complex technological environment that has become part of our lives today. [R: BL, 15 Feb 99, pp. 1093-1094] —**Varadaraja V. Raman**

486.   **Experiment Central.** John T. Tanacredi and John Loret, eds. Farmington Hills, Mich., Gale, 2000. 4v. illus. index. $110.00/set. ISBN 0-7876-2892-1.

This 4-volume set provides 100 science projects, designed for students in middle school and up, that will allow users to gain a better understanding of a variety of science fields. The nine key curriculum fields discussed are astronomy, biology, botany, chemistry, ecology, geology, meteorology, physics, and scientific method. The book is divided into 50 chapters developed around the 9 science fields, and the work is arranged alphabetically by scientific concept. There are two experiments per chapter. The chapters begin with a basic overview of the scientific concept and then go on to describe the concept's history and individuals involved. The experiments provide a hypothesis, timetable, an indication of level of difficulty, materials needed, budget involved, instructions, and what will happen if the variables are changed. There are several sidebars called "Troubleshooter's Guide" throughout the work that will help students prevent problems within the experiments. Each volume begins with a glossary of words used throughout the work and each chapter ends with a bibliography of more information. A budget index, level of difficulty index, timetable index, and a general index conclude each volume of the work. The same indexes are repeated in each volume.

This set will be used mainly in middle and some high school libraries. The experiments are simple and use common products in most cases. [R: BL, 1 Oct 2000, p. 377; VOYA, Oct 2000, p. 300; SLJ, Nov 2000, pp. 96-97]—**Shannon Graff Hysell**

487. **The Handy Science Answer Book.** 2d ed. Compiled by the Science and Technology Department of the Carnegie Library of Pittsburgh. Detroit, Visible Ink Press/Gale, 1997. 580p. illus. maps. index. $16.95pa. ISBN 0-7876-1013-5.

It is often said that this is an age of information explosion. That statement may be true, but there never was an age when a single human being could have absorbed all available human knowledge. Although it is accurate that the twentieth century has witnessed a mushrooming of knowledge and information such as never before in recorded human history, it is no less correct that never before was information more easily available or accessible.

The Handy Science Answer Book is one of hundreds of efforts to make knowledge and science easily available to anyone who will take the trouble of opening the pages of a book. The more than 1,400 questions have been culled from inquiries directed by the general public to the staff of the Science and Technology Department of the Carnegie Library of Pittsburgh. All are interesting questions, but not all of them truly pertain to science, even though they are presented under the broad headings of physics and chemistry, space, Earth, biology, and the like. Some questions are of purely historical interest (e.g., What is phlogiston?), while some have only terminological value (e.g., What is an adiabatic process?). Some are purely informative (e.g., What is the composition of air?) and some have no more than numerical significance (e.g., What are the relative gravitational pulls on planets?).

Despite the fact that many of the questions are not purely scientific, books such as this one can provoke the curious, inspire the young, or liven up conversations at the dinner table. At a time when the United States has become aware of how low the nation's level of scientific literacy is, this work can come in handy indeed.—**Varadaraja V. Raman**

488. **Inventions & Inventors.** Danbury, Conn., Grolier, 2000. 10v. illus. index. $319.00/set. ISBN 0-7172-9384-X.

Aimed at upper elementary, middle school, and junior high students, each 72-page volume in this 10-volume set addresses a different topic related to the history; scientific principles; biographies; science concepts; and social, economic, and political factors influencing the origin, development, and significance of major technologies. The chief focus is on how various technologies have evolved over time. The chapters and volumes may be read independently.

Each volume offers cross-references, a glossary, and set index. Chapters are lavishly illustrated with black-and-white and color photographs and diagrams. In-depth information boxes explain scientific principles, key components, society and inventions, and facts and figures. Volume 1 covers air and space technologies, such as the jet age, space age, and "flying without wings" (i.e., balloons and airships). Volume 2 focuses on buildings, homes, and structures (e.g., bridges and tunnels). Volume 3 looks at communications, such as television, computers, photography, and the movies. Volume 4 centers on farming, food, and biotechnology including hunting, food, drink, and agriculture. Volume 5 considers instruments and measurement, such as time, navigation, cartography, and scientific investigations. Volume 6 moves on to land and water transportation, including animal power, human power, trucks, trains, and ships. Volume 7 concentrates on manufacturing and industry, such as tools, chemicals, metals, and clothing. Volume 8 focuses on medicine and health, including drugs, diagnosis, modern surgery, reproduction, and genetics. Volume 9 reflects on the military and security, such as warfare before and after the Civil War, sea warfare, and locks and keys. Volume 10 explores power and energy, including fuels, heating, lighting, engines, and electricity. This set will prove useful for browsing and writing research papers, especially in science and history classes. [R: BR, May/June 2000, p. 81]—**Esther R. Sinofsky**

489.   Malone, John. **Predicting the Future: From Jules Verne to Bill Gates.** New York, M. Evans, 1997. 194p. index. $19.95. ISBN 0-87131-830-X.

Humans have been trying to predict the future for ages, whether motivated by reasons of religion, science, imagination, entertainment, or commerce. Furthermore, some of the predictions to date have been spectacularly correct (e.g., the atomic bomb) and incorrect (e.g., space travel). These facts, along with our endless fascination with such predictions, are the motivation behind this book. It is a collection of more than 100 predictions, many scientific in nature, arranged chronologically by year from 1858 through 1996. For each prediction there is a date in which it was made, the name of the predictor, and a one-to two-page summary of the reasons for the prediction and its success or failure. Many notable fiction writers are included (e.g., H. G. Wells and Jules Verne), as are diplomats and politicians (e.g., Benjamin Disraeli and Grover Cleveland), corporate moguls (e.g., Henry Ford), and scientists and inventors (e.g., Thomas Edison and Albert Einstein). The predictions themselves relate primarily to the areas of science, medicine, and technology, although there are a few that deal with politics and social life. Indexes to predictions and predictors are included as well as a bibliography of consulted and relevant works.

Given the nature of the topic and the level of the writing, the book's target audience appears to be secondary school students. But there is little scientific or educational purpose to these stories. They are isolated vignettes, with no discussion of underlying processes involved in creative writing, scientific research, or invention. Most certainly the book does not address "where we've been, how we got to where we are, and where we may go yet," as the dust jacket suggests. Students fascinated with science may find this an additional boost to their interests, particularly if they consult some of the works cited in the bibliography. Other than that, the book is what it appears to be at first glance, a quirky and readable overview of scientific facts. School and public libraries may find it of interest.—**Stephen H. Aby**

490.   **Science Activities.** Danbury, Conn., Grolier, 2002. 10v. illus. index. $365.00/set. ISBN 0-7172-5608-1.

Each of the 10 volumes in this set addresses a different subject of science: "Electricity and Magnetism," "Everyday Chemistry," "Force and Motion," "Heat and Energy," "Inside Matter," "Light and Color," "Our Environment," "Sound and Hearing," "Using Materials," and "Weather and Climate." The volumes have a table of contents, a two-page introduction of its subject, and a half-page "Good Science Guide" describing the processes of science, such as documentation, repeatability, and data analysis. These processes are often grouped under the controversial heading, "The Scientific Method." Each of the 10, 64-page volumes contains a 2-page glossary of terms from only that volume and a 1-page (superficial) index for the entire set. The volumes are well illustrated by diagrams and color photographs. Units of measurement are given in both English and SI (metric) units. Historical connections are frequently made. In volume 6, "Light and Color," the 300-year-old debate about the nature of light is chronicled and the historical development of telescopes and cameras is discussed. The first photograph (an eight-hour exposure through a pinhole camera) is also reproduced.

As indicated by the title of the series, the core of each volume is a group of 10 activities reflecting the subject of the volume. The text surrounding each activity reinforces and enhances the subject of the activity. For instance, the activity "Wind Direction" (in volume 10) is preceded by two pages of text describing what causes wind and global wind systems. The activity itself is "Making a Weather Vane." The activity is succeeded by a "Follow Up" section to the weather vane and an "Analysis" section of prevailing global wind patterns. The activities are illustrated by sequential photographs of a student completing each step.

The vast majority of supplies for the activities are readily available materials, but obtaining some unique items (such as polarizing filters, four-foot-long balsa wood, a collection of glass or plastic lenses, foot squares of Plexiglas, swanee whistles, and methylated spirits) could cause frustration. The publisher describes the activities as innovative, but several (such as making a pinhole camera, heating water with food, testing for starch with iodine, or building an electromagnet by coiling copper wire around a nail) are much less innovative than others.

This series could be very useful as a reference in an elementary or middle school media collection. Students looking for a class or science fair project could gain both project ideas and background knowledge. While the content is good, at a time of tightening education budgets, the price might provide a reason for pause to carefully consider its value. [R: SLJ, Nov 02, pp. 105-106]—**Craig A. Munsart**

491.   **Science Matters!** Brian Knapp, ed. Bethel, Conn., Grolier Educational, 2003. 25v. illus. maps. index. $279.00/set. ISBN 0-7172-5834-3.

Science Matters! is an all-inclusive series of books designed to teach elementary-aged children the basics of science. The set does not select one discipline of science to focus on but instead discusses aspects of biology, earth sciences, chemistry, and health sciences to give readers an overview of all aspects of science.

Each volume in the 25-volume set is a mere 24 pages in length. The basic layout of each volume is also similar; each includes a timeline that shows the major historical events of the research in the area discussed, a glossary of words, and a short index. The text is presented in two-page spreads on specific topics or which answer specific questions. The text is very simplistic and the use of color photographs and illustrations aid in the understanding of often difficult-to-understand topics.

Although this set would be a useful addition to elementary school libraries, most libraries will have resources on many of the topics discussed here. The price, a rather high $279, will be the deciding factor for most school libraries. [R: SLJ, April 03, p. 98]—**Shannon Graff Hysell**

23 Biological Sciences

BIOLOGY

Atlases

492. **Facts on File Wildlife Atlas.** rev. ed. By Robin Kerrod and John Stidworthy. New York, Facts on File, 1997. 80p. illus. maps. index. $18.95. ISBN 0-8160-3714-0.

A comprehensive study of animals, plants, habitats, evolution, and threats to nature, this Facts on File compendium undertakes a grand study for only 80 pages. In full color and at a modest price, this work begins instruction on the front cover and continues all the way to the back cover. A small box on page 2 explains how to access data. A locator map of the world indicates the pages on which readers can find maps and data. A 10-part introduction to terms and themes on pages 4 through 23 covers the world's habitats and biota. The authors present seven continent-by-continent studies, including maps and scale charts, sketches of habitats, and appealing color photographs of animals in the wild with each caption marked by an arrow to connect to the appropriate illustration. The volume concludes with a 3-part index of place-names, plants and animals, and wildlife locator maps by continent.

Overall, the book is well written for young readers and features straightforward composition, suitable diction and models, and tasteful commentary. Inclusion of such examples as the capercaillie, guillemot, and surf scoter augments more familiar reptiles, insects, and mammals. Two hindrances weaken the effect and may prove troublesome for disadvantaged or ESL readers—small typeface, particularly in the index, maps, and sidebars, and text overwhelmed by sidebars. The layout makes it difficult to follow the commentary among a dizzying array of captions and illustrations. There is one unacceptable illustration, the drawing of Charles Darwin (p. 19). Despite flaws, the work is a worthy addition to school and public libraries, classrooms, and home reference collections.—**Mary Ellen Snodgrass**

Dictionaries and Encyclopedias

493. **Exploring Life Science.** Tarrytown, N.Y., Marshall Cavendish, 2000. 11v. illus. index. $329.95/set. ISBN 0-7614-7135-9.

Exploring Life Science is a colorful, fact-filled encyclopedia for young readers to learn about the environment around them. More than 300 articles cover animals, plants, bacteria, fungi, single-celled organisms, the earth and the environment, and the study of life. Each article contains color illustrations including photographs and diagrams, a brief definition of the subject, a pronunciation guide, and a "Highlights" box that lists key information. There are also other dialog boxes scattered throughout the volumes. "Look Closer" boxes contain an in-depth discussion about a particular point covered in the main text. Another box entitled "Discoverers" features notable scientists, while "Out of the Past" boxes focus on how living creatures evolve. "Warning!" boxes discuss animals and plants in danger of extinction and "Everyday Science" boxes show how life science is applied in areas such as medicine.

Each volume has a glossary and its own index. The last volume contains a complete glossary and a comprehensive index. It also contains other information such as a brief explanation of weights and measures, a description of taxonomic classification, and individual sections on the various kingdoms (i.e., moneran, fungus, plant, and animal). This volume also features sections on places to go in each state to observe subjects featured in the set and another section listing other resources for further study. These resources include books, Websites, and television channels and programs.

Marshall Cavendish has become well respected for their young reader reference publications. This set is another example of how they provide easy-to-understand information in a fun and eye-catching format. *Exploring Life Science* is highly recommended for school libraries and juvenile reference collections in public libraries. [R: BL, 1 Mar 2000, pp. 1279-81]—**Cari Ringelheim**

494.   **The Facts on File Dictionary of Biology.** 3d ed. Robert Hine, ed. New York, Checkmark Books/Facts on File, 1999. 361p. $17.95pa. ISBN 0-8160-3908-9.

As the revised, updated, and expanded edition of an established reference work, this dictionary retains the basic format of previous editions, with some 3,300 alphabetically arranged headwords. Appendixes giving succinct diagrams of the animal and plant kingdoms and amino acid structures have been added. Definitions, usually encyclopedic in scope (one or two paragraphs) are clearly written for the intelligent layperson and are fairly nontechnical. Many cross-references are provided. Entries have been revised and updated when needed. A few illustrations of chemical or cellular structures have been included.

The Facts on File Dictionary of Biology remains a good basic dictionary for school and public library use, particularly where budgets are limited and works such as the *McGraw-Hill Dictionary of Scientific and Technical Terms* (5th ed.; see ARBA 95, entry 1493) and the *Concise Encyclopedia Biology* (see ARBA 97, entry 1226) are not readily available.—**Jonathan F. Husband**

495.   **Wildlife and Plants of the World.** Tarrytown, N.Y., Marshall Cavendish, 1999. 17v. illus. index. $329.95/set. ISBN 0-7614-7099-9.

Wildlife of the World (see ARBA 95, entry 1561) has been updated and expanded for this set. Biomes (e.g., desert, grassland) and moneran, protoctist, fungi, and plants (e.g., bonsai, ginkgo) have been added. The original set was limited to only animals and most of that information has not changed.

The 17-volume set contains more than 400 alphabetically arranged entries. Animals are still the primary focus of the set and comprise approximately 75 percent of the articles. Volume 1 provides general information on the 5 kingdoms, classifying organisms and a table of contents for all volumes. The information on the kingdoms is repeated at the beginning of volumes 2 through 16. Each volume is individually indexed. Articles follow a prescribed format. Each is two pages in length with two color photographs or detailed drawings, a distribution map, cross-references, and a key facts side box. Key facts include but are not limited to scientific name, range, habitat, appearance, life cycle, uses, status, food, and breeding. Color-coding is used to indicate the type of organism, biome, or habitat. A color bar is used at the top of the page and in the key facts box; a legend of the code is provided at the beginning of each volume. Volume 17 has more in-depth information on classifying organisms, including essays on various classes of organisms, which are structured in the same page format as the other articles. A glossary, bibliography, and 5 indexes (geographic, biome, classification, scientific name, and comprehensive) complete volume 17. These indexes aid the user in locating information from various vantage points, such as the plants and animals found in Australia. Although the set is not comprehensive, it does contain lesser-known as well as common plants and animals. The alphabetic, concise format and visually pleasing layout will appeal to elementary and middle school students for research. [R: BL, 1 Mar 99, p. 1254; SLJ, Feb 99, p. 136]—**Elaine Ezell**

Handbooks and Yearbooks

496.   McPhee, Andy. **A Student's Guide to Biotechnology.** Westport, Conn., Greenwood Press, 2002. 4v. illus. index. $160.00/set. ISBN 0-313-32256-2.

In spite of the current debate, biotechnology has been around for as long as people have been trying to grow a better tomato and even longer. This four-volume set, *A Student's Guide to Biotechnology*, gives a well-rounded view of both the subject area and the issues surrounding the use of biotechnology. Written for the middle school reader, the writing is straightforward and the presentation interesting. Each volume has a clearly defined purpose and, as a package, the set provides a well-rounded introduction. The volume titled "Words and Terms" is precisely what it advertises itself to be. It is an encyclopedic dictionary, focusing on the biotech definition of the term, its pronunciation, use in a sentence, and a short discussion of the connection or history of the term in biotechnology. Some of these entries, like the one on stem cell research, provide more substantial detail. The volume titled "Important People in Biotechnology" provides biographical, career, and research information on notable individuals. Both historic (1600s) and current researchers associated with biotechnology are included. The reader can get insight into the scope and range of biotechnology through the volume that focuses on its history. Ancient practices of fermentation are discussed, along with genetic engineering in plants and biological warfare. Students can read the history of small pox as a dreaded disease, a weapon, and the subsequent development of the vaccine. Critical analysis of the controversies produced by the application of biotechnology is the focus of the volume on debatable issues. This volume is a good place to browse when looking for a paper or essay topic, as it covers a wide range of issues. Sufficient depth is provided for a good understanding of the complexities surrounding biotechnology applications. Every topic includes a brief pro and con essay and a discussion of major concerns, such as allergies and genetically modified foods. Each volume contains its own index, a glossary of terms, and a timeline that covers 600 B.C.E. to the year 2000.—**Lorraine Evans**

497.   Whitfield, Philip, Peter D. Moore, and Barry Cox. **Biomes and Habitats.** New York, Macmillan Reference USA/Gale Group, 2002. 220p. illus. maps. index. (Macmillan Living Universe Series). $95.00. ISBN 0-02-865633-4.

This is the fourth and final volume of the Macmillan Living Universe Series, a series originally conceived, edited, and designed by Marshall Editions of London, England. This volume examines, in five multichapter, narrative sections, the various biomes and habitats (e.g., deserts, tropical forests) in which the various life forms on Earth have developed, the human impact upon them, and their possible futures. Appendixes include basic charts of the plant and animal kingdoms and geological time frames; selective lists of successful, threatened, and endangered plants and animals; and a 53-item list for further reading.

Biomes and Habitats is well illustrated and its text is readable and accurate, but it assumes a readership scientifically more sophisticated than the high school audience for which the book is intended (no glossary is provided). The fact of evolution is assumed, which might be a sticking point for some U.S. school systems where equal time for "Creationists" is mandated. The qualifications of the authors are not spelled out beyond identifying them as "Dr." and "Professor" on the title page. The charts and lists of plants and animals are too selective to be of much reference value. The further reading list, an eclectic mix of field guides, scholarly, and popular titles, contains nothing published after 1988. This titles is, therefore, appropriate mainly for secondary school and public library circulating collections. [R: VOYA, Oct 02, pp. 318-319]—**Jonathan F. Husband**

ANATOMY

498. **DK Encyclopedia of the Human Body.** By Richard Walker. New York, DK Publishing, 2002. 304p. illus. index. $29.99. ISBN 0-7894-8672-5.

This encyclopedia is written for a juvenile audience grades 4-7. While written simply, it does not talk down to its audience. As a result, it is also a good reference tool on the human body for any age group not familiar with how the human body is constructed and how it works.

The book is divided into seven sections, the first five dealing with the body itself and the last two being a history and a glossary. Section 1 covers the cells and microscopic level of the body. The next section covers the moving framework, including skin, bones, joins, and muscles. The third section covers the nervous system, the brain, endocrine glands, and the senses. Section 4 is called "Supply and Maintenance" and covers circulation, the immune system, the GI system, the respiratory system, and nutrition. Section 5 covers reproduction. And section 6 provides a historical timeline of key medical events and an overview of knowledge through the ages.

The book uses color very effectively to show the different parts of the body, such as the different areas of the spine. Key common diseases, such as asthma and diabetes, are highlighted. While the subject of the human body and how we have learned about how our bodies work is not covered in depth, this encyclopedia provides a very good overview for an audience with little knowledge about the human body. This book is a useful edition to a home library or school media center.—**Leslie M. Behm**

BOTANY

499. **The Usborne Internet-Linked Library of Science World of Plants.** By Laura Howell, Kirsteen Rogers, and Corinne Henderson. Tulsa, Okla., EDC Publishing, 2001. 64p. illus. index. $9.95pa. ISBN 0-7945-0086-2.

This slim volume is designed for middle school and high school students studying plant life and the role it plays in ecology. The book itself provides concise information on all aspects of plant life, from plant cell structure to plant classification and from flowering plants to fungi. Each discussion is two pages in length and provides photographs and illustrations to enhance the information. Words in bold throughout the text can be referenced to the glossary at the back of the volume. What makes this book ideal for student research are the Internet sites provided at the bottom of each page. These sites are designed for this age group and provide users with further information on the topics and oftentimes science experiments and reproducible charts and photographs for research projects. The publisher has set up a Website specifically for this series of books, which provides links to the Websites listed here so that students do not have to directly type in links. The publisher also ensures that any updates to URLs are made immediately here so that the book will not become too quickly dated.

This work will be useful for students researching plant life for class projects as well as for teachers looking for useful Websites for their students. At the low price of $9.95 this work will be a valuable addition to middle and high school libraries.—**Shannon Graff Hysell**

NATURAL HISTORY

500.   **DK Nature Encyclopedia.** New York, DK Publishing, 1998. 304p. illus. index. $29.95. ISBN 0-7894-3411-3.

Lovely to look at and a delight to browse, this reference guide to the world of plants and animals covers a wide range of life on Earth. Although it may not provide enough information for many reports, it can serve to provide ideas for topics and provide adjunct information. To get the most out of it students will need to read the double-page spread titled "How to Use This Book."

In traditional DK style, each page is a montage of text and illustrations that include photographs, drawings, cutaways, paintings, maps, and charts. Organized into 2-page spreads, the first third covers topics concerning the beginning of life and how living things work—ranging from a spread on cells through respiration; reproduction; movement; communication; defenses; homes; and ecology, including nutrient cycles and the food chain as well as several different habitats and the relationships between people and nature. The major portion of the book examines living things arranged by classification, starting with spreads on bacteria and viruses, single-celled organisms, and fungi. Plants, with topics ranging from algae and lichens to carnivorous plants, are covered in a dozen 2-page spreads. Animals from invertebrates to mammals are covered in increasing depth. Sometimes the divisions seem somewhat arbitrary; owls merit a 2-page spread of their own, but all other birds of prey are given only one 2-page spread. The classification charts in the reference section at the end of the book are rather confusing in that monerans, protists, fungi, and plants are on one 2-page spread and animals on another. Credentials for the authors and consultants are listed on the back flap of the cover. [R: BL, 1 Dec 98, p. 690]—**Diana Tixier Herald**

501.   **Extinct Species Series.** Bethel, Conn., Grolier Educational, 2002. 10v. illus. maps. index. $269.00/set. ISBN 0-7172-5564-6.

This 10-volume set from Grolier Educational explores how extinction occurred, the species that existed before humans, and prehistoric man. The volumes are written with elementary-age children in mind so definitions are simplistic and illustrations are plentiful. Titles in this set include: "Why Extinction Occurs," "Prehistoric Animal Life," "Fossil Hunting," "Extinct Mammals," "Extinct Birds," "Extinct Underwater Life," "Extinct Reptiles and Amphibians," "Extinct Invertebrates and Plants," "Hominids," and "Atlas of Extinction." The volumes are arranged so that specific issues are addressed on a two-page spread. This layout will make it useful for teachers to use because it breaks down each concept into a format that children will easily understand. The use of illustrations, maps, and informational sidebars add to the set's usefulness. Each volume provides a glossary of terms used within that volume and an index for the entire set. This resource will be useful in elementary school libraries and the children's collections of public libraries.—**Shannon Graff Hysell**

502.   **Oryx Guide to Natural History: The Earth and All Its Inhabitants.** By Patricia Barnes-Svarney and Thomas E. Svarney. Phoenix, Ariz., Oryx Press, 1999. 252p. illus. index. $62.50. ISBN 1-57356-159-2.

Oryx Press began in the mid-1990s to publish a series of guides to educational training programs (e.g., community colleges and distance learning) and guided to ethnic genealogy (e.g., Chinese American and Jewish American). This latest Oryx guide has been directed to the study of natural history and reflects a major new category of coverage. This volume is a cross-disciplinary approach to the natural world that "offers the reader a condensed version of the most important topics—from the beginnings of the universe and our planet, to the plants and animals inhabiting our world," and is meant only to be "a compendium of the highlights" (p. xi).

Barnes-Svarney and Svarney have strong backgrounds in the physical sciences, geosciences, engineering sciences, physics, and the materials sciences and have written numerous popular science books and articles. This title is organized under 30 topics, each providing a concise introduction; a stand-out tabular presentation of the timeline of the topic; a detailed, encyclopedia-type entry describing the "highlights" of the topic, including discoveries, expeditions, publications, and breakthroughs; and an alphabetic list with definitions of key terms.

Also included are 44 tables (e.g., "Human Taxonomy," "Ocean Trenches" and "Closest Stars Compared") , appendixes on "Careers in Natural History" and "Natural History Sites on the World Wide Web," a glossary, selected references, and an index. Inserted in selected topics is a sidebar that is deemed of significance to the authors. For example, two-thirds of a page is devoted to "Talking Time" under the chapter on the geologic time scale. Although the volume is nicely designed, location of information will depend heavily on experience. No obvious logic dictates the rationale for separate chapters. However, the attractive presentation and readability may be suitable for users in public libraries and school media centers, although advanced students will seek other sources focused on their specialized needs.—**Laurel Grotzinger**

503.   **People and the Earth: An Environmental Atlas.** Andrea Dué, ed. Danbury, Conn., Grolier, 1999. 6v. illus. maps. $225.00/set. ISBN 0-7172-9204-5.

No introductory material anywhere in the set explains the editor's intent. But the range of this colorfully illustrated set, designed for middle school and somewhat older students, is the history of the world; the development of animal, plant, and human life; and the effect human activity has had on the environment. The volumes are titled Prehistoric Times, Ancient Times, Medieval Times, Age of Expansion, Age of Revolutions, and The Modern World. Numerous two-page spreads deal with life and human development in the indicated time period, but may or may not have anything to do with the environment. Coverage is often not in proportion to events' relative importance. The final volume, in the printed material surrounding glitzy illustrations, hits very hard at modern humans' degradation of the environment, and may leave young people with hopeless feelings. This set is not especially useful for reference (despite a list of topics, a source list, a glossary, and an index in each volume), but it would serve as an excellent general browser for students who may then refer to other sources. For example, the Prehistoric Times volume has globe-shaped world maps showing the positions of the world's plates throughout its history. Medieval Times has a spread on the design of windmills and another on wars, plagues, and famines that would catch the interest of many young students despite their inexact fit with the theme of the set. [R: BR, Sept/Oct 99, p. 70]—**Edna M. Boardman**

504.   **Pockets: Nature Facts.** By Scarlett O'Hara. New York, DK Publishing, 1997. 128p. illus. maps. index. (DK Pockets). $6.95pa. ISBN 0-7894-1494-5.

DK Publishing has enlarged its original selection of 4-by-5-inch, full-color pocket book titles with a guide to nature facts. The choices of topics, pleasing layout, crisp-clear photographs, and labeled drawings and schematics are well worth the dollar increase in price over the original set, which sold for $5.95. Each book follows a pattern: color-coded sections, illustrated text, running heads, and annotations. The reference section at the end stresses peripheral information on species classification. The writers anticipate the kinds of questions children will ask about different types of mammals. The glossary and index introduce children to the types of data that quality reference works should include.

DK continues to respect the intelligence and to anticipate the needs of children by challenging and enticing the reader to turn another page, read another fact, and add to a growing base knowledge of the subject, for instance, the types of reproduction in fruit. The entries are brief enough to cover central facts and to raise a few points that readers may not have encountered in science class or personal encounters with nature.

Since the publication of the first set of pocketbooks, DK's editors have made no attempts to address weaknesses, particularly the lack of phonetic spellings of such daunting terms as *rhizoid*. Also puzzling is the deletion of color in the reference section. Still muddling the quality of DK reference works in the heyday of inclusion is the absence or de-emphasis of important women scientists and researchers.—**Mary Ellen Snodgrass**

505. Sherry, Clifford J. **Endangered Species: A Reference Handbook.** Santa Barbara, Calif., ABC-CLIO, 1998. 269p. index. (Contemporary World Issues). $39.50. ISBN 0-87436-810-3.

Sherry, a senior scientist and principal investigator with Veridian, has written a convenient introduction for eager youth working on merit badges, undergraduates, scholars, activists, and general readers confronting this complex problem. After explaining how species becomes endangered, major protection measures and controversies surrounding organisms, such as the darter and the northern spotted owl, are presented in a chronology of 21 biographical sketches of conservationists, illustrators, legislators, and researchers. Researcher Jean Goddall discusses U.S. legislation and international treaties and summarizes complex issues such as the Endangered Species Reauthorization Act of 1997. The author provides print resources such as books on endangered species, extinction, biodiversity, conservation, ecology, federal publications, and law school reviews. The constantly evolving Internet is often unable to locate the Internet addresses Sherry's provides for researchers. Those persevering will reach the excellent Amazing Environmental Organization Web Directory at http://www.webdirectory.com, or Institute for Global Communications Discussion Groups Page at http://www.igc.org/igc/issuees/habitats to find a cornucopia of fascinating hyperlinks. Unfortunately, this reviewer was unable to examine the authors CD-ROMs and computer simulation programs or virtual reality examples. Finally, a glossary, geological timeline, and index conclude this brief overview that is recommended for high school, public, and undergraduate collections. [R: SLJ, Nov 98, pp. 134, 136; BL, 1 Dec 98, p. 698] —**Helen M. Barber**

506. **U*X*L Encyclopedia of Biomes.** Weigel, Marlene. Farmington Hills, Mich., U*X*L/Gale, 2000. 3v. illus. maps. index. $95.00/set. ISBN 0-7876-3732-7.

As defined by this encyclopedia, a biome is a "distinct, natural community chiefly distinguished by its plant life and climate" (p. xiii). This 3-volume set treats 12 of the world's major biomes, 4 per volume: coniferous forest, continental margin, deciduous forest, desert, grassland, lake and pond, ocean, rain forest, river and stream, seashore, tundra, and wetland.

Duplicated in all three volumes are a reader's guide to the set, a color map of the world's biomes, a glossary, a bibliography (with publications, organizations, and Websites), and an index to the entire set. Each volume has a 16-page, full-color photographic insert, captioned black-and-white photos, tables, figures, maps, and sidebars of interesting facts. Topics covered under each biome chapter are: development of the biome; its major types; its climate; its geography; its plant, animal, and human life; the food web; a "spotlight" on specific regions of that biome; and sources for more information. The photo reproductions are not top quality, but adequate for the subject and audience, and the line illustrations, though very simple, seem to support the text well.

All in all, *Encyclopedia of Biomes* has lots of good information for middle and high school students. The layout is clean, the writing uncluttered, and both English and metric units are given for numerical data. [R: SLJ, May 2000, p. 94; BR, May/June 2000, p. 81]—**Lori D. Kranz**

ZOOLOGY

General Works

507.   Dalton, Stephen. **Secret Worlds.** Willowdale, Ont., Firefly Books, 1999. 159p. illus. index. $35.00. ISBN 1-55209-384-0.

This beautiful book is a collection of Dalton's nature photographs. Most of the photographs are of animals near his home in Sussex, England, with a few scattered over the rest of the world. Dalton has a particular interest in photographing animal flight, and there are numerous stunning pictures of flying insects, birds, and bats. There are about 140 photographs of 111 subjects, including 21 mammals, 21 birds, 7 reptiles, 12 amphibians, 1 fish, 38 insects, 4 spiders or spiderwebs, 1 mollusk, 11 plants, and 5 landscapes. The photographs are accompanied by short accounts of the creature or of the taking of the photograph. There is an index in which creatures are listed under both common and scientific names.

Although not primarily a reference work, this book may be useful in reference collections as a source of images of the natural world. As such, it is not comprehensive, and many taxonomic groups are not represented. The quality of the images is quite spectacular.—**Frederic F. Burchsted**

508.   **Dorling Kindersley Animal Encyclopedia.** New York, DK Publishing, 2000. 376p. illus. index. $29.95. ISBN 0-7894-6499-3.

Once again, Dorling Kindersley has published a captivating book on animals for children. The volume is divided into two main sections. The "Animal Life" section covers 19 topics on animal classification, anatomy, behavior, habitats, adaptation, migration, and conservation issues. Animal classification is not only explained in understandable terms but is illustrated with pictures of the Manx species of cat belonging to each group from the genus through the animal kingdom. The user can easily visualize how groups narrow from the kingdom down to the species.

The main section is the alphabetic arrangement of information for more than 2,000 animal species. Animal group pages on amphibians, birds, fish, mammals, and reptiles are also included. Each entry covers from one to three pages. Each photograph has a caption that is the main source of information. Annotations and labels provide extra details. Fact boxes provide essential data, such as family name, habitat, distribution, food, number of young or eggs, life span, and size. At-a-glance scale indicators compare the animal to a human hand or an average adult human male. The "Find Out More" boxes refer the user to pages of related topics.

The photography is outstanding. It includes close-up shots of animals, animals in their natural habitat, and detailed artwork. Through time-lapse photographs the reader can view each sequence in the movement of a kangaroo hopping and dolphins and penguins moving through water. The number and quality of the photographs is the strongest feature of the book. Many of the photographs of the animals in their natural habitat are full page.

The "How to Use This Book" section introduces the book with clear explanations of how the entries are arranged. A glossary and index are also provided. The encyclopedia is fully cross-referenced. This volume is reasonably priced and suitable for home, school, or public library use.—**Elaine Ezell**

509.   Nagel, Rob. **Endangered Species.** Farmington Hills, Mich., U*X*L/Gale, 1999. 3v. illus. maps. index. $84.00/set. ISBN 0-7876-1875-6.

This is a nicely laid-out book for middle school students. The general overviews and species accounts are easy to understand. The book covers 200 endangered species from a broad taxonomic range: mammals, birds, reptiles, amphibians, fish, mollusks, insects, arachnids, crustaceans, and plants. There are 3 volumes. The 1st covers mammals; the 2d covers arachnids, birds, crustaceans, insects, and mollusks; and the 3d covers amphibians, fish, plants, and reptiles. Each volume has the same helpful glossary; introductory sections; a further research section with books, journals, and Internet addresses; and an index, making it easy to navigate between books or to review general information.

The introductory sections are titled "Reader's Guide"; "Endangerment and Its Causes: An Overview"; "Endangered Species Fact Boxes and Classification: An Explanation"; "International Union for Conservation of Nature and Natural Resources (IUCN–The World Conservation Union)"; and "Endangered Species Act." Within each book, sections are organized by class and within class. Accounts are alphabetic by common name.

Each species account contains the common and scientific names of the species, classification information, current status in the wild according to the International Union for Conservation of Nature and Natural Resources and the United States Fish and Wildlife Service, the country where the species currently lives, and locator maps with the range. Each account has 3 sections: "Description of Biology," "Habitat and Current Distribution," and "History and Conservation Measures." Most entries have color or black-and-white photographs. This is a good purchase for any school library. [R: BL, 15 April 99, pp. 1544-1546; BR, Sept/Oct 99, p. 70; SLJ, Aug 99, p. 186]—**Constance Rinaldo**

510.   Pringle, Laurence. **Scholastic Encyclopedia of Animals.** New York, Scholastic, 2001. 128p. illus. index. $17.95. ISBN 0-590-52253-1.

This volume is an alphabetic arrangement of information on 140 fairly common animals of all species, such as large bears, sand dollars, millipedes, flies, frogs, and hummingbirds. The entries range in length from two to four paragraphs. The information is presented in an interesting, but factual, manner for children and includes information on habitats, physical characteristics, diets, life cycles, and behaviors of the animals. It does not include details such as scientific names and classifications of these animals. The pronunciation of the animal's name and a color picture of the animal in its natural habitat are given in each entry. Words in bold typeface in the text are defined in the glossary, which then provides a page number reference back to the first use of the word in the body of the book. An index and a pronunciation guide are also included. Although not an extensive, nor an in-depth, reference resource, young children will be drawn to the simple arrangement; colorful pictures; and brief, easy-to-read text. This title will be most useful in collections for elementary school age children. [R: SLJ, Feb 02, p. 90]—**Elaine Ezell**

511.   **World Book's Animals of the World Series.** Chicago, World Book, 2000. 10v. illus. maps. index. $139.00/set. ISBN 0-7166-1200-3.

World Book's Animals of the World Series is a 10-volume set designed to appeal to young students' curiosity about the animal kingdom. Each volume focuses on a group of animals with something in common, such as marsupials, pennipeds, birds of prey, and wild dogs. Information is given about the various groups in an easy-to-follow and eye-catching format. Numerous color photographs and illustrations will capture the attention of young readers. The question-and-answer format promotes critical thinking by presenting similarities and differences among members of the animal groups. Each volume begins with animals that are most familiar to children—such as ants, kangaroos, owls, and wolves—and then advances to less-familiar members of the featured groups (e.g., lantern sharks, capuchins, bandicoots). Each book concludes with a volume-specific glossary and index.

Specifically geared toward children in grades one through four, this set will be ideal for elementary school libraries and children's reference collections in public libraries. Many children will enjoy learning about their favorite animal and other animals related to it. This reference set is highly recommended for teachers, librarians, and parents who want to introduce the fascinating world of the animal kingdom to young learners. —**Cari Ringelheim**

Insects

512.   **Insects and Spiders of the World.** Tarrytown, N.Y., Marshall Cavendish, 2003. 11v. illus. maps. index. $329.95/set. ISBN 0-7614-7334-3.

The first 10 volumes in this set (volume 11 is the index volume) contain approximately 200 alphabetically arranged articles about insects and spiders—from Africanized bee to Zorapteran. While most articles are about individual insects or spiders, there are some "overview" articles that discuss broad categories or topics such as arthropod, biological control, coloration, endangered species, insect life cycle, or swarming. Each article is profusely illustrated with captioned color photographs and artwork. Most also have a map that shows where the insect or spider lives in the world.

Every article in the set can be grouped into one of four thematic categories: insects, spiders, other arthropods, and overview. These categories are color-coded. You can see at a glance which category an article belongs to by looking at the color of the heading that runs along the top of every page. Articles are divided into smaller sections, which are introduced by bold headings. There is a "Key Facts" section with each article that provides basic pieces of information, and many articles have boxed insets that focus on special subjects in greater detail. Every article contains a *see also* section that refers the reader to related articles elsewhere in the set. Each volume includes a contents page, a glossary where important terms are identified and defined, and an index for that volume. Volume 1 provides a "Set Contents" overview and a "Contents by Category." Volume 11 includes the comprehensive index for the entire set as well as several smaller indexes broken down into subjects.

This set is easy to read and has colorful, authoritative, accessible, and timely information (even West Nile Virus is included). All of these features make this a useful reference for students from grades 7-12 who are doing reports, the layperson who needs information on insects or spiders, or the casual browser who simply likes insects and spiders and wants to read more about them.—**Dana McDougald**

513.   **National Audubon Society First Field Guide: Insects.** By Christina Wilsdon. New York, Scholastic, 1998. 159p. illus. index. $10.95pa. ISBN 0-590-05483-X.

This book is one of the selections in the First Field Guide series from the National Audubon Society aimed at children age eight and older. The guide covers 12 insect orders, containing information on 50 of the most widely found insects of North America plus 125 additional species. Introductory pages in the guide define what insects are, how to tell them apart, and explain and give examples of what the 12 insect orders are. In the field guide portion, brief descriptions of the insect or related species include information on the common and scientific name, habitat and range, identification cues, and examples of similar insects or arthropods. The appendix includes a reference section, which offers a glossary; additional books and tapes, organizations, and Website resources; and an index of species listing the common and scientific name. Lots of large and small colorful pictures and illustrations are used effectively throughout the work.

This book offers a lot of information for children interested in the topic. The pictures alone will keep any reader entertained. This resource is recommended for purchase by school, public, and personal libraries. [R: SLJ, Oct 98, p. 160]—**Julia Perez**

Mammals

514.   **Encyclopedia of Mammals.** Tarrytown, N.Y., Marshall Cavendish, 1997. 17v. illus. maps. index. $459.95/set. ISBN 0-7614-0575-5.

The 17-volume *Encyclopedia of Mammals* is a treat to browse, with its high-quality photographs, drawings and graphics, and its lively informational style. It also provides copious information about mammals from aardvarks to zebras. The set will meet the needs of students from elementary through high school levels as well as the casual reader. Each volume is manageable, with fewer than 200 pages. The A to Z organization is easy to navigate. More than 1,700 photographs add both interest and information to the set. Introductory material explains the characteristics of mammals, where mammals fit on the geologic timeline, how mammals are categorized into orders, and where mammals live in the six zoogeographic regions.

Each entry has 3 sections: profile, behavior, and survival. The profile provides a physical description of the animal and describes different varieties of the mammal. The behavior section investigates all aspects of the animal's life from reproduction and raising its young to its habitat and life cycle. The survival section looks at both endangered animals as well as species that are flourishing. Each volume is indexed, and the final volume contains a comprehensive index and six specialized indexes covering classes of mammals, endangered species, geographic locations, scientific organizations, scientific names for species, and wildlife preserves and parks. The format, quality and depth of information and the fact that mammals are a fascinating and frequently requested topic will make this set popular and useful in any school or public library. —**Lynda Welborn**

515.   Grassy, John, and Chuck Keene. **National Audubon Society First Field Guide: Mammals.** New York, Scholastic, 1998. 159p. illus. index. $10.95pa. ISBN 0-590-05489-9.

More than 450 color photographs make this slim volume a gold mine for budding ecologists and children. Published under the auspices of the reputable and long-standing children's press, Scholastic, and in conjunction with the National Audubon Society, this guide makes an ideal starting place for children with an interest in mammals and their place in nature.

This book is part of the National Audubon Society's First Field Guide series, which includes companion guides on wildflowers, birds, insects, weather, and rocks and minerals. It is intended, as its name implies, to be used not only for reference, but as an outdoor tool. At only $5\frac{1}{4}$-by$7\frac{1}{4}$-inches and 159 pages, it will fit into a big pocket or daypack for easy portability. A removable water-resistant spotter's card, about the size of a sheet of microfiche, is tucked into a convenient flap inside the back cover and features postage-stamp size photographs of 50 North American mammals.

Although this book is aimed at children, it makes an ideal learning tool for people of all ages, as it does not talk down to its audience. The guide is divided into 4 sections: "The World of Mammals," which defines the term and describes such characteristics of mammals as social life, eating habits, and mating behavior; "How to Look at Mammals," an analysis of habitat and a "detective work" section that teaches the reader to track and identify various mammals; "Field Guide," the heart of the book, which consists of two-page summaries for each profiled animal that include a large color photograph, habitat map, Latin nomenclature, and "look-alikes," which are subspecies or near relatives; and "The Reference Section," which includes a glossary and a bibliography of related videos, CD-ROMs, books, and Websites. Pages 154-157 index the work.

Because any book endorsed by the National Audubon Society will enjoy almost instant credibility and name recognition with most patrons, *First Field Guide: Mammals* should be considered for purchase by all public libraries, no matter how small. The adult version of nearly the same title by John O. Whitaker Jr., *The Audubon Society Field Guide to North American Mammals*, which expands coverage to more than 700 pages, may be considered a companion volume. In addition, parents may want to purchase a personal copy for their adventurous offspring.
—**Linda D. Tietjen**

516.   **World of Animals: Mammals.** By Pat Morris, Amy-Jane Beer, and Erica Bower. Bethel, Conn., Grolier Educational, 2003. 10v. illus. maps. index. $419.00/set. ISBN 0-7172-5742-8.

This 10-volume set from Grolier is the first of a 5 part series they have planned on the animal kingdom. The next 4 sets will focus on birds (10 volumes), reptiles (5 volumes), amphibians (3 volumes), and fish (10 volumes). This set on mammals is designed with middle to high school age students in mind. It focuses mainly on animals the students will be interested in but includes some from all of the major groups—carnivores, primates, rodents, marsupials, and marine animals.

The set begins with an introduction to the set and information on the scientific naming of animals, a general introduction on how an animal is classified as a mammal (e.g., body temperature, reproduction), and information on extinction of mammals. Each volume of the set is designated a specific type of mammal. For example, volume 1 covers small carnivores, with information on raccoons, weasels, and the mongoose family. Other volumes provide information on large carnivores (e.g., cat family, dog family), sea mammals (e.g., whales), primates, large herbivores (e.g., elephant family, horse family), insectivores and bats, rodents 2 (porcupines, hares and rabbits), rodents (squirrels, mice), ruminant (horned) herbivores, and marsupials. Each volume provides colorful photographs and illustrations, sidebars with specific information on families of mammals and interesting facts, a list for further reading and a list of Websites, and a glossary specific to that volume. Each volume contains the set index.

This set will be most useful in middle school libraries and the children's collections of public libraries. Children will be fascinated by the colorful photographs and the set is written in a language that will be easy for them to understand.—**Shannon Graff Hysell**

Marine Animals

517.   **Sharks.** 2d ed. John D. Stevens, ed. New York, Checkmark Books/Facts on File, 1999. 240p. illus. maps. index. $39.95. ISBN 0-8160-3990-9.

Sharks have become cultural icons, much like dinosaurs. The public is fascinated with strange, primitive, and menacing beasts; and scientists have found many clever ways to use this interest to teach physiology, ecology, and evolution. This book is a superb example of how quality science can be presented attractively and effectively. Most libraries have dozens of shark books on their shelves, and this one should join them. It is profusely and beautifully illustrated with color diagrams and photographs, and the text is readable and highly informative.

This book contains the contributions of almost two dozen shark experts, from paleontologists to marine photographers. It is edited so well that the prose flows smoothly between chapters and sections. The first third of the book is devoted to the origin of sharks, their classification, shark physiology and behavior, and shark ecology. The systematic section is especially important, since general readers rarely see the details of a formal classification. One of the basic premises of the book is that the first step in predicting a shark's behavior is knowing what kind of shark it is. And that mistaken identity provokes most shark scares. The diversity of shark adaptations is very impressive, and the authors use this extraordinary variety to dispel many myths about sharks. Only some, for example, must keep moving in order to breathe, and some nourish their unborn young with placentas analogous to our own. The middle third of the book covers "encounters" with sharks around the world. The reader learns that shark attacks are horrible but relatively rare compared to so many other hazards in the water. The last section of the book is an eclectic set of myths, stories, and observations of sharks. Here is where readers see that people are far more of a threat to sharks than they are to people. Sharks are used for meat, fertilizer, biochemicals, abrasives, cosmetics, paint base, and even corneal transplants. Several species of sharks now face extinction because of overexploitation. The book ends with a short guide to shark resources, including reference books, Websites, and a list of institutions with shark exhibits.—**Mark A. Wilson**

518. **Whales, Dolphins, and Porpoises.** 2d ed. Carwardine, Mark, ed. New York, Checkmark Books/Facts on File, 1999. 240p. illus. maps. index. $39.95. ISBN 0-8160-3991-7.

This encyclopedic work is organized into three parts. The first part, "Whales of the World," has a chapter on the origin and evolution of whales, and a chapter with descriptions of most cetacean species (including dolphins and porpoises as well as whales). Each entry contains a color illustration and covers appearance, size, habitat, distribution, reproduction, and diet. One chapter covers the general biology of baleen (whalebone) whales. The capabilities of these whales for swimming, feeding, and other functions are discussed as well as population, losses due to whaling, and other information. A similar chapter covers the toothed whales, dolphins, and porpoises. Distribution and ecology are treated in depth in another chapter. Each chapter is written by a different contributor—a recognized expert in that area. "Whales up Close" covers anatomy, senses, reproduction, growth, intelligence, and social behavior. The final part, "Whales and People," covers legends about whales, whaling, cetacean training, and other areas such as stranding. A checklist of living species and a guide to further resources are provided.

The coverage of cetaceans is excellent. Written for the general public yet written by experienced researchers in the field, the work contains many original observations and enough material to be useful in academic as well as public libraries. The color illustrations and photographs are excellent. This book is well written and provides the reader with a lot of information about cetacean biology. [R: BL, 1 Dec 98, p. 682]—**John Laurence Kelland**

Reptiles

519. **Reptiles and Amphibians.** Tarrytown, N.Y., Marshall Cavendish, 2003. 11v. illus. maps. index. $459.95/set. ISBN 0-7614-7390-4.

This 11-volume encyclopedia provides in-depth information on every family of reptiles and amphibians. The scope of the set is worldwide with species ranging from the common pond turtle to geckos and caecilians. The introduction to the set provides the reader with unique facts, environmental effects and factors, and indicators of the health of the environment as related to reptiles and amphibians. Volume 1 also contains a table of contents, a reptile family tree, and an amphibian family tree. Each volume contains 144 pages divided into 7 articles of approximately 18-20 pages each. The volumes are arranged by the commonly used English names of families. Each article follows a standard format beginning with a profile that lists shared features and behaviors of individual species, as well as variety within the family, relationships to other groups, and classification information. This is followed by two-page spreads featuring such topics as family tree, habitats, anatomy, habitat, food and feeding, flight, visual signals, reproduction, survival, and endangered environments. Topics are further enhanced by sidebars of key facts, informational boxes, and distribution maps. Each article is well illustrated with photographs and artwork. Volumes are indexed individually and cover the species, places, and behaviors mentioned in that particular volume. The comprehensive index is located in the last volume. Volume 11, however, is much more than an index volume. Besides providing thorough definitions of reptile and amphibian, risk categories, a glossary, a list of contents by category, bibliographic resources, and subject indexes are given. Resources include books, journals, Internet Websites, places to visit, organizations, and a separate bibliographic list for younger readers. Especially useful will be the subject indexes providing scientific names, biological classification, habitats, geographical distribution, and behaviors. This set has an excellent binding that will withstand the repeated use it will receive. Each volume's cover also has attractive illustrations.

The publisher recommends this set for grades 8 and up; however, the illustrations, key facts, and arrangement of the topics will appeal and be useful to students in lower grades as well. Public libraries will also find this a useful addition. This is a well-researched and thorough set and is highly recommended. [R: SLJ, April 03, pp. 100-101]—**Elaine Ezell**

24 Health Sciences

GENERAL WORKS

Dictionaries and Encyclopedias

520.   Levchuck, Caroline M., Michele Drohan, and Jane Kelly Kosek. McNeill, Allison, ed. **Healthy Living.** Farmington Hills, Mich., U*X*L/Gale, 2000. 3v. illus. index. $95.00/set. ISBN 0-7876-3918-4.

This three-volume set is one element of U*X*L's Complete Health Resource series. The companion sets are *Sick! Diseases and Disorders, Injuries and Infections* (see entry 526) and *Body by Design: From the Digestive System to the Skeleton* (see entry 524).

Each volume is divided into five chapters. The 1st volume addresses nutrition, hygiene, sexuality, fitness, and environmental health. The second volume discusses health care systems, health careers, preventive care, over-the-counter drugs, and alternative medicine. And the third volume covers mental health, mental illness, eating disorders, and mental health therapies.

A cumulated table of contents and a glossary are repeated at the beginning of each volume. Each chapter begins with a summary, a table of contents, and a glossary of terms specific to that chapter's main subject. However, chapter tables of content are lacking page numbers, decreasing its usefulness. There are inset boxes throughout the chapters that offer interesting facts and health and safety tips relevant to the discussion. The further readings and pertinent Websites listed at the end of each chapter provide additional information, but are limited. Each volume ends with a repeated cumulated bibliography and index. The very useful index is cross-referenced and denotes illustrations associated with a subject. The text is liberally sprinkled with photographs and illustrations to visually demonstrate the main points of the text. The text itself is organized more like a textbook than an encyclopedia.

There is a definite bias toward alternative forms of health care and medication. The book devotes 12 pages to a history and discussion of homeopathy and naturopathy. More conventional physician training, both traditional medical doctor and osteopathic physician, comprises a mere four pages of text. In addition, at the beginning of the section on herbal medicine there is a one-sentence blanket statement that the "benefits of herbal medicine and their effectiveness and safety have not been proven," but the subsequent discussions of individual herbal medicines is written as if the information were verified by proven research.

Overall, *Healthy Living* presents a balanced discussion of most topics and is suitable for high school libraries, especially if a thorough discussion of alternative health care and medicine is desired. [R: BL, 1 Oct 2000, p. 372; SLJ, Nov 2000, pp. 92-94]—**Bronwyn Stewart**

Handbooks and Yearbooks

521.   **Adolescent Health Sourcebook.** Chad T. Kimball, ed. Detroit, Omnigraphics, 2002. 658p. illus. index. (Health Reference Series). $78.00. ISBN 0-7808-0248-9.

A new addition to Omnigraphics' Health Reference Series, this volume presents holistic coverage of adolescent health issues ranging from physical, sexual, and emotional health to social concerns such as safety, education, violence, and disasters. Like others in the popular series of about 100 subject volumes, it is written in clear, nontechnical language aimed at general readers; here, especially, parents and caregivers of teenagers. The material is up-to-date, comprehensive, and mainstream, making it a convenient first-step resource for consumers wanting basic understanding (not in-depth knowledge) of health care issues facing today's youth.

The book is arranged in 7 parts and contains 93 articles and excerpts originally published by government agencies, professional medical associations, and other nonprofit groups. Chad T. Kimball, editor of several other books in the series, selected the documents. The parts are: "Emotional and Mental Health Issues Affecting Adolescents," which discusses normal development as well as specific disorders; "Physical Health Issues Affecting Adolescents," covering common diseases and health risks like loud music, tattooing, and tanning; "Adolescent Sexual Health"; "Drug Abuse in Adolescents"; "Social Issues and Other Parenting Concerns Affecting Adolescent Health and Safety," including driving, gangs, and the Internet; "Adolescent Education," from school failure to preparing for college; and "Additional Help and Information." The latter comprises a glossary as well as contact information for agencies, organizations, Websites, and publications. A list of references and sources for additional reading, all pertaining to topics discussed in the book, is also provided. The *Adolescent Health Sourcebook* is recommended for public libraries, community colleges, and other agencies serving health care consumers. [R: SLJ, Nov 02, p. 102]—**Madeleine Nash**

522.   Field, Shelly. **Career Opportunities in Health Care.** New York, Facts on File, 1997. 228p. index. $29.95; $18.95pa. ISBN 0-8160-3381-1; 0-8160-3382-Xpa.

People seeking information about careers in health care may not realize that so many options are available. In addition to the usual physician, nurse, pharmacist, and dentist, one can consider health services administrator, music therapist, director of hospital funding, biomedical equipment technician, and medical records technician. This book discusses more than 70 different jobs involving direct patient care as well as administration.

The book is divided into 18 sections covering broad areas: medicine, vision care, geriatrics, long-term care, and so on. Within each section, job profiles are listed alphabetically. Each entry is approximately two pages in length. The entries begin with two charts that are next to each other. The "career profile" summarizes the main points of the article, and the "career ladder" shows the path from entry level to the highest position in the field. The narrative portion of the article contains a detailed job description in lay language; salary range; employment prospects; advancement prospects; education and training required; experience, skills, and personality traits useful for the job; best geographic location for employment; unions and professional associations; and job-hunting tips. Appendixes contain a list of education programs for selected occupations by state, a list of trade associations and unions, a brief bibliography, and a glossary of abbreviations and terms.

Career Opportunities in Health Care is a helpful starting point for those exploring options in the job market. It is reasonably priced, so both reference and circulating copies can be purchased. Libraries that own any of the larger career encyclopedias, such as those from J. G. Ferguson or VGM (see entry 93), will not need a reference copy.—**Barbara M. Bibel**

523. **Health Matters!** William M. Kane, ed. Danbury, Conn., Grolier, 2002. 8v. illus. index. $409.00/set. ISBN 0-7172-5575-1.

This eight-volume combination health encyclopedia and health class text is aimed at the middle school and high school audience. The language and reading level is fairly simple and will be easily comprehended by most students. Each of the eight volumes covers a different health-related topic, which include "Addiction"; "Sexuality and Pregnancy"; "Physical Activity"; "Weight and Eating Disorders"; "HIV, AIDS and STDs"; and "Diseases and Disabling Conditions."

Each volume starts off with a several page introduction titled "Healthy Living: Teen Choices and Actions," followed by a test for the readers to assess their own behavior relating to health issues. An alphabetic encyclopedia follows, with one to several paragraph entries on terminology, health statistics, and historical facts relating to the topic of the volume. There are numerous tables, illustrations, and cross-references to other volumes. Several appendixes to each volume relate the issue to teen life through stories of teens whose lives have been affected by health problems and question-and-answer essays on difficult topics and choices. The editor also includes glossaries and lists of hot lines, Internet sites, and organizations relating to each volume's topic.

Although this set is well written, well researched, and attractively presented, the mixture of factual information with persuasive essays and arguments may turn older, more sophisticated teens off. Teenagers have a very sensitive radar to adult preaching and may tend to doubt the factual nature of information if it is presented with a clearly stated point of view. This is always a danger when presenting such information to the young. The best teachers can present the facts and let them speak for themselves. The right balance between education and advocacy is difficult to achieve. In *Health Matters!* this balance may be satisfactory for the middle school audience but not necessarily for older readers.—**Carol L. Noll**

524. Nagel, Rob. Des Chenes, Betz, ed. **Body by Design: From the Digestive System to the Skeleton.** Farmington Hills, Mich., U*X*L/Gale, 2000. 2v. illus. index. $79.00/set. ISBN 0-7876-3897-8.

Body by Design is described by the publishers as a "medical reference product designed to inform and educate readers about the human body," and is considered "comprehensive, but not necessarily definitive" (p. xiii). Distributed in the United States by Gale Group, it is one of several new titles produced out of London by U*X*L, an imprint of Gale. Another introductory note points out that it "is only one component of the three-part U*X*L Complete Health Resource" (p. x). The two other titles are *Sick! Diseases and Disorders, Injuries, and Infections* (see entry 526) and *Healthy Living* (see entry 520).

The medical information found in *Body by Design* can be found in many other books, but not in two volumes that are attractively designed and written for students or nonprofessional users. A check of the last five years of ARBA disclosed three well-reviewed atlases of anatomy (see ARBA 99, entry 1415; ARBA 98, entry 1499; and ARBA 96, entry 1694) that would certainly provide better details on anatomical design. However, this title is designed to supplement organ and structure design with three additional narratives (physiology or "Workings," diseases or "Ailments," and keeping healthy or prevention). Each of the 12 chapters (one for each of the 11 organ systems and a final chapter on special senses) describes an organ system. Volume 1 covers cardiovascular, digestive, endocrine, integumentary, lymphatic, and muscular systems, and volume 2 is devoted to the nervous, reproductive, reparatory, skeletal, and urinary systems plus the chapter on special senses.

Each chapter also includes illustrations; photographs; "words to know"; assorted historical, biographical, and informational inserts (e.g., in the respiratory system section there are sidebars on the composition of air, breathing underwater, how fish and plants breathe); and a section of book references and Websites. The first and second volumes include the same overview section and a general, medical "Words to Know" section. Both volumes conclude with the same general (and short) bibliography and Website listing as well as the same index.

The volumes are replete with reference data, although the specificity and value of the information will depend completely on the nature of the question. The "ailments" in the section on the lymphatic system include AIDS/HIV (with data through 1997), allergies, autoimmune diseases, lymphadenitis, lymphoma, and tonsillitis. Each category is described in less than a few hundred words regardless of complexity. For example, autoimmune disease includes only Graves' disease, multiple sclerosis, and lupus. The index provides a brief entry on the common cold but not the common cold sore, and carpal tunnel syndrome is referenced but not bursitis or tendonitis. All in all, school and public libraries may purchase this set, but may not find the work of major reference value except as the two volumes provide a basic overview of the human body. [R: BL, 1 Oct 2000, p. 372; BR, Nov/Dec 2000, pp. 77-78; SLJ, Nov 2000, p. 94]—**Laurel Grotzinger**

MEDICINE

General Works

525.   **Human Diseases and Conditions.** Neil Izenberg, ed. Farmington Hills, Mich., Charles Scribner's Sons/Gale Group, 2000. 3v. illus. index. $245.00/set. ISBN 0-684-80543-X.

The human body and its ailments are fascinating subjects for most people. Much of the literature in this area is very technical and difficult for lay readers to understand. *Human Diseases and Conditions*, although edited by a group of physicians, is written for readers from middle school to adult level. The 3-volume set has information on 294 diseases and conditions.

An introduction provides a very basic overview of physiology, the health care system, and medical research. The alphabetical entries that follow are two to six pages long. They include a definition of the disease or condition; an explanation of what it does to the body; and information on the causes, symptoms, diagnosis, and treatment. Many articles also have short scenarios describing people who have had or currently live with the illness. Pictures of Stephen Hawking, Magic Johnson, and Jackie Joyner-Kersey accompany the entries on amyotrophic lateral sclerosis, AIDS, and asthma, respectively. References to Michael J. Fox, Muhammad Ali, and Janet Reno in the article on Parkinson's disease demonstrate that serious illness does not have to interfere with life. Articles on chronic diseases such as diabetes and cystic fibrosis explain what it is like to live with the illness. All articles have brief bibliographies and referral lists.

There are ample cross-references and a comprehensive index to lead users to the information they need. A bibliography of recent medical textbooks appears in the third volume. Several color photographs, charts, and illustrations augment the text. Sidebars in the margins provide definitions and keywords for searching other reference sources and the Internet. Fact boxes offer historical information and literary quotations about diseases. These features enliven the text.

While *Human Diseases and Conditions* is an attractive encyclopedia that is easy to use, it provides very basic information that is readily available in many other sources. It is also rather expensive. The *Harvard Medical School Family Health Guide* (Simon & Schuster, 1999) and the *American College of Physicians Complete Home Medical Guide* (DK, 1999) provide more information in a single volume at a fraction of the price. The *Gale Encyclopedia of Medicine* (see ARBA 2000, entry 1413) is a multivolume set that covers this material in greater depth. *Human Diseases and Conditions* and its supplemental volume (see ARBA 2002, entry 1472) are optional purchases for school and public libraries. [R: SLJ, May 2000, pp. 86-88; BL, July 2000, p. 2062;

VOYA, Aug 2000, p. 212; RUSQ, Sept 2000, pp. 413-414; BR, Sept/Oct 2000, p. 66]—**Barbara M. Bibel**

526.   **Sick! Diseases and Disorders, Injuries and Infections.** David Newton, Donna Olendorf, Christine Jeryan, and Karen Boyden, eds. Farmington Hills, Mich., U*X*L/Gale, 2000. 4v. illus. index. $115.00/set. ISBN 0-7876-3922-2.

Sick! Diseases and Disorders, Injuries and Infections is a four-volume set covering a wide range of health-related topics of interest for students from middle school to adult readers. More than 100 entries are arranged alphabetically, with information on causes, symptoms, diagnoses, tests, and treatments and prognoses. Entries include sidebars on related people and topics and words to know, as well as a list of sources for further research. The Websites and organizations after each topic will be useful to the layperson. Research and activities for classes would be helpful for the classroom teacher. It is comparable to D. W. Griffith's *Complete Guide to Symptoms, Illness, and Surgery* (Perigee, 2000) but it is more current. It would be an excellent resource for a juvenile health section for public libraries although cost could be a deterrent at a $115 for the set. [R: SLJ, Aug 2000, p. 134; BL, 1 Oct 2000, p. 372; VOYA, Oct 2000, p. 300; BR, Nov/Dec 2000, p. 71]—**Theresa Maggio**

25 High Technology

INTERNET

527.   Gralla, Preston. **Online Kids: A Young Surfer's Guide to Cyberspace.** rev. ed. New York, John Wiley, 1999. 276p. index. $14.95pa. ISBN 0-471-25312-X.

This is the revision of the widely reviewed and widely acquired 1996 edition of the same title. Like the original edition, the more recent effort introduces the young reader (and the reader's parents) to the world of cyberspace. This is not a book filled with unintelligible jargon and technical information. It provides the basics within the context of entertaining, yet informative articles and annotations.

The chapters cover a wide range of topics within the parameters of cyberspace. For instance, one chapter speaks of what cyberspace is and defines its various capabilities, including chat, downloading software, and video or sound clips. But it is not a "how to" guide. Another chapter discusses equipment requirements, but does not delve into detail beyond the basics. It appears the book is written with the assumption that an adult will guide any child embarking into Internet explorations. With adult supervision in mind, an entire chapter is devoted to online etiquette and a child's safety on the Internet. There is discussion on the site blocking software available, plus how various services provide for protecting children.

The best parts of the book are the chapters devoted to Websites. They are chosen with children in mind, but many are equally as interesting to adults. Each entry includes the address of the site, plus brief annotations describing what is on the site. For quick reference, there is the "Usefulness Index" and the "Coolness Index." According to the introduction, the author's children rated each site. Some of these entries did have drawbacks. Not all of them were readily available unless one is a subscriber to a service such as America on Line (AOL) or CompuServe. Also, a random check showed that some sites are no longer active. But then, that is a problem of the medium. No book of this type will be completely accurate.

Like the well-received, earlier edition, this book achieves exactly what it is designed to do. It provides the young reader a well-organized, well-presented, and informational introduction to the cyberworld.—**Phillip P. Powell**

528.   Polly, Jean Armour. **The Internet Kids & Family Yellow Pages.** 3d ed. New York, McGraw-Hill, 1999. 744p. illus. index. $34.99pa. ISBN 0-07-211849-0.

The 3d edition of these yellow pages is a directory of 4,000 educational or entertainment-oriented Internet sites for children in grades K-8. The arrangement is alphabetic by broad subject headings. An index is provided for those who wish to locate a Web page by specific topic. An electronic CD-ROM version of the yellow pages is furnished with keyword search capability to enable direct access to listed Websites. Special features include a short list of the 100 best sites on the net, a list of Websites for countries of the world, and a "net files" section to illustrate how the Internet can be browsed to locate trivia. The audience for these yellow pages seems to be apprehensive parents with little direct knowledge of the Internet who fear that their children will access inappropriate material while surfing the Web. The compiler, Jean Armour Polly, a former librarian and self-titled "net mom," assures parents that she has personally reviewed each Website to verify that it is "family friendly" and free of any offensive content. Perhaps her distaste for controversy explains why a good number of sites in these yellow pages come under the heading of fun and games. For example, there is a generous list of links to commercial Disney Online sites, which may not be surprising considering that Polly works for the corporation as a private consultant. So great is her maternal concern that she includes advertisements for "net-mom"-endorsed products that parents may purchase to guarantee the safety of their kids on the Internet.

All good intentions aside, currency is the unavoidable problem with all Web directories in print format. To compensate for this weakness, the author directs us to her personal homepage for free updates to track changes to Web addresses listed in the yellow pages. While consulting her Web page for updates, however, one cannot fail to notice the "net-mom" bookstore link where one can purchase the new 4th edition of her yellow pages through Amazon.com just in time for the millennium. For reference staff who use the Internet on a daily basis in public and school libraries to satisfy the information needs of young patrons, these yellow pages will contain no surprises because the educational sites identified by Polly are already well known by librarians and are usually accessible as bookmarks or links on most library homepages.—**David G. Nowak**

PHYSICAL SCIENCES

Chemistry

Dictionaries and Encyclopedias

529.   **Chemical Elements: From Carbon to Krypton.** By David E. Newton. Lawrence W. Baker, ed. Farmington Hills, Mich., U*X*L/Gale, 1999. 3v. illus. $84.00/set. ISBN 0-7876-2844-1.

This young person's guide (high school level) to the chemical elements is thoughtfully designed and attractively produced. Entries are alphabetic by element name, and there is a table of contents by atomic number as well as one by periodic group. Each volume includes the same timeline of the discovery of the elements, glossary, index to the set, and bibliography that includes Websites as well.

Entries are self-contained, and technical terms are explained within them, although that can lead to slight misstatements. For example, the entry for argon defines fractional distillation as the process of letting liquid air slowly warm up, but fractional distillation is a more general term that includes separations of components in any temperature range. Each profusely illustrated entry contains the atomic symbol; atomic number; mass; periodic family; the pronunciation of the element's name; the history of knowledge; and use of the element, physical, and chemical properties, occurrence in nature, isotopes, extraction processes, compounds of the elements, health effects, and more. There are plentiful cross-references and informative sidebars. Each entry also gives a simple shell diagram for the electronic energy levels, but because the meaning of this diagram is not explained it may be simply puzzling. An explanation would also help the reader to understand what is meant by the periodic group into which the element is placed and to understand the periodic table itself, which is printed on the front and back endpapers of each volume. This is my only real quibble about the set, which would be a useful resource in any public or school library.

Finally, the subtitle is a bit of a mystery. Possibly carbon is there as the element forming the largest number of chemical compounds, but krypton is not quite the element forming the fewest compounds, since helium, neon, and argon form no stable compounds at all. [R: BL, 1 May 99, pp. 1606-1608; BR, Sept/Oct 99, p. 79; SLJ, Aug 99, pp. 186-87]—**Robert Michaelson**

530.   **The Facts on File Dictionary of Chemistry.** 3d ed. John Daintith, ed. New York, Checkmark Books/Facts on File, 1999. 266p. $17.95pa. ISBN 0-8160-3910-0.

Produced for use in schools, this dictionary, first published in 1980 (see ARBA 82, entry 1436), has been revised and extended. It now contains more than 3,000 entries covering the terminology of modern chemistry; some 250 new terms have been added. Line drawings interspersed throughout the text serve to illustrate chemical structures. Useful tables in the appendix include the chemical elements, the Greek alphabet, fundamental constants, elementary particles, and the periodic table.

Arranged in alphabetic order, each page includes guide words. Entry words are in bold typeface, and each entry is separated by a generous space. Type size is sufficient enough to allow for easy reading. Features include cross-references and *see* references. Definitions are presented in a clear and concise style that is accessible to the beginning chemistry student or layperson, and are frequently enhanced with formulas, the above-mentioned line drawings, and practical applications. This is an affordable and useful reference that will be welcome in both secondary school and public libraries.—**Dana McDougald**

531.   Knapp, Brian. **ChemLab Series.** Danbury, Conn., Grolier, 1998. 12v. illus. index. $299.00/set. ISBN 0-7172-9146-4.

Colorful, informative, detailed, and practical are all good descriptors for Grolier's 12-volume set, *ChemLab*. Aimed at middle school and high school students, each of the 12 volumes covers one aspect of chemistry: gases, liquids, and solids; elements, compounds, and mixtures; the Periodic Table; metals; acid, bases, and salts; heat and combustion; oxidation and reduction; air and water chemistry; carbon chemistry; reaction rates and electrochemistry; preparations; and standard laboratory tests.

The 12 clearly written volumes feature vivid, close-up photography detailing step-by-step chemical reactions and changes, including the exact color a substance will become when another substance is added or the form an element may be expected to take when heat is applied. In volume 8, "Air and Water," it is possible to read text material about the reaction of water with metals and to see, at the same time, a series of illustrations revealing just what happens when sodium metal is added to water or when calcium metal is introduced. The standard apparatus shown in the experiments is helpfully defined in the master glossary for those who might need to find alternative equipment. Each volume's index serves the entire set, which is an asset when browsing through all 12 volumes. Biographies of "Great Experimental Scientists" are scattered throughout in inset boxes at appropriate places, serving to make the work and processes being explained with such care more relevant. In many cases, chemical formulas are provided along with their atomic diagrams so the reader can visualize the written formulas for elements and their combinations. *ChemLab* is a hands-on, useful reference tool and an excellent purchase for middle school, high school, and public libraries.—**Marcia Blevins**

Handbooks and Yearbooks

532.   **Elements.** By Brian Knapp. Danbury, Conn., Grolier, 1996. 15v. illus. index. $269.00/set. ISBN 0-7172-7572-8.

This highly illustrated set of 15 volumes provides students with in-depth information about individual and groups of elements. The main format of each book is two-page spreads focusing on one aspect of the element in question. In each volume, the reader can find out the definition, natural occurrences, extractions/preparation, uses, and compounds. Colorful photographs and diagrams make it easy for the reader to get an idea about the relevant information. A key feature of this set is the gradation in typeface size, which corresponds to the level of information. At first glance, one may think that the book is for younger readers because of the introductory large type-face, but the smaller print material can challenge the thinking of most high-schoolers. Each volume includes key facts about the specific elements and then provides the same following pages for each: periodical tables (and explanation), how to read equations, and a glossary. In that way, each volume may be used independently without having to refer to a separate key legend volume. The individual volumes also have indexes.

Each volume is slim, with a glossy cover. The binding is stitched. The books do not lie flat easily. Finding good, accessible information on elements can be a daunting task. This set will be most welcome in junior and senior high school library collections. [R: SLJ, May 97, p. 160]—**Lesley S. J. Farmer**

533.   Newton, David E. **Chemistry.** Phoenix, Ariz., Oryx Press, 1999. 294p. illus. index. (Oryx Frontiers of Science Series). $44.95. ISBN 1-57356-160-6.

This volume provides readers with an overview of developments in the fields of chemistry and chemical engineering from 1996 to 1998. The author summarizes about two dozen research studies, covering areas such as buckyballs, reactions at the atomic scale, protein folding, nerve cell growth, and chlorofluorocarbon (CFC) disposal. The topics were selected because they appeared in science journals designed for the general reader, such as *Scientific American* and *Science News*. Readers will need to have a basic knowledge of chemistry to understand the text. Since the author intended to provide only a brief synopsis of each topic, the references at the end of each summary are valuable sources of additional information.

The rest of the book has more general information about the field of chemistry. Newton includes a chapter on controversial issues such as pollution, ozone depletion, greenhouse effect, chemical weapons, and food quality protection and a chapter with excerpts from congressional hearings on these controversies. The biography section provides brief biographies of important chemical researchers in recent years, so the names may not be familiar. There are also sections on the future of chemistry, career information, organizations and associations, a glossary, and an index. Newton also includes a section of statistics on various aspects of the chemical industry and a good list of print and electronic information sources.

Even though Newton gives the reader a good overview of recent advances in chemistry, the organization of the book is a bit confusing. The biographical section separates the chapter on social issues from the congressional hearings on the same topics. Although it may not be the intention, Newton's book is a source of career information. He gives a nice overview of the fields of chemistry and chemical engineering, the kinds of people who work in these fields, and several good information sources. Students considering a science career will find his book very useful. Recommended for high school and undergraduate students.—**Teresa U. Berry**

534.   Stwertka, Albert. **A Guide to the Elements.** 2d ed. New York, Oxford University Press, 2002. 246p. illus. index. $18.95pa. ISBN 0-19-515027-9.

It is easy to be enthusiastic about Stwertka's new edition of *A Guide to the Elements*, although it has not increased much in bulk since the 1st edition (1996). The author starts with an explanation of the periodic table and its development, followed by brief, one-to seven-page descriptions of each element that concentrate on their history, chemical and physical properties, and usage. Stwertka writes in a clear and nontechnical style that is appropriate for middle and high school students as well as adults with a minimal (or long-forgotten) background in chemistry. The black-and-white and color illustrations that accompanying many of the elements' descriptions add to the pleasing visual effect. A glossary, chronology of the discovery of the elements, and slightly updated list for further reading complete the volume. The 1st edition was received with enthusiasm and won several book awards. This edition has only eight additional pages, most of which are dedicated to the 1999 discovery of Element 114, Ununquadium, an epilogue detailing the 2001 retraction of the announced discovery of Element 118, and a brief list of Websites. For the updating, a paperback copy is still a worthwhile purchase for libraries with the 1st edition. While more information for young readers is available in multivolume sets such as Knapp's *Elements* (see entry 532) and Newton's *Chemical Elements: From Carbon to Krypton* (see entry 529), Stwertka provides most of the essential information within a consistent, attractive, and easy-to-read format —and at a fraction of the price. [R: SLJ, Nov 02, p. 106]—**Barbara MacAlpine**

Earth and Planetary Sciences

General Works

535.   **Earth Science: Discovering the Secrets of the Earth.** Danbury, Conn., Grolier, 2000. 8v. illus. maps. index. $269.00/set. ISBN 0-7172-7499-3.

Titles of the eight volumes in this set are "Minerals," "Rocks," "Fossils," "Earthquakes and Volcanoes," "Plate Tectonics," "Landforms," "Geologic Time," and "Earth's Resources." Each volume contains 72 pages, 13 of which are the identical end matter consisting of a glossary and set index (an unnecessary repetition occupying almost one-fifth of each volume). The 59 pages of the subject text in each volume are profusely illustrated with color photographs, maps, and explanatory diagrams. The British influence in the publication is obvious in the exclusive use of the metric system (with which this reviewer agrees) and the use of the term "nodding donkey" for an oil field pumping unit. Information boxes scattered through the text provide additional background information.

Minerals are discussed within their environment of formation, the process of identification, and their grouping by elemental composition. Rocks are introduced by a general discussion of the rock cycle and systems of formation and then discussed within their convention trinity—igneous, sedimentary, and metamorphic. The explanation of fossils includes illustrations of the living animal along with the fossil, an important relationship that is often not presented. The fossils are first presented as a catalog of common fossils, then related to the geographic record.

Indexing, a useful tool for students, is not as good as it might be. Excellent illustrations (and supporting text) of Point Reyes, California, are used to describe earthquake-generated landforms, but they are not found in the index. The White Cliffs of Dover are indexed in volume 7 (p. 52) but no reference is made of a photograph and information in volume 1 (pp. 34, 35). In some cases, photographs are repeated for multiple entries. Volume 3 deals with fossils, yet despite the importance of trace fossils, they are addressed with only two short sentences (and no illustrations) prefaced by the quixotic statement: "Fossils may not be of actual living things at all."

Perhaps the greatest flaw in this series of volumes is their title. The "Earth Sciences" are generally considered to include geology, astronomy, meteorology, and oceanography. This series touches on only geology and so misses the critical aspect of the interrelationship of all of the Earth sciences. The Earth influences all four disciplines and, in turn, is shaped by them. To narrowly focus on geology only sends a false message to students.

This is a resource that some secondary students may find useful as a limited initial reference, mostly for the excellent color photographs. It would have been much more useful to students had the publisher broadened the focus and opted for references or other sources at the end of each volume rather than repeating the glossary and set index. Other references, such as the four-volume encyclopedia *Earth Sciences for Students* by Macmillan (see entry 536), would probably serve student needs more completely.—**Craig A. Munsart**

536. **Earth Sciences for Students.** E. Julius Dasch, ed. New York, Macmillan Library Reference/Simon & Schuster Macmillan, 1999. 4v. illus. maps. index. $325.00/set. ISBN 0-02-865308-4.

This 4-volume set is a student version of the *Macmillan Encyclopedia of Earth Sciences* (see ARBA 97, entry 1391) and is designed for students in grades 5 and up. Articles are arranged alphabetically by topic and are cross-referenced. Vocabulary words are identified by bold typeface and defined immediately to the left of the text as well as in the glossary at the end of volume 4. Each volume contains front matter including the geologic timescale, measurements and abbreviations, and contributors. Volume 1 has a table of contents for the entire set. End matter for volume 4 consists of a glossary, bibliography (annotated to indicate references especially useful to students), photograph credits, and a cumulative index; other volumes contain only a volume index.

Biographical entries of scientists are arranged alphabetically within the text. There are 12 articles concerning careers in the earth sciences—an odd choice, however, was to place them under "C" for careers, rather than within their respective subjects. For instance, "Careers in Oceanography" is found under "C" for careers, rather than "O" for oceanography. Certain articles address social issues generally not associated with encyclopedias, such as "Minorities in the Earth Sciences," "Women in the Earth Sciences," or "Public Health and Earth Sciences."

Although there are many color photographs, some might have been better selected to illustrate the topic and some articles might have been more useful to students if illustrated with diagrams. For instance, to illustrate "Prospecting for Oil and Gas" one might have expected an illustration about a seismic crew or a drilling rig, not the construction of a natural gas pipeline. "Global Positioning System" is illustrated with a photograph of a shipboard scientist and a handheld GPS receiver, whereas a diagram of the signal path from satellites to receiver might help students better understand the determination of position. Similarly, diagrams might have made articles such as "Recovery of Oil and Gas" more student friendly. All cross-sections illustrating tectonics would have been even more useful with a vertical scale of kilometers; some have such a scale, some do not. Some supporting data are outdated. To demonstrate that abrasives are big business the "Abrasives" articles cites 1989 income.

This set could serve as an introductory earth sciences encyclopedia for middle grades and up. Although planned for students in fifth grade and above, some students in those lower grade levels may have difficulty with text comprehension.—**Craig A. Munsart**

537. Gates, Alexander E. **A to Z of Earth Scientists.** New York, Facts on File, 2003. 336p. illus. index. (Notable Scientists). $45.00. ISBN 0-8160-4580-1.

Alexander Gates has compiled a 336-page addition to the Notable Scientists series that profiles the lives of 192 people who devoted their careers to the disciplines and subdisciplines of the earth sciences during the 18th century to the present. Information about the scientists was gleaned through agencies, associations, older biographies, and written contributions from the scientists themselves. Gates also used the Google search engine on the Web to complement his research. This edition by no means includes profiles of all known deserving earth scientists. Those researchers would fill a subsequent volume, should there ever be one. As the author states, "earth science is largely responsible for sparking the scientific revolution of the 20th century."

Entries appear in alphabetic order under the name by which the scientist is most commonly known. Also included are birth date, date of death (if applicable), nationality, and earth science specialty. An essay containing more personal data, including an emphasis on the scientist's main work and contributions to the field follows this information.

Some of the scientists profiled are Albert Bally (petroleum geologist), Gerald Friedman (sedimentologist), Stephen Jay Gould (paleontologist), Teresa Jordan (stratigrapher), Barbara Romanowicz (geophysicist), and Mary Lou Zoback (seismologist). There are many other points of entry to help the reader find a specific researcher: the "Country of Birth" appendix, the country of major scientific activity index, the field index (to search by the specific earth science discipline), and the chronology index that lists entrants by dates of birth and death.

This volume was written for high school students, college undergraduates, and the general researcher. It is recommended for high school, undergraduate, and public library reference collections. —**Laura J. Bender**

538.   Llewellyn, Claire. **Our Planet Earth.** New York, Scholastic, 1997. 77p. index. (Scholastic First Encyclopedia Series). $14.95. ISBN 0-590-87929-4.

One of five books in the Scholastic First Encyclopedia Series, the volume begins with directions for use and tells what the book is about. The book divides the planet Earth into four general topics—an introduction, the Earth's surface, the changing planet, and life on Earth. Each of these divisions is further divided into colorful, two-page spreads, which discuss more specific topics. Each section is cross-referenced to topics in this and the other volumes in the series. Despite an introductory explanation of how to use the cross-references, the format of these references is rather confusing and, therefore, may be difficult for children to use. The book gives brief tidbits of information about a wide variety of subjects relating to Earth. It has value as an overview, but any child who wants or needs detailed information will not find much substance in this volume. The book includes both a glossary and index. [R: SLJ, Feb 98, p. 138]—**Janet Hilbun**

539.   Newson, Lesley. **The Atlas of the World's Worst Natural Disasters.** New York, DK Publishing, 1998. 159p. illus. maps. index. $50.00. ISBN 0-670-88330-1.

This book will convince anyone that the world can be a cold, cruel, dangerous place and that civilization does indeed exist only by "geological consent." The diagrams, photographs, and maps are spectacularly horrific and will be a jolt to anyone perusing this book in a quiet library far from nature's wrath.

The atlas is divided into two parts. The 1st and longest is a fully illustrated catalog of the woes visited upon us by our dynamic planet. This section begins with geological hazards, primarily earthquakes and volcanoes, with good but brief introductions to the physical mechanisms behind tremors and eruptions. Particular events are highlighted in text boxes, giving details of timing, magnitudes, damage, and casualties. Weather-related disasters (e.g., hurricanes, cyclones, blizzards) follow, with the same type of coverage and detail. The least cohesive portion is titled "Patterns of Chaos," which is a catch-all term for floods, droughts, fires, avalanches, landslides, mass extinctions, and patterns of global climate change. These are interesting but could have been placed in the geological and weather chapters. This would have provided more integration between natural systems and human catastrophes. The last descriptions cover biological hazards, from pests to disease epidemics. Here is the new frontier for cataclysms in the new century, particularly with the globalization of obscure and deadly tropical viruses.

The 2d part of the book is a gazetteer with maps covering most of the world. Each map is annotated with locations of natural disasters, numbered so that they can be looked up on an extensive descriptive list. The book ends with a short glossary of prominent terms and an index.—**Mark A. Wilson**

Astronomy and Space Sciences

540.   **Innovations in Astronomy.** Santa Barbara, Calif., ABC-CLIO, 1999. 328p. illus. index. (Innovations in Science). $50.00. ISBN 1-57607-114-6.

This book is part of a series whose apparent mission is to present a patchwork of information within various scientific disciplines. It contains an assortment of chapters on the field of astronomy. There are seven chapters. The overview chapter is the only chapter that is signed; however, there are no credentials provided for this author. Through 23 pages, the overview takes the reader on a tour of the various subdisciplines of astronomy; a bit of history, including related space programs milestones; and astronomical instrumentation. It is presented at the level of the interested layperson.

The remainder of the chapters are essentially lists. Chapter 2, "Chronology," lists by year the important advances of astronomy, beginning in 1903. Chapter 3 is a list of brief biographical sketches. Chapter 4 is a directory of organizations, observatories, and facilities. Conspicuously missing is anything about McDonald Observatory of the University of Texas, which has one of the largest land-based optical telescopes. The information here seems out-of-date. For information of this kind, the current volume of the *Astronomical Almanac* published by the U.S. Naval Observatory is reliable. Chapter 5 is a list of astronomy resources, some of which are certainly classics but may no longer be in print. Chapter 6 is a list of Websites. Unfortunately, the Internet changes so rapidly that many sites listed were out-of-date before it was printed. Chapter 7 is a dictionary.

A book like this that tries to bring together many different aspects of a discipline might be appropriate for school libraries where students just need a summary of a discipline for class projects or career information. [R: LJ, 1 Oct 99, pp. 80-82]—**Margaret F. Dominy**

541.   **Outer Space.** Danbury, Conn., Grolier, 1998. 12v. illus. $269.00/set. ISBN 0-7172-9179-0.

Each of the 12 volumes in this set contains a table of contents, a short introduction and conclusion, a glossary unique to that volume, and an index to the entire set. The first 4 volumes examine objects in our solar system; the next 3 examine the sky, stars, and astronomy in general; and the final 5 examine human presence in space, such as space flight and satellites. The text is printed in two columns, and items printed in bold typeface are explained in the glossary. Explanations of more complex concepts, such as parallax or the Apollo Lunar Launch System are given in large sidebars. Cross-references are also shown in bold print. The text is well-supplemented with color and black-and-white photographs, drawings, and data table

It is difficult to avoid the impression that the volumes are written independently with only minimal effort to coordinate among them. More stringent editing could have reduced many of the problems with improved indexing and cross-referencing and elimination of repetition. The same photograph of Mercury appears in two places (vol. 1, 16 and vol. 3, 14), as does discussion of the Barrington Meteor Crater in Arizona (vol. 1, 43 and vol. 3, 19; not indexed or cross-referenced). The captioned photograph of Venus de Milo is missing from the sidebar (vol. 3, 9)

Some index entries could be more helpful. On the pages given for "Jupiter, comet collision with" one might expect to find photographs of the dramatic Shoemaker-Levy impact sequence. Those photographs are merely cited in the Jupiter index citation but are shown in other discussions in different volumes and indexed under "Comet, Shoemaker-Levy." Although a short discussion of "Life in the Universe" can be found in volume 6, *Stars and Galaxies*, it cannot be found in the index.

An introduction explaining details of the format would have been helpful. For instance, the student must discover that bold text is explained in the glossary, or that all colored boxes with a solid line above are figure-captions and boxes surrounded by a dashed line (called sidebars) provide detailed explanations of items in the text. Although indicated by the publisher to be useful for students "in elementary school and up," the set may be of limited use to students in primary grades. The work is indicated to be "an engaging alternative to standard science textbooks," but most teachers might consider it a research supplement to other materials. Although there is much useful information here, students may have a difficult time finding and forming a comprehensive picture of what is available about a given subject. [R: SLJ, Nov 98, p. 158; BL, 1 Dec 98, pp. 700, 702]—**Craig A. Munsart**

Climatology and Meteorology

542.   Allaby, Michael. **Blizzards.** New York, Facts on File, 1997. 138p. illus. maps. index. (Dangerous Weather). $24.95/vol.; $149.00/set. ISBN 0-8160-3518-0.

543.   Allaby, Michael. **A Chronology of Weather.** New York, Facts on File, 1998. 154p. illus. index. (Dangerous Weather). $24.95/vol.; $149.00/set. ISBN 0-8160-3521-0.

544.   Allaby, Michael. **Droughts.** New York, Facts on File, 1998. 135p. illus. maps. index. (Dangerous Weather). $24.95/vol.; $149.00/set. ISBN 0-8160-3519-9.

545.   Allaby, Michael. **Floods.** New York, Facts on File, 1998. 135p. illus. maps. index. (Dangerous Weather). $24.95/vol.; $149.00/set. ISBN 0-8160-3520-2.

546.   Allaby, Michael. **Hurricanes.** New York, Facts on File, 1997. 136p. illus. maps. index. (Dangerous Weather). $24.95/vol.; $149.00/set. ISBN 0-8160-3516-4.

547.   Allaby, Michael. **Tornadoes.** New York, Facts on File, 1997. 131p. illus. maps. index. (Dangerous Weather). $24.95/vol.; $149.00/set. ISBN 0-8160-3517-2.

Extreme and dangerous weather phenomena are presented in this 6-volume series. *A Chronology of Weather* differs from the other volumes by taking an inclusive view of all dangerous weather conditions. It discusses how climates have changed and outlines how our understanding of the weather and our ability to forecast it have developed over time. Most of this volume is devoted to two chronological accounts: major weather disasters arranged by the year they occurred and important developments and improvements in the understanding and forecasting of weather. Chronological coverage goes back 10,000 years and includes the discovery of basic instruments, such as the barometer, hygrometer, and thermometer. The chronology of destruction not only lists major disasters beginning with the year 3200 B.C.E. but also explains how we know these events occurred so many years ago. The number of included events dramatically increases in the late 1800s because of better record keeping. There are 30 easy-to-perform experiments with step-by-step directions using basic household equipment that provide students and teachers with activities that will expand their understanding of weather principles. A glossary of 129 definitions of weather-related terms, a bibliography that also includes Websites, and an index complete the volume.

The remaining 5 volumes are each devoted to a single destructive natural weather occurrence. The science behind these dangerous weather occurrences is explained, including how, why, and where they are likely to take place. Information is included on how our lives are affected and what can be done to prepare for, cope with, and survive these destructive forces. Biographical information is provided on significant inventors, discoverers, and climatologists. Sidebars provide additional background information on meteorological concepts including adiabatic warming and cooling, cloud formation, and latent heat and dew point. When these sidebars pertain to more than one type of weather development, they are repeated in subsequent volumes. Extensive use of black-and-white maps, diagrams, charts, and photographs provide further information and enhance the text. Although each of these 5 volumes includes a section on the history of these occurrences, the topic is not sensationalized. Rather, the reader will gain a lot of information regarding the topic in an understandable presentation. Each volume is indexed individually, and there is no comprehensive index to the set. An excellent resource for grades 6 through 12.—**Elaine Ezell**

548.   Davis, Lee. **Natural Disasters.** rev. ed. New York, Facts on File, 2002. 420p. illus. index. (Facts on File Science Library). $60.00. ISBN 0-8160-4338-8.

Davis divides this revised edition of his work (see ARBA 94, entry 468, for a review of the 1st edition published in 1992) into broad natural disasters: avalanches and landslides, earthquakes, famines and droughts, floods, plagues and epidemics, cyclones, hurricanes, ice storms and snow-storms, tornadoes, storms, typhoons, volcanic eruptions, and natural explosions. At this point, the book sort of becomes a natural disaster on its own. First of all, the target audience of the book is hard to determine. Assumedly, it is aimed at a general interest science reader (perhaps middle and high school). However, the author fails to state this objective, and a number of the articles appear to have local northeastern U.S. emphasis. The articles written on individual disasters have no ref-erences or citations given, so scholars are unable to verify any of the facts presented. The bibliog-raphy also gives little clue as to the target audience. Some works cited are general, while others are advanced scientific works. Also, most of the black-and-white photographs come from agencies like the United Nations, the American Red Cross, and other general sources.

The arrangement of the articles is confusing to say the least. For example, under "Floods" the articles are arranged alphabetically by the country involved, then the state or geographic place, and then by date. This arrangement means that readers get all the hurricanes on the East Coast ar-ranged by date, then those in Florida arranged by date, then those in Hawaii, and so on. The reader going through the East Coast hurricanes finds many missing, only to discover them later under specific states. This odd arrangement is confusing and perhaps not the best for general readers. At times the arrangement is also very frustrating. Furthermore, some articles have an odd twist, either to their content or their length. For example, the "Hurricane Floyd" article devotes a large portion to chronicling the damage in the northeastern United States while giving scant mention to the dam-age in North Carolina, which was just as (if not more) extensive. The "Blizzard of '88" receives a short half page, while an earthquake in Peru in 1970 gets a three-page spread.

The volume is hard bound with an attractive cover. There is an index, a bibliography, and a list of Websites. The choice of some Websites is somewhat unusual, such as "Action Against Hun-ger Announces Release of Two Fieldworkers" and "Micronesia." A number of the Web links have expired or are not complete. Some of the stories make interesting reading, but the lack of useful or-ganization and any reference to sources used in the text limit the book's usefulness. These con-cerns cast the scholarship and editing of this work in doubt. Libraries that have patrons with general interest in disasters will find the volume light reading. Anyone but the most casual browser will lament the lacunae noted.—**Ralph Lee Scott**

549.   Lyons, Walter A. **The Handy Weather Answer Book.** Detroit, Visible Ink Press/Gale, 1997. 397p. illus. maps. index. $16.95pa. ISBN 0-7876-1034-8.

This entertaining work is a collection of 1,055 questions and answers on weather written in nontechnical language for the general reader. The author's stated purpose is to interest the reader in weather and related phenomena. His definition of *related phenomena* includes aspects of ocean-ography, seismology, volcanology, and environmental science. This broad definition is evident in the titles of the 17 sections: "Weather Fundamentals"; "Instruments and Observations"; "The Up-per Atmosphere and Beyond"; "Clouds"; "Hurricanes and Tropical Storms"; "Thunderstorms, Floods, and Hail"; "Lightning and Thunder"; "Optical Phenomena"; "Tornadoes"; "Cold and Winter Storms"; "Heat and Humidity"; "Earthquakes and Volcanoes"; "Air Pollution and the En-vironment"; "Weather and the Human Body"; "Weather Forecasting"; "Climate Change"; and "Careers in Meteorology." The questions and answers are not arranged in an organized manner within each section, but an excellent index makes it easy to locate the desired pieces of information.

The questions included in the book vary in relevance to the topic. Although the appropriateness of most of the questions is obvious, there are some that are truly trivial and irrelevant (e.g., "Is there malaria in Switzerland?") . Unfortunately, the answers do not include bibliographic source information, even though there is an 8-page bibliography. The author also notes in the introduction that he was unable to verify some of the weather phenomena that are included in this book. These shortcomings limit the book's usefulness as a reference tool, but school and public libraries should consider purchasing a copy for their circulating collection.—**John R. Burch Jr.**

550.   **National Audubon Society First Field Guide: Weather.** By Jonathan D. W. Kahl. New York, Scholastic, 1998. 159p. illus. index. $10.95pa. ISBN 0-590-05488-0.

Field guides are written for any number of subjects found in nature; many include the night sky and the weather along with companion volumes on mammals, birds, insects, rocks, flowers, and the like. This small book is thorough, with any number of color photographs illustrating the types and classifications of clouds, fog, rainbows, and even examples of air pollution and smog. This is not the book for those with an interest in climate and its changes. Such issues as global warming, acid rain, and ozone depletion are treated only briefly here, if at all. The book is intended for the observer of weather phenomena, who wishes to understand what can be seen in the sky. For this purpose, the book is as good as any and is up-to-date. This is an excellent addition to any school or public library.—**Arthur R. Upgren**

551.   **Weather Watch: A Month-by-Month Guide to World Weather.** Danbury, Conn., Grolier, 2000. 12v. illus. maps. index. $285.00/set. ISBN 0-7172-9458-7.

In this 12-volume set, 1 for each month of the year, the weather patterns, derived from a 30-year study of 72 major cities around the world, are described. Each volume details characteristics, for the specified month, of the six main temperate zones: North America, South America, Europe, Africa and the Middle East, Oceania and Hawaii, and Asia. These zones are then further divided into major cities for more in-depth coverage of individual regions. Longitude, latitude and position above sea level are listed as well as an airflow map for the month and temperature and rainfall charts for the year. Basic information is given to introduce students to the many differences and similarities in climate regions around the world. The informal, yet informative, style of writing provides the reader with a sense of how world climates determine the lifestyles of the regional culture groups. Colorful, eye-catching photos, illustrations, graphs, charts, and satellite images supply the browser with a sense of familiarity with the area studied.

Each volume contains a glossary of terms and a cumulative index. The sewn binding adds to the practical durability of the set for classroom use. The "Quick Reference," or preface, at the beginning of each volume defines symbols consistently used throughout the set. Though some of the concepts seem lofty due to the immensity and complication of the subject, this is a delightfully informative set that would complement classroom studies in such varied subjects as science, geography, and the environment. Recommended for large public, middle school and junior high collections or as a special classroom supplement. [R: BR, May/June 2000, pp. 81-82]—**Kimberley D. Harris**

Ecology

552. **Small Worlds Series.** By Jen Green and James W. R. Martin. New York, Crabtree, 2002. 4v. illus. index. $15.96/vol. (reinforced library binding); $8.06pa./vol. ISBN 0-7787-0138-7 (v.1); 0-7787-0141-7 (v.2); 0-7787-0140-9 (v.3); 0-7787-0139-5 (v.4).

These four volumes from Crabtree's Small Worlds series are designed to introduce elementary-aged learners to ecology and ecosystems. Like other volumes in the series, these new additions focus on various habitats: coral reefs, backyards, houses, and the Tundra. Following general introductory material, the books discuss the different life forms found in that particular habitat and how they interact and coexist with each other. For example, the *Coral Reef* volume covers the coral polyps, filter feeders, coral eaters, and an array of colorful fish that make up this underwater habitat. The *Backyard* volume includes information on insects, birds, and wild and domestic mammals and amphibians (squirrels, snakes, and cats) commonly found in backyards. Somewhat like the *Backyard* volume, the *House* volume covers the insects, birds, and rodents that are often hiding in and around homes. Lastly, the *Tundra* volume provides material on the plants, insects, birds, and mammals that inhabit this Northern region year-round and seasonally.

All of the volumes contain educational fact boxes and numerous color photographs and illustrations. A table of contents, a glossary, and a brief index are also included. The glossary is especially useful since many young readers will be unfamiliar with some of the scientific terms used throughout the text. This series is recommended for elementary school libraries and juvenile reference collections in larger public libraries.—**Cari Ringelheim**

Geology

553. **National Audubon Society First Field Guide: Rocks and Minerals.** By Edward Ricciuti and Margaret W. Carruthers. New York, Scholastic, 1998. 159p. illus. index. $10.95pa. ISBN 0-590-05484-8.

The beginning rock hound needs a field guide that gives some basic information on geology, provides information on types of rocks and minerals, and helps the beginner identify common rocks and minerals. A useful field guide has good quality photographs against which one can compare finds. It should also fit into a pocket or backpack.

This field guide meets the above criteria. For each of the 50 highlighted rocks or minerals there are photographs that covers three-fourths of the double-page spread; its name, whether it is a mineral or an igneous, metamorphic, or sedimentary rock; its properties, such as color, texture, and hardness; and information on where it is found and how it is used. Brief descriptions and small photographs of an additional 120 rocks and minerals occupy the remaining one-quarter of the double-page spreads. These appear near rocks and minerals of a similar type.

This first book, intended for the budding scientist, is clearly and simply written without talking down to the reader. With a few exceptions—galena, rhodochrosite, muscovite mica, and talc—the photographs are an accurate depiction of the mineral and can be easily used to identify a specimen. The photographs of rocks are of particularly good quality.

Additional information includes a glossary of commonly used terms, a short list of common minerals and their chemical formulas, a bibliography of items for further study by the young rockhound, some noted organizations in the field, and a selection of Websites. It lives up to its title as a "First Field Guide" and is the appropriate first guide to give today's hobbyists and tomorrow's geologists. Because this guide is limited in scope, it will not satisfy the serious rockhound for very long, so be prepared to provide a higher-level field guide.—**Ann E. Prentice**

Oceanography

554.   **Library of the Oceans.** Ellen Dupont and others, eds. Danbury, Conn., Grolier, 1998. 12v. illus. maps. index. $289.00/set. ISBN 0-7172-9180-4.

From the deepest trenches to the shallowest lagoons, a world as complex and compelling as life on land exists. Now students have the perfect resource to discover the secrets of the deep with Grolier's outstanding new set, *Library of the Oceans*. This 12-volume, comprehensive set presents oceanography, sea exploration, and the development of the oceans as factors in human life. Organized topically to cover all of the science and other aspects of the seas, each volume in *Library of the Oceans* includes a clear introduction that sets the stage for the information to follow. The set offers many pictures and photographs to intrigue elementary students, while at the same time providing solid information to be useful for high school students.

Each volume is 64 pages in length. There are easy-to-use features, such as lists of subjects covered and box features in each volume. A thorough glossary, bibliography, and full set index are found in every volume. There are informational boxes with related topics in every chapter and many illustrations and photographs to bring the topics to life. This 12-volume set is divided into 12 specific topics: the shape of the ocean (sea floor, ocean floor, rocks, fossil evidence); the restless waters (water in motion, tides, undersea avalanches, global warming); the prehistoric ocean (geological time, fossil record, evolution of life, Darwin's travels); life in the ocean (food webs, gray whales, migration); hunters and monsters (sharks, man-eaters, monsters of the deep, poisonous animals); the cold seas (kingdom of ice, the Arctic, the Antarctic, penguins); the warm seas (coral reefs, the giant clam, ospreys in danger, green turtles); the shallow seas (rocky shores, tide pools, algae on the shore, estuaries); exploring the oceans (the Bermuda triangle, great voyages, measuring longitude, sounding the depths); the world's oceans (the Atlantic, the Pacific, El Niño, the polar oceans); coasts and islands (islands, coasts, deltas, destruction by erosion); and the future of the ocean (the sea's riches, fish and fuel, sea salt, the dirty sea).

Library of the Oceans is one of those rare sets of books that students hope for and teachers dream of owning. From the deepest trenches to the shallowest lagoons, the world below provides substantial material to be incorporated into both science and geography lessons. Grolier Educational produces books aimed at helping students of all ages expand their understanding of the world and its history. This latest offering will have students on the edge of their seats in anticipation of what will come next. [R: BR, Nov/Dec 98, p. 76]—**Barbara B. Goldstein**

Paleontology

555.   **The Kingfisher Illustrated Dinosaur Encyclopedia.** By David Burnie. New York, Larousse Kingfisher Chambers, 2001. 224p. index. $24.95. ISBN 0-7534-5287-1.

The Kingfisher Illustrated Dinosaur Encyclopedia is yet another volume intended to appeal to dinosaur-crazed people older than eight years. It is not unique among works of this type in that the title does not reflect the complete contents, since only 98 of its 224 pages discuss dinosaurs. Geologic time periods and other prehistoric life are also covered in depth. The work is filled with high-quality color illustrations including many full-page color drawings of dinosaurs in their prehistoric environments.

The book begins with a section on life in the distant past, including a brief overview of the Earth's origins, the first living creatures, evolution, and fossil formation. Next is a detailed discussion of the geologic time periods and the animals that inhabited them. The following sections include plant-eating giants, ornithopods, the meat eaters, giant meat eaters, armored dinosaurs, reptiles in the air, reptiles in the sea, and the age of mammals. There is a nice discussion of the debate about cold-blooded versus warm-blooded dinosaurs, indicating that the content is relatively current. One significant flaw, however, is that this book does not make clear exactly which prehistoric creatures are and are not dinosaurs except in a brief, easily overlooked sentence in the introduction to one of the sections. Flying and swimming reptiles are not dinosaurs by definition, but it is possible to miss this distinction entirely based upon the book's organization and table of contents. There is a brief, two-page glossary, an index, and a list of nine recommended Websites at the end of the book. While this encyclopedia is a nice volume overall, there are better choices among the many works published in this area. The distinction between dinosaurs and other prehistoric reptiles needs to be made explicit. [R: SLJ, May 02, p. 92]—**Arlene McFarlin Weismantel**

556.   Matthews, Rupert. **Dinosaurs A-Z.** Woodbridge, Conn., Blackbirch Press/Gale Group, 2002. 64p. illus. index. $24.94. ISBN 1-56711-548-9.

This thin 64-page reference source on dinosaurs is designed with elementary school children in mind. The book begins with simple definitions of what dinosaurs are, when they lived, and how they lived. It also defines what dinosaurs are not by describing the other life forms living at the same time, including birds, lizards, and turtles. Short explanations about the evolution of dinosaurs as well as the evolution of the Earth and shifting continents are then explained.

The bulk of the book consists of an A to Z listing of dinosaurs written in terms that young children will understand. For each dinosaur there is information on where they lived, how they got their name, and their eating and living patterns. Each dinosaur has a color illustration as well as a diagram showing how its size relates to that of an adult human. Throughout the book are small sidebars under the heading "Dig It!" that provide additional information on topics such as dinosaur anatomy, the Earth's evolution, and how dinosaur bones and fossils were found. The book concludes with a glossary and a two-page index.—**Shannon Graff Hysell**

557.   Parker, Steve. **The Age of Dinosaurs.** Danbury, Conn., Grolier, 1999. 12v. illus. index. $249.00/set. ISBN 0-7172-9406-4.

The Age of Dinosaurs is a comprehensive reference series for young readers. Students can follow the development of dinosaurs from early origins to their eventual extinction. Basic information about a multitude of subjects is provided such as dinosaurs' similarities to birds and other animals, eating habits, skeletal structure, and the study of fossils.

In each of the 12 volumes there is a chart illustrating the dinosaur family tree and its place in the evolution of the world. Each volume also contains a complete index for the set. Individual volumes provide data on armored dinosaurs, hadrosaurs, ornithopods, sauropods, carnosaurs, and much more. Vivid illustrations and clear explanations encourage young readers to explore the field of paleontology. Highly detailed drawings, paintings, photographs, diagrams, maps, graphs, charts, sidebars, and boxes augment the abundance of learning opportunities.

The author writes with a coherent viewpoint and uses language that is clear and accessible to young students. He successfully demystifies the similarities and differences of various dinosaurs, climate and vegetation, and how and why evolution occurred as it did. This reference set is recommended for young reader reference collections in schools and public libraries. [R: BL, Aug 2000, p. 2194]—**Cari Ringelheim**

558.   Svarney, Thomas E., and Patricia Barnes-Svarney. **The Handy Dinosaur Answer Book.** Farmington Hills, Mich., Visible Ink Press/Gale, 2000. 493p. illus. index. $19.95pa. ISBN 1-57859-072-8.

This is one of a series of books written by two scientists, one a science writer, aimed at informing young adults about an important area of science. Simply and accurately written, it presents material in an easy-to-use and readable format.

The question-and-answer format works well as it breaks topics into discrete items, each represented by a question and its answer. While the focus is on dinosaurs, the context is the broader fields of geology and natural history. The authors begin with a description of the solar system and the formation of the Earth and other planets, then move to a discussion of geologic time and the formation of fossils. At that point they focus on the evolution of dinosaurs and their presence during the Triassic, Jurassic, and Cretaceous periods. They discuss the geologic events during these periods, and the rise and fall and extinction of dinosaurs. Additional chapters focus on what can be learned from dinosaur bones, dinosaur anatomy, and about dinosaur behavior such as what they ate, how fast they moved, and if they were intelligent.

A valuable set of lists is included: dinosaur finds in the U.S. and internationally, whom to contact if one wishes to go on a dig, locations of museums with dinosaur exhibits, publications with addresses and Websites, an annotated list of videos, an annotated list of films with dinosaurs as part of the story line, Internet sites, a bibliography, and so on. These lists would benefit from some reorganization to put like materials together such as combining the listing of state museums with those of national museums and outdoor sites. Putting all bibliographic lists together and all video lists together would also make use simpler. The title promises handy answers and it delivers them.—**Ann E. Prentice**

MATHEMATICS

559.   Bruno, Leonard C. Baker, Lawrence W., ed. **Math and Mathematicians: The History of Math Discoveries Around the World.** Farmington Hills, Mich., U*X*L/Gale, 1999. 2v. illus. index. $63.00/set. ISBN 0-7876-3812-9.

This encyclopedic set contains 50 biographies of mathematicians alternating with 34 essays describing math concepts and principles important in the middle school curriculum. In choosing the mathematicians to include, an effort was made to choose people from many different periods and countries as well as men and women over these same periods. The biographies include representatives from every major part of the world (ancient and modern) as well as mathematicians who are young or old, male or female. Covering the early life, influences, and career of each individual, it summarizes and describes the lives of well-known mathematicians, and also tells the stories of other greats and near-greats whose contributions have become an integral part of our popular mathematical knowledge. The 50 biographies include 14 people who were born or did their major work in the twentieth century, 6 of whom are still living. This should suggest that not all the great mathematicians are musty names found in old history books. The oldest historical figure included, Thales of Miletus, harks back to the seventh century B.C.E., whereas the youngest living mathematician, Andrew Wiles, was born in 1953. The common thread that links all these biographies is that genius, hard work, determination, inspiration, and courage are multicultural, multiracial, and ignorant of gender. The result is a broad spectrum of mathematicians. This broad spectrum is emphasized by a table of contents by mathematical field and ethnicity. Difficult, technical, and scientific words are defined in the text and sidebars.—**Janet Mongan**

27 Resource Sciences

ENVIRONMENTAL SCIENCE

560. **The Grolier Library of Environmental Concepts and Issues.** Danbury, Conn., Grolier, 1996. 8v. illus. maps. index. $249.00/set. ISBN 0-7172-7518-3.

The Grolier Library of Environmental Concepts and Issues is not really an encyclopedia but more of a series of mini-textbooks, each dealing with a specific segment of the environment. Starting with the broad topic "Ecosystem Earth" and going through various resources such as water, air, and energy, the reader can learn about the Earth and its people. Within each volume, readers will find chapters on specific aspects of that particular resource. For example, in the volume on living resources, chapters dealing with topics such as farming techniques and soil are found. This method provides for an interdisciplinary approach and makes the text very readable. It also allows an educator to work on a specific topic from a number of angles, providing students with the opportunity to see the whole picture. The final volume pulls all the topics together, showing the interrelations between all parts of the environment.

There is an index in each volume, and the final volume has a cumulative index as well as a glossary of selected terms. Photographs and diagrams illustrate various concepts, and "envirobits" provide interesting sidebars of information. The series should prove a useful springboard for a school's environmental program. [R: BR, Sept/Oct 96, p. 58; SLJ, Aug 96, p. 181]—**Angela Marie Thor**

Author/Title Index

Reference is to entry number.

Subject Index

Reference is to entry number.

MEDICINE -POPULAR
Adolescent health sourcebk, 521
Health matters! 523
Human diseases & conditions, 525

MEDICINE -VOCATIONAL GUIDANCE
Career opportunities in health care, 522

MESOPOTAMIA
Daily life in ancient Mesopotamia, 244

METEOROLOGY
Atlas of the world's worst natural disasters, 539
Blizzards, 542
Chronology of weather, 543
Droughts, 544
Floods, 545
Handy weather answer bk, 549
Hurricanes, 546
National Audubon Society 1st field gd: weather, 550
Natural disasters, rev ed, 548
Tornadoes, 547
Weather watch, 551

MIDDLE AGES
History of the ancient & medieval world, 280
Middle Ages, 286

MILITARY BATTLES
Encyclopedia of battles in N America: 1517-1916, 325
Modern campaigns, 324

MILITARY BIOGRAPHY
Generals in muddy boots: a concise ency of combat commanders, 321

MINERALOGY
National Audubon Society 1st field gd: rocks & minerals, 553

MONEY. *See also* **BANKS & BANKING**
Encyclopedia of money, 89

MULTIMEDIA -CAREERS
Career opportunities in TV, cable, video, & multimedia, 4th ed, 95

MUMMIES
Encyclopedia of mummies, 196

MUSIC -DICTIONARIES
Baker's student ency of music, 429

MUSIC INDUSTRY

Career opportunities in the music industry, 4th ed, 101

MUSIC -POPULAR
DK ency of rock stars, 430
Parents aren't supposed to like it, v.4-6, 431

MUSICIANS
Young musicians in world hist, 428

MYTHOLOGY
Illustrated dict of mythology, 434
Kingfisher bk of mythology, 2d ed, 433
Myths & hero tales, 399

NATURAL DISASTERS
Atlas of the world's worst natural disasters, 539
Natural disasters, rev ed, 548

NATURAL HISTORY
Extinct species series, 501
Illustrated bk of questions & answers, 37
Oryx gd to natural hist, 502
Pockets: nature facts, 504
U*X*L ency of biomes, 506

NEW DEAL, 1933-1939
Great Depression & New Deal: almanac, 206
Great Depression & New Deal: biogs, 207
Great Depression & New Deal: primary sources, 208
Historic events for students: the Great Depression, 221

NORSE
Historical atlas of the Viking world, 265
Vikings, 297

NORTH AMERICA
Encyclopedia of N American hist, 278
Peoples of the Americas, 130

NUBIA
Ancient African kingdom of Kush, 298

OCCULTISM. *See also* **WITCHES & WITCHCRAFT**
Wizards & sorcerers, 331

OCCUPATIONS. *See* **CAREERS**

OCEANIA -JUVENILE LITERATURE
Literature for children & YAs about Oceania, 81

OCEANOGRAPHY
Library of the oceans, 554